THE COINS

OF THE

MOGHUL EMPERORS OF HINDUSTAN

IN THE

BRITISH MUSEUM

THE COINS

OF THE

MOGHUL EMPERORS OF HINDUSTAN

IN THE

BRITISH MUSEUM

BY

STANLEY LANE-POOLE

EDITED BY

REGINALD STUART POOLE, LL.D.

GYAN

Published by

GYAN

Gyan Publishing House
5, Ansari Road
Daryaganj, New Delhi-110002
Phone: 011-47034999, 9811692060
E-mail: books@gyanbooks.com

Distribution Network
gyanbooks.com
India, USA, Canada, UK, Australia, France

ISBN: 978-81-212-7210-0 (PB)
First Published, 1892

2nd Impression 2023

Printed at: Gyan Press, Delhi.

THE COINS OF THE MOGHUL EMPERORS OF HINDUSTAN IN THE BRITISH MUSEUM

Author: STANLEY LANE-POOLE, Editor: REGINALD STUART POOLE

CATALOGUE

OF

INDIAN COINS

IN THE

BRITISH MUSEUM

THE MOGHUL EMPERORS

LONDON
PRINTED BY ORDER OF THE TRUSTEES
Longmans & Co., Paternoster Row; B. Quaritch, 15, Piccadilly;
Henry Frowde, Amen Corner; Archibald Constable & Co., Westminster;
Kegan Paul, Trübner & Co., Paternoster House, Charing Cross Road;
A. Asher & Co., 13, Bedford St., Covent Garden, and at Berlin;
Rollin & Feuardent, 19, Bloomsbury Street, and Place Louvois, Paris.
1892

THE COINS

OF THE

MOGHUL EMPERORS OF HINDUSTAN

IN THE

BRITISH MUSEUM

BY

STANLEY LANE-POOLE

EDITED BY

REGINALD STUART POOLE, LL.D.

KEEPER OF COINS

CORRESPONDENT OF THE INSTITUTE OF FRANCE

LONDON

PRINTED BY ORDER OF THE TRUSTEES

1892

EDITOR'S PREFACE.

The present volume of the Catalogue of Indian Coins contains the description of the issues of the Moghul Emperors of Hindústán, from the foundation of the Empire by Bábar, Humáyún, and Akbar, down to its gradual absorption into the realm of the Honourable East India Company. It also includes such coins of the Company as were issued in imitation of the currency of the Moghuls.

The transliteration of Arabic and Indian names of persons, places, &c., in this volume, is in accordance with the latest official system of the Indian Government. Familiar names of places are spelt in the ordinary English way.

The metal of each specimen is stated, and its size in inches and tenths of inches. The weight of the gold and silver examples is given in English grains. Tables for converting grains into grammes, and inches into millimètres as well as into the measures of Mionnet's scale, are given at the end of the volume.

A comparative table of the years and months of the Hijrah and of the Christian era has been added, with a view to facilitating reference to the standard works on Indian history where the European computation is adopted.

A specially prepared map of India is inserted to illustrate the distribution of the mint-cities throughout the Empire.

Typical specimens are figured in the thirty-three plates which are executed by the autotype mechanical process from casts in plaster.

The whole work is written by Mr. Stanley Lane-Poole, and I have carefully collated it with the coins.

REGINALD STUART POOLE.

AUTHOR'S INTRODUCTION.

§ 1. *HISTORICAL OUTLINE.*

THE history of the Moghul Empire of Hindústán, which nominally extends from 1525 to 1857, is really contained in much narrower limits. The assured domination of the Moghul Emperors begins with the building-up of the empire by Akbar (1556-1605) and practically ends with the death of Aurangzíb, the last autocrat of their line, in 1707. Before Akbar there was no Moghul Empire, but only the attempt to create one. After Aurangzíb there was still for awhile the framework of an empire, but no emperor: the power fell into the hands of Ministers and Viceroys, and political disintegration prepared the way for British expansion. Not much more than half a century had passed since Aurangzíb 'Álamgír was carried to his tomb near Aurangábád, when the East India Company began to gather up the fragments that remained of Akbar's empire, and the Emperor himself became their pensioner (1765).

The historical founder of the empire was Akbar; but the first of his line to assert imperial power in India was his grandfather Bábar; unless, indeed, the precedence belongs to his ancestor Tímúr, in virtue of his earlier raids upon Hindústán. BÁBAR, or "Tiger," also called Muhammad and surnamed Zahír-ad-dín, "Upholder of the Faith," was the son of 'Umar Shaikh, the son of Abú-Sa'íd, seventh Khán of Transoxiana; and Abú-Sa'íd was the son of Muhammad Sultán the son of Miran Sháh, the son of Tímúr. Bábar thus lineally descended in the fifth generation from Tímúr, on his father's side; on his mother's, he traced his pedigree to Chingis Kaán. He was born in 1482 (A.H. 888) in the province of Farghánah, then ruled by his father, whom he succeeded as chieftain about the age of twelve. Henceforward his precocious youth was spent in strife and war. He successfully withstood his envious kinsfolk in Farghánah, and even made incursions into the territory of Samarkand at the age of fifteen; but was eventually defeated and driven from Transoxiana by Shaibání and his Uzbegs about 1504, and forced to console himself with the subduing of Afghánistán and Badakhshán (A.H. 911). For twenty years he remained outwardly content with the kingship of Kábul and the country round about; though he confesses in his *Memoirs* that from the first he had meditated the invasion of India, but "sometimes from the misconduct of my Amírs and their dislike of the project, sometimes from the cabals and opposition of my brothers, I was prevented from prosecuting the expedition."* He was forty-three years of age before he was able to realize his dream.

At the close of 1525 (Safar 932)† he began to occupy the Panjáb with the connivance of the Afghán governor of Lahore. The disunited state of the so-called "Pathán" kingdom offered little resistance to the invader: India

---

* *Túzak-i Bábarí*, Erskine's (1829) translation, 290. These *Memoirs* were written in Chagatai Turkish, and have been translated into French by M. Pavet de Courteille (1871). The Persian version, which dates from the time of Akbar, was done into English by W. Erskine and J. Leyden (Or. Translation Fund, 1826); and extracts from both versions are given in Sir H. M. Elliot and Prof. Dowson's invaluable *History of India as told by its own Historians*, iv. 218-287. The latter will be frequently referred to by the abbreviation ED.

† *Ibid.* ED. iv. 239 ff.

GENEALOGICAL TREE OF THE MOGHUL EMPERORS.*

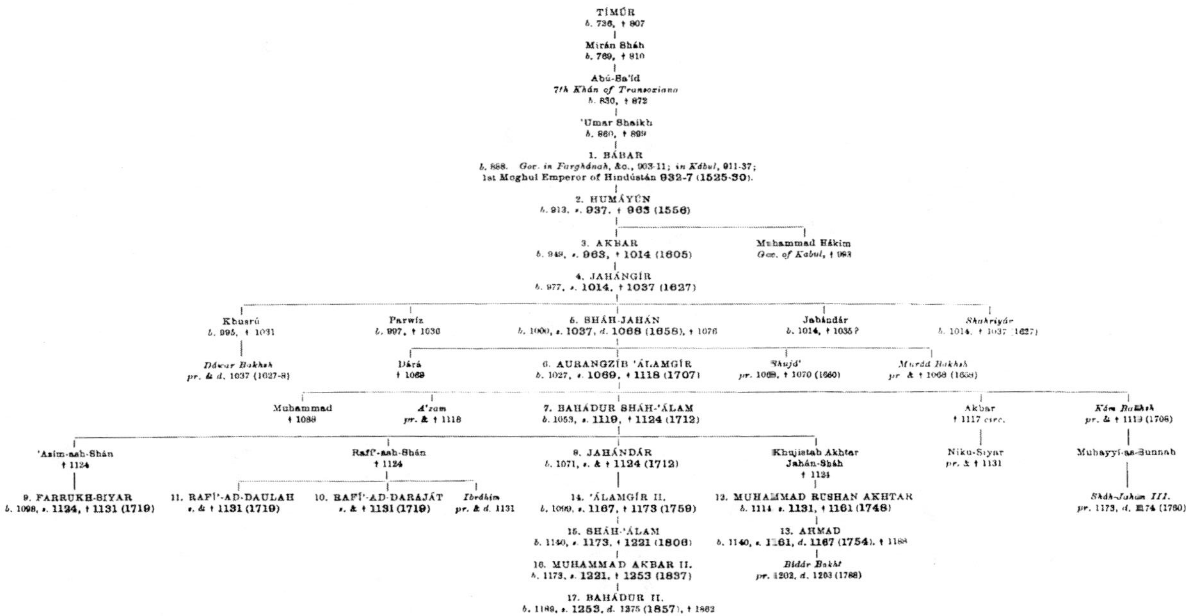

* The Emperors' names are printed in capitals; those of temporary or usurping rulers in italics. *b.* born; *s.* succeeded; *pr.* proclaimed; *d.* deposed; † died. For various collateral members of the family, not necessary to the pedigree of the Emperors, see the fuller genealogical table at the end of Vol. I. of H. Blochmann's translation of Abu-l-Fazl's *Áin-i Akbari*.

was divided amongst numerous petty rulers, and the authority of Sultán Ibráhím Lódí of Dehlí was worth little, except in the provinces adjoining his capital. Nevertheless, with the aid of his nobles and feudatories, Ibráhím contrived to bring together an army reckoned by his enemy at 100,000 men, with a thousand elephants. The decisive battle took place on the historic plain of Pánípat, 20th April, 1526, and the defenders were routed with the loss of their king and 15,000 men.* Bábar quickly occupied Dehlí and Agrah, and after defeating the Rájputs under Sanka Rána of Udaipúr, reduced Chánderí, their stronghold, in the following spring. Three years later he died at Agrah, 29th December, 1530 (9 Jumádá I., 937),† aged 48, sovereign "of a vast though incoherent empire, extending from Badakhshán and Kunduz, beyond the Hindú Kúsh, including all Afghánistán, the Panjáb, Hindústán, Rájputána, and Bihár."‡ The kingdoms of Bengal, Gujarát, and Málwah, and the Deccan (Dákhin) formed no part of his dominions.

Bábar's *Memoirs* form a refreshingly frank and vivid autobiography. They give one the impression on the one hand of a gallant and daring soldier, and on the other of a jovial, heedless, boon-fellow. A great change had come over the Mongols, or Moghuls,§ since the days when Tamerlane led his savage pagans on their skull-hunts. The "Tiger's" Moghuls were comparatively civilized Muslims. "Contemporary writings and drawings show Bábar and his followers as a jovial crew of men-at-arms, with fair and ruddy complexions, and

---

* *Túzak-i Bábarí* (Erskine), 304.

† Nizám-ad-dín, *Tabakát-i Akbarí*, ED. v. 188.

‡ H. G. Keene, *Sketch of the History of Hindustan* (1885), 70.

§ The Arabic name is Mughal, but the form Moghul or Mogul is consecrated by long usage in English. Bábar himself detested the Moghul race, as "the authors of every kind of mischief and devastation," and always called his own people "Turks."

unveiled wives; delighting in brocaded garments and gilded armour, using artillery in war, loving to carouse in the intervals of peace by the banks of streams or in shady gardens."* We read in the *Memoirs* of continual drinking bouts, in which the conqueror of Hindústán sometimes contrived to become thoroughly intoxicated four times in twenty-four hours,—and thus sowed the seeds of a vice which became hereditary in later generations of his descendants. Only his remarkable bodily vigour enabled him to trifle thus with his health. We hear of his riding from Kálpí to Agrah, a distance of 160 miles, in two days; and to his death he combined extraordinary activity with intervals of reckless self-indulgence, which must have hastened his end. His character is a singular mixture of rollicking good-humour, chivalrous generosity, and now and then truly Asiatic ferocity. His portrait, which has been preserved in the copy of his *Memoirs* which belonged to Sháh-Jahán, shows us "a thoughtful gentleman, with pale, oval face, and small, pointed, black moustache." Some notion of his standard of civilization may be derived from his criticism of the shortcomings of the Hindús, of whom he entertained a very mean opinion.

"Hindústán," he says, "is a country that has few pleasures to recommend it. The people are not handsome. They have no idea of the charms of friendly society, of frankly mixing together, or of familiar intercourse. They have no genius, no comprehension of mind, no politeness of manner, no kindness or fellow-feeling, no ingenuity or mechanical invention in planning or executing their handicraft works, no skill or knowledge in design or architecture; they have no good horses, no good flesh, no grapes or musk-melons, no good fruits, no ice or cold water, no good food or bread

* Keene, *op. cit.*, 53.

in their bazars, no baths or colleges, no candles, no torches, not a candlestick."*

Bábar's successor was his eldest son, Muhammad† Humáyún ("Augustus"), surnamed Násir-ad-dín, "Defender of the Faith," who had taken part in his father's Indian campaigns. He was born 6th February, 1511 (916 A.H.),‡ and was, therefore, not yet twenty when he came to the throne. His first enterprise was an unsuccessful attempt to conquer the united kingdom of Gujarát and Málwah, whence his attention was called away by the advance of Shér Khán § with the Afghán forces of Bengal. After a prolonged struggle Humáyún was decisively worsted in 1542 (949), and took refuge in Sind. For thirteen years the son of Bábar remained in exile, ruling his father's old kingdom of Kábul, whilst Shér Sháh, by his admirable organization of the government of Hindústán, laid the foundations of the future empire of Akbar. In 1555 Humáyún recovered Lahore, and after a sharp contest drove the Pathán forces to the eastward and occupied Dehlí, where an accident ended his life in January, 1556 (963). He was a generous and amiable profligate, much addicted to opium.

With the accession of Humáyún's son, Akbar ("Maximus"), surnamed Jalál-ad-dín, or "Glory of the Faith," the greatest epoch of the Moghul Empire begins. Born on 15th October, 1542 (5 Rajab 949 ‖), Akbar was only in his fourteenth year when he came to the throne; but he possessed a capable guardian in the

---

* *Túzak-i Bábarí* (Erskine), 333.

† It was the fashion of the Moghul Emperors to include Muhammad among their names.

‡ Abu-l-Fazl, *Akbarnámah*, ED. v. 188, *note*. Abu-l-Fazl's optimism is effectually counteracted by the cynicism of Badáóní, ED. v. 477-549.

§ See my *Catalogue of the Coins of the Sultans of Dehlí*, 105 ff.

‖ Nizám-ad-dín, *Tabakát-i Akbari*, ED. v. 214.

Turkomán Bairám Khán, who commanded the Moghul army and acted as Prime Minister during the Emperor's minority. The Hindú general, Hímú, had already seized Dehlí, when Bairám gave him battle, and utterly defeated him (5th November, 1556) on the field of Pánípat—the scene of so many eventful conflicts in Indian history ; and the boy-emperor found himself, at a single blow, master of most of Hindústán, though his authority in distant parts of his nominal dominions was at first somewhat shadowy. Akbar soon took the reins of power into his own hands. Henceforward for many years his career is a long record of conquest and annexation. Dehlí and Agrah were his from the day of Pánípat ; Gwálior was subdued in 1558 (966), Jaunpúr and Rantambhór in 1559 ; in 1561 Málwah was overrun, and Burhánpúr in Khandésh fell in 1562 (969) ; in 1567 (975) Chitór, the stronghold of the Rájputs, commanded by their Rájá, Jai Mal, was besieged and stormed, and Rájputána for a while submitted to the Moghuls.* Gujarát, nominally a province of the empire, rebelled, but was brought into subjection in 1572 (980) : Akbar entered its capital, Ahmadábád, and reduced Súrat, Cambay, and Baroda.† Júnágarh, the stronghold of Káthiáwár, was annexed in 1591 (999).‡ Bengal was another province held on an illusory tenure. It was still ruled by the Patháns in nominal dependence upon the empire. But when Dáúd, of the family of Shér Sháh, succeeded to the viceroyalty, he waxed contumacious, and rose in arms. A policy of conciliation proved unavailing, and Dáúd was overthrown in a battle near Jalasúr (1575), and finally killed in 1577 (984). Akbar's authority was thus established in Bengal, though this and other provinces (such as Orissa, Gujarát, and Rájputána) were disturbed from time to

---

* *Tabákát-i Akbarí*, ED. v. 327-328.

† *Ibid.* v. 350.

‡ *Ibid.* v. 461, 466.

time by temporary insurrections. Badakhshán was abandoned to the Uzbegs in 1585 (993), but, by way of compensation, Kashmír was annexed in 1587, and Kandahár six years later.

In the Deccan, Akbar's power was, so far, scarcely felt: he had, indeed, occupied Khandésh and Berár, and taken Burhánpúr and Elichpúr; but he had reinstated the native Rájás, whose tribute was intermittent and fealty barely nominal. In 1593 he had again to reduce Khandésh, and to occupy Ahmadnagar, the capital of Berár; but in each case he adhered to his policy of reinstating the native rulers as feudatories of the empire. The Rájá of Khandésh for a time justified Akbar's clemency, but Berár was soon in rebellion, partly by reason of the incompetence of Prince Murád, the drunken viceroy of the Deccan. The Emperor's trusted Minister, Abu-l-Fazl, author of the famous *Áín-i Akbarí*, or "Institutes of Akbar," was appointed to supersede him in 1599,* and Akbar himself moved south. Daulatábád had already fallen; Asírgarh, the formidable stronghold of Khandésh, endured a six months' siege, and only surrendered at last to the indomitable persistence of Abu-l-Fazl; while Ahmadnagar fell in 1600 (1008). An inscription at Fathpúr records how "His Majesty the King of Kings, whose court is Paradise, the shadow of God, Jalál-ad-dín Muhammad Akbar Pádisháh, conquered the Deccan and Dándésh,† which was heretofore Khandésh, in the Iláhí year 46, which is the year of the Hijrah 1010," &c.‡

---

* Murád died soon afterwards of delirium tremens.

† The name was temporarily changed in honour of the new governor, Dániyál, Akbar's son, a drunkard like his brothers. Like Murád, he fell a victim to his vice. Though kept under restraint, his servants smuggled liquor for him in a match-lock barrel, which the prince facetiously called his "bier." Keene, *op. cit.* 157.

‡ The conquest of Asírgarh took place in the 45th year, as recorded by the commemorative coin No. 166, but the honours were distributed some months later. On the Ilahí era and reckoning see below, § 4, p. lxi.

In many of these successful sieges the guns were served by English artillerymen. The Deccan provinces, however, in spite of this triumphant record, were still in a disturbed state at the time of Akbar's death, which occurred in October, 1605 (1014), when he was sixty-three years of age.

The preceding brief catalogue of Akbar's campaigns, by which he obtained and kept control over an empire which stretched from Kábul to Dhákká and from Kashmír to Ahmadnagar, is necessary to the numismatist;* but these warlike triumphs form but a small part of his claim to our admiration. In dealing with the difficulties arising in the government of a peculiarly heterogeneous empire, he stands absolutely supreme among oriental sovereigns, and may even challenge comparison with the greatest of European rulers. It may be true, as Mr. Keene urges, that he owed much of his success to the example of organization set by his able predecessor, Shér Sháh; and it is certain that he was deeply indebted to the talents of advisers like Todar Mal and Abu-l-Fazl; but the wisdom of the monarch is shown in the choice of his ministers and in his receptivity to the teaching of history. A dozen Burleighs could not have built up the power of England in the sixteenth century without the vigorous mind of Elizabeth to inspire and control them; and all the Todar Mals in Hindústán could not have welded together into an abiding empire the races, states, and religions of India in the sixteenth century without the aid and countenance of the commanding genius of Akbar. He was himself the spring and fount of the sagacious policy of his government; and the proof of the soundness of his system is the continuance of the Moghul Empire after his death, in spite of the follies

* See the records of these conquests on the coins themselves, *infra*, p. li.

and vices of his successors, until it was undone by a deliberate reversal of his policy in the bigoted reaction of his great-grandson Aurangzíb. To have united under one firm government Hindús and Muhammadans, Shí'ah and Sunnís, Rájputs and Afgháns, and all the numerous races and tribes of Hindústán, was a Herculean task the difficulty of which can be adequately appreciated only by those who know the force of caste prejudices and religious obstinacy in Indian history. Akbar was the first Indian sovereign who solved the problem, if only temporarily. Our own administrators have perhaps at length succeeded in mastering it after a century of perplexing experience.

To comment in detail on Akbar's system of government is beyond the present purpose. It will be sufficient to indicate a few salient features in his policy. His chief difficulties lay in the diversity and jealousies of the races and religions with which he had to deal. He met them by wise toleration. In religion, his latitude went to perhaps fantastic lengths. He encouraged Portuguese priests and Christian pictures and statues; established a hall, called the Díwán-i Khás or 'Ibádat Khánah, "Hall of Worship," for the discussion of philosophical and religious problems by men of diverse opinions; sanctioned something approaching sun-worship, and introduced the solar reckoning of time and the Persian months; abolished* the *Kalimah*, or Muhammadan profession of faith, on the money and in state documents, &c., and substituted the simple formula, *Allahu Akbar*, "God is most great," with the response, *Jalla Jaláluhu*, "Glorified be his glory." In short, he set up an eclectic pantheism, in the place of Islám, and selected from various creeds what he thought worthy of admiration, just as he selected

* See below, p. lxvii.

his wives from different nations and creeds, Hindú, Christian, and Muslim, with an impartiality never ventured upon by previous Muhammadan sovereigns. Whatever good or harm his *Dín* or *Tauhíd Iláhí,* "Divine Monotheism," may have done, the practical side of it, as shown in the abolition of all taxes upon religious non-conformity, was a strong influence towards consolidating the empire by making all subjects equal in the sight of the tax-gatherer. To conciliate the prejudices of race, he adopted the principle of reinstating evicted Rájás as tributary chiefs of the empire. He employed Hindús, Shí'ah, and Sunnís equally, and conferred like honours upon each denomination. To form the leading men of all races and creeds into a loyal body, he established a sort of feudal aristocracy, called *mansabdárs,* who were in receipt of salaries or held lands direct from the crown, on condition of supplying men and elephants for the imperial armies: the ranks were graduated like the degrees of *chin* in the modern Russian bureaucracy, and, like them again, the rank was not hereditary. A similar system was employed in Egypt at the time of the Mamlúk Sultáns, from whom Akbar may have derived the idea. Its merits in India were unquestionable. Hindús and Moghuls and Persians stood on an equality as "Amírs of 5000" or "of 500" men, and all were under the command of one of the chief officers of the empire, the Amír-al-Umará, or Premier Noble—the Earl Marshal of Hindústán. The dangers of a territorial aristocracy (which in some form the *mansabdárs* were sure to become) were minimised by a rigorously equitable inspection and collection of the land rents, which formed the bulk of the state revenue (about 10 *crores** of rupees).

* The crore (*karór*) is 100 *lákhs* of 100,000 rupees, and is therefore equal to 10,000,000 rupees, or, taking the rupee at 2*s.* 3*d.* of English money of the time, 1,125,000*l.* sterling.

Other duties had been extensively remitted, and the taxation on the whole was light, the currency was admirable, and the laws were improved.

Akbar's portrait has been drawn by his son Jahángír. He was somewhat over the middle height, with a wheat-coloured complexion, inclining to dark; his eyes and eyebrows were black; his body stout, the chest and brow open; and his arms and fingers were long. His voice was ringing, and in spite of his lack of education his speech was elegant. "His manners and habits were quite different from other people's, and his countenance was full of godlike dignity."*

Akbar was followed by his son Salím,† born of a Rájput princess in 1569 (977), who was proclaimed Emperor, 21st October, 1605 (8 Jumádá II., 1014), with the style of Núr-ad-dín ("Light of the Faith") Muhammad Jahángír ("World-grasper"). He was thirty-seven years old, and maturity had in some degree mellowed his character. He had more than once broken into open insurrection against his father; he was suspected on very good grounds of having instigated the murder of Akbar's trusted friend and minister, Abu-l-Fazl; he was possessed of a violent and arbitrary temper; and he was a notorious and habitual drunkard. After his accession, however, he displayed little or nothing of his former ferocity, and became almost amiable. Indeed, Sir Thomas Roe describes him, after dinner, as "very affable, and full of gentle conversation."‡ He treated rebellious officers with clemency; and he not only issued a treatise against tobacco and an edict against intemperance, but himself set the example by seriously reforming his own habits. In his marvellously candid

* *Túzak-i Jahángírí*, ED. vi. 290. † See the coins, Nos. 288, 289.

‡ Letter to Archbp. of Canterbury, 29 Jan. 1615, *apud* Pinkerton, *Coll. of Voyages*, viii. 46.

*Memoirs** he relates how (like his wretched brothers, Murád and Dániyál) he had been addicted to intoxicating liquors from the age of eighteen, and used to drink as much as twenty cups a day, at first of wine, then of "double-distilled liquor," of such potency that it made Sir Thomas Roe sneeze, to the delight of the whole Court. But as time went on, he says, he became sensible of the injury he was doing himself, and in seven years he reduced his allowance to six or seven cups; restricted his potations to the evening; and finally, he avers, he drank only to assist digestion,† though he admits that he indulged excessively in the use of opium. William Hawkins, (a cousin of the famous Sir Richard) who lived for two years in intimate attendance upon "the Mogul," confirms, in the main, these alcoholic statistics, but makes it clear that even the five or six cups of the Emperor's reduced allowance overcame him to such a degree that "being in the height of his drink," he fell into heavy sleep, from which he was roused for supper by his attendants, who had to feed the incapable monarch.‡ "This done," adds Sir Thomas Roe, "he turned to sleep; the candles were popped out: and I groped my way out in the dark."§ The subject possesses a numismatic interest, inasmuch as Jahángír, with the unabashed frankness for which he is noted, had himself portrayed upon some of his coins in the attitude of holding a drinking-cup in his hand.||

---

* There are two distinct versions of the *Túzak-i Jahángírí* (also called the *Wákí'át-i Jahángírí*), or *Memoirs of Jahángír*. One was translated by Major David Price (Or. Transl. Fund, 1829); the other by Atkinson (*Asiat. Misc.* ii. 77). The latter is the better version, and was continued by Muhammad Hádí. Extracts are given in ED. vi.

† *Wákí'át-i Jahángíri*, ED. vi. 285, 341, 500.

‡ *The Hawkins' Voyages*, 437, edited by Clements R. Markham (Hakluyt Society, no. 57).

§ Sir Thomas Roe's *Journal*, *apud* Pinkerton, viii. 10.

|| See Coins, Nos. 317-321, and the remarks, p. lxxx.

He was, no doubt, influenced towards a healthier mode of life by his wife, the celebrated Núr-Mahall ("Light of the Palace"), afterwards called *Núr-Jahán* ("Light of the World"). This lady, whose maiden name was Muhr-an-Nisá, or "Seal of Womankind," had attracted the admiration of Jahángír when he was crown-prince; but Akbar married her to a young Turkomán and settled them in Bengal. After Jahángír's accession the husband was killed in a quarrel with the governor of the province, and the wife was placed under the care of one of Akbar's widows, with whom she remained during four years, and then married Jahángír (1610). There is nothing to justify a suspicion of the Emperor's connivance in the husband's death; nor do Indian historians corroborate the invidious criticisms of "Normal" by European travellers: on the contrary, they portray Núr-Mahall as a pattern of all the virtues, and worthy to wield the supreme influence which she obtained over the Emperor. "By degrees," says Muhammad Hádí, the continuer of Jahángír's *Memoirs*, "she became, except in name, undisputed sovereign of the empire, and the king himself became a tool in her hands. He used to say that Núr-Jahán Bégam has been selected, and is wise enough, to conduct the matters of state, and that he wanted only a bottle of wine and piece of meat to keep himself merry. Núr-Jahán won golden opinions from all people. She was liberal and just to all who begged her support. She was an asylum for all sufferers, and helpless girls were married at the expense of her private purse. She must have portioned about five hundred girls in her lifetime, and thousands were grateful for her generosity."* Her beauty and wisdom were universally extolled, and her devotion to her royal husband was attested by the

* ED. vi. 398-9.

white robes she wore in her long retirement during her eighteen years of widowhood till her death in 1645. Jahángír's queen, like his bottle, claims a place in numismatics, for the historian records that "coins were struck in her name, and the royal seal on firmáns bore her signature." That his statement as to coins is correct, the Catalogue will prove,* though Tavernier's story of her having designed and issued the famous zodiacal mohrs is certainly erroneous.†

Sir Thomas Roe gives a detailed picture of the Court and life of Jahángír, in which the daily levees of the Emperor formed a feature corresponding to our Court Circular. "The Mogul every morning shows himself to the common people at a window that looks into the plain before his gate. At noon he is there again to see elephants and wild beasts fight, the men of rank being under him within a rail. Hence he retires to sleep among his women. After noon he comes to the Durbar. After supper, at eight of the clock, he comes down to the Guzalcan, a fair court . . . where none are admitted but of the first quality, and few of them without leave. Here he discourses of indifferent things very affably. No business of state is done anywhere but at one of these two last places, where it is publicly canvassed, and so registered; which register might be seen for two shillings, and the common people know as much as the council. . . . This method is never altered unless sickness or drink obstruct it; and this must be known, for if he be unseen without a reason assigned, the people would mutiny; and for two days no excuse will serve, but the doors must be opened, and some admitted to see him to satisfy others. On Tuesday he sits in judgment, and hears the meanest person's complaints, examines both parties, and often sees execution done by his elephants."‡

* See Coins, Nos. 513-526. † See below, p. lxxxi.

‡ Sir Thomas Roe's *Journal, apud* Pinkerton, viii. 6.

Under Jahángír the Moghul empire retained almost the same boundaries as under his father. The Deccan provinces acquired more independence, however, and the Maráthas began to be heard of for the first time. Bengal and Udaipúr were, as usual, the scenes of insurrection, and Kandahár passed into the possession of the Persian Sháh in 1622, and remained lost to the Moghuls till 1637. The government of the country was carried on, at least nominally, on Akbar's lines, and no innovations, political or religious, were hazarded. Toleration was the order of the day, as in Akbar's time. Father Francisco Corsi was a *persona grata* at Court, and Jahángír appeared to favour Christianity, and had two of his nephews baptized: but the motive of this was said to be either to bar the possible succession of the two princes to the throne, or to provide a means of importing Portuguese wives into the family. When the Jesuits declined to sanction such alliances, the Christianated youths recanted without hesitation. * It is true the Hijrah reckoning was revived in place of the new Iláhí era, but the years of the reign still continued to be calculated on the solar principle, and the Persian names of the solar months were retained. The general tranquillity was due partly to the prestige of Akbar's example, and partly to the ability of Jahángír's queen and ministers, especially Mahábat Khán, an Afghán of Kábul, Ásaf Khán, Núr-Jahán's brother, and the Emperor's able son, Khurram, afterwards Sháh-Jahán, who combined valuable services as a general with frequent rebellion as heir-apparent. Nevertheless, the seeds of corruption were being profusely sown. The accounts of European travellers, such as James I.'s ambassador, Sir Thomas Roe, and his chaplain Edward Terry, William Hawkins, Sir Thomas Herbert, and Pietro della

---

* W. Hawkins, *l. c.* 438 ; Roe *ubi supra*, 47.

Valle, who visited the Moghul court at Agrah or Ajmír, or travelled in India between 1608 and 1626, unanimously condemn the venality and inefficiency of the administration. The provinces and *sirkars* were farmed by contractors, the military spirit was weakened, the country was a prey to brigands, and every one, from Núr-Jahán downwards, was greedy of gifts.* Travellers' tales are proverbially to be accepted with caution, but the picture of the court of Jahángír drawn by so capable an observer as Sir Thomas Roe cannot lightly be set aside, even when it forms a glaring contrast to that of the native chroniclers.†

Jahángír died in November, 1627 (28 Safar, 1037)‡ on his way back from one of his frequent visits to the cool valleys of Kashmír. His portrait, after a contemporary picture, is given by Terry, § and shows us a somewhat truculent *bon vivant.* He was buried in a splendid mausoleum at Lahore, and near him in a humbler tomb lies his renowned empress, Núr-Jahán. The last years of his reign had been clouded by intrigues for the succession, and his death was the signal for usurpation. His undoubted heir was Sháh-Jahán, but his youngest son, *Shahriyár*, had married Núr-Jahán's daughter, and by the mother's advice proclaimed himself Emperor at Lahore, whither he had lately retired in great confusion at the humiliating disappearance of his hair and eyebrows by the ravages of the "fox's disease." The dowager's

---

* Roe's *Journal, apud* Pinkerton, viii, 35.

† In his *History of Hindústán*, Mr. Keene follows the native chroniclers perhaps too exclusively. Mr. Wheeler, on the other hand, entirely repudiates them (except Badáóní, whose detractions fit in with his own views), and relies, with almost superstitious credulity, upon every scrap of European testimony.

‡ Mu'tamad Khán, *Ikbál-námah*, ED. vi. 435.

§ Terry's Voyage, 446, at end of *Travels of Pietro della Valle (a Noble Roman) into East-India*, &c., transl. G. Havers, 1665. Colonel Hanna possesses two admirable contemporary portraits of Jahángír.

brother, Ásaf, however, had scruples about prolonging her virtual reign, and possessed a royal son-in-law of his own in tho most capable of the princes, Sháh-Jahán: * accordingly, he set up a *fainéant* Emperor, Búlákí, a grandson of Jahángír, with the title of *Dáwar Bakhsh* ("God-given",) as a stop-gap, while he despatched an express to Sháh-Jahán to announce his father's death. Ásaf then defeated, blinded, and eventually executed Shahriyár—who was known by the nickname of *Ná-shudaní* ("Do-nothing"); the "Winter King," Dáwar Bakhsh, vanished—probably to Persia —after his three months' pretence of royalty; and on 25th January, 1628 (18 Jumáda I., 1037),† Sháh-Jahán ascended at Agrah the throne which he was to occupy for thirty years.

Sháh-Jahán Shiháb-ad-dín ("Lord of the World, Flame of the Faith") was born in 1592 (1000 A.H.), and was thirty-six when he came to the throne.‡ His mother was a Hindú, the daughter of the Rána of Marwar, and his paternal grandmother was also a Rájput, so that he was more Indian than Moghul. Nevertheless, by the influence of his Muhammadan wife, he acquired a certain tinge of intolerance entirely foreign to his indolent easy-going father and broad-minded grandfather. His bigotry was scarcely skin-deep, however; for he permitted Jesuit missions in his capital and at his eldest son's court, and placed Hindús in command of his armies. His wars were chiefly in the Deccan, where Bíjápúr and Golkondah were reduced to temporary submission and paid tribute,

---

* Arjmand Bánu, "Noble Princess," the daughter of Ásaf, and favourite wife of Sháh-Jahán, and mother of his eight sons and six daughters, died in 1631: her monument is the celebrated Táj-Mahall at Agrah.

† ED. vii. 6.

‡ There is an admirable portrait of him, reproduced in colours, from Colonel Hanna's collection, in Mr. Constable's scholarly edition of Bernier's Travels (*Constable's Oriental Miscellany*, vol. i.).

1635 (1045); and in Afghánistán, where the Moghul arms were unsuccessful, as they were also in some fruitless expeditions into Tibet. Kandahár, however, returned for a while to its allegiance in 1637, though recaptured by the Persians in 1648. Many of these campaigns were conducted by Sháh-Jahán's son, Aurangzíb, who proved himself a good soldier and able general, and, by winning the respect and devotion of his troops, prepared himself for an ambitious career.

Sháh-Jahán's reign is chiefly notable for the general tranquillity of the undiminished empire under the stable government of men like Ásaf Khán, Sa'd-alláh 'Allámí, and 'Alí Mardán. Tavernier eulogizes the paternal government of the Emperor, "like a father over his family," and testifies to the security of the roads, and the just administration of the law. A Hindú writer extols the equity of his rule, his wise treatment of his tenants and management of his estates, the probity of his courts of law, his personal supervision of the revenue accounts, and the general prosperity of the empire during his reign.* Sháh-Jahán was a great builder, as his works at Agrah and New Dehlí, and his great canal, attest to this day. A single item in his budget is two and a half crores (nearly 3,000,000*l*) for public edifices. His court at Lahore, or in summer in Kashmír, or at his magnificent palace-suburb of New Dehlí, called Sháhjahánábád (which was completed in A.H. 1058, after building ten years), was splendid and refined, according to the accounts of European visitors. The Augustinian friar, Manrique, who came to inspect the Jesuit missions at Agrah, found the prime minister, Ásaf Khán, at Lahore in a splendid palace decorated with paintings, some of which were of scenes in Christian hagiology

* Rái Bhárá Mal, ED. vii. 171.

He dined with the minister and the Emperor himself, and observed that unveiled ladies were at the table.* The taxation must have been heavy to meet the outlay of this sumptuous court, and we read of no fewer than eighty varieties of imposts. The revenue is said to have risen during the reign from the value of about 17,000,000*l.* to 20,000,000*l.* We possess ample European evidence for the history and life of the period in the travels of Mandelslo, Bernier, Tavernier, and others, whilst a little later the Italian physician, Manouchi or Manucci, wrote his observations made during a long residence at the Moghul court.† Great variety of religious opinion prevailed among the imperial family. Dárá Shikóh, the eldest son, was a freethinker, with a leaning to Christianity, encouraged by three Jesuit priests in his suite. Two of the Emperor's daughters were Christians, and Aurangzíb was a bigoted Muslim. Murád Bakhsh and Shujá' were careless and self-indulgent.

The rivalry of the brothers broke out into open conflict in 1657 (1067), when Sháh-Jahán, who was residing at Dehlí, was attacked by strangury.‡ Dárá immediately took upon himself the office of Regent, and intercepted all communications with his brothers in the outlying provinces. When the news of the Emperor's illness at length became known, general confusion ensued, and

---

* *Itinerario* of F. Sebastian Manrique, Religioso Eremita de S. Agustin, 374 (Roma, 1649).

† They have all been translated into English. See *The Voyages and Travels of J. Albert de Mandelslo*, 1638-40, in Adam Olearius's *Voyages and Travels of the Ambassadors sent by Frederick, Duke of Holstein, to the great Duke of Muscovy and the King of Persia*, transl. J. Davies, 1662. Tavernier's *Six Voyages* have recently been re-translated by V. Ball, 1889, and Bernier has been excellently edited by Mr. Archibald Constable, 1891. Manucci's observations were edited and unfortunately garbled by Père François Catrou (1705) and translated into English in 1709.

‡ Kháfí Khán, *Muntakhab-al-lubáb*, ED. vii. 214-19.

rebellion, long pent up, burst forth. Prince *Murád Bakhsh* ("Desire-attained") declared himself King in Gujarát, and struck coins in his own name.* *Shujá'* did the like in Bengal, and advanced upon Agrah.† Aurangzíb was watching events from his camp in the Deccan. Dárá and his invalid father moved from Dehlí to Agrah to meet these dangers; an army under Jai Singh, the Rájá of Ambar, defeated Shujá', who, after some further resistance, fled to Burmah and disappeared (1660); and another army under another Hindú, Mahárájá Jaswant Singh, was sent against Murád, who was joined early in 1658 by his brother Aurangzíb, for his own ends, but nominally with the intention of supporting Murád's claim to the throne. A decisive battle was fought at Dharmátpúr, near Ujjain, in April, and the two brothers routed the imperial forces. A second victory near Agrah and the flight of Dárá opened the way to the royal city. Sháh-Jahán, though somewhat recovered from his illness, was made a prisoner, June, 1658 (1068), and remained in captivity at Agrah till his death eight years later, in 1666 (Rajab, 1076). Murád Bakhsh was rudely undeceived by his astute brother, and sent to a dungeon at Dehlí, where he was eventually murdered (1662). Dárá was caught later, paraded in ignominy through the streets of Sháhjahánábád, and executed in his prison (1659).‡

Aurangzíb's road to the throne was now clear. He pretended at first to be acting as his father's deputy; but the farce could not long be kept up, and in May 1659 (1069) he was proclaimed Emperor with the style of Muhayyí-ad-dín Aurangzíb 'Álamgír ("Preserver of the Faith, Throne-adorner, World-grasper"). Born

---

* See Coins, Nos. 692-700. † See Coins, Nos. 690, 691.

‡ Kháfí Khán, ED. vii. 221-46, 266, 275.

in A.H. 1028, he was forty years of age at his accession. His mother's strict Muslim teaching, derived from her aunt Núr-Jahán, bore fruit in the son. Aurangzíb was a fanatical Muslim, and a man of strongly marked character, with all the courage of his opinions, and one whose prejudices make themselves felt. Jahángír and Sháh-Jahán had not been at the pains to bring any original ideas to bear upon their government. They had no gift of initiative, but were content to take Akbar's empire as they found it, and let things go on as usual. Provided that Jahángír had his bottle and Sháh-Jahán his stately Peacock Throne and all that it implied, they were content to let well alone. But for the soundness of Akbar's polity, and the wisdom of a series of able ministers, the empire might hardly have survived two such easy-going monarchs.

In Aurangzíb the people soon found that they had to deal with a very different sort of ruler. Not only was he a man with an idea, but he possessed the business capacity and attention to details which enabled him to carry his idea into practice. To him the Moghul empire was not so much a possession to be skilfully managed with the wisdom of this world, as a trust from God to be watched over, as a province of Islám. His wars in the Deccan, which occupied much of his energy throughout his long reign, were not so much prompted by ambition or the spirit of aggrandisement, as inspired by the zeal of a propagandist eager to bring pagan provinces within the pale of a Muhammadan empire. In every department of government the puritanical and bigoted Musalman revealed himself. He began by abolishing the heretical solar year and Persian months of Akbar, and restoring not only the Hijrah reckoning (which Jahángír had reinstated), but the lunar system for the regnal years and the Arab names of the months.* The significant New Year's festival, or Nauróz, celebrated at the vernal equinox, was strictly prohibited. The worldly luxury of Sháh-Jahán's court was exchanged for an austerity worthy of a Wahhábí tent, and the Emperor himself not only practised extreme asceticism, but followed the Prophet's precept in plying a trade for his own support. He embroidered skull-caps, and, like a literary bootmaker of our own day, he doubtless achieved a *succès d'estime*. He disliked the ostentation of the daily levees, when crowds came to stare at the Emperor as he sat in his belvedere of state; and in abolishing the custom, which was as reassuring as a Court Circular, he materially diminished his personal influence over the people. He stirred up religious jealousies, by taxing Muslim traders less than Hindús, and exasperated the latter, who formed the large majority of his subjects, by demolishing hundreds of their temples and throwing down their idols. He infuriated the Rájputs by attempting to circumcise the Rájá of Marwar's sons and make Muslims of them. He crowned his oppression of the Hindús by reimposing the poll-tax, a duty on heresy, which had never been levied since Akbar abolished it. For such measures as these he was finally mobbed in the streets, but the stern old bigot trampled down the crowds by a charge of his war-elephants. Such a policy in the land of the Hindús was madness, and led surely to the loosing of those ties which Akbar had striven to knit. Nor could it be consistently carried out, as Aurangzíb confessed by his own acts. He had himself married two Hindú wives, and he wedded his son Mu'azzam (afterwards the Emperor Bahádur) to a Hindú princess, as his forefathers had done before him, and thereby promoted

* Kháfí Khán, ED. vii. 241.

a mixture of blood which had conduced in a high degree to the improvement of their race ; he employed Hindús, like Jaswant Singh and Jai Singh and others, in positions of high trust, and graciously adopted a condescending attitude towards the English of Bombay and Calcutta.

By his strenuous advocacy of Muhammadanism he alienated the Hindús and paved the way for later disaffection. By his continual aggression and interference in the Deccan he brought the Moghul empire into contact with forces which it could neither assimilate nor subdue, and thus really weakened while he seemed to extend his realm. He stirred up the Maráthas, whom he never overcame, but left as a disastrous heritage to his successors. By his ineradicable habit of mistrust and suspicion he disheartened his ministers, and alienated his sons, one at least of whom, Mu'azzam, was inclined to be dutiful to the point of excess. Of his five sons, the eldest, Muhammad (sometimes called Mahmúd) threw in his lot with Shujá', and died in prison (1677). The second, of a Hindú mother, was Mu'azzam, who succeeded him : he, too, was imprisoned for some time by his father on groundless suspicion. The third and fourth, A'zam and Akbar, were children of a Persian lady. Once at least A'zam was on the verge of rebellion, and *Akbar* in 1682 openly espoused the cause of the insurgent Rájputs, assumed the attributes of sovereignty, and was driven into exile and died in Persia about 1706. The youngest, Kám Bakhsh, whose mother was a Hindú, became insubordinate in the Deccan and was put under arrest, only to fall later on in a rebellion against his brother.

In the midst of such troubles, but brave, resolute, and resourceful to the last, Aurangzíb 'Álamgír died, March 1707 (28 Zú-l-ka'dah 1118), * at the age of

* Kháfí Khán, ED. vii. 386.

almost ninety. "The instant which has been passed in power," he wrote, "has left only sorrow behind it. I have not been the guardian and protector of the empire." With all his marvellous vitality and power of work, he had failed to achieve success, and had placed his empire on the verge of a slope down which it slid irresistibly to dissolution. His narrow and suspicious nature could not inspire enthusiasm or devotion. "The period," Mr. Keene says,* "is dull and depressing; barren of great ideas, great transactions, and great men. With an abundance of energy and many talents and even virtues, the Emperor was one of those singular human beings who combine a hot head with a cold heart, and, having the courage and ambition to achieve power, lack the unscrupulousness by which alone—in such conditions as his—power can be permanently supported and exercised. To this day his name retains its hold in the memory of Indian Muslims as that of the greatest of their rulers; and writers nearer the time can hardly find words to express their admiration of him who unquestionably prepared the ruin of his dynasty. His misfortunes were those of a bold, narrow-minded, suspicious, and centralising egotist. As his father said of him, in terms that he himself records, 'Aurangzíb excelled both in action and in counsel and was well fitted to undertake the burden of affairs; but he was full of subtle suspicion, and never likely to find any one whom he could trust.'"

Yet when this last of the truly Great Moghuls died in 1707 there was little to indicate that the wide empire which he had ruled for half a century was destined to crumble in hardly more than the same period before the inroads of savage mountaineers and the steady encroach-

* *Op. cit.* 220. See his character in ED. vii. 157 ff.

ment of European traders. All the old provinces of Hindústán remained in undisturbed tranquillity. His money bears witness to the extent of his dominions. We find his name on coins issued at nearly forty different mints :* Kábul and Kashmír; Lahore and Multán in the Panjáb; Bhakkar on the Indus; Tattah further south in Sind; Júnágarh in Káthiáwár; Ahmadábád, Súrat, and Cambay in Gujarát; Ajmír in Rájputána; Sháhjahánábád, Sirhind, and Barailí in the *súbah* or province of Dehlí; Akbarábád (Agrah), Nárnól, Etáwah, in the province of Biána; Lucknow in Oudh; Zafarábád in the Alláhábád *súbah;* Akbarnagar and Patnah in Bihár; Makhsúsábád (*i.e.* Murshidábád), Jahángírnagar (Dhákká), and Islámábád (Chittagong), in Bengal. South of the Vindhya mountains, the testimony of the currency to the Emperor's sway is equally positive. We have coins bearing his name from the mints of Burhánpúr in Khandésh, from Ahmadnagar and Aurangábád in Berár; further south, from Sholápúr, Golkondah, Bíjápúr, and Haidarábád; and even from Masulipatan and Chínápatan (Madras), far down on the Coromandel coast. All India, save the very apex of the Deccan triangle, owned the authority of Aurangzíb.

In Akbar's reign, India had been originally divided into twelve *súbahs* or provinces: Agrah, Alláhábád, Oudh, Bihár, Bengal, Dehlí, Lahore, Multán, Ajmír, Málwah, Gujarát, Kábul (with Kashmír); to which were added at a later date Khandésh, Berár, and Ahmadnagar. In Aurangzíb's time there were twenty provinces: Gondwána, Aurangábád, Bíjápúr, Haidarábád, and Bídar were added in the Deccan. The mode of government in these provinces has been ably described by Bernier in a

---

* In the British Museum and in the list published by Mr. C. J. Rodgers in the *Proceedings of the Asiatic Society of Bengal* for 1883.

letter to the French minister Colbert.* The system of military feofs continued much as in Akbar's time, and many of these territorial lords were Hindús; they received high salaries, sometimes paid in land, in return for which they maintained a body of retainers, well armed and mounted for the service of the Emperor. The provinces, districts, and cities had their governors, and the administration by all accounts appears to have been fairly good for an oriental system: Manouchi indeed thought it "little inferior to that of other nations," though murder and robbery were undoubtedly far from infrequent crimes.

The history of the Moghul empire after the death of Aurangzíb is a chronicle of weakness in the sovereigns and disintegration in the realm. Seventeen princes exercised the royal prerogative of coinage between 1707 and 1857 (some of whom, however, were usurpers or unsuccessful claimants for the throne), and not one of these displayed the capacity of a ruler. Aurangzíb's eldest surviving son, Mu'azzam ("Very Mighty"), who had been given the title of Sháh-'Álam or "Lord of the World," was governor of Kábul at the time of his father's death, and in his absence, and in default of evidence of the late Emperor's having named a successor, the next brother, *A'zam* ("Mightiest") Sháh, assumed the functions of royalty and struck coins, 1707 (1118),† supported by Asad Khán and his son Zú-l-Fikár, who led what may be called the Persian faction, as opposed to that of the Afgháns and Turks, in the internal politics of Hindústán. Meanwhile Mu'azzam, accompanied by his sons, came down from Kábul, and, joined by the able governor of the Panjáb, Mun'im Khán, occupied Dehlí and Agrah.

---

* Bernier's *Travels* (*Constable's Oriental Misc.* i.), 200 ff.

† See Coins, Nos. 847-851.

Then, with the magnanimity which was his best characteristic, the gentle prince offered to share the empire with his brother. A'zam would not listen to terms, however, and the brothers fought on the plains near Agrah, where A'zam was slain and his army defeated, June, 1707 (18 Rabí' I. 1119).* Asad and Zú-l-Fikár were treated with the new emperor's habitual clemency, and the former was reinstated as prime minister. Mu'azzam then ascended the throne under the title of Sháh-'Álam Bahádur ("Valiant") Sháh. He was then a man of sixty-four; naturally of a conciliatory and merciful disposition, the blood he drew from his Hindú mother made him benignant to his Indian subjects, and should have recommended him to his kinsmen, the refractory Rájputs. His philosophical studies indeed laid him open to the charge of being too much of a Hindú for the approbation of honest Muslims. Nevertheless, the seeds of disaffection sown by the exclusive policy of Aurangzíb bore fruit, and in spite of the new Emperor's concessions, and especially his prudent consent to rescind the hated faith-tax on non-Muslims, the Rájputs continued to nurse their awakened suspicions. Another race, the Játs, a tribe of brigands, nominally Muslims, who had their centre about Bhurtpúr, also became troublesome at this time. A new and dangerous power, that of the Sikhs, sprang up in the Panjáb, sacked Sirhind and Sahéranpúr, and in spite of repulses succeeded in harrying the country up to the gates of Lahore. Finally, the Maráthas were waxing stronger and more outrageous every year. The Deccan was the weakest point in the empire from the beginning of the reign. Hardly had Bahádur appointed his youngest brother, *Kám Bakhsh* ("Wish-fulfiller"), viceroy of Bíjápúr and Haidarábád, when that infatuated

* For this period see Kháfí Khán, ED. vii. 387-533.

prince rebelled and committed such atrocities that the Emperor was compelled to attack him. Zú-l-Fikár engaged and defeated the rebel king (who was striking coins in full assumption of sovereignty)* near Haidarábád, and Kám Bakhsh died of his wounds (1708, A.H. 1120).

In the midst of this confusion, and surrounded by portents of coming disruption, Bahádur died, 1712 (1124). He left four sons, who immediately entered with the zest of their race upon the struggle for the crown. The eldest, *'Azím-ash-Shán* ("Strong of heart"), first assumed the sceptre, but Zú-l-Fikár, the prime minister, opposed and routed him, and the prince was drowned in his flight. The successful general next defeated and slew two other brothers, Khujistah Akhtár Jahán-Sháh and Rafí'-ash-Shán, and placed the surviving of the four sons of Bahádur on the throne with the title of JAHÁNDÁR ("World-owner"). The new Emperor was an irredeemable poltroon and an abandoned debauchee. He divided his time between a dancing-girl and low taverns, whence he was brought home in a cart, and on one occasion by inadvertence left there outside his own palace to cool till the morning. "Night and day," says Kháfí, "were devoted to the lusts of this vile world. It was a fine time for dancers and singers and all the tribe of actors. There seemed to be a likelihood that the Kázís would turn tosspots and the Muftís become tipplers."† Such profligacy speedily aroused the contempt of his subjects, and two ambitious brothers, Abdallah and Husain, the chiefs of the Sayyids of Bárha, who held the posts of governors of the provinces of Alláhábád and Bihár, and belonged to the Persian sect of the Shí'ah, selected a new candidate for the Peacock Throne.

---

* See Coins, Nos. 852, 853.

† Kháfí Khán, ED. vii. 432-3.

This was Farrukh-siyar ("Happy-natured"), son of the late 'Azím-ash-Shán, and formerly governor of Bengal under Bahádur.* The conspirators were successful; the imperial troops were defeated; the slaughtered body of Jahándár was placed on an elephant, and Zú-l-Fikár's corpse tied to its tail in a mock funeral procession (January, 1713, A.H. 1124). Farrukh-siyar was almost as effeminate as his predecessor, but his ministers and generals were men of pith. They were able to make head against the Rájputs, who gave a daughter of the Rájá of Jodhpúr in marriage to the Emperor, whilst the Sikhs were seriously discomfited and their Guru or prophet was put to death with horrible barbarity. An English embassy from Calcutta was in 1715 received with courtesy at Dehlí, and, after considerable delay, obtained certain concessions which, however, they owed mainly to the diplomatic skill evinced by their surgeon Hamilton in operating upon a tumour which hindered the consummation of the Emperor's marriage with the Rájput princess.

An estrangement had by this time grown up between Farrukh-siyar and the two Sayyids, and Husain, who had been appointed Viceroy of the Deccan, having made a humiliating peace with the Maráthas, marched upon Dehlí, assisted by a contingent of these marauders, who for the first time enjoyed the delight of exercising their predatory propensities in the capital of the Moghul empire. No opposition was attempted; Farrukh-siyar hid himself among his women, whence he was dragged forth, thrown into prison (February 1719, Rabí' II.

* Kháfí Khán states that, on hearing of the death of Bahádur, Farrukh-siyar struck coins in the name of 'Azím-ash-Shán, and, after the latter's death, in his own name. No coins, however, have hitherto been published with the name of 'Azím-ash-Shán; but the mohr No. 890, struck at Murshidábád, with the regnal year 1, may have been issued prior to Jahándár's death. Farrukh-siyar ignored Jahándár's eleven months' reign, and reckoned his own from his father's death. ED. vii. 439, 478, *note*.

1131), and after some months executed. The same year witnessed the remarkable spectacle of four princes successively assuming the crown. Two of these were set up in rapid sequence by the Sayyid brothers: they were both sons of the late prince Rafí'-ash-Shán, the son of Bahádur, and were styled RAFÍ'-AD-DARAJÁT ("Summit of Degree") and RAFÍ'-AD-DAULAH ("Summit of the State") Sháh-Jahán II. The first died in four months, and the second followed him to the grave after holding the nominal sceptre from May to September (20 Rejeb to 11 Zú-l-Ka'dah, 1131). Meanwhile, another claimant appeared in the person of *Nikusiyar* ("Excellent in disposition") a son of Akbar, the rebel son of Aurangzíb, but he was soon disposed of, though not before he had exercised the coveted privilege of issuing his own money.* The empire had fallen into confusion; the contumacy of rájás was condoned with the governorship of provinces; and most of the western part of Hindústán became almost independent in the hands of Hindús, while the Maráthas did what they pleased in the Deccan.

In the midst of this anarchy MUHAMMAD Sháh ascended the throne (Sept., 1719, 11 Zú-l-ka'dah, 1131).† He was a son of Khujistah Akhtar and grandson of Bahádur, and consequently first cousin to the three preceding puppet-kings. He appears to have been only sixteen years of age when he became Emperor, and at first he was forced to acquiesce in the tyranny of the Sayyid brothers; but the Turkish party, headed by Chin Kulich Khán, soon put an end to the domination of these Persian dictators. Their armies were defeated; Sayyid Husain was treacherously murdered, while his brother 'Abdallah, after

* See Coin No. 953, and Kháfí Khán, ED. vii. 480-2.

† Kháfí Khán, ED. vii. 485.

setting up *Ibráhím*, a brother of Rafí'-ad-daulah, on the throne in 1720, which he occupied for only a month (9 Zú-l-Hijjah, 1132, to 12 Muharram, 1133), died in captivity in 1723. Chin Kulich Khán, henceforth to be known as Ásaf Jáh Nizám-al-Mulk, became viceroy of the Deccan, and prime minister, but soon departed south to administer the important province which is still ruled by one of his descendants. He was, perhaps, the only really great and powerful man of the reign. His government of the Deccan, though always hampered by the exactions of the Maráthas, was generous and enlightened; he was a patron of poor scholars, and an author himself; and he improved his dominions by building public works, bridges, canals, and mosques. He died in the plenitude of power in June, 1748, at the age of over a hundred years. The struggle for the throne once over, Muhammad Sháh gave himself up to the self-indulgence which had become the birthright of Moghul Emperors, and left his kingdom to be overrun by the Maráthas, and to be broken up into numerous petty principalities, more or less independent, from which most of the present native states of India trace their origin.

The Emperor was aroused from his lethargy by an overwhelming catastrophe. Nádir Sháh, the usurping sovereign of Persia, in response apparently to an invitation from the Persian party in Hindústán, suddenly seized Kandahár and Kábul in 1737, and, after laying waste the Panjáb, entered Lahore. The Moghul army advanced to repel him, but was defeated after an obstinate battle near Karnól. Negotiations for peace were already in progress when Muhammad cut them short by surrendering himself in Nádir's camp. The two armies fraternized and entered Dehlí together on 19 March, 1738 (Zú-l-Hijjah, 1151).

* See Coins, Nos. 954-7; Kháfí Khán, ED. vii. 509.

Here a passing brawl led to a tumult, and Nádir ordered the streets to be swept with grape-shot. An indiscriminate massacre of the inhabitants ensued for nine hours, during which 120,000 people are said to have been slaughtered. In May the Persians marched out of Dehlí,* taking with them a Moghul princess and a treaty by which they obtained all territories west of the Indus, and leaving the Moghul empire quaking and tottering after this unprecedented shock.

Ten years later Ahmad Khán the Durrání, founder of the modern Afghan dynasty, attempted to emulate Nádir's example by invading the Panjáb and occupying Lahore (1748). He was beaten off, for the time, by the Moghuls; but such invasions are a true index to the decay of the empire. Muhammad Sháh died of grief, feeble and passive to the end (April, 1748, 27 Rabi' II. 1161). He is the last of the Moghuls who enjoyed even the semblance of power, and has been called "the seal of the house of Bábar," for "after his demise everything went to wreck."†

His son and successor AHMAD Sháh occupied the throne for fourteen years: but they were all "labour and sorrow." The history of the reign is made up of the continual jealousies and intrigues and open conflicts of the rival Persian and Turkish factions, who fought in the streets of Dehlí; the turbulence of the Játs and of the Rohilas, or Afgháns of Rohilkhand, an added element of anarchy; quarrels between Rájput rájás; incursions of the Maráthas, who, led by chiefs of the Holkar and

---

* See Nádir's coins, struck at Sháhjahánábád in 1152, Bhakar 1156, and Pesháwar, in the *Catalogue of the Coins of the Sháhs of Persia in the British Museum*, by R. S. Poole, 80, 82; and others struck at Lahore 1151, and in Sind (but the reading is doubtful), published by C. J. Rodgers in *Numismatic Chronicle* III. ii. 319-26. See also ED. viii. 76.

† *Siyar-al-Mutaäkhirín.*

Sindhia lineage—names soon to become famous in the annals of British rule in India—overran Gujarát and Rájputána; and unwelcome visits from Ahmad Sháh Durráni, who again invaded the Panjáb, and only left it when the Moghuls consented to hold Multán and Lahore as tributary provinces of the Afghán kingdom.* The result of these various disturbing elements was that, while almost all India still professed fealty to the Moghul sovereign and impressed his name upon the local coinage, very little of the original empire really remained under his direct control, except the districts bordering upon the capital. "Gujarát was overrun by the Maráthas; Málwah and Rájputána had ceased to pay tribute or to acknowledge an imperial viceroy, the former being annexed to the Deccan, the latter held in sovereignty by its own rájás. The Játs were independent in the country south of Agrah, and the Bangash Patháns of Farrukhábád were equally so in the central Duáb. Oudh and Alláhábád were practically a kingdom in the hands of Safdar Jang [son of the Nizám]; the eastern Súbahs (Bihár, Bengal, and Orissa) were similarly subject to the dynasty of Iláhwírdí; the Panjáb was tributary to the Afghán state of Kandahár; the Maráthas were supreme elsewhere, save where the Nizám kept them at arm's length."†

At Dehlí itself the power was in the hands of Ghází-ad-dín, a nephew of Safdar Jang, whose youth (he was but sixteen when he was made Amír-al-Umará, or premier noble) was no measure of his audacity and ambition. Dissatisfied with the inefficiency of Ahmad, he deposed and blinded him; then, assuming the office of vazír, he set up a man of fifty-five, the exemplary son of the

---

* Ample numismatic evidence exists of the presence of the Durránís in the Indus provinces. See C. J. Rodgers in *Journal of the Asiatic Soc. of Bengal*, 1885; and M. Longworth Dames in *Num. Chron.* III. viii. 325-63 (1888).

† Keene, *op. cit.* 339.

scandalous Jahándár, with the title of 'Álamgír II. (June, 1754, 11 Sha'bán, 1167).* Whatever respect the new Emperor received in his diminished dominions was due less to his own undeniable amiability and piety than to the wisdom and courage of two men, Najíb-ad-daulah, the Afghán ruler of "the fifty-two Pargánas" or region about Sahâranpúr, who presently became vazír of the empire and its chief defender against the Maráthas; and Shujá'-ad-daulah, who had succeeded his father Safdar Jang as Nawáb of Oudh in October, 1754, and who joined Najíb in his efforts to withstand the domination of the southern invaders. It was not easy, however, to make even a show of imperial government in those evil times of Moghul history; and when Ahmad Durrání again came down from Kandahár and appeared at Dehlí in 1757, Najíb and Ghází showed their discretion in making an ally of a foe who was less to be dreaded than the Maráthas, inasmuch as he went off when he had got the plunder he came for, whereas the tribesmen of Holkar and Sindhia showed every disposition to stay. Having sucked Dehlí dry and drained the surrounding country as far as possible, the Durrání departed to Afghánistán in November, 1757, taking with him a few Moghul princesses for his family, and leaving Najíb as Amír-al-Umará to protect the Emperor against the encroachments of the ambitious and unscrupulous Ghází. The latter accepted the challenge and made war upon Najíb, and meanwhile had the harmless old Emperor brutally and treacherously murdered, November, 1759 (1173). 'Álamgír II. had sat on his tottering throne for five miserable years.

The vazír Ghází-ad-dín then set up a new puppet, a grandson of Kám Bakhsh, under the name of *Sháh-*

* *Taríkh-i 'Álamgír Sání*, ED. viii. 141.

Jahán II. (it should have been III., since Rafí'-ad-daulah was the second who used the title), and the administration at Dehlí was carried on in his name for a few months.* The rightful heir, however, was the son of the late Emperor, 'Alí Gaur, infelicitously styled SHÁH-'ÁLAM ("Lord of the Universe"), and he was at once recognized as emperor by the country at large and by its powerful neighbour, Ahmad the Durrání. This alarming protector was now again in Hindústán, and, after driving away Ghází-ad-dín and his mimic king, he inflicted a memorable and crushing defeat upon the Maráthas in January, 1761, upon the historical field of Pánípat: after which he returned to Afghánistán, leaving Najíb and Shujá' to make the best of their new Emperor.

When the news came of his father's murder, Sháh-'Álam was in Bihár, bent upon establishing his claim to the viceroyalty of the eastern Súbahs, where he thought he had a better chance of enjoying the pleasures of power than in the distracted capital of his ancestors. He soon found, however, that he was out in his reckoning. Since the battle of Plassey in 1757, Bengal (with Bihár and Orissa) had been under the authority of a Nawáb, under British control. The new Emperor, however, did not at once realize the full meaning of the situation. He invaded Bengal, only to be twice repulsed by the Nawáb and the English (1760-1). Aided by Shujá'-ad-daulah, he resumed the attack in 1764, and was utterly routed 23rd October, by Munro at Baksar (Buxar) near the confluence of the Karamnasa and the Ganges.† Next day he came into the British camp, and from that date (if not earlier) the Moghul empire became practically a thing of the past. By firmáns of 12th August, 1765, a treaty

---

* See Coins Nos. 1086-1092.

† ED. viii. 216 ff.

signed at Alláhábád on the 16th, and articles of agreement dated three days later, the East India Company was granted the Díwání or financial administration of Bengal, Bihár, and Orissa, in consideration of the Emperor's being allowed to retain the province of Alláhábád and the district of Korah, and being given a yearly subsidy by the Company, wherewith to maintain his dignity. In other words, the English annexed the three eastern provinces, and Sháh-'Álam, whilst nominally Emperor of India, became really a pensioner of the British Crown. He kept a sorry court for some years at Alláhábád, with an English resident to look after him, and then in 1771 returned to Dehlí, exchanging, as events proved, the protection of the British for the tyranny of the Maráthas. He enjoyed, however, a brief interval of prosperity, almost of power, during the able administration of Mírzá Najaf; but the gleam of sunshine was followed by darkness. Sháh-'Álam was barbarously blinded by Ghulám Kádir in 1788, and a new puppet, *Bídár-Bakht* ("Of wakeful fortune"), son of Ahmad, was set up.* Immediately afterwards the Maráthas entered into possession, avenged the crime, and deposed the usurper, but kept the unfortunate Emperor completely under control. Thus he remained till Lord Lake's victory in 1803 freed him and Hindústán from the southern pestilence.

From the Treaty of Alláhábád in 1765 onwards the history of India has little to do with the Great Moghul: it is the history of the struggle of many adventurers of various nations for the fragments of a broken empire,† and the record of the final triumph of the English. As

---

* He sat on the abased throne from Shawwál, 1202, to Jumádá II, 1203 (1788). See Coins Nos. 1206-9.

† Mr. Keene's *Fall of the Mughal Empire* (1887) gives a detailed and accurate account of this period.

such it need not be detailed in this place : such parts of it as are necessary to the numismatist will be found discussed in § 9, below. Here it is only necessary to add that Sháh-'Álam died in 1806 (1221), and was succeeded in his position of imperial pensioner of the British Crown by his son, MUHAMMAD AKBAR II.; who in turn was followed in 1837 (1253) by his son, BAHÁDUR II., whose participation in the Indian Mutiny led to his banishment in 1857 to Rangoon, where this last of the Moghul Emperors died in 1862.

The task of England has been to undo the disastrous work of Aurangzíb. "It was by the alienation of the native races that the Moghul Empire perished: it is by the incorporation of those races into a loyal and united people that the British rule will endure." * But whilst endeavouring to restore Akbar's empire by Akbar's policy of wise conciliation, we have to remember that neither empire nor policy could have existed without the strong dominant ascendancy of Akbar himself; nor can the Empress of India's domination in her eastern Empire dispense with a strong and absolute British authority, supreme and paramount over all.

---

* Sir William Wilson Hunter, *The Ruin of Aurangzeb, XIXth Century*, May, 1887.

§ 2. *THE CABINET OF MOGHUL COINS.*

THE series of coins of the Moghul Emperors of Hindústán in the British Museum has long been celebrated, and the important additions of the last ten years have placed it at the head of all similar collections. The nucleus of this unrivalled cabinet was the rich bequest of William Marsden in 1834. This was notably augmented by the purchase in 1847 and 1850 of coins collected by the *doyen* of Indian numismatists, Prinsep, and his worthy disciple, Edward Thomas, and by the acquisition in 1853 of the valuable Eden cabinet. Within the last decade the coins originally preserved at the India House and Office were transferred to the British Museum (1882); the fine collection of Mr. A. Grant was added in 1885; and the splendid Arabic and Persian cabinet of Gen. Sir Alexander Cunningham was purchased in 1888; while the Government of India, the Bengal Asiatic Society, the Bombay Branch of the Royal Asiatic Society, and the Archaeological Survey of the Panjáb, have largely contributed towards filling up the gaps in the National series. These are the chief constituents in the collection; but a number of officers, civilians, and travellers in India have continually brought a few rare specimens to the Museum, and many names well known to others than numismatists may be recognised among these collectors; such as Professor H. H. Wilson, Col. Guthrie, Col. Tobin Bush, Major Hay, Sir Bartle Frere, Mr. James Gibbs, Mr. James Burgess, Mr. Da Cunha, &c.; whilst among the early benefactors of the collection, though in small numbers, may be mentioned Miss Sarah Sophia Banks (1818), the Rev. Clayton Mordaunt Cracherode (1799), Mr. R. Payne Knight (1824), and his Majesty King

George III., who contributed four specimens. As a considerable interest attaches to many of the collectors whose cabinets have combined to form the series described in the present volume, it has been judged useful to affix their names to their coins, except in cases where there were but one or two specimens presented or purchased. Coins acquired in the ordinary market have as a rule no name attached to them in the Catalogue.

The relative strength of the various component elements of the Moghul series may be summarized as follows. Excluding the East India Company's coinage, the series consists of about 1250 coins. Of these the following collections contributed nearly 1000 :—

Marsden	173
Cunningham	147
India Office	132
Alex. Grant	101
Prinsep	65
Eden	57
Thomas	58
Government of India	34
Panjáb Archaeological Survey	30
Bengal Asiatic Society	28
Hay, Payne Knight, Gibbs, Playfair, Theobald, and Bombay Asiatic Society (from 10 to 20 each)	97
Banks, Prof. Wilson, Bank of England Coll., Cracherode, Bush, Stubbs, Pearse, Frere, Yeames, Cureton, Burnes, Stewart, De Bode, Guthrie, Da Cunha, & George III. (under 10 each)	74

About two-thirds of the Moghul coinage, as represented in the British Museum, falls under the third, fourth, fifth and sixth Emperors, Akbar, Jahángír, Sháh-Jahán, and

Aurangzíb, whose reigns cover rather more than half the interval between the accession of Bábar in 1525 (A.H. 932) and the death of Sháh-'Álam in 1806 (1221). The actual numbers of gold, silver, and copper coins of these four Emperors are as follows :—

	AV	AR	Æ	Total
Akbar	75	168	39	282
Jahángír	83	161	1	245
Sháh-Jahán	50	123	—	173
Aurangzíb	24	125	—	149
Total	232	577	40	849

In this table, the very large proportion of gold to silver (more than one-half in the reign of Jahángír, and ·4 on the whole number) and the extraordinary scarcity of copper will be observed. The latter subject will call for discussion later (§ 8).

The coins of the two Emperors preceding Akbar, Bábar and Humáyún, which are attributable to their Indian government, are very few, and partake of the character of the currency of Transoxiana, the province whence Bábar advanced to rule in India. Some Transoxine issues of Bábar are described in the *Catalogue of Oriental Coins*, Vol. vii, p. 163, and *Additions* part ii, p. 163, and in the *Catalogue of Persian Coins*, pp. xxv and 210. The Kashmír issues of Humáyún and Akbar are noticed in the *Catalogue of Indian Coins, Muhammadan States*, p. 80.

Of the seventeen Emperors and pretenders who struck coins between the death of Aurangzíb and the accession of Sháh-'Álam, only Muhammad Sháh appears to have issued a large currency (AV 20. AR 63 = 83); Farrukh-siyar is represented by 47 coins; and the others by numbers ranging from 1 to 29. Sháh-'Álam's coinage, numerous as it is, as will be explained further on (§ 9), cannot be regarded as his personal coinage in the same sense as that of Akbar.

§ 3. *MINT CITIES.*

The range of mints embraced in the rich series of coins from Akbar to Aurangzíb furnishes a faithful chart of the growth and extent of the Moghul Empire. In the following list the later Emperors are included, though they add little to the data. Bábar and Humáyún's mints are represented only by Lahore in the British Museum collection.

Akbar. 963—1014 (1556—1605)	Agrah, Lahore, Dehlí, Ahmadábád, Burhánpúr, Patnah, Tattah, Kábul, Multán, Alláhábád, Nárnól, Gwálior, Sárangpúr, Jaunpúr, Sirhind, Udaipúr, Fathpúr, Urdú-Zafar-Karín, Urdú, Asír, Sítápúr, Dógám, Malpúr, Bairátah.
Jahángír. 1014—37 (1605—27)	Agrah, Lahore, Dehlí, Ahmadábád, Burhánpúr, Patnah, Súrat, Tattah, Kábul, Ajmír, Jahángírnagar [Dhákká], Akbarnagar, Kashmír, Kandahár.
Dáwar Bakhsh. 1037 (1627-8)	Lahore.
Sháh-Jahán. 1037—68 (1628—58)	Agrah and Akbarábád, Lahore, Dehlí and Sháhjahánábád, Ahmadábád, Burhánpúr, Patnah, Súrat, Tattah, Kábul, Multán, Alláhábád, Jahángírnagar [Dhákká], Akbarnagar, Kashmír, Kandahár, Júnahgarh, Daulatábád, Bhakar.

Sháh Shujá'. 1068—70 (1656—60)	Akbarábád [*i.e.* Agrah].
Murád Bakhsh. 1068 (1658)	Ahmadábád, Cambay, Súrat.
Aurangzíb. 1069—1118 (1659—1707)	Akbarábád [Agrah], Lahore, Sháhjahánábád [Dehlí], Burhánpúr, Patnah, Súrat, Tattah, Kábul, Ajmír, Multán, Nárnól, Júnahgarh, Cambay, Etáwah, Khujistah-bunyád, and Aurangábád, Golkondah, Masulipatan, Ahmadnagar, Bíjápúr, Chínápatan [Madras], Nasratábád, Baraílí, Lucknow, 'Álamgírpúr, Zafarpúr, Zafarábád.
A'zam. 1118-19 (1707)	Ahmadábád, Burhánpúr, Khujistah-bunyád [Aurangábád.]
Kám Bakhsh. 1119-20 (1708)	Bíjápúr, Haidarábád.
Bahádur. 1119—23 (1707—12)	Akbarábád [Agrah], Lahore, Sháhjahánábád [Dehlí], Burhánpúr, 'Azímábád [Patnah], Súrat, Ajmír, Peshâwar, Khujístah-bunyád [Aurangábád], Sholápúr, Ujjain.
Jahándár. 1124 (1712)	Akbarábád [Agrah], Sháhjahánábád [Dehlí], Súrat, Khujistah-bunyád [Aurangábád].

FARRUKH-SIYAR 1124—31 (1713—19)	Akbarábád [Agrah], Lahore, Sháhjahánábád [Dehlí], Burhánpúr, Patnah and Azímábád, Súrat, Multán, Gwálior, Etáwah, Bíjápúr, Chínápatan [Madras], Barailí, Arkát, Katak, A'zamnagar, Imtiyázgarh, Gútí, Gangpúr, Murshidábád.
RAFÍ'-AD-DARAJÁT. 1131 (1719)	Akbarábád [Agrah], Lahore, Sháhjahanábád [Dehlí], Patnah, Mu'azzamábád.
RAFÍ'-AD-DAULAH. 1131 (1719)	Akbarábád [Agrah], Lahore, Sháhjahánábád [Dehlí], 'Azímábád [Patnah], Súrat, Khujistah-bunyád [Aurangábád], Barailí, Murshidábád.
Niku-siyar. 1131 (1719)	Súrat.
Ibráhím. 1132 (1720)	Sháhjahánábád [Dehlí].
MUHAMMAD. 1131—61 (1719—48)	Akbarábád [Agrah], Lahore, Sháhjahánábád [Dehlí], 'Azímábád [Patnah], Súrat, Tattah, Akbarnagar-Oudh, Kashmír, Etáwah, Khujistah-bunyád [Aurangábád], Barailí, Murshidábád, Kúrá, Ajáyúr, Islámábád [Chittagong], Benáres, Sháhábád, Siwáï-Jaipúr, Imtiyázgarh, Farrukhábád.

AHMAD. 1161—7 (1748—54)	Akbarábád [Agrah], Sháhjahánábád [Dehlí], 'Azímábád [Patnah], Murshidábád, Benáres, Ahmadnagar-Farrukhábád, Murádábád.
'ÁLAMGÍR II. 1167—73 (1754—60)	Akbarábád [Agrah], Lahore, Sháhjahánábád [Dehlí], Murshidábád, Ahmadnagar-Farrukhábád, Imtiyázgarh, Indrapúr [Indore].
Sháh-Jahán III. 1173 (1760-1)	Sháhjahánábád [Dehlí], Ahmadábád, Ahmadnagar-Farrukhábád, Indrapúr [Indore], Islámábád [Chittagong].
SHAH-'ÁLAM. 1173—1221 (1761—1806)	Akbarábád [Agrah], Sháhjahánábád [Dehlí], Ahmadábád, 'Azímábád [Patnah], Súrat, Murshidábád, Ahmadnagar-Farrukhábád, Etáwah, Benáres, Bahádurpatan, Dilshádábád, Jahángírnagar [Dhákká], Srínagar, Lucknow, Najíbábád.
Bídár-Bakht. 1202-3 (1788)	Sháhjahánábád [Dehlí], Ahmadábád.
MUHAMMAD AKBAR II. 1221—53 (1806—37)	Sháhjahánábád [Dehlí].
BAHÁDUR II. 1253—75 (1837—57)	Sháhjahánábád [Dehlí].

A glance at the accompanying map of India will immediately show the wide range of territory embraced by these mint-cities. In Akbar's time they spread from Kábul and Tattah on the west to Patnah on the east, and from Lahore in the north to Udaipúr in Rájputána, and Asírgarh in Khandésh. In the reign of Aurangzíb we find a large addition of Deccan mints, due to this Emperor's wars in the south. Under the pretender Kám Bakhsh, Haidarábád occurs for the first time; Arkát and Gútí appear under Farrukh-siyar, as well as the new fiscal capital of Bengal, Murshidábád, afterwards familiar on the coins of the East India Company.

The first appearance of many of these mints possesses an historical importance. The occurrence of the mint Ahmadábád on a gold mohr of 980 evidently marks the conquest of Gujarát, of which this city was the capital, in 980 (1572). Still more notable is the mohr no. 63. It bears the unique formula ضرب محمداباد عرف اديپور مفتوحة "Struck at Muhammadábád commonly called Udaipúr, conquered," with the date 984, which corresponds to the reduction of that frequently insurgent Rájput city by Akbar in 1577. The first rupee of Burhánpúr (no 197), issued in the month Dai of 38 Iláhí (1593), records the invasion of the provinces of Khandésh and Berár in 1001. The mohr of Asír (no. 166), again, with the curious device of a falcon, and the Iláhí year 45, clearly commemorates Akbar's later conquest of the fortress of Asírgarh, the strong place of Khandésh, and the discovery of immense treasure there, in the summer of 1600. Akbar's new palace of Fathpúr, or "Victory-town," which he founded at Síkrí, 27 miles south-west of Agrah in 976-9 (1569-71), is represented in his coinage only from 986 to 989, and thenceforth disappears from the series. Mr. Rodgers, however, has described * a Zodiacal mohr (Capricornus) of Jahángír's, bearing this mint and the 14th year of his reign, and 1028 A.H. The mint Urdu,

* *Journal of the Asiatic Society of Bengal*, lvii. 26.

or Urdú-Zafar-Karín ("Camp linked to Victory"), is supposed to indicate the striking of coins during Akbar's victorious progresses, in the north probably, on his way to his summer resort in the happy valley of Kashmír. It is possible, however, that the name Urdú-Zafar-Karín may possess some mystical import. All the coins bearing this mint, if such it be, present, in the place of the usual ciphers indicating the date, the single word الف, 1000. This is the only instance in the whole series (except احد in recording the first regnal year) of the use of an Arabic numeral in the place of ciphers, and it has a certain significance in view of the following circumstances recorded by the historian Badáóní. As early as 990 Akbar had convinced himself that the Muhammadan religion was destined to last exactly 1000 years from the Hijrah and no more. It was believed that the second advent would be inaugurated by the coming of the Mahdí, and Akbar appears to have encouraged the expectation. He ordered the "Era of the Thousand" to be engraved on the coins, and commanded a Shíya'í divine to write a *Tarikh-i Alfí* or "History of the Millennium" (A.H. 1-1000), and confided the completion of it to Badáóní himself. The work appeared in the year 1000 A.H. (1592); and in the same year Akbar called-in all the old coins of his predecessors and melted them down.* There may be some connexion between this "Era of a Thousand" and the year الف 1000 on the coins; and it may not be unreasonable to suggest that these millennium pieces with the word الف are the product of the melting down of older issues recorded to have taken place in the year 1000 of the Hijrah. If this be a correct surmise, the name Urdú-Zafar-Karín may bear some such signification, in the mystical phraseology of the Shí'ah, as "Camp of the approaching triumph of the Faith."

* Badáóní, ED. v. 534, 542.

Abu-l-Fazl's account of Akbar's mints in the *Áín-i-Akbarí* is very imperfect. He states that at the beginning of the reign gold was struck in many parts of the empire; but at the time he wrote, only at four places, the seat of government [Fathpúr], Bengál [*i.e.* Dhákká], Ahmadábád, and Kábul. Silver was also coined there, and likewise at ten other towns:—Iláhábás, Agrah, Ujjain, Súrat, Dehlí, Patnah, Kashmír, Lahore, Multán, and Tándah. Copper, however, he says, proceeded from twenty mints:—Ajmír, Oudh, Atak, Alwar, Badáón, Benáres, Bhakar, Bahrah, Patnah, Jaunpúr, Jálandár, Hardwár, Hisár Fírózah, Kálpi, Gwálior, Górakhpúr, Kalánwar, Lucknow, Mandú, Nágór, Sirhind, Siálkót, Sironj, Sahá-ranpúr, Sárangpúr, Sambal, Kanauj, Rantambhór.* A comparison with the coins will at once show the inaccuracy of these statements.

Few of Akbar's mints present difficulties in identification. The mohr no. 31 is ascribed to Sárangpúr, but it must be admitted that there is no trace of the ك in the mint, which reads merely سارنپور It may be urged, however, that as this city, the capital of Málwah, was annexed by Akbar in 969, according to the *Tabakát-i Akbarí*, the appearance of a solitary gold piece with its name in 972 (the date of this coin) was in character with Akbar's proceedings at Udaipúr and Asírgarh. All three are in the nature of commemorative medals, and we do not meet with these mints again in the series. The name سلور on no. 177 has been read پشاور Peshávar, but with little confidence; Mr. Rodgers,† however, suggests سیتاپور Sítápúr, and the diacritical points favour his interpretation. Mr. Rodgers and Mr. Oliver‡ have read the mint دوکام as دوکانو, Dóganw:

---

* See § 8 below.

† *Journ. As. Soc. Bengal*, lii. 97. ‡ *Ibid.* lv.

but, while it is most probably the same name, there can be no question that the last letter on the copper coins nos. 263, 271, is مر not نو. Several places called Deogaon are mentioned in Abu-l-Fazl's list of Todar Mal's rent-roll. Málpúr in Gujarát, and Bairátah, which Gen. Sir Alex. Cunningham supposes to be Vairáta, in Rájputána, noted for copper mines, are among the rarer mints which occur only among Akbar's copper currency. The mint Tattah has frequently been confused with Patnah: the distinction is explained in a footnote to p. 37.

Among Jahángír's mints we find evidence of this Emperor's well-known predilection for the cool valleys of Kashmír and Afghánistán as refuges from the summer heats of the Indian plains. Kashmír, Kandahár, and Kábul occur frequently upon his coins; and at first sight one is tempted to identify Jahángírnagar with Jahángírpúr, a familiar hunting-ground of the Emperor on the way from Lahore to Kashmír, especially as it first occurs at a time when he was frequently in that neighbourhood: but a comparison of the style of the engraving on the coins of this mint with that of the contemporary coins of Patnah, another mint of the Eastern Súbahs, leaves little doubt that Prof. Dowson* is right in identifying Jahángírnagar with Dhákká (originally Bengálah).† Jahángír not only celebrated his own name in the christening of the city of Jahángírnagar: he also named Akbarnagar (Rájmahall) after his father. So Sháh-Jahán called the new suburb he added to Dehlí in 1648 (1058) Sháhjahánábád, and renamed Agrah Akbarábád. In later times we meet with other eponymous mints, as Murádábád (so named after Murád Bakhsh), Aurangábád and 'Álamgírpúr (after Aurangzíb 'Álamgír),

* ED. vii. 241.

† Cunningham, *Arch. Survey*, xv. 127.

A'zamnagar (after A'zam), Mu'azzamábád (after Mu'azzam, Bahádur's original name), Farrukhábád (after Farrukh-siyar), and 'Azímábád (Patnah, after 'Azím-ash-Shán). In like manner Murshidábád (formerly Makhsúsábád) records the name of Mír Ja'far Khán, the Díwán or revenue officer and afterwards Nawáb Názim or military governor of Bengal (1704-1725), who received the title of Murshid Kuli Khán; while Najíbábád was the capital of the famous Rohila chief Najíb-ad-daulah, of the time of Sháh-'Álam. In still more recent days we meet with such combinations as Abbottábád. Some of these new names for old cities are difficult to identify: *e.g.* 'Álamgírpúr and Zafarpúr, in the time of Aurangzíb; Mu'azzamábád in that of Rafí'-ad-daraját, and Bahádurpatan in that of Sháh-'Álam. If we are permitted to regard such terms as -púr, -nagar, -garh, -patan, and -ábád, as interchangeable (which is doubtful), 'Alamgírpúr may stand for 'Alamgírnagar in Bengal, Zafarpúr for Zafarábád, in the province of Alláhábád (N.W.P.), or for Zafarnagar near Burhánpúr, and Bahádurpatan for Bahádurgarh, which is frequently mentioned in the wars of the time of Sháh-'Álam. Mu'azzamábád, however, cannot be explained by any such hypothesis; and Nasratábád, in Aurangzíb's reign, may represent any newly conquered city, or may be the modern Násirábád. Dilshádábád, again, "City of heart's content," is a species of pet-name.

Among Sháh-Jahán's mints is one which, even when compared with several other specimens of the time of Aurangzíb, is difficult to decipher, in consequence of the bad preservation of the marginal inscriptions. There can be no doubt, however, that it must be read جونه Júnah, and sometimes more completely جوبه کر[ه] Júnáh-garh, (compare Asír and Asírgarh). The extremely rude fabric of all the examples of this mint would be explained by the remote situation of Júnágarh, a fortress in Káthiáwár, renowned for its formidable strength, but taken by Akbar after three months' siege in 999 (early in 1591) and annexed to the empire.* It is true that Júnágarh is generally spelt with an alif (جونا کره, "Old Fort"), but it may nevertheless have been originally derived from the name Júnah, جونه, which belonged to Muhammad ibn Taghlak, and afterwards have been corrupted to suit the meaning of "Old Fort." Júnágarh was an important stronghold, the chief place in the district of Súrat in Káthiáwár (not to be confounded with the greater Súrat further to the south-east). Sir Thomas Roe † refers to it as the capital of "Soret," and Mandelslo mentions it under the name of "Jangar" as the chief city of that district. It is still a separate native state and has had a Nawáb of its own for the last century and a half. Akbar found here and at the greater Súrat (which he took in 980) some guns and mortars abandoned by the Ottoman Sultán Sulaimán the Great, after his fruitless attack on Diu in 1538. In Sháh-Jahán's reign may be noted an indication of the southward expansion of the empire in the occurrence of of the mint Daulatábád (the ancient Deogír) on coins of 1039 &c., the date of this Emperor's first campaign in the Deccan.

From the reign of Sháh-Jahán onwards a source of confusion is found in the similarity between the names Alláhábád (properly Iláhábád, originally Iláhábás), and Akbarábád, (written on the coins الد اباد and الك اباد) which differ merely in the absence or presence of the small ء after the ا which stands for ل in الد اباد and ك in الك اباد. It is commonly stated that the name of this city, founded by Akbar in 1572, and called by him Iláhábás,

* *Tabakát-i Akbarí*, ED. v. 461, 466.

† *Journal*, Pinkerton, viii. 55.

was changed to Iláhábád by Sháh-Jahán. The latter form, however, as well as Iláhábás, occurs on coins of Akbar himself.

The rival princes Shujá' and Murád Bakhsh divided the empire, before the triumph of Aurangzíb: Shujá's advance from Bengal is marked by his issuing coins at Akbarábád (Agrah); while Murád struck at the old and future capitals of Gujarát, Ahmadábád and Súrat, and also at Cambay. It should be noticed that in this, the earliest, occurrence of the mint Cambay, the name is spelt correctly كهنبايت Khanbáyat or Khanbáit (pronounced Khambáit). It is stated in the *Túzak-i Jahángírí* or "Memoirs of Jahángír" that Khambáit is derived from Khamb, a pillar; whence Khambáwatí and Khambáit.* On later coins the name is spelt كنبايت, without the *h*.

Aurangzíb's coinage exhibits several mints unused by his predecessors, chiefly situated in the Deccan, where, as has been seen, he waged continual war. The chief mint is Aurangábád (also called on coins and in Kháfí Khan's history, Khujistah-bunyád, or "Auspicious Structure,") named after himself, and henceforward the capital of the Moghul power in the Deccan,—a dignity previously enjoyed by Burhánpúr. Other Deccan mints now appearing for the first time are Golkondah,† Ahmadnagar, Bíjápúr, Chínápatan (the old name for Madras), and Masulipatan (Machhlipatan). In Hindústán we find

* ED. vi. 354. It should be added that no coins are known corresponding to the "gold and silver *tankas*" described in the *Memoirs* as having been struck at Cambay in A.H. 1027, regnal year 12, "ten and twenty times heavier than the current gold mohr and rupee," and with the remarkable legend (on the silver), "After the conquest of the Deccan he came from Mándú to Gujarát." Jahángír claims them as "an invention of my own," and calls them "Jahangírí tankas," adding that all previous tankas were of copper.

† The coin No. 726 is erroneously printed Calcutta: it should of course be Golkondah.

as new mints Lucknow, Barailí, Zafarábád, and the unidentified names already referred to:—Zafarpúr, 'Álamgírpúr, and Nasratábád.

Of the later Emperors and aspirants to the throne, A'zam and Kám Bakhsh struck coins only in the Dekhan, the latter adding Haidarábád to the list of Moghul mints; Bahádur struck at Sholápúr in the Deccan (ceded to Aurangzíb in 1668 by 'Alí 'Ádil Sháh of Bíjápúr), and Ujjain in Málwah; and re-named Patnah 'Azímábád, after his son 'Azím-ash-Shán. In Farrukh-siyar's currency Arkát, A'zamnagar, and Murshidábád appear for the first time; and a diminutive gold coinage, resembling that of southern India, forms a new feature; it issued from Imtiyázgarh ("Distinction-Fort," Aurangzíb's new name for Adoni, which I at first read Imtiyáz Karrah), Gútí, Gangpúr (in Chutiá Nágpúr), and another mint which is illegible. A similar issue, also from Imtiyázgarh, occurs in the coinage of Muhammad Sháh and of 'Álamgír II. Two new mints appear with the name of Rafí'-addaraját: Mu'azzamábád (unidentified) and Kúrá, which is probably not the Kúrá near Sironj, but the city spelt variously كورا and كوره, in the Duáb, and generally written Korah in the maps. Muhammad Sháh repeats the rare mints Kúrá and Imtiyázgarh, and adds Benáres, Akbarnagar-Oudh, Farrukhábád, Siwáï-Jaipúr (founded in his day by Siwái-Jai-Singh), Islámábád (the new name given to Chátgáon, or Chittagong, on its conquest in 1076), Sháhábád (an ancient city in the province of Oudh, with the addition on the coin of the word فتوح), and Ajáyúr, اجايور thus pointed, possibly Ajáyapúr, the old name of Bakror.* Murádábád, though by no means a new creation, first appears in this series on a coin of Ahmad Sháh; and Indrapúr (the old name of Indore*) on the issues of 'Álamgír II. In Sháh-'Álam's

* Cunningham, *Arch. Survey*, i. 13.

time the new mints of Bahádur-patan and Najíbábád (already referred to), Srínagar and Dilshádábád, appear for the first time.

Several of the principal mints are generally, but not invariably, provided with honorific prefixes. Thus Lahore is styled *Dár-as-Saltanah*, "Seat of Empire;" Dehlí, *Dár-al-Khiláfah*, "Seat of the Caliphate;" Bijápúr, *Dár-az-Zafar*, "Seat of Victory;" Ajmír, *Dár-al-Khair*, "Seat of Weal;" Kábul, *Dár-al-Mulk*, "Seat of Royalty;" Agrah, *Mustakarr-al-Khiláfah* "Resting place of the Khalifate;" Multán, *Dár-al-Amán*, "Seat of Safety." A list of these is given in Index II A. Mr. Rodgers* mentions *Bandar-al-Mubárak*, "the Blessed Port," as a prefix of Súrat (so termed because it was the Báb-al-hájj, or starting point of the Indian pilgrimage to Mekka), and *Baldat-al-Fákhirah*, "the Resplendent Town," as a prefix of Burhánpúr: neither of these occurs in the British Museum collection.

Abu-l-Fazl's *Áín-i Akbarí* contains some sections on Akbar's mints and their management, and the simple processes of assaying and coining; and the late Mr. Blochmann's translation reproduces some native drawings of the various operations in use in Akbar's time. The chief officer of the mint was the *dárógah*,† under whom were the *sairafí* or *sarráf* (assayer), the foreman, clerk, bullion-buyer, treasurer, weigher, melter, and plate-maker or flan-cutter (*zarráb*), and *sikkachí* or puncher. The best engraver of dies was 'Alí Ahmad, of Dehlí.‡

---

* *Proceedings As. Soc. Bengal*, Jan. 1883.

† Or *'darugha*, in Mongol ᠳᠠᠷᠤᠭᠠ, *lieutenant* or *governor*. The word occurs on coins of the Ilkháns of Persia: see my *Catalogue of Oriental Coins*, vol. vi. p. lxvi. &c. Sir William Hedges, in 1682-4, speaks of the "droga" of the mint (*Diary*, ed. Yule, i. 129, Hakluyt Society).

‡ *Áín*, transl. H. Blochmann, i. 18-22 (1873).

According to Lieut. Moor,* who wrote in 1794, the method of coining in Bombay was extremely primitive, and doubtless had remained unchanged for centuries: "the metal is brought to the mint in bars the size of the little finger, where are a number of persons seated on the ground provided with scales and weights, a hammer, and an instrument between a chissel and a punch: before each man's birth is fixed a stone by way of anvil. The bars are cut into pieces, by guess, and if, on weighing, any deficiency is found, a little particle is punched into the intended rupee; if too heavy, a piece is cut off, and so on until the exact quantity remains. These pieces are then taken to a second person, whose whole apparatus consists of a hammer and a stone anvil, and he batters them into something of a round shape, about seven eighths of an inch diameter, and one eighth thick; when they are ready for the impression. The die is composed of two pieces, one inserted firmly into the ground; the other, about eight inches long, is held in the right hand of the operator, who, squatting on his heels . . . fills his left hand with the intended coins, which he with inconceivable quickness slips upon the fixed die with his thumb and middle finger, with his fore finger as dexterously removing them when his assistant, a second man with a mall, has given it the impression, which he does as rapidly as he can raise and strike with the mall on the die held in the right hand of the coiner. . . . The rupee is then sent to the Treasury, ready for currency, as no milling or any farther process is considered necessary."

---

* *Narrative of the operations of Captain Little's Detachment, etc.,* 499, 500.

§ 4. *ERAS, REGNAL YEARS, AND PERSIAN MONTHS.*

THE era exclusively employed by all the Moghul Emperors, with the exception of Akbar, is the Muhammadan Hijrah. Akbar also made use of this reckoning up to the 28th (solar) year of his reign, beginning 11 March, o.s., 1583, A.H. 991,* when he instituted his *Iláhí* or "divine" epoch, composed of solar years, and dating from the vernal equinox of the first year of his reign (1556). The British Museum possesses one rupee of the 28th year of this epoch; and from this time to the end of the reign the Iláhí years were employed to the almost total exclusion † of the Muhammadan reckoning. Together with the use of the Iláhí epoch, the custom of recording the month of issue was introduced upon the currency. The months thus employed were those of the ancient Persian Kalendar, consisting of twelve solar months: Farwardín, Ardíbihist, Khúrdád, Tír, Mardád, Shahriwar, Mihr, Abán, Azur, Dai, Bahman and Isfandármiz.

The following table of Akbar's Iláhí years, from the 28th, when the new reckoning was introduced, will be found useful. It is taken from Sir Henry Elliot's table in the *History of India as told by its own Historians*, vol. iv., p. 246.

---

* Abu-l-Fazl, in the *Áín*, places the date of inauguration of the Iláhí era at A.H. 992. The discrepancy between this statement and the positive evidence of the rupee no. 177, which bears the regnal year 28, beginning 28 Safar, or March 10, 991, may be reconciled by supposing the change of reckoning to have taken place near the end of the solar year, which would bring it into the new Hijrah year 992, and A.D. 1584.

† See, however, pp. 20, 30-1, and 47.

AKBAR'S ILÁHÍ YEARS
from the 28th to the 50th
WITH THE CORRESPONDING HIJRAH AND CHRISTIAN YEARS.

ILÁHÍ		A.H.		A.D.
28	began	991 (28 Safar)	...	1583 (11 March,* o.s.)
29	„	992 (8 Rabí' I.)	...	1584
30	„	993 (19 „)	...	1585
31	„	994 (29 „)	...	1586
32	„	995 (11 „ II.)	...	1587
33	„	996 (22 „)	...	1588
34	„	997 (4 Jumádá I.)	...	1589
35	„	998 (14 „)	...	1590
36	„	999 (24 „)	...	1591
37	„	1000 (5 „ II.)	...	1592
38	„	1001 (17 „)	...	1593
39	„	1002 (28 „)	...	1594
40	„	1003 (9 Rajab)	...	1595
41	„	1004 (20 „)	...	1596
42	„	1005 (2 Sha'bán)	...	1597
43	„	1006 (13 „)	...	1598
44	„	1007 (23 „)	...	1599
45	„	1008 (4 Ramazán)	...	1600
46	„	1009 (15 „)	...	1601
47	„	1010 (26 „)	...	1602
48	„	1011 (6 Shawwál)	...	1603
49	„	1012 (17 „)	...	1604
50	„	1013 (28 „)	...	1605

* Beginning of course at sunset on the 10th, as the Muhammadan day begins at night.

When Jahángír succeeded his father, he abolished the Iláhí era, and reverted to that of the Hijrah, even specifying the word *Hijrí* هجری on some coins. But, whilst reverting to the *lunar* reckoning for the years counted from the Hijrah, or ordinary "date" of his coins, he still employed the *solar* year and Persian months in stating the year of his reign on the coinage, though without any pretence of establishing a new epoch, but simply as our own Acts of Parliament are dated by the Queen's regnal years. This singular juxtaposition of lunar and solar years on the currency has not, I believe, been noticed by numismatists; but the use of the Persian names of months would by itself suggest the employment of a solar reckoning, and the statement of Kháfí Khán the historian and the evidence of the coins themselves place the matter beyond a doubt. It will be found that as the lunar years are about ten days shorter than solar, and therefore advance more rapidly, so on the coins the Hijrah years overtake and finally overlap the regnal years. Thus the regnal year 22 appears on the coins in conjunction with the Hijrah years 1036 and 1037, *i.e.* it began in 1036 and ended in 1037; whereas, had the regnal reckoning been lunar, 1036-7 would have corresponded to parts of the regnal year 23 (beginning Ramazán 1036). Besides retaining Akbar's solar reckoning for regnal years, Jahángír preserved the special term *Iláhí* in connexion with the regnal year, using it in the same manner as *julús*—a term which he also occasionally employed. Thus he inscribed his coins with ضرب اکره ٦ ماه مهر الهی, and also with سنه ١ جلوس. The custom of recording the *julús* or regnal year was preserved by all succeeding Emperors and pretenders; but the solar years and Persian months were banished from the coinage and the exchequer by Aurangzíb, who was, as has been seen, a zealous Muhammadan, and thenceforward the lunar reckoning was strictly adhered to, together with the Arabian months, though these are never named on the coins. It should be observed that discrepancies between the Hijrah year and the regnal year are not infrequent. Sometimes this is due to the employment of an old die; sometimes it is caused by the carelessness of the mint-masters. The use of the solar reckoning for the regnal years, and the lunar for the Hijrah date, during Jahángír's and Sháh-Jahán's reigns, when the two were constantly shifting their relative positions, may reasonably have caused some confusion. The Hijrah and regnal dates are always expressed in figures, not words; except the first year of the reign, which is usually written احد, and the year 1000, الف;* and excepting also the Hijrah years on Akbar's copper coins, which are expressed in Persian numerals (نهصد وهشتاد وهفت, &c.).

---

* On a probable mystical interpretation of this numeral, in connexion with the anticipated end of the world at the thousandth year of the Hijrah, see above, lii.

§ 5. *INSCRIPTIONS, TITLES, WEIGHT, &c.*

THE earliest coins of the Moghul Emperors naturally followed the design and style, and adopted the broad thin shape, of the coins of the Transoxine Tímúrís from whom Bábar sprang. He and his son Humáyún placed the *Kalimah*, or profession of faith in God and his Prophet in the obverse area, and surrounded it with a marginal inscription containing the names and virtues of the first Four Khalifs. On the reverse were arranged, partly in the margin, partly in the area, the name, surname (*lakab*), and titles of the Emporor, which began with the usual Transoxine style of السلطان الاعظم الخاقان المكرم, "the mightiest Sultán, the honourable Khakán," Zahír-ad-dín Muhammad Bábar, or Abu-l-Muzaffar Muhammad Humáyún, and ended with the most general of all Moghul titles, *Pádisháh Ghází*, "Victorious King," together with the benedictory formula, خلد الله تعالى ملكه وسلطانه, or part of it. Humáyún on one coin introduced the innovation of سيد السلاطين, "Lord of Sultáns," into his title; and on another he used, once only, the Koranic verse يرزق الله من يشاء بغير حساب, "God rewards whom He wills without reckoning" (Kor. ii. 208).

Akbar for a short time followed the example of his predecessors and adopted the Transoxine style of coin, and the same elaborate titles; but already, by the influence of Todar Mal, Arabic was being superseded by Persian in the imperial bureaux and among the engravers of seals and coins;* and by this time Akbar had

* Some of the early Moghul coins evince an imperfect acquaintance with Arabic: as in the frequent confusion of ابو, ابى, and ابا, and the slip يحا ابا بكر, for يحياى ابى بكر; which, however, should be بصدق. The change from Arabic to Persian in the coin inscriptions has necessitated a corresponding change in orthography: *e.g.* the final ة is no longer to be dotted.

realized the wisdom of conforming to the traditional preference of his Indian subjects for thick dumpy coins, instead of the broad thin pieces of the Khalifs and their successors. Accordingly, we see him abandoning the Transoxine forms; first the *Khákán* disappeared, then the *Sultán*, and finally there remained only the title *Pádisháh Ghází*, which continued in vogue to the end of the Moghul empire. The *Kalimah* and Khalifs' names, however, still retained their place in the obverse area and margin, and the benediction, رضی الله عنهم or رضی الله بهم, was sometimes appended. At the same time he adopted the thicker form which continued henceforward to be characteristic of the Moghul currency. The coins of Akbar and of his successors, Jahángír and Sháh-Jahán, are splendid specimens of the moneyer's art. They may be compared advantageously in respect of execution and uniformity of standard with any contemporary European money, and far excel any other Oriental coinage. The inscriptions are boldly yet gracefully drawn in the roháni (and sometimes the ta'lík) character, and the borders and other ornaments are simple and artistic. The engraving was entrusted to men of reputation in their art, and the difference in their styles may be detected in the issues of the various mints, where a traditional character of writing evidently prevailed. It is easy to distinguish the issues of Kashmír from those of Lahore at a glance, and similarly those of Lahore from the coinage of Patnah, or from that of Burhánpúr, &c. The differences may be clearly traced in the Plates.

Akbar was troubled with a perpetual restless yearning after innovation, in small matters as well as great; and among the useless changes he devised (besides many exceedingly valuable reforms) was an alteration of the shape of the money. Coins had hitherto been usually round, which was a sufficient reason for their being now made square. Round coins were obviously the more convenient, but the square shape had the merits of eccentricity and originality, though unfortunately the form was not absolutely novel, seeing that it had already been employed by the kings of Kashmír and Málwah. Akbar first tried the experiment of an oblong coin with scolloped ends (see nos. 50, 51, and compare the lozenge-shaped coin, no. 168), known as *mihrábí*, because it resembled the arch of a prayer-niche; but in 986 he began to strike *square* coins in gold at Fathpúr, his new capital, and in silver at Fathpúr, Lahore, and other mints. The square-shape was not long retained for his gold currency, but in silver it lasted, together with the round, until the end of the reign. After Akbar square coins were seldom used; but Jahángír struck a few, and there are four square mohrs of Sháh-Jahán in the British Museum. On Akbar's square coins the long tail of the ے, &c., in the names or epithets of the Four Khalifs, is turned to account to form a sort of border between the margin and the area, which contains the *Kalimah*; at the same time the reverse margin is abolished, and the simple *Pádisháh Ghází* takes the place of the longer titles of the earlier coins.

Akbar's *Iláhí coinage*, begun in A.H. 992, is both round and square in silver (generally square up to the 40th year of the reign, 1003), but only round in gold. The inscriptions indicate the religious changes of the time. The Muhammadan profession of faith and the Four Khalifs and their virtues have vanished, and in their place appears the new Iláhí formula, الله اكبر جل جلاله, "God is most great: glorified be his glory." This formula either occupies the whole of the obverse, leaving the reverse for the Persian month and Iláhí year; or الله اكبر appears on the obverse, and جل جلاله and the Iláhí year on the reverse. The Emperor's name does not appear upon the Iláhí currency; but it has been pointed out that الله اكبر not only means "God is most great," but also may be interpreted "Akbar is God;" and the suggestion has been made that the Emperor played upon the double meaning. If he did so, the levity was wholly out of keeping with his character and conduct in all other respects. This coinage endured till the end of the reign, but was never imitated by Akbar's successors.*

With Jahangír's coinage (after the rupees, nos. 288-9, which appear to have been struck during his governorship of Gujarát, and on which he is styled *Salím Sháh Sultán* and *Málik al-Mulk*), a new phase in inscriptions begins. The Iláhí formula is abandoned, and the Muhammadan *Kalimah* rarely appears;† and their place is filled by a doggrel Persian rhyme which is dignified by the name of *distich* or couplet (in Arabic *bait*). The use of *Persian distichs* was begun on a coin of the time of Akbar,‡ but Jahángír employed them on the majority of his coins, and the Court poets were busily engaged in manipulating suitable verses. A list of these jingles is given in Index VI. Their meaning is generally nothing more than a euphuistic mode of expressing the fact that the Emperor caused the coin to be struck; the radiance of the sun and the gold, or the

---

* A curious little group of coins is described on pp. 47, 48, under the heading "Gujarát Fabric." They have all the appearance of the later Kachh coins, and some present the name of Akbar with the date 1215—in this respect also agreeing with the Gujarát habit of imitating old coins and inserting modern dates. See *Catalogue of Indian Coins, Muhammadan States*, lx.

† In the British Museum Collection it occurs only on a single mohr and ten rupees of the first two or three years of the reign.

‡ See the three specimens, Nos. 254, 254*a*, 254*b*. Mr. Rodgers, who describes dated specimens of this piece (Iláhí 44, 45), remarks that it is said to have been issued by Prince Salím (Jahángír) when in rebellion against his father Akbar; but does not cite his authority for the statement (*Journal of the Asiatic Society of Bengal*, lvii, 1888).

moon and the silver, supplying felicitous references to the glory of his Majesty's epoch. The florid inflation of the distichs, however, finds no counterpart in the enumeration of the Emperor's titles: *Pádisháh Ghází* is all he styles himself, and often plain *Sháh* suffices. When he joins his queen's name on the coins, she is described as *Núr-Jahán Pádisháh Bégam.*

Indeed the *titles* assumed by the Moghul Emperors from Jahángír onwards are singularly devoid of oriental bombast. They seldom used their proper name (as Salím, Khurram),* but employed the name assumed on (or before) coming to the throne, as Jahángír, Sháh-Jahán, together with the orthodox name Muhammad. To this they added their lakab or surname, as Núr-ad-dín, Shiháb-ad-dín; and sometimes a patronymic, as Abu-l-Muzaffar, Abu-l-Fath. Finally came the sovereign title, *Pádisháh Ghází,* used by all the Emperors, except Farrukh-siyar, who preferred to style himself پادشاه بحر و بر, "Monarch of sea and land," and Rafí'-ad-daraját, who claimed to be شہنشاه بحر و بر "Sháh of Sháhs of sea and land." Sháh-Jahán added a horoscopic title, *Sáhib Kirán Sání,* "Second Lord of [auspicious] Conjunction"—his ancestor Tímúr being the first; and the same style was adopted by Shujá' and Muhammad. Murád Bakhsh, who had the patronymic Abu-l-Muzaffar, and the unique lakab *Muzawwaj-ad-dín,* "Wedded to the Faith," (?) assumed the title of سکندر ثانی, "The Second Alexander." Aurangzíb was given to ostentatious humility, and beyond his throne-name 'Álamgír,

* Sháh-Jahán's first Lahore rupee is an exception to this rule: here he is styled Abu-l-Muzaffar Násir-ad-dín Muhammad Sháh-Jahán Khurram, though afterwards his lakab is always Shiháb-ad-dín, and his proper name, Khurram, never recurs. This coin may have been struck on the occasion of his first proclamation as Emperor, which took place at Lahore, 2 Jumádá I., 1037; and the style may have been altered when he ascended the throne at Agrah a fortnight later.

generally called himself plain *Sháh*, rarely *Pádisháh* or *Pádisháh Ghází*, and only twice or thrice engraved his lakab, &c., in the form Muhayyí-ad-dín Muhammad Bahádur. A'zam Sháh had a title of his own, *Pádisháh Mamálik*, "King of Realms." Jahándár was *Padisháh Jahán* and *Sáhib Kirán*. Niku-siyar was *Pádisháhi zamán Sháh bi-lutfi-lláh Muhammad*, "Monarch of the Age, King by the grace of God." Ahmad used the epithet *Bahádur*, and 'Álamgír II. was styled Abu-l-'Adl 'Azíz-ad-dín, "Father of justice, Honoured of the Faith;" while Sháh-'Álam invented a new formula, including the title حامی دین اله محمد شاه عالم پادشاه "Defender of the divine Faith," &c.

One of Jahangír's inscriptions contains an anagram: زروز ازل درعدد شد برابر حروف جهانگیر والله اکبر :—

> "The letters of *Jahángír* and *Alláhu Akbar*
> Are equal in value from the beginning of time."

This is explained by the fact that the letters ج (3), ه (5), ا (1), ن (50), ك (20), ی (10), and ر (200), of جهانگیر, and those of الله اکبر, ا (1), ل ل (30, 30), ه (5), ا (1), ك (20), ب (2), ر (200), when added together, respectively make up the sum of 289.

The general arrangement of the inscriptions after Jahángír is very regular. Persian distichs become rare, and the *Kalimah*, with the mint and month,* occupies the obverse, and the imperial titles the reverse of Sháh-Jahán's money, sometimes entirely in the area, sometimes divided between area and margin; while the Hijrah date and regnal year are variously distributed between the obverse and reverse: on some coins the Four Khalifs and their virtues, followed by the mint, surround the *Kalimah*. The inscriptions on the *Nisárs* (see § 7) are more elementary. The usurpers Murád and Shujá' imitated Sháh-Jahán's arrange-

* The names of months rarely occur after A.H. 1041.

ment. Aurangzíb, however, introduced a new style, and in spite of his orthodoxy, abolished the profession of faith. The reason was, however, a proof of reverence; for he was afraid lest the sacred words should pass with the coins into "unworthy places and fall under the feet of infidels."* The obverse contains the mint and the formula سنه . . . جلوس میمنت مانوس "In the year . . . of his reign of tranquil prosperity," while the reverse has the Emperor's simple titles or else the Persian distich,

سکه زد در جهان چو مهر منیر
شاه اورنگزیب عالمگیر

which has been rendered :†

Through all the world he struck his sun-like coin of golden ore,
Sháh Aurangzíb (throne-ornament) of earth the conqueror.

Marginal inscriptions were abolished (save on a few examples), and never reappear in the series.

The *julús* formula سنه جلوس میمنت مانوس and the mint continue to occupy the obverse to the end of the series. The reverse inscription of all the succeeding Emperors from Bahádur to Muhammad Akbar II. consists of the name and titles of the sovereign, preceded by the word سکه, or سکه مبارك, "Auspicious money;" except in the case of Jahándár, Farrukh-siyar, and Rafí'-ad-daraját, and some of Sháh-'Álam's coins, when Persian formulas were again employed. One Emperor alone, the devout 'Álamgír II., restored for a single year the Muhammadan *Kalimah* and the Four Khalifs with their virtues, which had been in disuse since Sháh-Jahán's reign.

The *names of the coins* of the Moghul Emperors appear

* Kháfi Khán, ED. vii. 241.

† R. S. Poole, *Cat. Coins of the Sháhs of Persia*, lxxxiv.

to have been numerous, if Abu-l-Fazl's account * of Akbar's coinage may be taken as typical of the whole series. The general term for a gold coin is *mohr*, commonly called mohur (a "seal" or "impression"); for a silver coin, *rupee* (or more accurately *rupíh*), and for the copper coin *dám*. But in Akbar's time the different varieties and subdivisions had separate names. Abu-l-Fazl's list of these names ought to be of great value to the numismatist, but, in fact, it forms but another instance of the incapacity of oriental (and for that matter most European) historians to describe accurately or systematically the coins which passed under their own eyes. Al-Makrízí's well-known treatise is a case in point. It is the best account we have of Arabic numismatics by an Arabic writer, but it is far from being what it might easily have been made, had the author made an adequate study of his subject. Abu-l-Fazl gives a long list of names, without supplying the necessary means of identifying the coins to which they belong. Many of the types he describes do not appear to have been preserved in any collection, whilst many existing coins are not described. His list may be conveniently arranged as follows. All are round coins, unless otherwise described.

AKBAR'S COINAGE.

GOLD.

Sihansah, or 100 *mohr piece*. (Maksúd's work.)

Obv. Kalimah. Margin, الله يرزق من يشاء بغير حساب (Kor. ii. 208).

Rev. Margin, السلطان الاعظم الخاقان المعظم خلد الله ملكه وسلطانه

---

* *Áín-i Akbarí*, Blochmann's trans., i. 31 ff. Compare E. Thomas, *Chronicles of the Pathan Kings of Delhi*, 418 ff.

100 *mohr piece* (improved by 'Alí Ahmad).

Obv. افضل دينار ينفق الرجل دينار ينفق على اصحاب في سبيل الله

Rev. السلطان العالى الخليفة المتعالى خلد الله تعالى ملكه وسلطانه وابد عدله واحسانه

A third variety was engraved with two Persian rubá'ís of Fáizí.

Rahas, or 50 *mohr piece*, was inscribed with a rubá'í of Fáizí.

Átmah, both round and square, had also a rubá'í.

Binsat, or 20 mohr piece, both round and square.

Chugal, or *double mohr*, square.

Round La'l-i Jalálí, or double mohr in weight and value; inscr. الله اكبر, and يا معين.

Of *single mohrs* there were eight :—

(1) Round :

Aftábí, worth 12 rupees : } obv. الله اكبر جل جلاله ;
Iláhí, worth 10 rupees : } rev. mint and date.

'Adlgutkah, worth 9 rupees : الله اكبر, and يا معين.

Mohr, worth 9 rupees : with *Kalimah*.

(2) Square :

Square La'l-i Jalálí, worth 10 rupees : obv. الله اكبر; rev. جل جلاله.

Mu'íní, worth 10 rupees : inscr. يا معين ; also *round*, worth 9 rupees.

(3) [Other shapes, not so stated] :

Mihrábí, worth 9 rupees.

Chahárgóshah, worth 12 rupees (Thomas says 30).

Of *half-mohrs*, three :—

Gird = ½ Iláhí, same inscriptions.

Dhan = ½ La'l-i Jalálí.

Salímí = ½ 'Adlgutkah.

Of *quarter-mohrs*, three :—

$\frac{1}{2}$ *Salímí.*

Rabí' = $\frac{1}{4}$ Aftábí.

Man = $\frac{1}{4}$ Iláhí and Jalálí.

Of other fractions :—

Panj = $\frac{1}{5}$ Iláhí.

Pandan = $\frac{1}{5}$ La'l-i Jalálí: lily and wild rose on two sides.

Sumní = $\frac{1}{8}$ Iláhí : obv. الله اكبر ; rev. جل جلاله.

Kalá = $\frac{1}{16}$ Iláhí : wild rose on both sides.

Zarah = $\frac{1}{32}$ Ilahi : „ „

SILVER.

Rupee, round } worth 40 dáms: obv. الله اكبر جل
Jalálah, square } جلاله ; rev. date.

Darb = $\frac{1}{2}$ Jalálah.

Charn = $\frac{1}{4}$ „

Pandú = $\frac{1}{5}$ „

Asht = $\frac{1}{8}$ „

Dasá = $\frac{1}{10}$ „

Kalá = $\frac{1}{16}$ „

Súkí = $\frac{1}{20}$ „

COPPER.

Dám, originally called *Paisah* or *Bahlólí*: obv. mint; rev. date.

Adhélah = $\frac{1}{2}$ dám

Páulah = $\frac{1}{4}$ „

Damrí = $\frac{1}{8}$ „

Abu-l-Fazl adds that *mohrs, rupees,* and *dáms* form the usual commercial currency. He also mentions that in the 27th year of Akbar's reign four kinds of mohr were allowed to be current, viz. the *La'l-i Jaláhí*, which was quite pure, and worth 400 dáms ; the *mohr* (360 dáms) ; the mohr reduced by wear (355 dáms), and the mohr much rubbed (350 dáms) ; also three kinds of *rupees*, viz. square, pure silver, worth 40 dáms ; the old round *Akbarsháhí* (39 dáms), and worn specimens of both (38 dáms). These regulations for passing worn coin were modified in the 29th and 36th years of the reign.

It is clear that Abu-l-Fazl is writing of Akbar's later coinage, after the introduction of the *Iláhí* issues, and that he does not concern himself much with the earlier coins, which he refers to under the name of "the old round *Akbarsháhí.*" In silver, he only mentions *Iláhí rupees* and *jalálahs*, though he refers to the older *Kalimah* coins in gold as *mohrs*. He is obviously wrong in attributing an issue of *La'l-i Jalális* to the 27th year of the reign, for it was not till the 28th year that the Iláhí era and the formula *Jalla Jaláluhu* were introduced. Of Akbar's large coins (100, 50, 20, and 2 mohr pieces) not one is known in modern collections; but a five mohr piece is preserved in the British Museum (no. 23), which is not mentioned in Abu-l-Fazl's list. A few of the single mohrs may be identified. Nos. 50 and 51 are undoubtedly *Mihrábís* from their shape, resembling the arch of a niche for prayer, and the lozenge-shaped coin no. 168 may be a variety of this species. The *Chahár góshah,* or "four-cornered," sounds very like the same thing. No coin of Akbar in the Museum bears the inscription يا معين (O Protector)* ; but it appears on some of Jahángír's issues. Of the Iláhí gold, no. 165 is an *Aftábí*, and 164 a *Rabí'* or quarter-Aftábí ; but no. 163 has the inscriptions of the square *La'l-i Jalálí*, only it is round, It seems probable that Abu-l-Fazl, whilst describing a round *La'l-i Jalálí*, equal to two mohrs, omitted to mention that there was also a round *La'l-i Jalálí single mohr*. He also entirely ignores the singular square issue of Fathpúr in 986, etc., and of Urdu-Zafar-Karín of 1000, though these have the peculiarities of a square form, and a heavier weight than the rest. The difference of value seems to have depended upon the purity, and

* One is described by Mr. Delmerick, with no mint, but year 981, in *J.B.A.S.* xlv.

not upon the weight, and this cannot be tested without injuring the coins. Of the silver pieces mentioned by Abu-l-Fazl, it is easy to recognize the *Rupee* in (*e.g.*) no. 177, and the square *Jalálah* in 179 and 185, etc.; the *Darb* in 184, the *Charn* in 188, the *Asht* in 202, etc.; Of the copper, the *Dáms* and *half Dáms* (*Adhélahs*), are called *fulús* on their inscriptions, and *tankahs* and double tankahs occur.*

In Jahángír's *Memoirs* † some names of his coins are recorded, but they only refer to phenomenal pieces. The *Núr-i Sháhí* was equal to 2000 tolahs, the *Núr-i Jahán* to 1000, the *Núr-i daulat* to 500, the *Núr-mohr* to 100. The *tolah* was substituted for the gold rupee (i.e. mohr). There were corresponding pieces in silver. The tolah was probably the heavier coin issued by Jahángír in the first five years of his reign.

The *weight* of the Moghul coinage, allowing for wear, is strikingly exact and uniform, as soon as the uncertainty of the earliest issues is passed. There are no gold coins of Bábar in the British Museum, but his silver pieces weighed from 69 to 73 grs., and were doubtless intended for dirhams of the Tímúrí standard, not rupees. Humáyún struck small gold pieces of 13 to 16 grs. and 8 grs. ($\frac{1}{4}$ and $\frac{1}{8}$ of dínár), and silver of 37, 47, 68, 71, 72, 73, 110, 112, 113, and 180 grs., in which we may perhaps trace a transition from the Transoxine dirham to the full rupee weight of 180 grs. Akbar, with his habitual comprehension of the exigencies of the time, began at once with an Indian standard, and his weights of 170 grs. for the gold mohr, and 180 for the silver rupee, continued to be the accepted model, with few exceptions, throughout the rule of his dynasty. His *gold* coins (in the British Museum series) vary in weight from 166 to

---

* See below, § 8.

† Transl. Major D. Price, p. 11.

169, and only a few worn coins drop to 164, 162, and one to 157. The square issue of Fathpúr and Lahore 986—8, and Urdú-Zafar-Karín rise to a different standard of 186 to 187 grs., with sub-divisions of 93 and 46 : but the object of this alteration is not known, nor is it referred to by the historians. In 992, the new *Ilahí* issue was introduced, with the weight at first of 187, and later of 168 (for 170). A few early gold coins weigh only 18 and 9 grs., like Humáyún's, and two of A.H. 988 weigh 15 grs. The *silver* coinage was clearly intended to weigh 180 grs., though most of the existing specimens are reduced a few grains by wear. The half rupee weighs from 86 to 89 grs.; the quarter from 42 to 44; and the eighth, from 19 to 21. Jahángír for the first five years of his reign, up to A.H. 1019, used a weight of 202, rising finally to 211 grs., for his gold coins, and 212, rising to 220, for his rupees (and 105-106 for the half-rupee) : but after 1019, except in the case of four coins of Kandahár and Kashmír, he reverted to Akbar's standard, and his mohr weighs about 168, and his quarter-mohr 42, while his rupee weighs about 176 grs., and the half-rupee, 89. One five mohr piece of his is preserved, weighing 843 grs., which gives $168\frac{3}{5}$ to the mohr. Sháh-Jahán, Aurangzíb, Bahádur, Muhammad, etc., follow the same standard; but a few of Farrukh-siyar's rupees, struck at Katak and Jahángírnagar, rise as high as 187 grs.

A curious variety of gold coin was issued by Farrukh-siyar, Muhammad, and 'Álamgír II., in addition to their ordinary *mohrs*. The coins of this type are very small, with a diameter of ·4 to ·5in. for the larger, weighing 51 to 53 grs., and of ·3 or ·35 for the smaller, weighing 22 grs. In the character of the engraving they resemble other small issues of Southern India, and two of their mints are in the Deccan, Imtiyáz-garh and Gútí. The former has always been read Karrah, کره, the city in the Duáb, and the word beneath it has been interpreted as referring to the coin : "decoration of Karrah." There can be no doubt, however, that the two form a compound name Imtiyáz-garh, امتیاز کره, "Distinction Fort," or "Fort *par excellence*," which, according to Mr. C. J. Rodgers, was a name given by Aurangzíb to Adwání, the Adóní of the maps, a little north of Gútí. The close similarity of its style would lead one to look for the third mint, Gangpúr, in the same neighbourhood : but the district of Gangpúr is in Chutiá Nágpúr. Possibly it has some traditional connexion with the old Ganga dynasty of Talkad in Mysore ; or it may relate to one of the sacred rivers of Southern India. Of its Deccan fabric there can be no doubt.

§ 6. *IMAGES AND ZODIACAL SIGNS.*

The Moghul Emperors, with the exception of Aurangzíb 'Álamgír and his name-sake 'Álamgír II., were far from strict in their observance of the laws of the Korán. As has been seen, they were commonly addicted to the use of intoxicating liquors; they married unbelieving wives, instead of making them merely concubine slaves in accordance with the orthodox custom of Islám, and their encouragement of the fine arts was free from the trammels of Koranic Puritanism. They were fond of pictures and sculpture, and paid no regard to the divine ordinance which prohibited the representation of living beings in art. They even delighted to adorn their palaces with paintings and statues portraying scenes which belong to the sacred traditions of Christianity, and images of the Blessed Virgin and portraits of St. John Baptist contributed to the decoration of their Court. The same disregard of orthodox prejudices may be occasionally observed on their coinage. So long, indeed, as the Muslim profession of faith occupied its rightful place on Akbar's coins, no profane image desecrated the formula: but after the Emperor had discovered the errors of Islám and had founded his own "Divine Religion," the objection to the representation of living things on the coins was no longer in force. Yet Akbar used images very sparingly. A falcon is depicted on the first and only coin of Asír (No. 166), possibly in allusion to the conquering swoop of the besiegers. On No. 173, a duck appears on a coin of Agrah. Another gold coin, without the name of the mint, bears a curious representation of a crowned archer, with stretched bow and sheaf of arrows, followed by a woman, who draws back her long veil from her face. This may refer to the submission (in A.H. 1013, the date of this coin) of the King of Bíjápúr, which was accompanied by the gift of his daughter to be the bride of Prince Dániyál, Akbar's son.

Jahángír's use of images on the coinage was much more marked than his father's. In the sixth year of his reign (1020) he ventured upon the daring innovation of engraving his own portrait on some of his gold coins. He is represented in bust with head turned to the left, and face wearing only a moustache; the shoulders are covered by a brocaded dress, and a turban adorned with the imperial *jikkah* or egret is on his head; his hand holds sometimes a book, sometimes fruit; and sometimes he holds a book in one hand and a goblet in the other. If, as is probable, the book is intended for the Korán, its combination with a wine-cup must have been regarded by orthodox Muslims as an outrage. In the following year (1021), and in 1023, Jahángír placed on some of his gold pieces his royal person seated cross-legged on a throne, with the inseparable goblet raised in his right hand, and with an aureole or nimbus round his head, which he probably derived from some Christian paintings, but which wears a singularly incongruous air in conjunction with the wine-cup and the Emperor's bacchanalian pose. On the reverse of most of these portrait coins is a lion surmounted by the sun, apparently setting behind it, or, in astrological language *Sol in constellatione Leonis*, the sun entering the sign Leo; but on some coins the sun appears without the lion. The presence of the sun has been explained as a reference to the fact that Jahángír was born on a Sunday; but it is more probable that the sun's image appears in virtue of the tendency towards solar worship which undoubtedly found encouragement under Akbar, and was never positively repudiated by his successor. It is possible that the choice of the zodiacal sign Leo may be connected with the month (rather than the day) of the Emperor's birth, which was surrounded by mysterious omens and spiritual agencies, if we are to believe the historians.

It is not probable that these "bacchanalian coins," as they have been called, were intended for general circulation. They would have caused deep umbrage to any orthodox Sunnís into whose hands they fell, and even Shíya'ís, with all their freedom from traditional prejudice, would hardly have relished these vinous representations. The portrait-coins were doubtless in the nature of medals or presentation pieces, rather than money for circulation. The ordinary coinage without images continued to be struck simultaneously with the "bacchanalian" issues.

On the other hand, the well-known *zodiacal* coins of Jahángír were certainly intended to pass as ordinary money, and generally took the place of the common coinage of the Agra mint during the eight years of their issue (1027-34). Tavernier, who visited the court of Aurangzíb in the middle of the seventeenth century, was the first to report the pretty legend that Núr-Jahán, the Emperor's gifted wife, begged her adoring husband to allow her twenty-four hours of supreme sovereignty, and, on obtaining his consent, immediately issued the celebrated zodiacal coins, having previously had the necessary bullion collected and the dies engraved with her own name and that of the Emperor. The story is refuted by the zodiacal coins themselves: they do not, as a rule, bear Núr-Jahán's name; and instead of being all of one date, and issued within twenty-four hours, they are spread over eight years.* Jahángír's own account of the origin

* Two zodiacal mohrs (not in the British Museum) present the name of Núr-Jahán as well as that of Jahángír, and bear the latest

of these pieces is doubtless correct and authentic. He says in his *Memoirs*,* "Formerly it was customary to strike my name on one side of the coin, and that of the place, and the month, and the year of the reign, on the obverse. It now occurred to my mind that, instead of the name of the month, the figure of the sign of the zodiac corresponding to the particular month, should be stamped. For instance, in the month of Farwardín, the figure of a ram, in Ardibihist that of a bull, and so on; that is, in every month in which a coin might be struck, the figure of the constellation in which the sun might be at the time, should be impressed on one side of it. This was my own innovation: it had never been done before."

The British Museum possesses an unrivalled series of these zodiacal issues.† It includes a complete set of all the zodiacal signs in genuine mohrs, with several varieties of each sign, in all forty-three specimens; seven signs (fourteen coins) of the silver zodiacal rupees, in which a complete set of the signs is not known to exist; ten gold and one silver specimen of mediæval forgeries, and a complete series of the signs in modern imitation half-rupees. Some of the signs are rarer than others, and Aquarius is especially rare in both metals. The figures of the various signs, combined with the solar rays, as a rule agree with their traditional representation. The ram, humped bull, embracing twins, crab, lion, scales, scorpion, centaur, capricorn, and two fish present no special peculiarities. But Virgo appears in three different forms on the genuine mohrs; first as the

---

known date, 1034. One of these, of the sign Cancer, and mint Ajmír, was described by Mr. Gibbs in *Proceedings of the As. Soc. of Bengal*, 1883. The other, in the Bibliothèque Nationale, is engraved in Bonneville, and mentioned by Marsden, *Num. Orient.* 630.

* *Túzak-i Jahángírí*, ED. vi. 357.

† It does not, however, possess any of the earliest year, 1027, nor of the latest, 1034.

traditional standing winged figure with ear of corn; secondly, as a squatting woman with a braid of hair down her back,—a typical Indian figure; and thirdly, as a woman with a pitcher on her head, who might be described as a female Aquarius; and a fourth form, of a dancing girl, appears on one of the forged mohrs. Aquarius is represented as an old man with a pitcher of water, or by the pitcher alone.

The zodiacal coins, both gold and silver, have always attracted much attention and emulation among collectors. The Hindús after a time came to regard them as talismans, to be worn prophylactically round the neck,* and English ladies have not despised them as ornaments. They have consequently been extensively forged, and few collections exist which do not contain some of these imitations. A distinction, however, must be drawn between different classes of these forgeries. There is (1) a small class of gold zodiacal mohrs which are clearly ancient, and in spite of their rude workmanship and the peculiar forms of the zodiacal signs, may not be forgeries at all, but merely trial-pieces of Jahángír's time: such are nos. 333*c*, 339, and 346*a*, all of the year 1030 and 16th of the reign, which are represented in the lowest line of Plate X. On the whole, I believe them to be almost contemporary imitations. Then (2) there are more recent forgeries, distinguished by a certain crudeness and sharpness in the drawing and execution of the figures, and a tendency to blunder in the Persian inscriptions; these are numbered, in the gold, 376 to 384 in the Catalogue; and there is but one silver forgery of

---

* Marsden states that his zodiacal coins came from Mr. Crow, formerly chief of the Súrat factory of the East India Company; and adds that the Hindús treated them as talismans. Lieut. Edward Moor (*Narrative of the operations of Captain Little's Detachment*, 490) mentions the sale of a set of zodiacal mohrs at Bombay in 1790 for the sum of 2500 rupees.

this class, the rupee no. 385. In the representation of Virgo, the forgeries show, besides the usual type (as the true coin 338, and the forgery 378), a curious figure of a dancing woman, which does not occur on any genuine mohr at present known. Finally (3), there is a class of modern half-rupees which, unlike the first two classes, can never have been intended to pass as counterfeit money, but must have been either an avowedly new currency, or else intended merely as ornaments. They are struck from the same dies as the imitation gold mohrs, or from dies closely resembling them; and thus bearing inscriptions peculiar to mohrs, and not borne by rupees, would have been immediately detected. They were probably struck to please somebody's fancy, and tradition ascribes them to a Frenchman, Colonel Martine, well known in the history of the Company's power in India; but Marsden denies this, on the authority of the Colonel's personal friends.

In spite of general indications in the style and fabric, there is often considerable difficulty in distinguishing the imitation from the genuine mohrs, and numismatists are frequently found to differ in their decisions. In distinguishing the British Museum forgeries, the late Mr. James Gibbs' experience has proved of value.*

* See *Journal of the Bombay Branch of the Royal Asiatic Society*, xiv. 155-160, and *Proceedings of the Asiatic Society of Bengal*, 1883.

§ 7. *NISÁRS OR PRESENTATION MONEY.*

Among the coins of the Moghul Emperors, from Jahángír onwards, certain pieces, generally of small size, bear the word *nisár* (نثار), which means "scattering." These coins were struck for the purpose of distribution among the crowd on the occasion of certain festivities, such as marriages, or progresses of state, and the like. They were in fact a species of Maundy Money. The custom is common in Eastern countries and survives to the present day. The Moghul coins struck for this purpose (except Aurangzíb's) are economically thin for their diameter, and weigh from 43 to 44 grains (*i.e.* ¼ mohr or rupee); but one weighs 88 grains, and another 22. They are executed with considerable elegance, and have a border of dots. Aurangzíb's, on the other hand, are clumsy and thick, of South Indian fabric, and weigh 44 grains. The British Museum contains no specimen of Jahángir's *nisárs*, but Mr. Rodgers has described three, of Ajmír in the 10th year of the reign, Ahmadábád in the 13th, and Agrah in the 14th year; and also two of Sháh-Jahán, of Kashmír and Lahore; and adds that he has never seen any others.* The British Museum, however, has ten of these coins, viz:—

Sháh-Jahán. Æ Agrah, 1038, Y.R. 2. (ↄ)
Æ Lahore, 1044, Y.R. 7. (ↄ)
Æ Lahore, 1049, Y.R. 13. (ↄ)
Æ Sháhjahánábád, 1060, Y.R. 24. (ↄ)
Æ Kashmír, 1061, Y.R. 25.
Æ Sháhjahánábád, 1067, Y.R. 31. (ↄ)
(posthumous) AV Sháhjahánábád, 1069. No regnal year (ↄ)

---

* *Proceedings of the Asiatic Society of Bengal*, 1883.

Aurangzíb.	AV Chínápatan, 1103, Y.R. 35.
	AV Chínápatan, 1111, Y.R. 4x.
Jahándár.	AR Sháhjahánábad, 1124. (ذ)
'Álamgír II.	AR Akbarábád, 1171, Y.R. 4.

All Sháh-Jahán's *nisárs* save one (where it may be obliterated) have an initial letter ذ over the ر. The same sign (or its points) appears on Jahándár's *nisár*, but not on those of Aurangzíb or 'Álamgír II. This abbreviation has not hitherto been noticed, and its meaning is enigmatical. As it occurs on coins of four different mints, and two different weights (44 and 88 grs.) it can neither be a mint-mark nor a sign of denomination.

Nisárs were used for other purposes than scattering among crowds. The word is also used as signifying the periodical tribute or gift, symbolical of homage, rendered to the Moghul Emperor on certain festivals, such as the anniversary of his coronation, or New Year's day. Mr. Delmerick says* that "coins used to be specially struck in his [Bahádur II.'s] name and offered as part of the customary *nazar* by the Resident on behalf of the British Government," until the practice was abolished by Lord Ellenborough "in the cold season of 1842-3." I have no doubt that the coins used for this purpose were the *thin* pieces issued in the name of Sháh-'Álam, of Muhammad Akbar, and of Bahádur II., at Sháhjahánábád, the residence of the titular Emperors under British protection. They are numbered in the Catalogue nos. 1104-9, 1210-16, 1221-2, and in style they closely resemble the thin half-rupee *nisár* of Sháh-Jahán, no. 669, which is 1·15 in. broad, yet weighs only 88 grs. They are not in the least like current coins meant for circulation, but they are unmistakeably like *nisárs*, though the name does not occur in their inscriptions.

---

* *Journal of the Asiatic Society of Bengal*, xlv. 295.

In connexion with occasional coins of this kind, mention should be made of certain abnormally large and heavy pieces, two of which, though not the largest, are found in the British Museum series. These are both five-mohr pieces, issued by Akbar at Agrah in A.H. 971 and by Jahángír at Agrah in 1028, and weigh respectively 838 and 843 grains. There are also preserved in the British Museum two casts of a gigantic 200-mohr piece of Sháh-Jahán, $5\frac{3}{8}$ in. in diameter, with mint Sháh-jahán-ábád, and date 1064, regnal year 28. It is represented in full size in pl. xxxiii. The inscriptions are as follows :—

Obv. Area, within square,

لا الــــه الا الـــلـــه
مــحـــــــــمـــــد
رســـول الـــلـــه ۱۰۶۴
ضـــرب
دار الخلافه شاه جهان اباد

Margin, in segments,

شـد ایمان از صدق ابـی بکر انور
شد از عدل عمر اسلام قوی دست
از شرم وحیای عثمان دین تازه شد
وزعـلـم عـلـی ولایت زیـــور یـــافت

Rev. Area, within square,

۲۸
پـــادشــــاه غــــازی
قــران ثــانی شاه جهان
حـــب
شهاب الدین محمد صا

Margin, in segments,

سکه بر مهر دو صد مهری زد از لطف اله
ثانی صاحب قران شاه جهان دین پـنـاه
روی زر بادا ز نقش سکه اش عـالـم فـروز
تا شود از پرتـو خورشید روشن روی مـاه

A drawing of a similar 200-mohr piece, of the same mint and date, but with the inscriptions slightly varied in arrangement, and ولایت انور در علم علی یافت instead of وز علم علی ولایت زیور یافت, was exhibited by Mr. J. Gibbs at a meeting of the Bengal Asiatic Society, and is engraved in the *Proceedings* of January, 1883. General Sir A. Cunningham states that the original coin was at Patnah some fifty to eighty years ago. According to Richardson, it weighed above 70 oz. (33,600 grs.), and had a diameter of 4 inches.*

Mr. Gibbs also published a photograph of a 100-mohr piece of Aurangzíb, struck at Sháhjahánábád, A.H. 1083, Y.R. 15, diameter 4 in., thickness ¼ in., weight 35 oz. 4 dwt., or 16,880 grs., belonging to the Mahárájá Sindhia.† One like it was at Benáres 45 years ago, according to Sir A. Cunningham. A *silver* coin of Aurangzíb's at Dresden, issued at Sháhjahánábád in the tenth year of his reign, has a diameter of 4·4 in., and a weight of 5·15 English lbs.‡

General Cunningham is of opinion that these large pieces were probably "Nazzarnána medals," given to the Emperor by nobles who paid their tribute in a single lump coin.§ That such large pieces were not infrequently struck is shown by the inventory of Jahángír's treasure given by William Hawkins, in which we find these items: "Of another sort of Coyne, of a thousand rupias [*i.e.* 100 mohrs] a piece, there are twenty thousand pieces. Of another sort, of halfe the value, there are ten thousand pieces. Of another sort of Gold, of twenty Tolas a piece, there are thirty thousand pieces. Of

---

* It is referred to by Tavernier, and described by Richardson, *Persian, Arabic, and English Dictionary*, art. سکه (ed. 1777); see Marsden, *Num. Orient.* 641; Thomas, *Chronicles*, 423.

† *Proceedings Asiatic Soc. Bengal*, March, 1885.

‡ Thomas, *l.c.*

§ *Proceedings of the Asiatic Society of Bengal*, 1883.

another sort of five Tolas, which is this King's stamp, of these there be fiftie thousand pieces." There were also, in silver, "of another sort of coin of Selim Sha this King, of an hundred Tolas a piece, forty thousand pieces,"* &c. Aurangzib, as he grew old, displayed a notable talent for hoarding money. According to the Venetian physician Manouchi, he devised peculiar safeguards for his treasure. "He caused to be constructed under his palace at Dely two deep caves, supported by vast marble pillars. Piles of gold were stored in the one, and of silver in the other; and to render more difficult any attempt to convey away his treasure, he caused, of both metals, pieces to be made of so prodigious a size as to render them useless for the purpose of commerce," meaning currency.† Such, no doubt, are the pieces belonging to the Mahárájá Sindhia and the Dresden Cabinet. Doubtless, the reason that so few of these unwieldy coins have come down to us is that they were melted down into the current coin of commerce.

---

* *The Hawkins Voyages* (Hakluyt Society), 421-2.

† See Appendix iv. to *Bernier's Travels*, edited by Arch. Constable (*Oriental Miscellany*), 476.

§ 8. *COPPER COINAGE.*

THE rarest of all Moghul coins are those of copper. The British Museum possesses seventeen specimens of the early local issues of the time of Bábar and Humáyún (pp. 262-4), thirty-nine copper coins of Akbar, one of Jahángír; but none of any other Emperor. The reason for this singular scarcity of copper is the general use of other substances for petty currency in India. Cowries formed the chief small change of Bengal, and bitter almonds of Bombay. Admiral John Splinter Stavorinus (1768-71) states that "copper coin is not seen in *Bengal.* For change they make use of the small sea-shells called cowries, eighty of which make a *poni*; and sixty, or sixty-five *ponis,* according as there are few or many cowries in the country, make a rupee. They come from the *Maldive* Islands. The money-changers sit upon all the *bazars* with quantities of them, to furnish the lower orders with change, for the purchase of necessaries."* The same authority says that at Súrat, "in the same way as cowries are made use of in *Bengal,* as the lowest medium of exchange, almonds, which are called *badams,* are employed for the purpose here."† Linschoten remarked in 1584 that almonds were used for coins at Súrat,‡ and the observation is confirmed by Mandelslo (1638), who says that thirty-six almonds or eighty "kauret" shells went to the pice.§ We read of ten tons of cowries being ordered by "our Honourable Masters" to be shipped in 1753, and of a tribute of "12,000 *kahuns* of cowries" in 1803.|| This accounts

---

* *Voyages to the East Indies,* 1798, i. 461-2. † *Ibid.* iii. 10.

‡ *Voyage of John Huyghen van Linschoten to the East Indies,* ed. A. C. Burnell and P. A. Tiele, i. 241 ff. (Hakluyt Society).

§ *Voyages,* 118. || *Hobson-Jobson, s.v.*

for the absence of copper coins in the series of the later Emperors.

The copper currency of Akbar, however, was abundant, as Mr. C. J. Rodgers has shown in his valuable papers in the *Journal of the Asiatic Society of Bengal* * and the *Indian Antiquary*.† Some obscurity exists as to the weights and denominations of these pieces. Abu-l-Fazl enumerates only the *dám* (or *paisah*), and its half, quarter, and eighth. But the word *dám* does not occur by itself on the coins. Instead, we find generally the vague term *fulús* فلوس, which means "money," the weight-denomination *tankah* تنکه, with its half نیم تنکه, نصفی, quarter چهارم حصه, eighth هشتم حصه, and sixteenth شانزدهم حصه; and the forms *dú tánkí* دو تانکی, or *double tánkí*, and what Mr. Rodgers reads as *chú tánkí* چو تانکی, *four tánkís;* though the Hindústání form چو for the Persian چهار is somewhat unexpected. The *muhr* مهر also occurs; and the *dámrá* دامرا, and *dámrí* دامری. These terms require consideration.

The thirty-nine specimens in the British Museum may be classified as follows :—

1. Fulús : 307 to 325 grs.‡

Ahmadábád A.H. 982 (wt. 312), 98*x* (314).
Dehlí, Iláhí 42-4 (37 = $\frac{1}{8}$).

---

* xlix. (1880) ; liv. (1885). † 1890, July, 220-224.

‡ Mr. Rodgers, in *Journal of the Asiatic Society of Bengal*, xlix. 213-7, and *Ind. Antiq.*, 1890, gives the following weights of *fulús* and their fractions:—Alwar, A.H. 968 (303); Ahmadábád, A.H. 980 (314), 986 (318); Ajmír, 988 (313); Attak Benáres, Iláhí 37 (316); Burhánpúr, Iláhí 48 (310); Chitór, A.H. 999 (314); Dehlí, A.H. 981 (311), Iláhí 38 (308); Fathpúr, A.H. 989 (319), 986 (78 = $\frac{1}{4}$); Gwálior, Iláhí 38 (315); Hisár Fírózah, A.H. 967 (320) 996 (314); Jaunpúr, 970 (307); Lahore, A.H. 987 (325), 970 (315), 976 (289), Iláhí 43 (295), 38 (39 = $\frac{1}{8}$); Lucknow, A.H. 989 (317); Málpúr, 985 (309); Multán, *Iláhí* 41 (312); Nárnól (?), A.H. 969 (37 = $\frac{1}{8}$); Urdú-Zafar-Karín, Iláhí 42 (315), &c. These are all regular in weight, and in accord with the weights of fulús in the British Museum.

Dógám, A.H. 983 (312), 994 (321).
Fathpúr, A.H. 987 (309), 988 (311).
Gwálior, A.H. 9*xx* (309).
,, Iláhí 38 (316).
Jaunpúr, A.H. 98*x* (312).
Kábul, Iláhí 32, 33 (155 = ½).
Lahore, A.H. 97*x* (310).
,, Iláhí 39 (312), 43 (78 = ¼), 36 (40 = ⅛).
Málpúr, A.H. 985 (319).
Multán, Iláhí 37 (310).
Nárnól, A.H. 963 (325), 965 (317), 980 (311), 982 (312).
,, Iláhí 36 (128).
Urdú-Zafar-Karín, A.H. 1000 (307).
Mint obliterated A.H. 966 (315), 980 (314), 987 (314, 318).

2. Tankah.*

Bairátah, Iláhí 44 (634, 644, 316).
No Mint, Iláhí year obliterated (36 : $\frac{1}{16}$th شانزدهم حصت).

3. Tánkí (all *Agrah*).†

1 Tánkí, Iláhí 47 (58).
2 ,, ,, 46 (116); 47 (120); 50 (122).
4 ,, ,, 47 (244).

4. Mohr.

Iláhabás, Iláhí 31 (315).

5. No Denomination.

Agrah, Iláhí 4*x* (67).

---

* Mr. Rodgers (*ubi supra*) describes tankahs of 618, 620, 623, 625·5, and 626 grs., and of 327 and 315 grs.; half-tankahs (so specified in their inscriptions), of 317, 309, and 318 grs.; a quarter-tankah of 158 grs.; an eighth of 39·5 grs. (*sic*); and sixteenths of 37·5 and 38·5 grs., all so specified.

† Mr. Rodgers (*ubi supra*) publishes a 1 tánkí piece of Lahore (? Iláhí 46 (59 grs.), and others of 59, 58·8 grs.; 2 tánkí pieces of Agrah of 108 and 109 grs.; 4 tánkí pieces of 237-244·5 grs., agreeing with the weights in the British Museum.

According to the *Áín-i Akbarí* the *dám* or copper unit of Akbar weighed 1 *tolah,* 8 *máshas,* 7 *ratis,* or, at Mr. Thomas's estimate of the rati, 323·5 grs. It is therefore clear that the coins which are named *fulús* in their inscriptions, and weigh from 307 to 325 grs., are *dáms,* whilst the Kábul specimen of 153 grs. is an *adhélah* or half-dám ; the Lahore piece of 78 grs. a *páulah* or quarter-dám ; and the two coins of 36 and 37 grs. *dámrís* or eighths of a dám. Mr. Rodgers has published a half-dám (نیم دام, specifically so named) of 148·7 grs., a *dámrí* of 40 grs., and a *dámrá* (presumably two dámrís, or 1 paúlah) of 76 grs. The *mohr* of Iláhábás (315 grs.) is also clearly a dám, and the word *mohr* is probably used, not as a denomination, but merely as meaning "stamp."

The term *tankah* appears to be used just as vaguely as *fulús,* both for dáms of 315 to 327 grs. and double dáms of 618 to 644 grs. Mr. Rodgers states that his weights prove that the tankah was equal to two dáms: but I do not draw the same inference. All his weights prove is that some tankahs weighed about 630 grs., and others about 320. He publishes a coin specifically named an *eighth* of a tankah, weighing nearly 40 grs., which brings the tankah to 320 grs., and also *sixteenths* of 38·5 grs., which would make it 616 grs.

The *tánkí* is quite distinct from the *tankah.* It weighs 58 or 59 grs., and its double weighs 108 to 122 grs. ; while *four-tánkí* pieces weigh 237 to 244 grs. According to Mr. Rodgers the *tánkí* is a weight, not a coin, and he endeavours unsuccessfully to reconcile its weight (say 62 grs. when unworn) with the "jeweller's tank," which is stated in the *Áín* to be of 24 *ratis* (42 grs). A more probable hypothesis would be that, just as there were *fifth* parts (*panj, pandan, pandú*) of the mohr and rupee, so the *dám* had its fifth, called a *tánkí.* The weight, of 63 grs. or so, corresponds fairly well with one-fifth of the dám of about 320 grs.; and the *dú tánkí* and *chú tánkí* pieces would correspond to $\frac{2}{5}$ths and $\frac{4}{5}$ths of the dám.

To sum up, allowing for wear, we have roughly—

The *Dám* (*paisah, fulús, tankah*), about 320 grains.
$\frac{1}{2}$,, (*adhélah, ním dám, nasfí*), 160 grs.
$\frac{1}{4}$,, (*paúlah, dámrá*), 80 grs.
$\frac{1}{8}$,, (*dámrí, hashtum hissah*), 40 grs.
Tankah, large (*double dám*), 640 grs.
,, *small* (*dám*), 320 grs.
$\frac{1}{4}$ *tankah, large* (*chuhár hissah*), 160.
$\frac{1}{8}$,, *small* (*hashtum hissah*), 45.
$\frac{1}{16}$,, *large* (*shánzdahum hissah*), 40.
Tánkí, fifth of dám, 63.
Double tánkí, 125.
Quadruple tánkí, 250.

Further investigation and the discovery of more specimens may confirm or modify these conclusions.

§ 9. *COINAGE OF THE EAST INDIA COMPANY.*

In the latter part of this volume will be found descriptions of various coins issued by the East India Company in imitation of the Moghul currency. According to the principle of classification adopted in the Department of Coins, all clearly European issues, by which are meant coins issued with European legends or images, struck in the colonies and British possessions abroad, are placed among what is termed the British Colonial Series; and accordingly the early issues of Elizabeth, the obviously English coins of the Bombay factory, and the Imperial currency instituted by the Company in 1835, with the head of the King or the Lion on the obverse, etc., are omitted from the present volume and included in the Colonial Series. But when the Company's coins bear the name of an Indian sovereign, and were intended to pass among the people as though they had been struck by that sovereign himself, they cannot be regarded as part of the regular Colonial Series, but must be classed along with the coins which they avowedly counterfeit. Thus the coins issued by the Madras and Calcutta authorities, nominally from the mint of Arkát, in 1815, etc., are included in this Catalogue, because they bear the name of 'Álamgír II.; and similarly the Company's well-known "19 san" rupee of 1793—1835 is described in this volume, because it bears the name of Sháh-'Álam, though it continued to be issued long after this Emperor's death.

The task of distinguishing the Company's imitations from the Moghul issues is not always easy, and sometimes is impossible. Considerations of fabric, mint-marks, &c., are of assistance, but a knowledge of the mint records is essential to a final and permanent classification, and it may be doubted whether even these would avail to solve a large proportion of the complicated problems presented by the coinage. At present, however, this branch of information has been but imperfectly investigated. A considerable number of important facts has been collected by Prinsep, Marsden, Ruding, Atkins, and Sir Walter Elliot, &c.; and recently a valuable addition has been made to our sources by Mr. Edgar Thurston, the superintendent of the Madras Central Museum, who has explored the archives of the Madras mint.* It is much to be desired that similar researches should be made at Calcutta and Bombay; for until this is done more completely than Prinsep was able to do it, any detailed classification must be more or less tentative.

A cursory glance at the history of the Company's coinage will show the causes of this difficulty of classification. Although the first charter of the "Old"† or London East India Company (styled in full, "The Governor and Company of Merchants of London trading into the East Indies,") dates from the close of the year 1600, the Directors never assumed the right to authorize the issue of a universal currency for India, *bearing the Company's name*, till 1835. During this long interval several methods were employed to meet the monetary exigencies of their trade. For example, special coins with the device of a portcullis were exported from England in Elizabeth's reign for use in the Company's factories:

---

* *History of the Coinage of the Territories of the East India Company in the Indian Peninsula*, &c., with 20 plates. Madras, 1890.

† So called to distinguish it from the later "English Company" or "General Society," founded in 1698. The two were united in 1708-9 under the title of "The United Company of Merchants of England trading to the East Indies," commonly called the Honourable East India Company. The natives called it *Jahán-Kumpant*, "Company of the World," whence the nickname "John Company."

such, however, would of course be employed only for trade with European nations, and would not pass in the interior of India. When Charles II.'s queen brought him, as part of her dowry, the port and island of Bombay (in 1661, but the place was not surrendered till 1665), the king by Letters Patent dated 27 March, 1669, transferred them to the Company, to be held "as of the Manor of East Greenwich" in free and common soccage at a farm rent of 10*l*. Bombay soon (1685) became the seat of the Western Presidency, and already in 1671 a mint was founded, where the Company's agents by royal permission issued a local coinage of their own with English inscriptions, for circulation in the island and the immediate neighbourhood. The Letters Patent of 5 October, 1677, contain the following clause on this subject: "**And also** of our farther especiall grace vertuwe knowledge and meere motion **We doe** by these presents for us our Heires and Successors give and graunt unto the said Governor and Company of Merchants of London trading into the East Indies and their Successors full and free liberty power and Authority from tyme to tyme and at all tymes hereafter within the Port and Island of Bombay in the East Indies and the Precincts and Territoryes thereof and thereunto belonging to Stamp and Coyne or Caused to bee Stamped and Coyned moneys of Gold Silver Copper Tynne or Lead or of any mixt mettall Compounded or made up of them or any of them to bee Currant within the said Port and Island Fort and Townes and the Precincts and Territories thereof And also in all the Islands Ports Havens Cittys Creeks Townes and Places whatsoever within the East Indies Expressed mentioned or contayned in our said severall Charters or Letters Patents herein before mentioned or either of them with such Impression and

Inscription thereupon to bee made and to bee called or knowne by the Name or Names of Rupees Pices and Budgerookes," etc.* The historian Kháfí Khán records that "some rupees which the English had coined at Bombay with the name of their impure king," were shown to the Emperor Aurangzíb in 1694 (A.H. 1105); but when Khafí Khán was sent to expostulate, the chief of the Bombay factory explained that these pieces were only "current in our own jurisdiction."† Such coins are, therefore, properly classed as English colonial currency. For circulation among the natives in India, the Company were forced either to send their bullion to be minted by the Moghul governors, or to imitate at various local mints the common coins of the contemporary Moghul Emperor. The native princes having raised objections to this exercise of the privilege of coining, the Company obtained further powers by Letters Patent from James II., dated 12 April, 1686 (A.H. 1097), by which they were authorized to issue at all their forts copies of the current native coins, on the condition that they maintained an equal weight and fineness with the pieces they copied. The Bombay factory was directed to use "such stamps, dies, and tools, as were common in the country."‡ In 1688-9, the native authorities, anxious to obviate the exercise of this royal permission, granted the Company the right to send their bullion to be coined at the Moghul mint at Súrat; but it appears they preferred to continue their practice of coining at Bombay.

At this early period there is no means of distinguishing between the Moghul issues and the Company's

* Facsimile in *Journal of Indian Art*, No. 31. See also Sir G. Birdwood, *Report on the Old Records of the India Office*, 2nd reprint, 219, &c.

† Kháfí Khán, ED. vii. 351.

‡ Parchment Records, India Office: Birdwood, *op. cit.*, 285.

imitations. Nor can we be certain that a coin bearing the name of a certain city was struck at that mint. We read, for example, that the Bengal Council in 1707 (1119), sent a specimen of the new Emperor Bahádur's rupees to Fort St. George to be copied for use in the trade with Bengal.* But it is specially mentioned that this rupee was not to be used at Madras, because it might give offence to the rival Emperor, or pretender, Kám Bakhsh, whose influence was then predominant in the Deccan. Thus Bengal rupees † might be coined at Madras, and (as will be seen) Madras rupees at Calcutta.

So far all coining by the Company at their own mints was carried on with difficulty and interruption, and against the will of the Moghul rulers; indeed, the Company's coinage was at this period simple forgery, though the fact that it passed among the natives shows that it was intrinsically as good as the imperial currency, from which it apparently could not be distinguished. But in 1717 (1129) the Company were permitted to escape from this invidious position. In that year the Emperor Farrukh-siyar, yielding, no doubt, to substantial persuasions, and perceiving the futility of resistance, granted a firmán by which the English were allowed to coin money of the Empire in the island of Bombay.‡ The permission, however, is said to have not been practically put in force till 1725 (1137), when the Bombay mint, which had apparently fallen into disuse, no doubt by reason of the Emperor's opposition, was rebuilt.§ In 1742 (1154–5) the Company were also granted permission to coin rupees in imitation of those struck by the Imperial

---

* Thurston, *op. cit.*, 24.

† The word rupee is often officially used in a general sense to include both gold and silver coins; and we come across the term "gold rupee" in the writings of European travellers.

‡ Thurston, *op. cit.*, 25.

§ In contradiction of this statement, see below, p. cvi.

governors at Arkát,* and they issued rupees, with the name of the nominal mint Arkát, at Fort St. George for circulation in the Deccan, and later on, at Calcutta and Dhákká for use in Bengal. The French Compagnie des Indes exercised a similar privilege of issuing "Arkát" rupees at Pondicherry. The Arkát rupees struck at Madras had the mark of a *trisúl*, or "Siva's trident"; those struck at Calcutta, a *rose*; and the French, a *crescent*.†

In Bengal the Company were for a long time obliged to send their bullion to be coined at the mints of the Nawáb of the province, which were at Dhákká, Patnah, and Murshidábád. But at length in 1759 (1171-2), the Nawáb Siráj-ad-daulah gave them permission to establish a mint of their own at Calcutta.‡ In 1764 (1176), after the battle of Buxar, the Moghul Emperor Sháh-'Álam submitted to the English, who in 1765 took over the administration of what remained of his realm, but assigned to him the province of Alláhábád with the district of Korah, together with a subsidy for his establishment.§ In taking over the administration, the Company also assumed the right of coinage. At first, indeed, the Nawáb of Bengal continued to strike coins, whilst agreeing to pass Calcutta rupees as equal to those of his own mint of Murshidábád; but the mints at Patnah, Dhákká, and Murshidábád were soon abolished, and all the coins for Bengal were struck at Calcutta, whatever supposititious mint name they might bear.||

---

* Prinsep, *Useful Tables*, 24.

† Thurston, *op. cit.*, 50; 102 *note*. ‡ *Ibid.* 33.

§ This was arranged by the Treaty of Alláhábád, dated 16 Aug., 1765, between the English and the Nawáb Vazír of Oudh, and by "Articles of agreement," dated 19 Aug., 1765, confirming certain firmáns of the 12th of the same month. The Treaty is given in facsimile in the *Journal of Indian Art*, No 31. The coin issued in the Emperor's name at Calcutta in A.H. 1176, the only piece of its kind, seems to have been struck in commemoration of this event. It is in the nature of a medal.

|| Thurston, *op. cit.*, 34, 38.

Here, then, we come upon one of the perplexities of this period. For some years after 1765 there appears to have been a double issue in Bengal,—the Nawáb's and the Company's; and no record so far has been published of the distinction between the two. In the classification of these issues in the present volume, the principal guide has been the style and fabric of the coins themselves.

In 1793 (1207-8) the Company endeavoured to put an end to the existing confusion and discrepancies of weight and purity by establishing a standard currency which should supersede the various local issues. For this purpose they selected the coinage struck at Murshidábád in the 19th year of Sháh-'Álam's reign as the most suitable for imitation,—presumably because the most correct in standard and the most perfect in design and execution. The result was the coin familiar to Anglo-Indians under the name of the "19 san" or "sikkah" rupee (and mohr) of Murshidábád, which was now fixed as the standard coin to the exclusion of all others in Bengal, though the old rupees of the 11th, 12th and 15th year were still to pass current until there should be a sufficiency of the new coinage.* The old mints at Dhákká, Patnah, and Murshidábád are said to have been revived for this issue: but Marsden asserts that it was all coined at Calcutta. The 19th year of Sháh-'Álam's reign was retained on the obverse, whatever Hijrah year might appear on the reverse, and this absurd anachronism went on until the true colonial coinage of 1835 was introduced.

So much for the foundation of the Lower Bengal coinage which formed the chief currency of Calcutta until 1835, though modified, from time to time, notably in 1818 and 1832. The upper country in Bengal, however, was served from other mints, of which the chief were Benáres and Farrukhábád, and these were the only two

---

* Marsden, *Num. Orient.*, ii. 688. Prinsep, *op. cit.*, 24.

up-country mints used by the Company until 1830. The Benáres mint was established by Rájá Balwant Singh in 1730 (1142), and remained under native control for twenty years after the Company took over the administration of the province in 1765.* The Company's Farrukhábád mint was founded in 1803 (1218), about a year after the Duáb had been ceded to the English, and issued its "45 san" rupee, in imitation of what was known as the "Lucknow 45 san sikkah"† struck at the Fathgarh mint of the Moghul: the 45th year of 'Sháh-Álam corresponding to the year 1218 of the Hijrah (1803). The Benáres mint which had for some time been issuing the Nawáb of Oudh's rupees, in 1806 was made to coin Company's coin, with the mint-mark of the trisúl or Siva's trident. Neither mint enjoyed a long existence. That at Farrukhábád was closed in 1824 (1240) and that at Benáres in 1830 (1246):‡ but, in accordance with the anomalous ways of the time the Benáres mint ceased to issue its own rupees in 1819, and substituted an issue of *Farrukhábád* rupees from 1819 till its suppression in 1830. After that date, Ságar § and Calcutta took up the duty of issuing *Farrukhábád* coins for the up-country circulation, until this branch of the coinage was suppressed in 1835. The various difficulties in the classification of the coins arising from this confusion of mints will be noticed further on.

The following table, based upon Prinsep's data,|| shows the different classes of the Company's Bengal

---

* Prinsep, *op. cit.*, 26. Thurston, *op. cit.*, 43.

† It is not explained why it was called a "Lucknow" rupee, although it bore the name of Ahmadnagar Farrukhábád, and was struck at Fathgarh; but this is merely an example of the confusion of the subject.

‡ Prinsep, *op. cit.*, 26.

§ Ságar was established as a native mint in 1779 (1193) by the Peshwá's officer at Garrah Mandlah; and was ceded to the English in 1818.

|| *Op. cit.*, 3.

issues, so far as they adopted the European style of a collar, rim, or milled edges, by which they may be distinguished. That there were other issues after the native style will be shown later.

<table>
<tr><th></th><th>Milling, etc.</th></tr>
<tr><td>Murshidábád :—</td><td></td></tr>
<tr><td>Old standard sikkah rupee of 1793-1818.</td><td>////////////////</td></tr>
<tr><td>New " " " " 1818-1832.</td><td>||||||||||||</td></tr>
<tr><td>Later standard sikkah rupee of 1832-5.</td><td>No milling, but a dotted rim on the face.</td></tr>
<tr><td>Farrukhábád :—</td><td></td></tr>
<tr><td>Old standard Farrukhábád rupee (or "45 san Lucknow rupee") of 1803-19. . . . .</td><td>////////////////</td></tr>
<tr><td>New standard Farrukhábád rupee (coined at Farrukhábád, 1819-24, at Benáres 1819-30; and at Ságar and Calcutta, 1819-33).</td><td>||||||||||||||||</td></tr>
<tr><td>Later Farrukhábád rupee 1833-5. .</td><td>Plain edge and plain rim.</td></tr>
<tr><td>Benáres :—</td><td></td></tr>
<tr><td>Benáres rupee 1806-1819 . . . .</td><td>////////////////</td></tr>
</table>

It will be noticed that oblique milling prevailed in all three mints until 1818-9, straight milling from 1819 to 1832-3, and plain edges from 1833-5.

In September 1835 the Company established an English coinage with the head of William IV. in place of the name of the Moghul Emperor, and all the older issues were ordered to be suppressed.

Turning to Bombay, we find that the plan of a uniform and fixed coinage was adopted there rather later than the establishment of the "19 san Murshidábád" currency in Bengal (1793). The mohrs and rupees of

Súrat had long been the models on which the Bombay coins had been imitated; but there arose discrepances in the fineness which obliged the Company to have their coins restruck at Súrat. It was not till 1800 (1214) that the Bombay mint recommenced the issue of Súrat rupees,* and not till 1804 (1219), the 46th year of Sháh-Álam, that a fixed coinage was established.† The Bombay-Súrat coins, both in gold and silver, bearing this year, were distinguished by a crown, but this mark was soon abandoned, and the familiar "46 san Súrat rupees" are only distinguishable by their date from the native issues. Like the "19 san" rupee of Murshidábád, the "46 san" rupee of Súrat continued to be struck, irrespective of the true date, until the establishment of a general British currency in 1835.

The Madras coinage, with the nominal mint Arkát, has already been mentioned.

The foregoing summary of the history of the coinage of the East India Company up to the establishment of an English currency in 1835 prepares the way for an examination of the reasons which have ruled the classification of these issues in the present volume, and of the means of distinguishing between them and the contemporary native coinages.

The history of the Company's coinage (for circulation among natives) before 1835 has been seen to fall into three periods:—

1. The Period of Prohibition; when the Company either sent its bullion to be coined at the Moghul mints, or else issued illicit imitations, *i.e.* forgeries.

---

* Prinsep, *op. cit.*, 24. This year is the date of the suppression of the native Nawáb or governor at Súrat.

† Atkins, *Coins of British Possessions and Colonies* (1889), says that Súrat rupees were copied by the Company from 1733 to 1780 (1146—1194), and then the 46 san rupee was introduced. This last statement is irreconcilable with the fact that Sháh 'Álam's 46th year corresponds to 1804.

2. The Period of Concession; when the Company obtained limited rights of coining, viz. :—

a. To coin at Bombay, 1716 (1129), but not exercised until 1725 (1137).

b. To copy Arkát rupees, 1742 (1154).

c. To establish a mint at Calcutta, 1759 (1171).

3. The Period of Administration; when the Company practically took over the administration and minting of the Moghul Empire, 1765 (1178).

In classifying the coins these three periods must be treated in succession :—

(1.) During the *first* of these periods it is obviously impossible to distinguish between the Moghul and the Company's issues. The latter were forgeries, and forgeries that were so good that they apparently could not be detected.

(2.) In the *second* period there are only three mints to be considered: Bombay, Arkát (Madras), and Calcutta, corresponding to the three chief factories of the Company and to the three modern Presidencies.

We are not informed what coin the Bombay mint was authorized to issue in 1716, but it is termed "coin of the Empire," which must indicate coin such as the Moghul Emperor issued from his own mints: and any doubt which might be entertained on the subject is removed by the discovery, in the British Museum, of the very coins in question. They will be found described on pp. 278-9, and all bear the mint name منبی (or منبے) *Munbai*, pronounced *Mumbai* (Bombay).* The earliest, three in number, are dated A.H. 1131 (1719), and the year 1 [of Muhammad Sháh], which shows that the

* Marsden read this as "*the Moneer of the maps*," and Mr. Thurston, *op. cit.*, describes his no. 39 (Pl. xvi. 4) as a *Súrat* rupee, though it reads Munbai and is similar to nos. 79 and 80, p 279, in the present volume.

privilege of coining, granted in 1716, was speedily exercised, and not postponed till 1725 as stated in the records. These coins, and one of 1143 (1730), do not bear the name of a Moghul Emperor on the reverse, but merely the inaccurately engraved inscription سکه مبارك شا5ن شاه غازی. What the figure 5 represents is a difficult problem, unless it be a bad copy of the ها in شاهان شاه. It may refer to the relation of the coins to the rupee: for they all weigh 37 grains, which is about one-fifth of the full weight of a rupee. The 1725 issue, recorded in the annals, is represented by the rupee no. 72, p. 278, which bears the name of Muhammad Sháh and the regnal year 7, corresponding to 1137 (1725). A later rupee is dated in the eighteenth year of Muhammad Sháh, and A.H. 1148 (1735), with a counter-stamp, probably a shroff-mark of a Moghul money-changer. A gold mohr is dated the 9th of Sháh-'Álam, A.H. 1182 (1768); and a rupee bears the same regnal year, but the Hijrah date is 1188 (1774), an error not infrequent on Anglo-Moghul coins. Finally, two very badly engraved rupees, having no dates, and wearing a modern look, appear to have been issued at Calcutta for Bombay in 1800.*

As to Arkát, there is little difficulty in distinguishing the coins struck with this name at Madras, Calcutta, and Pondicherry, from those issued by the Moghul authorities at Arkát itself. The latter have no particular mark, whilst there is ample authority for identifying the trisúl, rose, and crescent, as the respective symbols of the three European mints. Examples of the native issues are described on p. 239, and illustrated on Pl. xxvii. The Company's coins all bear the name of 'Álamgír II., and the sixth year of his reign (whatever the Hijrah year),

* See the footnote, p. 279.

which seems to suggest that the issue of Arkát rupees, though authorized in 1742 (1154), was not actually carried out till the reign of that Emperor 1754—61 (1167—75). The earliest dated issues in the British Museum are of A.H. 1213—4 (1798—1800), and are precisely similar to the contemporary native coinage of Arkát, with the addition of the trisúl Ψ. In 1815 a milled coinage was established (with the name of 'Álamgír II., and years 1172 and 6 of reign) which lasted until 1835, and was issued at Madras with the trisúl and at Calcutta with the rose. The Calcutta issues have a straight milling, which, on the analogy of the Company's Bengal currency, would suggest that they were struck between 1818 and 1832. (See pp. 282—5, and Pl. xxxii.). The French rupees, with the mint Arkát and the crescent, bear the name of Sháh-'Álam more usually than that of 'Álamgír II., and, unlike the English issues, they vary the regnal years on the obverse nearly in accordance with those of the Hijrah on the reverse.* (See pp. 286-7 and Pl. xxxii.) The same symbols, the trisúl and the crescent, appear on some rupees of Masulipatan, but here both belong to the period of the English occupation; though the crescent is doubtless a survival from the French conquest. (See p. 288, Pl. xxxii.)

Of the Calcutta mint, authorized in 1759 (1171), very little is known in this *second* period. The only† occurrence of this name is on the commemorative piece of 1176 already referred to (ante, p. lxxxv., note), and on some copper coins (p. 289). The Calcutta mint was almost exclusively employed in issuing coins bearing the names of

* M. Zay's work on the French colonial coinages is weak in the Indian section.

† The rupee no. 726, described by an oversight on p. 143 as of Calcutta, is, of course, of Golkondah.

other mints (*e.g.* Arkát, and later on Murshidábád, Furrukhábád, &c.).

(3.) The *third* period presents the chief difficulties in classification. It extends from the assumption of administrative powers by the Company in Bengal in 1765 to the inauguration of a European currency in 1835, during the whole of which interval the name of Sháh-'Álam appears on the Company's coinage (except that of "Arkát"), although this Emperor died in 1806. As Sháh-'Álam's authority was purely nominal, and he was generally under British or Marátha control, it is idle to seek for any individual exercise of monetary powers by the Emperor personally. All that has to be done is to draw the line between the coinage issued in his name by the provincial governors (however independent, or however much under the real authority of the English) and the coinage issued at the Company's mints, which were few and well known. (See table above, p. ciii.) The latter alone can be properly termed Company's coins, however much other money may have been supervised by their officers.

We have first to determine what coins must be placed under *Sháh-'Álam*. Under this head are classed all those coins which bear his name, and have legible mints and consistent dates (*i.e.* dates in which the regnal and Hijrah years are in accord). A large number of these coins were issued by one or other of the numerous quasi-independent states which sprang up all over India upon the decay of the Moghul authority; but so long as they show the Emperor's name, and so long as their dates tally with his reign, they must be classed as his coinage, though he was only a figure head. This principle of classification excludes a large number of coins which do not fulfil the conditions here laid down: these will be referred to later. Sháh-'Álam's coinage is essentially of a local character, and is therefore divided under the several mints.

It is curious that there seem to be no specimens of Sháh-'Álam's coinage issued at his first capital, Alláhábád. His most important coinage was at *Sháhjahánábád*, modern Dehlí, where he can hardly be said to have been master; since he was a puppet there in the hands of the Maráthas from 1771-88 (1185-1203) and their prisoner from 1788 until Lord Lake's victory over them, March 14, 1803 (1217), when Delhí was administered for a year or two by a British resident. There are very few coins of this mint belonging to the Marátha period, and these present no peculiarities: but the British occupation is prominently signalized on the coinage. The British lion, which was the Company's crest, appears to the right of the imperial umbrella on rupees of 1218 (which year began in April 1803), but in deference, it is said, to the prejudices of the blind Emperor, who was told that the English had engraved an unclean animal on the coins, the lion gave place to the cinquefoil (the badge adopted on the coinage by the Company)* on rupees of 1218 and 1219 (1803-4). In the same way, on the large thin issues (probably *nisárs*, see above, p. lxxxvi.) of this mint, instead of the tree which usually stands beside the umbrella, we find the

---

* Although a rose with five petals formed part of the arms of the "Old" Company, at least as early as 1677 (cf. plate in *Journal of Indian Art*, no. 31), it was not found in the arms of the "New" Company, or of the Honourable United Company. The new arms granted in 1698 were: Argent a cross gules, on a shield in the dexter quarter the arms of France and England quarterly within a compartment, adorned with an Imperial crown; for the crest, upon a helm on a torse or wreath argent and gules, a lion rampant gardant or, holding between his paws an imperial crown proper, mantled gules, doubled argent; supported by two lions gardant or, each holding a banner argent charged with a cross gules. (See facsimile of the Grant in *Journal of Indian Art*, no. 31.)

cinquefoil * introduced on rupees of 1218 to 1221, while a truly British wreath, composed of roses, thistles, and shamrocks, encircles the coinage of A.H. 1219 to 1220. (See pp. 234-6 and Pl. xxvii.) Sháh-'Álam's coinage at Etáwá, Ahmadábád, Arkát, Akbarábád, Najíbábád (the capital of the Rohila chief Najíb-ad-daulah) and other mints, calls for no special notice; he died in 1221 (1806).

We now come to *mints which passed from native control into the Company's*, such as *Benáres*, and the problem to be determined is where the native coinage ends and the Company's begins. The older Benáres type (represented in the Museum from A.H. 1183 to 1196) was exchanged for a new issue, distinguished by a large flower of four petals, at or before 1203 (1787-8). These coins bear a double regnal year, one referring to Sháh-'Álam, the other invariably 17. Marsden † explains this latter as being the date of the succession (1191 A.H.), of Ásaf-ad-daulah, the Nawáb-Vazír of Oudh, under whose authority these coins were issued: the year 1191, of course, being the 17th year of Sháh-'Álam, who came to the throne in 1173. This type of Benáres coinage runs on, as to regnal years, to the 49th year of Sháh-'Álam, which corresponds to 1221, the year of his death; but the Hijrah dates include 1222, 1224, and 1225 (1810 A.D.), all later than the Emperor's death. (See p. 244, Pl. xxviii.)

Now we have already seen that Prinsep says that the Benáres mint remained under native control for twenty years after the Company took over the administration of Bengal in 1765. It is distinctly stated by the Indian historians that on the death of the Nawáb Vazír Shujá'-

* The same arrangement was adopted by Muhammad Akbar II. and Bahádur II., the two puppet Emperors who succeeded Sháh-'Álam, until the Indian Mutiny brought about the end of the effete dynasty.

† *Num. Orient.* 693.

ad-daulah in A.H. 1191, the English received the districts of Benáres, Jaunpúr, Gházípúr, and Chunár, from his successor Ásaf-ad-daulah, in consideration of his being confirmed in his post, and these parts were accordingly annexed. The coins with the special year of the Nawáb of Oudh seem to disprove this statement: the native control, according to them, must have lasted up to 1810. On the other hand, the only milled Benáres rupee in the collection (no. 66, p. 277, Pl. xxxi), clearly belonging to the Company's issue of 1806—1819, bears the Nawáb's number 17 and the four-petal flower, exactly like the earlier issues, but the Hijrah year 1229 (1814). Moreover, it is distinctly stated that the Company issued coins at Benáres from 1806. We must therefore conclude either that the Company permitted the Nawáb to go on coining till 1810, or that they began their own coinage at Benáres by copying his. But that the Company did issue coins of a pronounced native type, without the collar or milled edge, is shown by the series of eleven coins described on p. 276 (Pl. xxxi). These belong to the older Benáres type, prior to the four-petal-flower type, but the fabric is unquestionably more modern, and the fact that a fixed regnal year (26) is retained, whilst the Hijrah years range from 1212 to 1233 (1797 to 1817), is a probable indication of European negligence. These are, in my opinion, Company's coins. And if so, this is a reason why the flower type should not be theirs, for it is improbable that they issued both simultaneously. Thus we have—

Old Benáres type	1183-1196.
Flower-type (with Nawáb's year 17) . . .	1203-1225.
Company's *native style* and regnal year 26 .	1212-1233.
,, *milled* flower type and Nawáb's year 17,	1229.

The next transitional mint, first native, then belonging

to the Company, is *Súrat*. The Company coined here at the native mint and imitated native Súrat coins at Bombay in the first and second periods (see above, p. xclvii. ff.), but illegally: they only possessed the right to coin at Bombay for internal circulation. Whatever coins they may have issued before 1800 with the name Súrat are indistinguishable, so far as I know, from the Moghul coinage. Prinsep tells us that in 1800 the Bombay mint recommenced the issue of Súrat rupees,* and the date is confirmed by the circumstance that the English, who had owned the fort of Súrat since 1611 (1020), and had become supreme in the city since 1759, took the final step of abolishing the nominal authority of the native Nawáb in 1800.† The earliest specimen of this new issue of Súrat rupees and mohrs by the Company is the quarter-mohr, No. 81, p. 280. It shows but a portion of the usual inscription, and no Hijrah or regnal year; but it is marked with a crowned head, in token of English fabrication, and it has the figures 1802 engraved (not counterstruck) on a label on the reverse. The next dated specimens have the regnal year 46 (which, as has been seen, was a fixed date), a crown in place of the third point over شاه, and (on the silver coins) the Christian date 1825. The next issue resembles this last, except in the absence of the crown: there is nothing to show that it is a Company's coinage except the year 46 (1804) which is posterior to any native rule in Súrat. The style and fabric of all these coins is native. In Nos. 87 ff., however, the milled edge is employed, and coins of this type continue down to the establishment of the European currency of 1835.

The Company's "*Murshidábád*" coinage is known to

---

* *Op. cit.*, 24. Rupee, here as before, is used as a generic term for coin, and includes gold mohrs.

† Hunter, *Imp. Gazetteer of India*, *s.v.*

have begun soon after their assumption of administrative authority in Bengal in 1765 (1178), but it does not follow that it began at Murshidábád itself. The Nawáb of Bengal undoubtedly continued to issue Sháh-'Álam's money at Murshidábád, Patnah (also called 'Azímábád), and Dhákká, for some time later.* The Murshidábád coins Nos. 1188-1198, ranging from A.H. 1180 to 119x (1766-1776 ff.), which I have ascribed to the native mint, are of a totally distinct fabric from any of those on pp. 267 to 273, which belong to the Company's coinage. The regnal and Hijrah years, moreover, are consistent, which cannot be said of many of the Company's issues. If it be urged that the Company's badge, a cinquefoil, occurs on Nos. 1195-6, the natural reply is that the cinquefoil, like everything else in the Company's imitative issues, must have existed on the native currency before it could be copied.

On the other hand, the issues of the regnal year 10, 1182-3 (1768) with dotted rims, described on pp. 267-8, although they present consistent regnal and Hijrah years, are marked by their fabric as the work of the Company's servants. The same fabric as that of the year 10 is seen in the issue of the year 11 (p. 269), and 12, 13, 15, and 19; but in those of 19 the regnal year for the first time remains stationary, while the Hijrah years move on through 1196, 1197, 1198, 1201, 1202, to 1203, a tolerably sure sign of the Company's handiwork. If these last belong to the Company's series, so do those of the regnal year 10. They are doubtless the coins referred to in the Company's regulation of 1793, in issuing the "19 san" coinage: "the rupees of the 11th, 12th, and 15th sun were indeed directed to be received equally with the 19th sun sicca rupee, but this

* See above, p. lxxxv.

was a temporary measure." A glance at Plates xxix and xxx will show the difference between this fabric and that of the native issues.

The deduction from what has been said above is that the Nawáb went on coining at Murshidábád for some years, whilst the Company were simultaneously striking coins, with the name of Murshidábád, at Calcutta. This was the result of the treaty made in 1765 between the Governor and Council of Fort William and the Nawáb of Bengal by which the latter agreed to "cause the rupees coined at Calcutta to pass in every respect equal to the Siccas of Moorshedabad, without any deduction of Batta."* It is true that the native mints were withdrawn "soon after the commencement of the Company's administration,"† but the phrase is elastic, and the native mints may have continued to issue Murshidábád rupees for a dozen years, whilst the Company was going through the experiments of the regnal years 10 to 15, leading up to the well-known "19 san sikkah," the various stages of which are described on pp. 272-3.

The trial piece of 1784, p. 271, is included in this volume as the earliest milled coin of the Company. The inscription on the edge ("United East India Company"), however, would not have commended it to natives.

The Farrukhábád issues call for little notice. The native coinages run from A.H. 1179 to 1218, though the regnal year 39 is misused on the last four coins. The Company's issues of "45 san" rupees, with three successive varieties of milling or plain rim, are represented on pp. 274-5 and Pl. xxxi.

---

* Thurston, *op. cit.*, 34.

† Regulation of 1793: Ibid. 38.

§ 10. *LOCAL COINAGE.*

In spite of this somewhat intricate examination of the various issues of the 18th and 19th centuries in India, a considerable number of coins have necessarily been omitted. These are what are known as "Indian Local Coinages."

They consist of the issues of the numerous petty states which attained to various stages of semi-independence or nominal dependence during the decay of the Moghul empire, and especially during the reign of Sháh-'Álam. They generally bear this Emperor's name, often long after his decease, but their dates are frequently fictitious, the regnal year bears no agreement with that of the Hijrah, and worst of all the mint itself is often wanting, or is merely represented by a symbol, which not seldom stands for more than one mint, and which too often it is impossible to identify with any mint. Had these local issues been carefully described and engraved when they were current, there would be no difficulty in the subject; and the plain reason that they defy classification is that all those who were living at the time when they were in circulation are long dead, and even Prinsep, with all the materials which were at his hand in 1833, was compelled to acknowledge the hopeless confusion of this branch of the coinage. What Prinsep could not effect with his opportunities in 1833, no one can accomplish after sixty years have diminished or abolished every source of information. The complexity of the subject may best be illustrated by a quotation from Prinsep's work.* He based his remarks on reports presented by government officers in

---

* *Useful Tables*, 27 ff.

Ajmír, Málwah, and the Narbada provinces in reply to questions circulated though the Mint Committee in 1818 and 1823; but in spite of such valuable materials he was forced to admit the incompleteness of his information.

"We have before remarked," he says, "that none of the coins now [1833] forming the circulation of Hindústán bear any other name than that of Sháh-'Álam,* and although we have no perfect information of the origin or date of the mints of Púnah, Nágpúr, or of the principal states of Rájputána, still we may safely assume that, until the authority of Dehlí was annihilated, the representative of the monarch in the various *súbahs*, or provinces, alone exercised the privilege of coining; and that even when it was assumed by chieftains already in actual independence, the form of a *sanad* or permission was obtained from the Emperor by purchase or extortion. The petty Rájá of Dattiah, for instance, was indignant [in 1824] at the supposition that he had opened his mint without authority, and of all the chiefs within Lieut. Moody's agency [at Bangál and Kantál], Rájá Pratáp Singh of Chatrapúr was the only one who could not produce his authority. The chiefs of Jhánsí and Jálaon cited the sanction of the Peshwá; the Tahrí Rájá, the tacit permission of the English. No notice, however, of mints was found in any of the *sanads* or treaties to which that officer had access.

"When first established, the mints were no doubt in most cases made the source of fraudulent profit to the government, by the issue of a debased coin, which was supported at an enhanced nominal value through the interdiction of the purer standards of neighbouring districts. A Hindú prince, or the minister who rules for him, is in general a money-dealer: thus at Kotá the executive authority has a shroff in each town, and participates in all the benefits arising out of money operations in the market . . . . . .

"The list of mints which have sprung up in Central India is so formidable that it is difficult to attempt any classification of

---

* This is not strictly accurate. The Arkát rupees, for example, bore the name of 'Álamgír II.

them. Mr. Wilder, in 1819, enumerates the following rupees current in Ajmír:—Old Ajmír, Srísáhí, Krishnagarh, Kochanam, Chitor, Jaipúr, Hálí, Jodhpúr, Udaipúr, Sháhpúrah, Pratápgarh, Kotá, Búndí, and Bhilwárá.

"Mr. Maddock furnishes an equally long list from the Narbada:—Panná, Chatrapúr, Sironj, Shánsí, Chanda, Srínagar, Nágpúr, Garrah-Kotá, Bálásáhí, Ráthgarh, Tahrí, Bhopál, Sohágpúr, Sudhaurah, Jálaon, Ujjain, Iságarh.

"The difficulty is also increased by the threefold appellations given to coins: first, from the place of fabrication, as Indore, Ujjain, Ságar proper, etc.; second, from the person issuing them, as Sindhiasáhí from Sindhia, Bálásáhi from Báláji Pandit, Gaur Sáhí from 'Alí Gaur, afterwards Sháh-'Álam, Mutí-Sáhí, a well-known Alláhábád coin of Mr. Achmuty; third, from some distinguishing symbol impressed on the field, as Trisúlí, from the 'trident' of Siva; Shamshírí from the figure of a 'sword' on the Haidarábád coin; Machhlisáhí and Shírsáhí from the 'fish,' and 'tiger' of the old and new Lucknow rupee, etc. There are also other titles common to different localities, as Chalan, 'current,' Hálí, 'of the present time;' and the distinction into Sans or different years of Sháh-'Álam's reign. . . . . .

"In Ajmír the Srísáhí rupee, coined by Tantia, formed in 1815 the principal currency; it has been partly supplanted by the Farrukhábád rupee since the province came into our possession.

"In Kotá there are three mints, at Kotá, Tantia Patan, and Gangroun, coining on an average thirty-six lákhs per annum; the currency is not debased.

"The Holkar currency of Indore, Hardá, and Makeswar and Ujjain rupee, are nearly at par with the Farrukhábád, but they maintain an unequal contest with the Sálimsáhí rupee, coined by the Rájá of Pratápgarh, of which there are three kinds . . . . .

"The northern parts of the Narbada territories were supplied with a base currency struck at Jabalpúr by Nána Ghatka in 1800; this mint was suppressed on cession to the English. The southern part (Dakhantír) had a rupee of still lower value struck at Sohágpúr, where a mint was established in 1810: it was abolished in 1818 by Mr. Molony. These rupees passed at par with Chanda and Nágpúr rupees, the chief issue of Berár.

"The Ságar mint was set up in 1779 by the Peshwa's officer at Garrah Mandlah, and coined about seventeen lakhs of Bálásáhí rupees per annum. Its operation continued under Mr. Maddock, who, to counteract the forgery going on at Garrah, inserted the word 'Sagar' in small English characters on the die. The new Ságar mint, erected in 1824, is now rapidly removing all the old coins from circulation.

"The standard of the Maráthí Government at Nágpúr, to which all the neighbouring mints were doubtless intended to conform, presents itself [even since the appointment of a British resident] one of the worst examples of irregularity and depreciation . . . . .

"In the Haidarábád country the government of the Nizám or of his Hindú minister has not been behindhand with its Maráthí rivals in the adulteration of the local currency; and by way of introducing greater confusion and vexation, there is a superior standard for the Palace and the Residency, an inferior for the city, and a *hukm chalami*, or forced token, the precise nature of which is dubious. The worst species are struck at Náráyanpat.

"In Bandalkhand the circulation consisted chiefly of Bálá Ráo's rupee, struck at Srínagar, near Panná. This mint issued at the time of its institution, in 1794, about eighteen lákhs per annum, but after 1819 the coinage fell to four lákhs. The same prince set up a mint at Jálaon, his capital, in 1809; its issue was at first six lákhs, and is now diminished to one-third of that amount.

"The Hánsí mint of Ráo Raín Chand dates from 1780; it issued three lákhs. Kuár Pratáp Singh's at Chatrapúr dates from 1816. The mints of Panná (1780), Samtar (of 1808) were on a most insignificant scale and have been put down. The Dattiah mint dates from 1784."

The Korah, Alláhábád, Agrah, Sahéranpúr, Barailí, Kálpí, Etáwá, Mathurá, Pánípat, and other rupees, belonging "more immediately to the Dehlí group," were coined only on particular occasions or for short periods, and the mints "have long disappeared from our list."

It is obvious that the local issues described in the

preceding extracts cannot properly be classed with the imperial currency of the Moghuls, but form a series apart. On this ground, and on account of the impossibility of identifying most of the mints with any approach to precision, they have been excluded from the present Catalogue. Their proper place would be in a catalogue of the minor coinages which sprang up on the decay of the central power, in which the coins of the Sikhs, the Maráthas, and other modern Indian money, would also find a place. It must be confessed, however, that the line between the local and imperial coinage is hard to draw during Sháh-'Álam's reign, and some of the coins described under this Emperor might perhaps be classed with equal reason among the local issues.

In conclusion I have to thank Dr. Rieu and the Keeper of Coins for reading and interpreting the Persian distichs; and Mr. E. J. Rapson for deciphering the Nágarí and Bengálí inscriptions on the copper coins of the East India Company. My indebtedness to various books and articles is duly recorded in numerous references in the preceding pages.

STANLEY LANE-POOLE.

ATHENÆUM CLUB,
May 30, 1892.

TABLE

OF THE

METHOD OF TRANSLITERATION ADOPTED IN THIS CATALOGUE.

أ	a,	ظ	z
ب	b	ع	'
پ	p	غ	gh
ت	t	ف	f
ث	th	ق	k
ج	j	ك	k g*
چ	ch	ل	l
ح	h	م	m
خ	kh	ن	n
د	d	ه	h
ذ	z	و	w
ر	r	ی	y
ز	z		
س	s	ـَ a	ـَا á
ش	sh	ـِ i	ـِی í
ص	s	ـُ u	ـُو ú
ض	z	ـَی ai, é	ـَو au, ô
ط	t		

* The distinction between the letters ك and گ is not shown on the coins, and therefore is not marked in the Catalogue.

CONTENTS.

THE COINAGE.

CONTENTS OF PLATES.

PLATE I.—BABAR, HUMÁYÚN.

No.	Metal.	Emperor.	Mint.	A.H.
1	Æ	Bábar	——	933
2	,,	,,	——	935
3	,,	,,	Lahore	936
8	AV	Humáyún	——	—
9	,,	,,	——	—
11	Æ	,,	——	962
12	,,	,,	——	—
13	,,	,,	Lahore	—
18	,,	,,	——	942
19	,,	,,	——	—

PLATE II.—AKBAR: GOLD.

No.	Metal.	Emperor.	Mint.	A.H.
23	AV	Akbar	Agrah (Five Mohrs)	971
24	,,	,,	Agrah ?	,,
25	,,	,,	Lahore	,,
26	,,	,,	——	,,
31	,,	,,	Sárangpúr	972
37	,,	,,	——	975
38	,,	,,	Dehlí	,,
40	,,	,,	Agrah	976
43 R	,,	,,	Lahore	977
46 R	,,	,,	Jaunpúr	978
48	,,	,,	Ahmadábád	980
50	,,	,,	Agrah	981

PLATE III.—AKBAR: GOLD.

No.	Metal.	Emperor.	Mint.	A.H.
52	AV	Akbar	Agrah	982
58	"	"	Jaunpúr	983
59	"	"	Lahore	"
61	"	"	Sirhind	984
63	"	"	{ "Muhammadábád called Udaipúr" }	"
64	"	"	——	"
65	"	"	——	985
66	"	"	Fathpúr	986
70	"	"	Lahore	988
71	"	"	——	"
73	"	"	Urdú-Zafar-Karín	1000
79	"	"	"	"
81	"	"	"	"
82	"	"	"	"
83	"	"	Patnah	—

PLATE IV.—AKBAR: SILVER.

No.	Metal.	Emperor.	Mint.	A.H.
84 R	AR	Akbar	——	963
86	"	"	Agrah	967
88	"	"	Jaunpúr	96*x*
90 R	"	"	——	970
96 R	"	"	Jaunpúr	974
97 R	"	"	Dehlí	975
105	"	"	Ahmadábád	982
108 R	"	"	Jaunpúr	983
119 R	"	"	——	986
122	"	"	Lahore	"
124 R	"	"	Fathpúr	"
127 R	"	"	Ahmadábád	987
128	"	"	Urdú	"
131 R	"	"	Patnah	"
132 R	"	"	——	"
151	"	"	Urdú-Zafar-Karín	1000

PLATE V.—AKBAR: GOLD WITH ILÁHÍ YEARS.

No.	Metal.	Emperor.	Mint.	Iláhí year and month =	A.H. (not on coins.)
163	AV	Akbar	——	32	995
164	"	"	Agrah	42 Bahman	1005
165	"	"	"	44 Ardíbihist	1007
166	"	"	Asír	45 Isfandármiz	1008
167	"	"	Agrah	49 Farwardín	1012
168	"	"	"	" Amardád	"
169	"	"	"	" Azur	"
170	"	"	"	50 Amardád	1013
171	"	"	Lahore	" "	"
172	"	"	——	" Farwardín	"
173	"	"	Agrah	" Khúrdád	"
175	"	"	"	51	1014
176	"	"	——	—	—

PLATE VI.—AKBAR: SILVER WITH ILÁHÍ YEARS.

No.	Metal.	Emperor.	Mint.	Iláhí year and month =	A.H. (not on coins.)
177	AR	Akbar	Sítapúr	28	991
178	"	"	Ahmadábád	30 Dai	993
184	"	"	——	34	997
191	"	"	Ahmadábád	37	1000
194	"	"	Lahore	38 Tír	1001
197	"	"	Burhánpúr	48 Dai	"
199	"	"	Tattah	40 Khúrdád	1003
202	"	"	——	"	"
204	"	"	Lahore	41 Isfandármiz	1004
209	"	"	Patnah	42 Shahriwar	1005
215	"	"	"	43 Khurdád	1006
218	"	"	——	" Shahriwar	"
221	"	"	Kábul	44 Abán	1007
233	"	"	Lahore	46 Azur	1009
238	"	"	"	47 Khúrdád	1010
241	"	"	Burhánpúr	48 Mihr	1011
243	"	"	Lahore	" Abán	"
250	"	"	Agrah	50 Amardád	1013

PLATE VII.—AKBAR:

SILVER AND COPPER.

No.	Metal.	Emperor.	Mint.	A.H.
252*a*	Æ	Akbár	——	992
252*b*	,,	,,	——	997
252*c*	,,	,,	——	1215 (*sic*)
254	,,	,,	Alláhábád	—
255	Æ	,,	Nárnól	963
257	,,	,,	——	966
258	,,	,,	Lahore	97*x*
261	,,	,,	Ahmadábád	982
263	,,	,,	Dógám	983
264	,,	,,	Málpúr	985
266	,,	,,	Fathpúr	987
270	,,	,,	Jaunpúr	98*x*
272	,,	,,	Gwálior	9*xx*
273	,,	,,	Urdú-Zafar-Karín	1000

COPPER WITH ILÁHÍ YEARS.

No.	Metal.	Emperor.	Mint.	Iláhí year and month	= A.H. (not on coins.)
273*a*	Æ	Akbar	Alláhábád	31 Mihr	994
274	,,	,,	Kábul	32	995
275	,,	,,	Lahore	36 Dai	999
282	,,	,,	Dehlí	42-4 Dai	1005-7
283	,,	,,	Agrah	46 Abán	1009
287	,,	,,	,,	4*x*	10*xx*

PLATE VIII.—JAHÁNGÍR:

SILVER, WITH NAME SALÍM; GOLD, WITHOUT PORTRAIT.

No.	Metal.	Emperor.	Mint.	Regnal year and month.	A.H.
288	AR	Jahángír	Ahmadábád	2 Farwardín	*x*
290	AV	,,	Agrah	—	1015
291	,,	,,	Lahore	1	,,
292	,,	,,	,,	,,	,,
294	,,	,,	,,	3	1016
295	,,	,,	Agrah	4	1017
297	,,	,,	,,	6 Mihr	1020
300	,,	,,	,,	7 Ardíbihist	1022
302	,,	,,	Ajmír	—	1025
306	,,	,,	Ahmadábád	14	1028
308	,,	,,	Jahángírnagar	19 Isfandármiz	1033-[4]
310	,,	,,	Lahore	22	1036
311	,,	,,	Burhánpúr	— Abán	—

PLATE IX.—JAHÁNGÍR:

GOLD, WITH PORTRAIT (except 305).

305	AV	Jahángír	Agrah	14	1028
312	,,	,,	——	6	1020
313	,,	,,	——	,,	,,
314	,,	,,	——	,,	,,
315	,,	,,	——	,,	,,
317	,,	,,	——	7	1021
318	,,	,,	Ajmír	8	1023
319	,,	,,	,,	9	,,

PLATE X.—JAHÁNGÍR:

ZODIACAL MOHRS.

No.	Metal.	Emperor.	Mint.	Zodiacal sign.	Regnal year.	A.H.
322	AV	Jahángír	Agrah	Aries	14	1028
323	,,	,,	,,	,,	16	1030
324 } 325 }	,,	,,	,,	Taurus	14	1028
328	,,	,,	,,	,,	16	1030
331	,,	,,	,,	Gemini	,,	1031
332	,,	,,	,,	,,	18	1032
333*a*	,,	,,	,,	Cancer	15	1029
333*c*	,,	,,	,,	,,	16	1030
334	,,	,,	,,	Leo	14	1028
337	,,	,,	,,	,,	17	1031
339	,,	,,	,,	Virgo	16	1030
340	,,	,,	,,	,,	,,	1031
341	,,	,,	,,	,,	19	1033
343	,,	,,	,,	Libra	16	1030
346	,,	,,	,,	Scorpio	—	1030
346*a*	,,	,,	,,	,,	16	,,
348	,,	,,	,,	Sagittarius	,,	1031
350	,,	,,	,,	Capricornus	14	1028
353	,,	,,	,,	,,	16	1031
355	,,	,,	,,	Aquarius	,,	,,
356	,,	,,	,,	,,	18	1032
357	,,	,,	Ahmadábád	,,	—	—
358	,,	,,	Agrah	Pisces	13	1028

PLATE XI.—JAHÁNGÍR:

ZODIACAL RUPEES.

No.	Metal.	Emperor.	Mint.	Zodiacal sign.	Regnal year.	A.H.
362	Æ	Jahángír	Ahmadábád	Aries	13	1027
364	"	"	"	Taurus	"	"
369	"	"	"	Gemini	"	"
370	"	"	"	Cancer	"	"
374	"	"	"	Scorpio	—	"
			IMITATIONS OF ZODIACAL MOHRS.			
376	*N*	Jahángír	Agrah	Cancer	—	1028
377	"	"	"	Leo	—	1032
378	"	"	"	Virgo	14	1028
379	"	"	"	"	17	1033
380	"	"	"	Scorpio	12	1028
381	"	"	"	Sagittarius	17	1033
382	"	"	"	Capricornus	16	1031
383	"	"	"	Aquarius	13	1028
384	"	"	"	Pisces	"	"
			IMITATION OF ZODIACAL RUPEE.			
385	Æ	Jahángír	Ahmadábád	Leo	13	1027
			LATE IMITATION HALF-RUPEES.			
386	Æ	Jahángír	Agrah	Aries	14	1028
387	"	"	"	Taurus	"	"
388	"	"	"	Gemini	15	1029
390	"	"	"	Cancer	17	1031
391	"	"	"	Leo	16	1029
393	"	"	"	Virgo	17	1033
395	"	"	"	Libra	18	1032
397	"	"	"	Scorpio	12	1028
398	"	"	"	Sagittarius	17	1033
399	"	"	"	Capricornus	18	1033
400	"	"	"	Aquarius	13	1028
401	"	"	"	Pisces	"	"

PLATE XII.—JAHÁNGÍR: SILVER.

No.	Metal.	Emperor.	Mint.	Regnal year and month.	A.H.
402	Æ	Jahángír	Agrah	1	1014
403	„	„	„	„	„
404	„	„	Akbarnagar	—	„
405	„	„	Kábul	1	„
411	„	„	Ahmadábád	2	1015
413	„	„	Patnah	2 Isfandármiz	„
414	„	„	Lahore	1	„
415	„	„	„	2	„
424	„	„	„	5	1017
425	„	„	Ahmadábád	„	1018
432	„	„	Agrah	„ Isfandármiz	1019
433	„	„	Kashmír	—	„
438	„	„	Lahore	5 Bahman	„
439	„	„	Agrah	6 Abán	1020

PLATE XIII.—JAHÁNGÍR: SILVER.

No.	Metal.	Emperor.	Mint.	Regnal year and month.	A.H.
440	Æ	Jahángír	Kandahár	6	1020
441	„	„	Agrah	„ Isfandármiz	1021
442	„	„	„	7 Ardíbihist	„
444	„	„	Dehli	„ Mihr	„
445	„	„	Kandahár	„ —	„
447	„	„	Lahore	„ Farwardín	„
451	„	„	Kandahár	8 Ardíbihist	1023
455	„	„	Lahore	9 „	—
460	„	„	Ajmír	11	1025
461	„	„	Ahmadábád	— Abán	„
463	„	„	Lahore	11	„
467	„	„	Patnah	12 Shahriwar	1026
468	„	„	Tattah	„ Khúrdád	„
472	„	„	Kandahár	13	1027
473	„	„	Kábul	„ ? Shahriwar	„

PLATE XIV.—JAHÁNGÍR: SILVER.

No.	Metal.	Emperor.	Mint.	Regnal year and month.	A.H.
475	AR	Jahángír	Ahmadábád	13	1027
488	"	"	Lahore	15	1029
491	"	"	"	16	1030
498	"	"	Súrat	18	1033
501	"	"	Jahángírnagar	19 Shahriwar	—
510 R	"	"	"	20 ? Mihr	—
			COPPER.		
512	Æ	"	Agrah	7	1021
		WITH NAME OF NÚR-JAHÁN.			
513	AV	Jahángír and Núr-Jahán	Súrat	—	1036
515 R	AR	"	Ahmadábád	—	1034
516	"	"	Lahore	20	"
518	"	"	"	—	"
519	"	"	Súrat	2[0]	"
523	"	"	Agrah	22	1037
525	"	"	Patnah	"	"
526	"	"	"	"	—

DÁWAR BAKHSH.

No.	Metal.	Emperor.	Mint.	Regnal year and month.	A.H.
527	AR	Dáwar Bakhsh	Lahore	1	1037

PLATE XV.—SHÁH-JAHÁN: GOLD.

No.	Metal.	Emperor.	Mint.	Regnal year and month.	A.H.
529	AV	Sháh-Jahán	Ahmadábád	2 Khurdád	1038
530	"	"	Daulatábád	"	—
534	"	"	Akbarábád	—	1042
536	"	"	Lahore	5	"
541	"	"	Akbarábád	—	1043
544	"	"	Ahmadábád	8	1045
549	"	"	—	12	1049
551	"	"	Akbarábád	14	1050
563	"	"	Burhánpúr	25	1061
566	"	"	Daulatábád	27	1063
568	"	"	Sháhjahánábád	30	1066
577	"	"	—	—	—

PLATE XVI.—SHÁH-JAHÁN: SILVER.

No.	Metal.	Emperor.	Mint.	Regnal year and month.	A.H.
578	Æ	Sháh-Jahán	Lahore	1	1037
580	„	„	Burhánpúr	„	„
581	„	„	Agrah	„	1038
582*	„	„	„	2	„
583	„	„	Akbarábád	„ Tír	„
584	„	„	Patnah	2	„
585	„	„	Súrat	1	„
588	„	„	Akbarábád	2	1039
589	„	„	Akbarnagar	„	„
603	„	„	Dehlí	3 Dai	1040
605	„	„	Akbarábád	5	1041
606	„	„	Alláhábád	4 Azur	„
608	„	„	Patnah	„ „	„
621	„	„	Akbarábád	6	1043
622	„	„	„	„	„

PLATE XVII.—SHÁH-JAHÁN: SILVER.

No.	Metal.	Emperor.	Mint.	Regnal year and month.	A.H.
623	Æ	Sháh-Jahán	Alláhábád	6	—
625	„	„	Bhakar	„	1043
626	„	„	„ ?	„	„
629	„	„	Akbarnagar	7 Farwardín	„
632*	„	„	Lahore	„	1044
634	„	„	Bhakar	8	1045
643	„	„	Tattah	10 Khurdád	1047
651*	„	„	Lahore	13	1049
659	„	„	Súrat	20	1057
666	„	„	Júnahgarh	—	1059
669*	„	„	Sháhjahánábád	24	1060
671*	„	„	Kashmír	25	1061
676	„	„	Daulatábád	31	1067
678*	„	„	Sháhjahánábád	„	„
681	„	„	„	32	1068
689*	AV	Anonymous	„	—	1069

* The coins distinguished by an asterisk are denominated in their inscriptions نثار *nisár*, *i.e.* presentation pieces, or coins for distribution as largesse or for the annual tribute, &c.

PLATE XVIII.—SHUJÁ', MURÁD BAKHSH, AND AURANGZÍB 'ALAMGÍR: GOLD.

No.	Metal.	Emperor.	Mint.	Regnal year.	A.H.
690	Æ	Shujá'	Akbarábád	—	1068
691	,,	,,	Jalaonábád?	1	,,
692	AV	Murád Bakhsh	Ahmadábád	1	,,
694	Æ	,,	,,	,,	,,
696 R	,,	,,	Súrat	,,	,,
699	,,	,,	,,	,,	—
700 R	,,	,,	Cambay	,,	—
701	AV	Aurangzíb	Tattah	5	1072
702	,,	,,	Aurangábád	6	1074
706	,,	,,	Akbarnagar	12	—
708	,,	,,	Golkondah	20	1086
709	,,	,,	Sháhjahánábád	24	1091
711	,,	,,	Bíjápúr	31	1099
715*	,,	,,	Chínápatan	35	1103
719	,,	,,	Khujistah-bunyád (Aurangábád)	4x	1109
721*	,,	,,	[Chíná]patan	,,	1111

PLATE XIX.—AURANGZÍB 'ALAMGÍR: SILVER.

No.	Metal.	Emperor.	Mint.	Regnal year.	A.H.
725	Æ	Aurangzíb	Akbarábád	1	—
726	,,	,,	Golkondah	1	1069
728	,,	,,	Patnah	1	1070
729	,,	,,	Multán	3	,,
732	,,	,,	——	4	1071
733	,,	,,	Akbarábád	,,	,,
734	,,	,,	Júnahgarh	—	,,
739	,,	,,	,,	6	1074
742*a*	,,	,,	Akbarnagar	9	107*x*
743	,,	,,	Sháhjahánábád	,,	1076
745	,,	,,	Akbarábád	—	1077
748	,,	,,	Golkondah	14	1076 (*sic*)
749	,,	,,	,,	15	—
762	,,	,,	Súrat	24	1091
772 Obv.	,,	,,	'Álamgírpúr	—	1096
777	,,	,,	Nárnól	3*x*	1098
781	,,	,,	Zafarpúr	32	1100
782	,,	,,	Kábul	,,	—

* *Nisár.*

PLATE XX.

AURANGZÍB 'ALAMGÍR: SILVER; AND A'ZAM.

No.	Metal.	Emperor.	Mint.	Regnal year.	A.H.
788	Æ	Aurangzíb	Chínápatan	35	—
796	„	„	Súrat	37	1105
798 Obv.	„	„	Ajmír	38	„
804 „	„	„	Barailí	39	1107
805 „	„	„	Nasratábád	3*x*	—
808 „	„	„	Zafarábád	40	1107
809	„	„	Ahmadnagar	„	1108
811	„	„	Etáwah	41	„
814	„	„	Lahore	„	„
819	„	„	Júnahgarh	4½	1109
821	„	„	Cambay	43	1111
822	„	„	Masulipatan	44	„
847	AV	A'zam	Khujistah-bunyád	1	1118
849	„	„	Burhánpúr	1	1119
850	Æ	„	Ahmadábád	„	„
851	„	„	Burhánpúr	„	„

PLATE XXI.—KÁM BAKHSH, BAHÁDUR.

No.	Metal.	Emperor.	Mint.	Regnal year.	A.H.
852	AV	Kám Bakhsh	Haidarábád	2	1120
853	Æ	„	Bíjápúr	„	„
854	AV	Bahádur	Pesháwar	„	„
856 Obv.	„	„	Sháhjahánábád	„	„
858	„	„	Lahore	„	„
861	„	„	Khujistah-bunyád	4	1121
862	„	„	Ujjain	—	1122
863	„	„	Akbarábád	5	1123
866	Æ	„	Ajmír	1	1119
867	„	„	Sháhjahánábád	„	„
868	„	„	'Azímábád (Patnah)	2	1120
870	„	„	Akbarábád	„	„
873	„	„	Burhánpúr	4	1121
874	„	„	Sholápúr	„	1122
875	„	„	Súrat	6	1123

PLATE XXII.—JAHÁNDÁR, FARRUKH-SIYAR: GOLD.

No.	Metal.	Emperor.	Mint.	Regnal year.	A.H.
877	AV	Jahándár	Khujistah-bunyád	1	1124
878	"	"	"	"	"
880	"	"	Sháhjahánábád	"	"
885	AR	"	"	"	"
887	"	"	[Akbarábád]	"	"
889*	"	"	Sháhjahánábád	—	"
890	AV	Farrukh-siyar	Murshidábád	1	—
891	"	"	Sháhjahánábád	4	1127
892	"	"	Lahore	5	1129
893	"	"	Barailí	"	—
894	"	"	Burhánpúr	6	—
897	"	"	Multán	7	1130
898	"	"	Bíjápúr	"	—
900	"	"	——	—	1125
900*a*	"	"	Imtiyázgarh	3	—
901	"	"	Gútí	5	1128
902	"	"	Gangpúr	"	"

PLATE XXIII.
FARRUKH-SIYAR: SILVER, RAFÍ-AD-DARAJÁT.

No.	Metal.	Emperor.	Mint.	Regnal year.	A.H.
903	AR	Farrukh-siyar	Jahángírnagar	1	1124
907	"	"	Katak	2	1125
918	"	"	Etáwá	5	1128
920	"	"	Chínápatan	"	"
924 Obv.	"	"	Akbarábád	"	1129
925 "	"	"	Sháhjahánábád	"	"
927 "	"	"	Gwálior	6	"
928 "	"	"	Lahore	"	"
931 "	"	"	Murshidábád	"	—
933 "	"	"	Arkát	7	1130
935 "	"	"	Multán	"	"
936 "	"	"	A'zamnagar	—	—
937	AV	Rafí'-ad-daraját	Sháhjahánábád	1	1131
937*a*	"	"	Mu'azzamábád	"	"
938	AR	"	Akbarábád	"	"
941	"	"	Sháhjahánábád	"	"
942	"	"	Kúrá	"	"
943	"	"	Lahore	"	"

* *Nisár.*

PLATE XXIV.

RAFÍ'-AD-DAULAH, NÍKÚ-SIYAR, IBRÁHÍM.

No.	Metal.	Emperor.	Mint.	Regnal year.	A.H.
945	AV	Rafí'-ad-daulah	Sháhjahánábád	1	1131
946	„	„	Khujistah-bunyád	—	„
947	AR	„	Akbarábád	1	„
948	„	„	Barailí	„	„
950	„	„	'Azímábád (Patnah)	„	„
951	„	„	Lahore	„	„
952	„	„	Murshidábád	„	„
953	AV	Níkú-siyar	Súrat	1	—
955	AV	Ibráhím	Sháhjahánábád	1	1132
956	AR	„	„	„	„

PLATE XXV.—MUHAMMAD.

No.	Metal.	Emperor.	Mint.	Regnal year.	A.H.
958	AV	Muhammad	Khujistah-bunyád	1	1131
959	„	„	Sháhjahánábád	3	1134
967	„	„	Akbarábád	17	1147
968	„	„	Etáwá	20	1150
973	„	„	Kashmír	24	1154
974	„	„	Lahore	25	1155
976	„	„	Imtiyázgarh	—	1161
977	„	„	„	—	—
985	AR	„	Akbarnagar-Oudh	5	1135
998	„	„	Kúrá	11	1141
1011	„	„	Ajáyúr	1x	1148
1019	„	„	Sháhábád	21	1151
1029	„	„	Farrukhábád	25	1155
1032 Obv.	„	„	Siwái-Jaipúr	26	1156
1035 „	„	„	Barailí	27	115x

PLATE XXVI.

AHMAD, 'ALAMGÍR II, SHÁH-JAHÁN [III].

No.	Metal.	Emperor.	Mint.	Regnal year.	A.H.
1039	AV	Ahmad	Sháhjahánábád	1	1161
1040	"	"	Benáres	2	1162
1044	"	"	——	—	—
1045	AR	"	'Azímábád (Patnah)	1	1161
1047 Obv.	"	"	Farrukhábád	"	"
1057 "	"	"	Murádábád	6	1167
1059	AV	'Álamgír II.	Sháhjahánábád	1	11*xx*
1060	"	"	"	2	1168
1062	"	"	Indrapúr	4	11*xx*
1065	"	"	Lahore	5	1171
1066	"	"	Ahmadnagar-Farrukhábád	6	"
1069	"	"	Imtiyázgarh	—	—
1077*	AR	"	Akbarábád	4	1171
1082	"	"	Sháhjahánábád	5	1172
1086	AV	Sháh-Jahán [III.]	Islámábád	1	1173
1087	"	"	Ahmadnagar-Farrukhábád	"	"
1090	AR	"	Indrapúr	"	"

PLATE XXVII.—SHÁH-'ÁLAM.

No.	Metal.	Emperor.	Mint.	Regnal year.	A.H.
1093	AV	Sháh-'Álam	Sháhjahánábád	3	1176
1094	"	"	"	32	1205
1099 } 1100 } †	AR	"	"	46	1218
1104	AV	"	"	"	"
1110	"	"	"	47	1219
1118	AR	"	Etáwá	18	—
1121	"	"	Ahmadábád	16	118*x*
1122	"	"	Arkát	12 ?	119*x*
1129	"	"	Akbarábád	26	1198

* *Nisár.* † Struck on occasion of Lake's entry, 1803.

PLATE XXVIII.—SHÁH-ÁLAM.

No.	Metal.	Emperor.	Mint.	Regnal year.	A.H.
1135	AR	Sháh-'Álam	Benáres	17	1189
1137	,,	,,	,,	19	—
1138	,,	,,	,,	23	1196
1139	,,	,,	,,	30	1203
1143	,,	,,	,,	45	1217
1157	AR	,,	Jahángírnagar	10	1183
1159	,,	,,	Srínagar	2	—
1160	,,	,,	Súrat	4	—
1161	,,	,,	,,	5	—
1163	,,	,,	,,	6	—
1166	AV	,,	'Azímábád (Patnah)	2	1174
1167	,,	,,	,,	10	1182

PLATE XXIX.
SHÁH-'ÁLAM, BÍDÁR-BAKHT, AKBAR II, BAHADUR.

No.	Metal.	Emperor.	Mint.	Regnal year.	A.H.
1171	AV	Sháh-'Álam	Ahmadnagar-Farrukhábád	23	1196
1172	AR	,,	,,	6	1179
1182	,,	,,	,,	39	1218
1185	AV	,,	Murshidábád	—	1181
1188	AR	,,	,,	8	1180
1193	,,	,,	,,	19	—
1200	,,	,,	Najíbábád	22	1195
1205*a*	AV	,,	No mint	—	1183
1206	,,	Bídár-Bakht	Sháhjahánábád	1	1202
1207	,,	,,	Ahmadábád	,,	1203
1210	AR	Muhammad Akbar II.	Sháhjahánábád	1	1221
1217	AR	Bahadúr II.	,,	5	1257

PLATE XXX.—EAST INDIA COMPANY.

MURSHIDÁBÁD.

No.	Metal.	Denomination.	Mint.	Titular Emperor.	A.D. circ.
Appendix.					
1	AV	½ Mohr	Murshidábád	Sháh-'Ālam	1768
3	,,	⅛ ,,	,,	,,	,,
5		4 Annas	,,	,,	,,
8	AV	Mohr	,,	,,	1770
14	AR	Anna	,,	,,	,,
17	AV	Mohr	,,	,,	1773
20	,,	,,	,,	,,	1782
22	,,	¼ Mohr	,,	,,	1787
28	AR	Rupee	,,	,,	1784
29	AV	Mohr	,,	,,	1793-1818
33	,,	¼ Mohr	,,	,,	,,
35	AR	Rupee	,,	,,	,,
37	,,	,,	,,	,,	,,
39Obv.	,,	½ ,,	,,	,,	,,
43	AV	¼ Mohr	,,	,,	1818-32
47Obv.	AR	Rupee	,,	,,	1832-35

PLATE XXXI.—EAST INDIA COMPANY.

FARRUKHÁBÁD, BENÁRES, CALCUTTA, BOMBAY.

No.	Metal.	Denomination.	Mint.	Titular Emperor.	A.D. circ.
50	AR	Rupee	Farrukhábad	Sháh-'Ālam	1803-19
52	,,	,,	,,	,,	1833-35
54	,,	¼ ,,	,,	,,	,,
61	,,	Rupee	Benáres	,,	1811
66	,,	,,	,,	,,	1806-19
67	,,	,,	Calcutta	,,	1763
68	,,	¼ Rupee	Bombay	Sháh	1719
71	,,	,, ,,	,,	,,	1730
72	,,	Rupee	,,	Muhammad	1725
76	AV	Mohr	,,	Sháh-'Ālam	1768
77	AR	Rupee	,,	,,	1774
79	,,	Rupee	,,	,,	1800
80	,,	¼ ,,	Bombay-Súrat	,,	1718

PLATE XXXII.—EAST INDIA COMPANY.

SURÁT, ÁRKAT (MADRAS, CALCUTTA), MASULIPATAN.

FRENCH COMPANY.

ARKÁT (PONDICHERRY).

No.	Metal.	Denomination.	Mint.	Titular Emperor.	A.D.
Appendix.					
81	AV	$\frac{1}{4}$ Mohr	Súrat	Sháh-'Álam	1802
82	,,	Mohr	,,	,,	1825
85	AR	Rupee	,,	,,	1825
87	AV	Mohr	,,	,,	——
96	AR	Rupee	,,	,,	1818-32 ?
98	,,	,,	,,	,,	1832-35 ?
103	AR	Rupee	Arkát (Madras)	'Álamgír II.	1798-99 ?
109	AV	$\frac{1}{2}$ Mohr	,, ,,	,,	1815 ?
111	AR	Double rupee	,, ,,	,,	,, ?
122	,,	$\frac{1}{2}$ Rupee	,, (Calcutta)	,,	1818-33
127	,,	Rupee	,, (Pondicherry)	,,	1755
128	,,	,,	,, ,,	Sháh-'Álam	1763
145	,,	Double rupee	Masulipatan	'Álamgír II. (*sic*)	1780
148	,,	Rupee	,,	Sháh-'Álam	1797

PLATE XXXIII.

SHÁH-JAHÁN.

Page.					A.H.
lxxxvii	AV	200 Mohrs	Sháhjahánábád *From a cast.*	Sháh Jahán	1064

CORRIGENDA.

The reader is requested to make the following corrections before using the Catalogue.

PAGE.	NO	
8		*heading : for* 960 and 1554 *read* 963 and 1556.
13	31	*for* سار[ك]پو[ر] *read* سار[نك]پو[ر].
19	68	*dele* Pl. III.
32		*note, for* April 1st *read* March 11th.
35	177	*for* (*sic.*) پشلور *read* سیتاپور ; *for* Pesháwar ? *read* Sítápúr.
36		*heading : transpose* Obv. and Rev.
37	196	*dele* Pl. VI.
,,	197	*for* ٣٨, 38, *read* ۴٨, 48.
53	273*a*	,, الهاباد *read* الهاباس.
54	284	,, دو تانکی *read* چو تانکی ; *for* two *read* four.
55	287*b*	,, Tanka *read* $\frac{1}{16}$ Tanka, *and for* حص]ت *read* حص]ة
58	295	,, شاه *read* پناه
59	298	,, Wt. 16 *read* Wt. 163.
,,	300	,, (regnal year) 7 *read* 8,
60	302	,, برز *read* بزر.
62	310	,, میمنت *read* همیشه.
64	318	,, روز نو زینت *read* زیب و زیور.
66	328	*transfer* Pl. x. Marsden, *to* 327.
68,75	341,378	*for* 339 *read* 338.
71	357	*for* جنانك *read* جنانات اله.
80	405-7	*add in first col.* $\frac{1}{2}$.
93	476	,, Wt. 17, *read* Wt. 175.
94,95	488, 491	*for* میمنت *read* همیشه.
99	512	*add* Wt. 315.

PAGE.	NO.	
114		*heading : for* Kharram *read* Khurram.
135	691	*for* Jalúnábád *read* Jalaonábád ?
137	699	„ فت[یا] and غازی *read* فت[کر] and شه.
143	726	„ Calcutta *read* Golkondah.
„	„	„ کلکته *read* [ه]کلکند.
183	900*a*	„ Karrah *read* Imtiyázgarh (Adóní).
		ـــب ـــت
191	937	„ هراران *read* هزاران.
202	975*a*	*omit this coin : it is transferred to p.* 251, 1171*a*.
203	967-7	*for* Karrah *read* Imtiyázgarh (Adóní).
212	1019	„ فنوج *read* فتوح.
223	1063	„ وچو *read* همچو.
224	1068-70*a*	*for* Karrah *read* Imtiyázgarh (Adóní).
226	1077	*first col. add* $\frac{1}{8}$.
227	1085*b*	*for* Karrah *read* Imtiyázgarh (Adóní).
229, 230		*heading of first col. : for* AV *read* Æ

In several instances Daulatábád is spelt Dawlatábád, and Azur, Adhur.

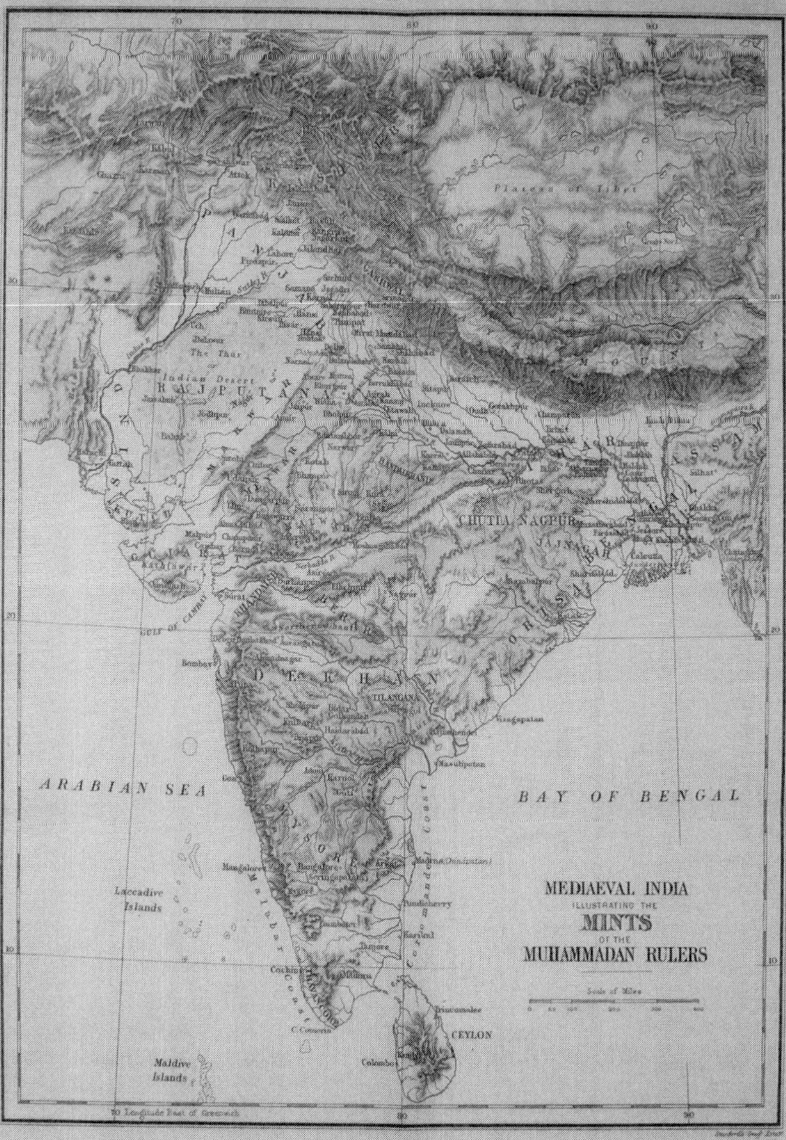

MEDIAEVAL INDIA
ILLUSTRATING THE
MINTS
OF THE
MUHAMMADAN RULERS
Scale of Miles
ARABIAN SEA
BAY OF BENGAL
Plateau of Tibet
RAJPUTANA
DEKHAN
CHUTIA NAGPUR
TILANGANA
Laccadive Islands
Maldive Islands
CEYLON
Bombay
Calcutta
Colombo
Trincomalee
Pondicherry
Bangalore
Mangalore
Cochin
C. Comorin
Masulipatam
GULF OF CAMBAY
Longitude East of Greenwich

THE MOGHUL EMPERORS
OF HINDUSTAN.

MOGHUL EMPERORS

OF HINDUSTAN.

		A.H.	A.D.
I.	Bábar, Zahír-ad-dín . . .	932	1525
II.	Humáyún, Násir-ad-dín . .	937	1530
III.	Akbar, Jalál-ad-dín . . .	963	1556
IV.	Jahángír, Núr-ad-dín . . .	1014	1605
	Dáwar Bakhsh	1037	1627-8
V.	Sháh-Jahán, Shiháb-ad-dín .	1037	1628
	Shujá' (in Bengal) . . .	1068-70	1658-60
	Murád Bakhsh (in Gujarát) . .	1068	1658
VI.	Aurangzíb 'A'lamgír, Muhayyí-ad-d.	1069	1659
	A'zam Sháh	1118	1707
	Kám Bakhsh	1119-20	1708
VII.	Bahádur Sháh-'A'lam, Kutb-ad-dín	1119	1707
VIII.	Jahándár Sháh, Mu'izz-ad-dín .	1124	1712
IX.	Farrukh-siyar	1124	1713
X.	Rafí'-ad-daraját, Shams-ad-dín .	1131	1719
XI.	Rafí'-ad-daulah Sháh-Jahán II. .	1131	1719
	Niku-siyar	1131	1719
	Ibráhím	1132	1720
XII.	Muhammad, Násir-ad-dín . .	1131	1719
XIII.	Ahmad	1161	1748
XIV.	'A'lamgír II., 'Azíz-ad-dín . .	1167	1754
	Sháh-Jahán [III.] . . .	1173-4	1759-60
XV.	Sháh-'A'lam, Jalál-ad-dín . .	1173	1759
	Bídár Bakht	1202-3	1788
XVI.	Muhammad Akbar II. . .	1221	1806
XVII.	Bahádur Sháh II.	1253	1837
	Deposed by the British Government	1275	1857

I.—ZAHÍR-AD-DÍN BÁBAR.*

A.H. 932—937 = A.D. 1525—1530.

No.	Mint.	Year.	
Æ			SILVER.
1	—	933	Obv. Area, within square,† لا اله الا الله محمد رسول الله Margin, in segments, divided by ornaments, ابو بكر الصديق | [عمر] الفاروق | عثمان العفان | على المرتضى Rev. Area, within twelve-foil, محمد بابر ح ظهير الدين Margin, ... السلطان ا.......... اعزه(؟) الله ٩٣٣ ..... PL. I. *CUNNINGHAM.* Æ 1·0, Wt. 70

* The following coins were presumably struck by Bábar about A.H. 917, when in alliance with the Safaví Sháh Ismá'íl. See R. S. Poole, *Catalogue of Persian Coins*, Introduction, pp. xxv. ff., and 210. They are also published in my *Catalogue of Additions*, part ii., p. 163, where two of them (134[v] and 134[x]) are figured in Pl. xxxi.

Æ

SILVER.

134[t] No mint or date.

Obv.		Rev., within square,	
	لا اله الا الله		سلطان
	محمد رسول الله		بابر*
	على ولى الله		بهادر

Around, names of the twelve Imáms, partly obliterated.

Æ ·95, Wt. 78.

† This common formula is arranged in various ways, as a reference to the plates will show; but these slight variations are disregarded in the descriptions, so long as the general division of the formula into three lines is maintained.

No.	Mint.	Year.	
Æ 2	—	935	Obv. as 1 : but twelve-foil border (ابابكر, instead of ابو) Rev. Area, within circle, غازی شـــــاه ٩٣٤ الدین محمد باد ظهیر بابر Margin, .. الله تعا .... Pl. I. *CUNNINGHAM.* Æ ·95, Wt. 71

134v No mint or date.

Obv. Area, within square, لا اله الا الله / محمد رسول الله

Margin obliterated.

Rev., as 134t; but no star, and order of Imáms varied.

Æ ·8, Wt. 79

134w No mint or date.

Coin similar to 134v, struck over coin of Sháh Rukh, similar to 58, mint and date obliterated.

Æ ·95, Wt. 76

134x No mint or date.

Obv. Area as 134t, but within square, and divided by lines; margin obliterated.

Rev. Area, in pear-shaped border,

سلطان
بابر بها
در

Margin, عظم خلد الله ملکه وسلطانه........

Æ ·95, Wt. 79

No.	Mint.	Year.	
Æ 3	Lahore	936	Obv. as 1: but area enclosed in circle (ابابكر) Rev. ا]سلطان الاعظم خاقان المكرم ٩٣٦ ظهير الدين محمد بابر پادشاه غازى ... الله ملكه [و س]لطانه . . . لاهور Pl. I. *CUNNINGHAM.* Æ 1·0, Wt. 69
4	—	936	As 3: mint obliterated. *PEARSE.* Æ ·9, Wt. 72
5	—	—	Obv. as 1: but area enclosed in circle. Rev. السلطان الاعظم الخاقان المكرم ظهير الدين محمد بابر پادشاه خلد الله مل . . . . *CUNNINGHAM.* Æ 1·0, Wt. 72
6	—	—	As 2: but no date. Rev. margin shows [السلطان ا] لاعظم خاقان المكرم خلد الل . . . . Æ 1·15, Wt. 73
7	—	—	Obv. as 2. Rev. Area, within eight-foil, پادشاه محمد ظهير الدين بابر Margin as 6. Æ 1·0, Wt. 73

II.—MUHAMMAD HUMÁYÚN.*

A.H. 937—960 = A.D. 1530—1554.

No.	Mint.	Year.	
AV			GOLD.
8	—	—	Obv., within octagon, لا اله الا الله محمد رسول الله Rev., within circle, غازى محمد همايون پادشاه ابو المظفر PL. I. *AV* ·5, Wt. 14
9, 10, 10*a*	—	—	Obv., within circle, as 8. Rev., within circle, خلد الله تعالى پادشاه غازى محمد همايون ملكه . . . . PL. I. *CUNNINGHAM.* *AV* ·55, Wt. 16 *I.O.C.* *AV* ·5, Wt. 13 *I.O.C.* *AV* ·45, Wt. 8

* For coins of Humáyún struck in Kashmír (in 953?), see my *Catalogue of Indian Coins, Muhammadan States*, p. 80.

No.	Mint.	Year.	
Æ			SILVER.
11	—	962	Obv. Area, within looped square, لا اله الا الله سول الله محمد ر Ψ Margin, ابابكر الصديق | عمر الفاروق | عثمان العفان | على المرتضى Rev. Area, within looped square, پادشاه غازى محمد همايون ۹٦۲ Margin, ابو المظفر | العادل | ...... | .... Pl. I. *CUNNINGHAM.* Æ ·95, Wt. 180
12	—	—	Obv. Area, within looped circle, لا اله الا الله محمد رسول الله Margin, ابا بكر الصديق | عمر الفاروق | عثمان العفان | على المرتضى Rev. Area, within eightfoil, محمد غازى همايون Margin, السلطان الاعظم الخاقان المكرم[خلد الله تع]الى ملكه و[س]لطانه ض...... Pl. I. *CUNNINGHAM.* Æ 1·05, Wt. 113

No.	Mint.	Year.	
AR 13	Lahore	—	As 12: but . . ضرب لاهـ at end of rev. margin. PL. I. *HAY.* AR 1·0, Wt. 111
14-17	—	—	As 12: rev. area in different border; margin varied in arrangement, and partly obliterated. *BOMBAY AS. SOC.* AR 1·0, Wt. 112 *HAY.* AR ·8, Wt. 110 AR ·8, Wt. 37 *EDEN.* AR ·9, Wt. 47
18	—	942	Obv. as 12. Rev. Area, within ornamented oblong border, محمد همایون پادشاه غازی سید السلاطین Margin, السلطان الا]عظم الخاقان ال[کرم] خلد الله تعالی ملکه سنة ۴۲ PL. I. *BUSH.* AR ·85, Wt. 72
19	—	—	Obv. Area, within looped circle, لا اله الا الله محمد رسول الله الله بغیر حساب یرزق من یشا Margin as 12. Rev. as 12. PL. I. *CUNNINGHAM.* AR 1·05, Wt. 72
20	—	—	Obv. Area as 19. Margin, ... | بعدل عمر | بحیای عثمان | .... Rev. as 11: but barbarous. *CUNNINGHAM.* AR 1·0, Wt. 68
21	—	—	Obv. as 20. Rev. as 12. AR 1·0, Wt. 73
22	—	—	As 12. *CUNNINGHAM.* AR ·95, Wt. 71

III.—JALÁL-AD-DÍN AKBAR.

A.H. 963—1014 = A.D. 1556—1605.

No.	Mint.	Year.	
N			**I.—WITH HIJRAH YEARS.** GOLD.
23	Agrah	971	Obv. Area, within ornamented pentagon, لا اله الا الله محمد رسول الله Margin, in segments, | ابی بکر صدیق | عمر الفاروق | عثمان العفان | علی المرتضی | [ر]ضی الله عنهم Rev. Area, السلطان الاعظم الخاقان المکرم | اکبر پادشاه غازی | الله محمد | خلد تعالی | جلال الدین | ۹۷۱ اکره ملکه وسلطانه ضرب (Five Mohrs.) PL. II. *I.O.C.* *N* 1·75, Wt. 838

No.	Mint.	Year.	
AV 24	Agrah?	971	Obv. Area as 23. Margin, بصدق ابابکر | اصسا (؟) عمر | بحیای [عثم]ان | بعل[م] علی | دل الله بهم Rev. السلطان الاع[ظم] خلد الله ے پادشاه ۹۷۱ غاز جلال الدین محمد اکبر لے تعا ملکه [و]سلطا[نه . ک .. (السلطان written السلطان) PL. II. AV 1·05, Wt. 165
25	Lahore	,,	As 24: mint, .. لاه PL. II. *BENGAL AS. SOC.* AV 1·05, Wt. 168
26-28	—	,,	Obv. as 23: no margin. Rev. غازی اکبر پادشا[ه مد ∴ مد ۹۷۱ جلال الدین (Year imperfect on 27 and 28; dots omitted on 29.) PL. II. *I.O.C.* AV ·5, Wt. 18 ,, ·5, Wt. 18 ,, ·45, Wt. 9
29	—	972	As 26: but year ۹۷۲ ,, ·5, Wt. 18
30	Ag[rah]	,,	As 24: [ر]ضی الله عنهم instead of دل; year and mint ۹۷۲, .. ضرب اک. *BENGAL AS. SOC.* AV 1·1, Wt. 168

No.	Mint.	Year.	
AV 31	Sárang-púr ?	972	As 24 : obv. margin partly obliterated ; year ۹۷۲, and lowest line of rev., ـــــــــــــلے تعا ملکه سار[ك]پو[ر] Pl. II. *I.O.C.* AV ·9, Wt. 164
32	—	973	As 24 : obv. margin (as 30) partly obliterated ; on rev., year ۷۳ : mint obliterated. *MARSDEN.* AV 1·05, Wt. 168
33	Lahore	974	As 24 : obv. margin partly obliterated ; year ۹۷۴ : mint .رب .. هور *BENGAL AS. SOC.* AV 1.05 Wt. 169
34	—	975	As 24 : inscriptions barbarous ; year ۹۷٤ : mint illegible. AV 1·2, Wt. 169
35	—	„	As 24 : obv. margin obliterated ; year ۹۷۵ ; mint obliterated. *MARSDEN.* AV 1·05, Wt. 169
36	—	„	As 24 : obv. margin, | ...ق ابا بكر و | . . ا . عمر | . ى ...ان | بعـ[ـلم علـى] | [ر]ضى عنـهم : year ۹۷٤ : mint obliterated. *STUBBS.* AV 1·05, Wt. 167
37	—	„	As 36. Pl. II. *BENGAL AS. SOC.* AV 1·05, Wt. 168
38	Dehlí	„	As 30 : year and mint ۹۷۵, ضرب حضرت دهلی. Pl. II. *BENGAL AS. SOC.* AV 1·1, Wt. 169

No.	Mint.	Year.	
AV 39	—	976	As 24 : obv. margin barbarous ; year ٩٧٦ : mint obliterated. *MARSDEN.* AV 1·0, Wt. 162
40	Agrah	,,	Obv. as 24, within ornamented quatrefoil ; margin omits benediction. Rev. ملكه خلد الله تعا[ا] ٩٧٦ پادشاه غاز جلال الدين محمد اكبر دار الخلافة اكره ضرب PL. II. *BENGAL AS. SOC.* AV 1·0, Wt. 169
41	Jaun- púr	977	As 24 : year and mint ٩٧٧, ضرب جونپور AV 1·0, Wt. 167
42	Dehlí	,,	As 40 : year and mint ٩٧٧, .. ضرب حضرت ده *BENGAL AS. SOC.* AV ·95, Wt. 169
43	Lahore	,,	٩٧٧ As 40 : year and mint دار الخلافة لاه[و]ر PL. II. *BENGAL AS. SOC.* AV 1·0, Wt. 169

No.	Mint.	Year.	
AV 44	—	977	Obv. Area, within dotted border, لا اله الا الله محمد رسول الله Margin obliterated. Rev. خاقان ؟ ... پا]دشاه غازی محمد اکبر جلال الدین ملکه سلط... ۹۷۷ Ornament, obv., *MARSDEN.* AV ·95, Wt. 157
45	Agrah	978	As 40 : but year and mint ۹۷۸, ..لخلافة اک.... *PRINSEP.* AV ·85, Wt. 168
46	Jaun-púr	,,	As 24 : but year and mint ۹۷۸, ضرب جونپور (In margin ابی بلر, and رضی الله عنهم) Pl. II. *CUNNINGHAM.* AV 1·0, Wt. 166
47	,,	97*x*	As 46 : but unit of year obscure. *PRINSEP.* AV 1·05, Wt. 166
48	Ahmad-ábád	980	As 40 : but year and mint ۹۸۰, ...[لخ]لافة احمدا .... Ornament, obv., Pl. II. *BENGAL AS. SOC.* AV ·8, Wt. 169
49	Agrah	,,	As 40 : but year and mint ۹۸۰, ..ر الخلافة اک.. *MARSDEN.* AV ·8, Wt. 168

No.	Mint.	Year.	
AV 50,51	Agrah	981	Obv. لا اله الا الله رسول الله محمد ٩٨١ ابی بکر عمر عثمان علی Rev. خلد ملکه پادشاه غازی محمد جلال الدین اکبر ضرب بلدة اکره Pl. II. *MARSDEN.* AV 1·3 × 8, Wt. 167 *MARSDEN.* AV 1·2 × 8, Wt. 167
52,53	„	982	Obv. Area, within triple square, لا اله الا الله محمد رسول الله ٩٨٢ Margin, in segments, | بصدق ابی بکر | . . . . . عمر | . . ی عثمان | [ب]عل[م]علی Rev. خل]د الله ملکه پادشاه غازی اکبر جلال الدین محمد د]ار الخلافة اکره Pl. III. *BENGAL AS. SOC.* AV ·9, Wt. 169 *MARSDEN.* AV ·95, Wt. 168

No.	Mint.	Year.	
AV 54	Agrah	982	As 52: barbarous. *MARSDEN.* AV ·95, Wt. 168
55	Ahmadábád	,,	As 52: but mint احمداba[د] . . . . . *BENGAL AS. SOC.* AV ·95, Wt. 169
56	,,	,,	As 55: barbarous. *MARSDEN.* AV 1·0
57	,,	983	As 52: year and mint, ۹۸۳, احمد ا[باد ...... *MARSDEN.* AV ·95
58	Jaunpúr	,,	As 52: year and mint, ۹۸۳, ضرب جـ[و]نپو[ر] PL. III. AV ·8, Wt. 169
59,60	Lahore	,,	As 52: year and mint, ۹۸۳, ضرب لاهور PL. III. *GOVT. INDIA.* AV ·85, Wt. 168 AV ·85
61	Sirhind	984	As 52: year and mint, ۹۸۴, شهرند . . . . PL. III. *YEAMES.* AV ·9, Wt. 169
62	—	,,	As 52: year ۹۸۴; mint obliterated. *LADY FRERE.* AV ·9, Wt. 165
63	Muhammadábád Udaipúr	,,	Obv. عمر ۳ لا اله الا الله محمد رسول الله Margins: بصدق ابي بكر — بحيا عثمان — علي — بعلم ۹۸۴ Rev. پادشاه غازى جلال الدين محمد اكبر مفتوحة اباد عرف اديپور محمد ضرب Commemorative of the reduction of Muhammadábád, commonly called Udaipúr. (Persian style.) PL. III. *I.O.C.* AV ·9, Wt. 169

No.	Mint.	Year.	
AV 64	—	984	Obv. Area, within triple eightfoil, لا اله الا الله محمد رسول الله Margin obliterated. Rev. Area, within triple square, پادشاه اکبر غازی محمد ٤ ٨ جلال الدین ٩ Margin obliterated. Pl. III. *MARSDEN.* AV ·95, Wt. 166
65	—	985	Obv. Area, within triple square, لا اله الا الله محمد رسول الله ٩٨٤ Margin obliterated. Rev. Area, پادشاه غازی اکبر جلال الدین محمد Margin obliterated. Pl. III. AV ·9, Wt. 169

No.	Mint.	Year.	
AV 66* square	Fathpúr	986	Obv. 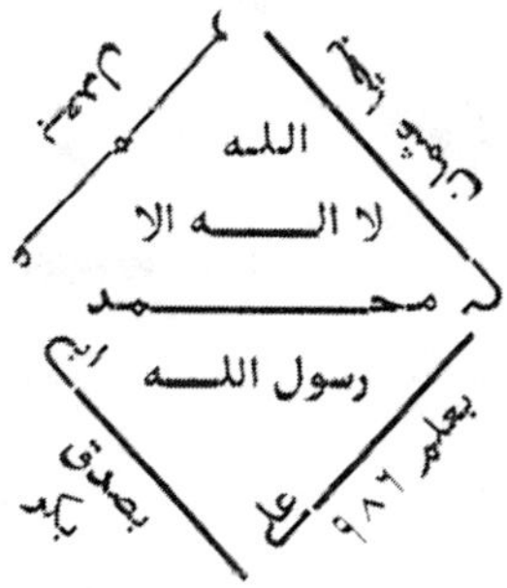 Rev. خلد الله تعا ملكه محمد اكبر پادشاه جلال الدين غازي ضرب دار السلطنة فتحپور Pl. III. *PRINSEP.* AV ·75, Wt. 186
67 sq.	Fathpúr	987	As 66 : but year ٩٨٧ *on reverse.* AV ·7, Wt. 187
68 sq	Lahore	„	As 66 : year ٩٨٧ on reverse ; and lowest line, ضرب دار السلطنة لاهور Pl. III. *PRINSEP.* AV ·75, Wt. 187
69 sq.	Fathpúr	988	As 66 : year ٩٨٨ on reverse. *MARSDEN.* AV ·75, Wt. 187

* In this volume all coins are assumed to be round, unless distinguished as square (sq.) beneath the number in the first column. The fractions ½ or ¼ beneath the number indicate a half or a quarter mohr or rupee as the case may be.

No.	Mint.	Year.	
AV 70 sq.	Lahore	988	As 66 : year ٩٨٨ on reverse; and lowest line, . . ضرب دار السلطنة لاهـ Pl. III. *MARSDEN.* AV ·75, Wt. 188
71,72	—	„	As 26, but —ꝏ— divides reverse; date ٩٨٨ Pl. III. *I.O.C.* AV ·45, Wt. 15 *I.O.C.* *Pierced.* AV ·55, Wt. 15
73-77 sq.	Urdú-Zafar-karín	1000	As 66 : year الف on reverse; lowest line, ضرب اردو ظفر قرين Pl. III. *MARSDEN.* AV ·75, Wt. 186 AV ·75, Wt. 186 *I.O.C.* AV ·8, Wt. 186 *MARSDEN.* AV ·75, Wt. 187 *I.O.C.* AV ·7, Wt. 183
78 sq.	„	„	As 73 : no year. AV ·7, Wt. 187
79,80	„	„	As 73 : but round. Barbarous. Pl. III. AV ·8, Wt. 166 AV ·8, Wt. 164
81 sq. ½	„	„	As 73. Pl. III. *CUNNINGHAM.* AV ·55, Wt. 93
82 sq. ¼	„	„	Obv. اكبر / الله / الف — Rev. قرين / ظفر / اردو Pl. III. *CUNNINGHAM.* AV ·4, Wt. 46
83 sq.	Patnah	—	As 73 : lowest line of rev., الضرب پتنه Pl. III. *MARSDEN.* AV ·65, Wt. 169

No.	Mint.	Year.	
			SILVER.
AR 84	—	963	Obv. Area, within looped circle, لا اله الا الله محـــــــمد رســـول الله Margin obliterated Rev. Above, عظم .... لطا ... Within square, پادشاه غازی محمد اکبر ۹۶۳ جلال الدین Beneath, inscription obliterated. PL. IV. *CUNNINGHAM.* AR ·9, Wt. 179
85	—	964	Obv. Area, within square, as 84; year ۹۶٤ Margin, ابابکر ال.............عد.ال.. تض . Rev. Area, within square, as 84, but no date. Margin, in segments, وسلطانه ....|......|.......|...... *CUNNINGHAM.* AR 1·0, Wt. 176

No.	Mint.	Year.	
Æ 86	Agrah	967	Obv. Area, within square, as 84. Margin, in segments,* | بصدق ابی بکر | بعدل عمر بحیای عثمان | بعلم علی Rev. Area, within square, اکبر پادشاه غازی ۹۶۷ محمد جلال الدین Margin, السلطان الاعظم | خاقان ..... | [خ]لد الله تعالی ملکه | وسلطانه ضرب اکره PL. IV. *PLAYFAIR.* Æ 1·2, Wt. 173
87	—	,,	As 86 : mint obliterated. *STUBBS.* Æ 1·1, Wt. 174
88	Jaun- púr	96*x*	Obv. Area, within wavy lozenge border, as 84. Margin, بحا (*sic*) ابابکر | بعدل عمر | بحیای عثمان | بعلم علی رضی الله Rev. ناصر الدنیا والدین محمد اکبر پادشاه غازی ۹۶ جلال الدین ابو الفتح (؟) ضرب جونپو[ر PL. IV. *BANKS.* Æ 1·2, Wt. 177

* Slight variations in this inscription (as omitting or inserting a ی or و), are not usually recorded in the Catalogue.

No.	Mint.	Year.	
AR 88[a]	Jaun- púr	96*x*	As 88: but ٩٦ in rev. area, and no trace of anything before ضرب *PANJ. ARCH. SURV.* AR 1·1
89	—	970	As 86: obv. margin obliterated; on rev. area, year ٩٧٠ margin obliterated. *MARSDEN.* AR 1·05, Wt. 170
90	—	970	Obv. as 86; margin as 88, ending عنهم Rev. Area, within eightfoil, خلد الله اکبر پادشاه غازی محمد ٩٧٠ جلال الدین Margin, ...ملكه وسلطانه..... Pl. IV. AR 1·1, Wt. 178
91	Agrah	970	As 86: year ٩٧٠; rev. margin partly obliterated; ..ب اکره *GRANT.* AR 1·05, Wt. 173
92	—	971	As 90: obv. and rev. areas inclosed in wavy border; year on rev. ٩٧١; margin obliterated. AR 1·1, Wt. 160
93	—	971	As 86: obv. area within circle; rev. area within wavy square; rev. margin obliterated; year on rev. ٩٧١ *I.O.C.* AR ·95, Wt. 177

No.	Mint.	Year.	
AR 94	Dehlí	971	Obv. as 84: within circle; margin ends رضی الله عنهم Rev., within ornamented square, ...طا. الاعظم الخاقان ال.... ... اکبر پادشاه الله ... محمد غازی خلد جلال الدین دهلی ضرب حضرت مم]لکه وسلطانه *THOMAS.* AR 1·1, Wt. 174
95	—	973	As 90: obv. border varied; year on rev. ۹۷۳, margin obliterated. (Formerly ringed). *EDEN.* AR 1·15
96	Jaun-púr	974	Obv. Area, within wavy pentagon, as 84. Margin obscure. Rev. الدنیا والدین ..صر ۹۷۴ ل الدین اکبر غازی جلا محمد پادشاه د]ا[ر] الخلافة جونپو[ر Pl. IV. *THOMAS.* AR 1·1, Wt. 177

No.	Mint.	Year.	
AR 97	Dehlí	975	Obv., within circle, as 86, adding رضی الله عنهم Rev. ا]سلطان الاعظم الخاقا[ن : الله | اکبر پادشاه : خلـ[د | محمد غازی : ده[لی | جلال الدین ۹۷٤ ضرب حضرة .... PL. IV. *CURETON.* AR 1·05, Wt. 174
98	Jaun-púr	„	Obv. as 86. Rev. as 96: year ۹۷٤ (Ringed.) *GRANT.* AR 1·1
99	—	„	As 90: mint obliterated; year ۹۷۵ (Obv. margin as 97.) AR 1·1, Wt. 169
100	—	976	As 90: mint obliterated; year ۹۷٦ *EDEN.* AR 1·05, Wt. 168
101	Agrah	977	As 86: year ۹۷۷ (Obv. in looped square; rev. margin varied in arrangement.) *THOMAS.* AR 1·0, Wt. 177
102	—	978	As 90: mint obliterated; year [۹]۷۸ *GRANT.* AR 1·05, Wt. 165
103	—	980	As 86: margins partly obliterated; year ۹۸۰ *I.O.C.* AR ·95, Wt. 174

No.	Mint.	Year.	
Æ 104	—	981	As 90: but year ٩٨١ (Borders varied.) Æ 1·0, Wt. 175
105	Ahmad-ábád	982	As 86: areas inclosed in triple squares; year ٩٨٢ Rev. margin, داراالسلطنة احمداباد | ضرب ..... | ...... Pl. IV. *GRANT.* Æ 1·0, Wt. 175
106	„ ?	„	As 105: mint partly obliterated. *THOMAS.* Æ 1·05, Wt. 174
107	—	983	As 86: margins chiefly obliterated; year ٩٨٣ (Borders varied.) *MARSDEN.* Æ ·95, Wt. 175
108-110	Jaun-púr	„	As 96: mint partly obliterated; year ٩٨٣ Pl. IV. *GRANT.* Æ ·85, Wt. 175; „ Æ ·85, Wt. 175; *EDEN.* Æ ·9, Wt. 173
111	Ahmad-ábád	„	As 105: year ٩٨٣ *STUBBS.* Æ 1·05, Wt. 175
112	—	„	As 90: year ٩٨٣; rev. margin nearly obliterated. Æ 1·0, Wt. 170
113	—	984	As 86: year ٩٨٤; mint obliterated. *THOMAS.* Æ ·9, Wt. 174
114	Dehlí	985	As 86: year ٩٨٥ Rev. Margin, | .. ضرب ده | وسلطانه.... | ...... | ...... *MARSDEN.* Æ 1·0, Wt. 175

No.	Mint.	Year.	
Æ 115-117	—	985	As 86 : year ٩٨٤ ; mint obliterated. *I.O.C.* Æ ·95, Wt. 173 *EDEN.* Æ ·95, Wt. 167 *PRINSEP.* Æ ·9, Wt. 173
118, 119	—	986	As 86 : year ٩٨٦ ; mint in rev. margin obscure. *EDEN.* Æ ·95, Wt. 175 PL. IV. Æ ·95, Wt. 174
120	—	„	As 105 : year ٩٨٦ ; margins obliterated. *STEUART.* Æ ·9, Wt. 177
121	—	987	As 105 : year ٩٨٧ ; mint obliterated. *GRANT.* Æ ·9, Wt. 170

No.	Mint.	Year.	
			SQUARE ISSUE.
Æ 122, 123 sq.	Lahore	986	Obv. (in square) لا اله الا الله / محمد / رسول الله; margins: بصدق ابي بكر / بعدل عمر / بحيا عثمان / بعلم علي
			Rev. خلد الله تعالى ملكه / ٩٨٦ / محمد اكبر پادشاه / جلال الدين غازى / ضرب دار السلطنة لاهور
			Pl. IV. *PRINSEP.* Æ ·8, Wt. 178
			(Formerly ringed.) *MARSDEN.* Æ ·85
124 sq.	Fath-púr	„	As 122 : but دار السلط[نة] فتحپور
			Pl. IV. *THOMAS.* Æ ·8, Wt. 174
125, 125*a*, 126 sq.	„	987	As 124 : but ٩٨٧
			MARSDEN. Æ ·75, Wt. 175
			PRINSEP. Æ ·75, Wt. 175
			I.O.C. Æ ·75, Wt. 175
127 sq.	Ahmad-ábád	„	As 122: but ...ب.. ...دار... احمدا... ; and ٩٨٧
			Obv. ornamented with branches.
			Pl. IV. *GRANT.* Æ ·8, Wt. 174

No.	Mint.	Year.	
AR 128 sq.	Urdú	987	Obv. Area, within quatrefoil, الله لا اله الا محمد رسول الله At corners, ابو بكر ,عمر ,عثمان ,على Rev., within square, اردو ضرب Margin, جلال الدين | محمد اكبر | پادشاه | غازى ۹۸۷ PL. IV. *MARSDEN.* AR ·85, Wt. 175
129, 130 sq.	Lahore	„	As 122 : year ۹۸۷ ; mint, دار السلطنة لا... *GRANT.* AR ·8, Wt. 175 *I.O.C.* AR ·75, Wt. 172
131 sq.	Patnah	„	As 122 : year *on obv.* ۹۸۷ ; last line of rev., ضرب پتنة PL. IV. *I.O.C.* AR ·8, Wt. 176
132 sq. ½	—	„	As 122 : year ۹۸۷ ; mint obliterated. PL. IV. *I.O.C.* AR ·65, Wt. 88
133 sq.	Lahore	988	As 122 : (letters form *diamond* instead of square on obv.); year ۹۸۸ AR ·75, Wt. 177
134, 135 sq.	Fath- púr	„	As 122 : year ۹۸۸ ; lowest line of rev., ضرب دار السلط[نة] فتحپور *BURNES.* AR ·75, Wt. 176 *THOMAS.* AR ·8, Wt. 173

No.	Mint.	Year.	
Æ 136 sq.	—	988	As 122 : year ٩٨٨ ; mint obliterated. *MARSDEN.* Æ ·8, Wt. 171
137 sq.	Lahore	989	As 122 : year ٩٨٩ ; mint partly obliterated. *PRINSEP.* Æ ·8, Wt. 173
138, 139 sq.	Fath- púr	,,	As 134 : year ٩٨٩ *I.O.C.* Æ ·95, Wt. 175 *MARSDEN.* Æ ·75, Wt. 171
140 sq.	—	990	As 122 : obv. margin (if any) cut off; mint obliterated; year ٩٩٠ *I.O.C.* Æ ·7, Wt. 161
141 sq.	—	992	As 122 : year ٩٩٢ ; mint obliterated. Æ ·7, Wt. 177
142 sq.	—	993	As 122 : year ٩٩٣ ; mint obliterated. *MARSDEN.* Æ ·7, Wt. 175
143 sq.	—	994	As 122 : year ٩٩٤ ; mint obliterated. *BURNES.* Æ ·7, Wt. 174
144, 145 sq.	—	995	As 122 : year ٩٩٥ ; mint nearly obliterated (probably Lahore). *I.O.C.* Æ ·75, Wt. 174 Æ ·75, Wt. 175
146 sq.	—	997	As 122 : year ٩٩٧ ; mint obliterated. *GOVT. INDIA.* Æ ·7, Wt. 177
147 sq. ½	—	,,	As 122 : year ٩٩٧ ; mint obliterated. *I.O.C.* Æ ·55, Wt. 86

No.	Mint.	Year.	
Æ 148, 149 sq.	—	998	As 122: year ٩٨٨; mint obliterated. Æ ·7, Wt. 175 *PRINSEP.* Æ ·7, Wt. 171
150 sq.	—	999	As 122: year ٩٩٩; mint obliterated. Æ ·7, Wt. 176
151-155 sq.	Urdú-Zafar-karín	1000	As 122: year الف; mint, ضرب اردو ظفر قرين Pl. IV. Æ ·75, Wt. 175 *EDEN.* Æ ·8 *I.O.C.* Æ ·7 *GOVT. INDIA.* Æ ·8 (Imitation.) Æ ·8, Wt. 175
156-159 sq. ½	,,	,,	,, ,, *I.O.C.* Æ ·55, Wt. 88 *THOMAS.* Æ ·5, Wt. 82 (Mint obliterated.) *PRINSEP.* Æ ·55, Wt. 83 *EDEN.* Æ ·5, Wt. 82
160 sq.	,,	—	,, no year *EDEN.* Æ ·7, Wt. 175
161 sq.	Fath-púr	—	,, ,, mint, فتحپور *EDEN.* Æ ·8, Wt. 178
162 sq.	—	—	,, rev. partly obliterated. *RIVETT-CARNAC.* Æ ·85, Wt. 180
			For square silver coins of Akbar struck in Kashmír, see *Catalogue of Muhammadan States*, nos. 221, 222.

No.	Mint.	Year: Month	Obv.	Rev.
			II.—WITH ILÁHÍ (SOLAR) YEARS.*	
			Obv. GOLD.	Rev.
AV 163	—	32 [995]	Within double square, with wavy border, الله اكبر	Border as obv., ۳۲ الهی جل جلاله Pl. V. AV ·8, Wt. 187
164 ¼	Agrah	42 Bahman [1005]	Within dotted circle, الله اكبر جل جلاله	Within dotted circle, بهمن الهی ۴۲ اکره ب ضر Pl. V. AV ·5, Wt. 42
165	,,	44 Ardibihist [1007]	,,	Within dotted circle, بهست اردی الهی ۴۴ ضرب اکره Pl. V. I.O.C. AV ·9, Wt. 187

* The Iláhí or 'divine' epoch of Akbar was introduced by this Emperor in the year 992 of the Hijrah, A.D. 1584, and dates from the 5th day of Rabí' II. of the year 963 (Feb. 1556, the first of his reign), being the time of the entering of the sun into the constellation Aries; and the Iláhí years are composed of twelve solar months, called by the names of the ancient Persian Kalendar :—

Farwardín	Mardád (Amardád)	Azur
Ardibihist	Shahriyar	Dai
Khúrdád	Mihr	Bahman
Tír	Abán	Isfandarmiz.

In giving the corresponding Hijrah year to any Iláhí year in this Catalogue, the Hijrah year in which the Iláhí year began (i.e., roughly, at April 1st) alone is given.

No.	Mint.	Year : Month	Obv.	Rev.
AV 166	Asír	45 Isfan-dár-miz [1008]	Hawk to right. Ornaments in field.	الله اکـــبـــر ۴۵ اسفندارمز الهی ضرب اسیر PL. V. *PAYNE KNIGHT.* AV ·8, Wt. 183
167	Agrah	49 Far-war-dín [1012]	As 164.	فروردیـن الهی ۴۹ اکـــره ـــــب ضـــر PL. V. *CUNNINGHAM.* AV ·75, Wt. 168
168	,,	49 Amar-dád [1012]	,,	امـــرداد الـــهی ضـــر ۴۹ اکره ـــــب (Lozenge shaped.) *MARSDEN.* PL. V. AV ·85 × 5, Wt. 168
169	,,	49 Azur [1012]	اســت ایـــن زر ی شاه اکبر ابرو مـــهـــر مهر ضرب اکره	ست انـــور زیورا مـــهـــر اســـمـــان را تا زمین والهی اذر ۴۹ PL. V. *PRINSEP.* AV 1·0, Wt. 166
170	,,	50 Amar-dád [1013]	As 164 : within octagram.	Within octagram, as 168, but ۵٠. PL. V. *MARSDEN.* AV ·9, Wt. 167

No.	Mint.	Year: Month	Obv.	Rev.
AV 171	Lahore	50 Amar-dád [1013]	As 164: within dotted circle.	Within dotted circle, امرداد الهی ضرب ۵۰ لاهور Pl. V. *I.O.C.* AV ·7, Wt. 168
172 ½	—	50 Far-war-dín [1013]	Within dotted circle, two figures: (1) a man, wearing crown of three cusps, and carrying a sheaf of arrows and a stretched bow; followed by (2) a woman, who draws back her long veil from her face.	Within dotted circle, ۵۰ الهی فروردین Pl. V. *PRINSEP.* AV ·8, Wt. 74
173	Agrah	50 Khúr-dád [1013]	Within dotted circle, duck to right. Ornaments in field.	الله اکبر ۵۰ خوداد الهی ضرب اکره Pl. V. *YEAMES.* AV ·8, Wt. 182
174	,,	,,	As 169:	As 169: but, ۵۰ خورداد *CUNNINGHAM.* AV 1·0, Wt. 167
175	,,	51 [1014]	نور شاه اکبر پاد مهر از ست زر ۵۱	نور علی بر ان زر نام شه نور ب ضر اکره Pl. V. *CUNNINGHAM.* AV ·85, Wt. 165
176	—	—	الله اکبر Borders as 163.	جل جلاله Pl. V. *I.O.C.* AV ·75, Wt. 187

No.	Mint.	Year: Month	Obv.	Rev.
			SILVER.	
Æ 177	Peshá-war(?)	28 [991]	الله اکبر جل جلاله	مهر الهی ۲۸ پشلور (*sic*) ب ضر PL. VI. *CUNNINGHAM.* Æ·85, Wt. 174
178	Ahmad-ábád	30 [993] Dai	,,	[د]ی الهی ۳۰ احمداباد ضرب PL. VI. *I.O.C.* Æ ·85, Wt. 175
179 sq.	,,	,, Mar-dád	,,	Same, but مرداد Æ ·7, Wt. 175
180 sq.	—	32 [995]	الله اکبر	۳۲ الهی جل جلاله *MARSDEN.* Æ ·7, Wt. 173
181 sq.	—	33 [996]	,,	,, but ۳۳ Æ ·7, Wt. 176
182, 183, 184 sq. ½	—	34 [997]	,,	,, but ۳۴ *GOVT. OF INDIA.* Æ ·65, Wt. 176 *EDEN.* Æ ·7, Wt. 175 PL. VI. *CUNNINGHAM.* Æ ·6, Wt. 87
185 sq.	—	35 Ardi-bihist [998]	As 177.	۳۵ الهی بهشت اردی Æ ·7, Wt. 174

No.	Mint.	Year: Month	Rev.	Obv.
Æ 186 sq.	—	35 Amar-dád [998]	As 177.	٣٥ الــــهی امرداد *CUNNINGHAM.* Æ ·7, Wt. 174
187 sq. ½	Lahore	36 Abán [999]	,,	ابـان الهی ٣٦ لاهـور ضرب *I.O.C.* Æ ·55, Wt. 88
188 sq. ¼	,,	36 Bah-man [999]	,,	Same: but به]من *CUNNINGHAM.* Æ ·4, Wt. 43
189 sq. ¼	Tattah	36 [999]	,,	٣٦ الــــهی تـتــــه Æ ·4, Wt. 44
190 sq. ½	—	37 [1000]	As 180.	As 180: but ٣٧ *I.O.C.* Æ ·55, Wt. 87
191 sq.	Ahmad-ábád	37 [1000]	As 122.	٣٧ محمد اکبر پادش]اه جــلال الــديـــن ضـ[ـرب احـمـدابـاد Pl. VI. Æ ·75, Wt. 172
192 sq.	,,	38 [1001]	,,	,, but ٣٨ Æ ·75, Wt. 177
193 sq.	,,	,, Bah-man [1001]	As 177.	بهمن الهی ٣٨ احمدابا[د ضرب Æ ·7, Wt. 169

No.	Mint.	Year: Month	Obv.	Rev.
Æ 194 sq.	Lahore	38 Tír [1001]	As 177.	تیر الہی ۳۸ لاهور ضرب Pl. VI. *CUNNINGHAM.* Æ ·7, Wt. 176
195 sq.	„	38 Farwardín [1001]	„	Same: but فروردین *CUNNINGHAM.* Æ ·7, Wt. 176
196 sq. ¼	„	38 Ardibihist [1001]	„	بہست اردی الہی ۳۸ لاهو[ر . . . Pl. VI. *THOMAS.* Æ ·45, Wt. 43
197	Burhánpúr	38 Dai [1001]	„	..دی ماه الہی ۳۸ برهانپور . . . (Ringed.) Pl. VI. *PLAYFAIR.* Æ ·8
198	Lahore	39 Azur [1002]	„	اذر الہی ۳۹ ضرب لاهور *PLAYFAIR.* Æ ·9, Wt. 174
199 sq.	Tattah*	40 Khúrdad [1003]	„	خورداد الہی ۴۰ تته ضرب Pl. VI. *PANJ. ARCH. SURV.* Æ ·6, Wt. 173

* This mint closely resembles Patnah, but has one upright stroke less: Tattah is ته and Patnah پته.

No.	Mint.	Year : Month	Obv.	Rev.
AR 200	Tattah	40 Bahman [1003]	As 177.	..ن الہی ۴۰ تتہ ضرب *I.O.C.* AR ·6, Wt. 175
201 sq. ½	—	,,	,, beneath, ضرب د...	۴۰ الہی ماہ بہمن *EDEN.* AR ·45, Wt. 86
202 sq. ⅛	—	40	,,	۴۰ الہی . . . PL. VI. *I.O.C.* AR ·35, Wt. 21
203	Ahmad-ábád	41 Khúr-dád [1004]	,,	خ]ورداد الہی ۴۱ احمدابا[د [ضر]ب (Ringed.) AR ·8
204	Lahore	41 Isfan-dár-miz [1004]	,,	اسفندار[مز] الہی ۴۱ لاہور ضرب PL. VI. *CUNNINGHAM.* AR ·9, Wt. 176
205 sq. ½	—	41 [1004]	As 180.	As 180 : but ۴۱ *I.O.C.* AR ·55, Wt. 88

No.	Mint.	Year : Month	Obv.	Rev.
AR 206	Ahmadábád	42 Khurdád [1005]	As 177.	خورداد الہی ۴۲ احمداباد ضرب AR ·85, Wt. 177
207	,,	42 Tír [1005]	,,	,, but تیر *CUNNINGHAM.* AR ·85, Wt. 176
208 ½	,,	42 Abán [1005]	,,	,, but ابان *EDEN.* AR ·7, Wt. 88
209	Patnah	42 Shahriwar [1005]	,,	شهریور الہی ۴۲ پتنه ضرب PL. VI. AR ·85, Wt. 175
210 sq.	,,	42 [1005]	,,	۴۲ الہی پتنه AR ·6, Wt. 176
211 ½	Lahore	42 Tír [1005]	,,	تیر الہی ۴۲ لاهور *GRANT.* AR ·65, Wt. 87
212	,,	42 Bahman [1005]	,,	بهمن الہی ۴۲ لاهور ضرب *CUNNINGHAM.* AR ·9, Wt. 175

No.	Mint.	Year : Month	Obv.	Rev.
Æ 213 sq.	Dehli?	42 Tír [1005]	As 177 : beneath دهلی ?	۴۲ الهی ماه تیر *PANJ. ARCH. SURV.* Æ ·65, Wt. 174
214 sq. ½	—	42 [1005]	As 180.	As 180 : but ۴۲ *I.O.C.* Æ ·55, Wt. 88
215 ½	Patnah	43 Khúr-dád [1006]	As 177.	خورداد الهی ۴۳ پتنه ضرب Pl. VI. Æ ·65, Wt. 88
216	„	43 Bah-man [1006]	„	Same : but بهمن *CUNNINGHAM.* Æ ·85, Wt. 175
217 sq. ½	—	43 [1006]	As 180.	As 180 : but ۴۳ *I.O.C.* Æ ·6, Wt. 88
218 sq. ½	—	43 Shah-ríwar [1006]	As 177.	۴۳ الهی شهریور Pl. VI. *THOMAS.* Æ ·55, Wt. 87
219	Ahmad-ábád	44 Amar-dád [1007]	„	امرداد الهی ۴۴ احمداباد ضرب *MARSDEN.* Æ 1·05, Wt. 180

No.	Mint.	Year. Month.	Obv.	Rev.
AR 220	Patnah	44 Shahriwar [1007]	As 177.	شهریور الہی ۴۴ پتنه ضرب AR ·95, Wt. 175
221 ½	Kábul	44 Abán [1007]	„	ابان الہی ضر کابل ۴۴ ب PL. VI. *GRANT.* AR ·75, Wt. 87
222	Lahore	44 Ardibihist [1007]	„	بہست اردی الہی ۴۴ لاهور ضرب *EDEN.* AR ·85, Wt. 174
223	„	44 Shahriwar [1007]	„	„ but شهریور *STEUART.* AR ·85, Wt. 174
224 ½	„	44 Abán [1007]	„	„ but ابان *GRANT.* AR ·65, Wt. 86
225 ½	„	44 Adhur [1007]	„	„ but اذر AR ·65, Wt. 89
226 ½	Kábul	45 Dai [1008]	„	دی الہی ضر کابل ۴۵ ب *EDEN.* AR ·7, Wt. 86

No.	Mint.	Year: Month.	Obv.	Rev.
AR 227 ½	Lahore	45 Dai [1008]	As 177.	دی الهی ۴۵ لاهو[ر] ضرب AR ·7, Wt. 88
228 sq. ⅛	,,	45 Bahman [1008]	,, partly obliterated.	ب[همن الہ]ی ۴۵ لاه[ور] ضرب *CUNNINGHAM.* AR ·35, Wt. 19
229	Ahmadábád	46 Tír [1009]	,,	تیر الهی ۴۶ احمداباد ضرب AR ·85. Wt. 176
230	Patnah	46 Adhur [1009]	,,	اذر الهی ۴۶ پتنه ٥ ضرب *CUNNINGHAM.* AR ·9, Wt. 176
231 ½	Kábul	46 Dai [1009]	,,	دی الهی ضر کابل ۴۶ ب *GRANT.* AR ·7, Wt. 87
232	Lahore	46 Khúrdád [1009]	,,	خورداد [الہ]ی ۴۶ لاهـو[ر] ضرب *PANJ. ARCH. SURV.* AR ·8, Wt. 175

No.	Mint.	Year: Month.	Obv.	Rev.
AR 233 $\frac{1}{4}$	Lahore	46 Adhur [1009]	As 177.	اذر الہی ۴۶ لاھ.. ضرب PL. VI. *GRANT.* AR ·5, Wt. 44
234 $\frac{1}{2}$	,,	46 Dai [1009]	,,	دی الہی ۴۶ لاهو[ر ضرب *STEUART.* AR ·65, Wt. 88
235	Ahmad-ábád	47 Bahman [1010]	,,	بہمن الہی ۴۷ احمداباد ضرب AR ·8, Wt. 175
236	,,	47 Mihr [1010]	,, within square enclosed in ornamented diamond border.	Within octagon enclosed in ornamented border, مہر الہی ۴۷ احمداباد ضرب *CUNNINGHAM.* AR ·8, Wt. 175
237 $\frac{1}{2}$	Kábul	47 Adhur [1010]	As 177.	اذر الہی ضر کابل ۴۷ ب *GRANT.* AR ·7, Wt. 88

No.	Mint.	Year: Month.	Obv.	Rev.
AR 238	Lahore	47 Khúr-dád [1010]	As 177, border as 236.	خورداد الہی ۴۷ لاهـــور ضرب Octagon and border as on 236. Pl. VI. *GRANT.* AR ·8, Wt. 171
239 ½	,,	47 Abán [1010]	As 177.	ابان ا[لہ]ی ۴۷ لاه]ور ضرب *I.O.C.* AR ·6, Wt. 87
240 ½	,,	47 Dai [1010]	,,	,, but دی *CUNNINGHAM.* AR ·65, Wt. 87
241	Burhán-púr	48 Mihr [1011]	,,	مہر ماه الہی ۴۸ برهانپور ضرب Pl. VI. *CUNNINGHAM.* AR ·75, Wt. 177
242	Lahore	48 Amar-dád [1011]	,, border as 236.	امرداد الہی ۴۸ لاهـــور ضرب Border as 236. *CUNNINGHAM.* AR ·8, Wt. 175
243 ½	,,	48 Abán [1011]	,, ,,	,, but ابان Pl. VI. *CUNNINGHAM.* AR ·65, Wt. 86

No.	Mint.	Year : Month.	Obv.	Rev.
Æ 244 ½	Lahore	48 Abán [1011]	As 177, without border.	As 243, but without border. *GRANT.* Æ ·55, Wt. 87
244*a* ½	„	„	As 177, border as 236.	As 243 ; border as 236. *STUBBS.* Æ ·55, Wt. 86
245 ½	Kábul	49 Abán [1012]	„	ابـــان الٰہ ..کابل ۴۹ ب *CUNNINGHAM.* Æ ·7, Wt. 86
246 ½	„	[4]9 Dai [1012]	„	دی الـــٰہ ضر کابل۹ ب *GRANT.* Æ ·7, Wt. 88
247	Lahore	49 Ardi-bihist [1012]	„ border as 236.	بـــہـــســـت اردی الـــٰہ ۴۹ لاهـــور ضرب Border as 236. *CUNNINGHAM.* Æ ·75, Wt. 175
248 ½	„	49 Abán [1012]	„ „	„ „ but ابان *THOMAS* Æ ·65, Wt. 88
249 sq.	Patnah?	49 Far-war-dín [1012]	„ without border.	فروردی(*sic*) ا[لہ]ی .. پـــتہ ۴۹ ضر . *MARSDEN.* Æ ·6, Wt. 174

No.	Mint.	Year: Month.	Obv.	Rev.
Æ 250	Agrah	50 Amar-dád [1013]	As 177, octagonal border, with quatrefoils outside.	امرداد الهی ٥٠ اکره ضرب Border as obv. PL. VI. Æ 1·0, Wt. 175
251	Lahore	50 Far-war-dín [1013]	„ border as 236	فروردین الهی ٥٠ لاهور ضرب Border as 236. *GRANT.* Æ ·8, Wt. 174
252 sq.	—	—	الله اکبر	جل جلاله *CUNNINGHAM.* Æ ·75, Wt. 175

No.	Mint.	Year : Month.	Obv.	Rev.
			III.—GUJARÁT FABRIC.	
Æ. 252*a* ½	—	992	Within dotted square, لا اله الا الله محمد رسول الله	بادشاه اكبر غازى محمد جلال الدين Pl. VII. *GRANT.* Æ ·65, Wt. 83
252*b* ½	—	997	,,	,, but ٩٩٧ Pl. VII. Æ ·6, Wt. 83
			Late Imitations.	
252*c* ½	—	1215	,,	,, but ١٢١٥ over جلال Pl. VII. Æ ·6, Wt. 87
252*d* ½	—	,,	,,	,, but ١٢١٥ *MARSDEN.* Æ ·6, Wt. 87
252*e* ½	—	,,	,,	,, but ١٢٥ *GRANT.* Æ ·6, Wt. 82
252*f* ½	—	—	,,	,, but within dotted square ; ہ over د of پادشاه ; no numerals over جلال *GRANT.* Æ ·6, Wt. 82
252*g* ½	—	—	,,	,, × over محمد *MARSDEN.* Æ ·6, Wt. 87

No.	Mint.	Year : Month	Obv.	Rev.
Æ 252*h* ¼	—	—	As 252*a*.	As 252*a*; no ० or × Æ ·55, Wt. 44
253 sq. ¼	—	—	Within dotted square, الله اكبر	جلاله جل ० *I.O.C.* Æ ·4, Wt. 44
254-254*b*	Allah-ábád	—	اله اباد سـكه ق جهان شـر بغرب و	ماه رايج باد مـهـر و زر هـمـچو هـمـيـشـه Pl. VII. *EDEN*. Æ ·9, Wt. 177 Æ ·9, Wt. 175 Æ ·8, Wt. 176

No.	Mint.	Year.	Obv.	Rev.
			IV. COPPER. A. WITH HIJRAH YEARS.	
Æ 255	Nárnól	963	نارنول فلوس ضرب	. . . . شصت نهصد ۹٦۳ Pl. VII. *PANJ. ARCH. SURV.* Æ ·9
256	,,	965	,,	,, but ۹٦٤ Æ ·85
257	—	966	لا اله الا الله الله سول محمد ر	صد ش . ۹٦٦ نه 卐 سنه ضرب . . . . . . Pl. VII. *PANJ. ARCH. SURV.* Æ ·9
258	Lahore	97x	لاهور ضرب س فلو	هفتا]د نهصد]و فی تاریخ Pl. VII. *THEOBALD.* Æ ·8
259	Nárnól	980	As 255.	هشتا]د نهصد ۹۸۰ فی س . . Æ ·85
260	—	,,	,, mint obscure.	Æ ·75

No.	Mint.	Year.	Obv.	Rev.
Æ 261	Ahmad-ábád	982	احمدابا[د دار السلطنه . . . . ضرب فلوس	. . . . هشتا . . . . فی نهصد و ۹۸۲ سنه Pl. VII. *HAY.* Æ ·85
262	Nárnól	982	As 255.	,, *PANJ. ARCH. SURV.* Æ ·8
263	Dógám	983	[ا]سلام (؟) د]ار (؟) فلـ]وس د]وکام ضرب	. . . هستا . . نهصد سنه فی ۹۸۳ Pl. VII. *HAY.* Æ ·8
264	Málpúr	985	ف]لوس مالپور ضرب	پنج هشتاد نهصد [۹]۸۵ Pl. VII. *PANJ. ARCH. SURV.* Æ ·85
265	—	987	. . . . . د[ار] السلط[نه فلوس ضرب	. . . . هشتاد ۹۸۷ و نهصد فی . . . Æ ·75

No.	Mint.	Year.	Obv.	Rev.
Æ 266	Fathpúr	987	فلوس فتحپور دا.....	.... هشتاد ۹۸۷ نهصد Pl. VII. *MARSDEN.* Æ ·9
267	—	987	... .السلطنه فلوس ضرب	هفت هشتاد و ۹۸۷ نهصد و *MARSDEN.* Æ ·85
268	Fathpúr	988	ف]لوس ف]تحپور دا[ر]ال....	۹۸۸ نهصد سنه *HAY.* Æ ·8
269	Ahmad-ábád	98*x*	احمداباد فلوس ضرب	... هشتاد ن]هصد و سنه *PANJ. ARCH SURV.* Æ ·85
270	Jaun-púr	98*x*	دا]ر الخلا[فه جونپو[ر ف]لوس	.... هشتاد ن]هصد و سنه Pl. VII. *PANJ. ARCH. SURV.* Æ ·9

No.	Mint.	Year.	Obv.	Rev.
Æ 271	Dogám	994	دار السلام ؟ ف]لـــوس دو]كـام	چهار نـ]ـود و ن]هصد و سنه *PANJ. ARCH. SURV.* Æ ·85
272	Gwálior	9*xx*	دار الخلافـه حـفـا ه كواليـ . . ضرب	. . . . نهـــصد فی تاریخ PL. VII. *PANJ. ARCH. SURV.* Æ ·9
273	Urdú-Zafar-Karín	1000	قرين ظـفـر اردو	ضرب الـف فلوس PL. VII. *THEOBALD.* Æ ·85

B. WITH ILÁHÍ YEARS.

No.	Mint.	Year : Month.	Obv.	Rev.
Æ 273*a*	Alláh-ábád	31 Mihr [994]	الهاباد مهر	سنة ۳۱ الهی Pl. VII. *PANJ. ARCH. SURV.* Æ ·85
274	Kábul	32 [995]	کابل فلوس	الهی ۳۲ سنه Pl. VII. *GRANT.* Æ ·7
274*a*	,,	33 [996]	,,	,, but ۳۳ *GRANT.* Æ ·75
275	Lahore	36 Dai [999]	لاهور فلوس	۳۶ الهی دی Pl. VII. Æ ·6
276	Nárnól?	36 [999]	الله اکبر جل جلاله	. . . الهی ۳۶ نارنول (؟) ضرب *EDEN.* Æ ·7
277	Multán	37 Dai [1000]	ملتان فلوس ضرب	۳۷ الهی دی *HAY.* Æ ·8
278	Gwálior	38 Shah-riwar [1001]	کوالی . . فلوس ضرب	۳۸ الهی شهرور *PANJ. ARCH. SURV.* Æ ·8

No.	Mint.	Year: Month	Obv.	Rev.
Æ 279	Lahore	39 Far-war-dín [1002]	لاهور فلوس ضرب	٣٩ الهی فروردین HAY. Æ ·9
279*a*	,,	43 Tír [1006]	,,	۴۳ الهی تیر Æ ·55
280	Bairá-tah	44 Amar-dád [1007]	تنکه اکبر شاهی ضرب بیراته	۴۴ الهی امرداد (*Tanka.*) *PLAYFAIR.* Æ 1·2
281	,,	,,	,,	,, but month . . . ماه ا (*Tanka.*) Æ 1·2
281*a*	,,	,,	,,	,, امرداد (*Tanka.*) *HAY.* Æ ·9
282	Dehlí	42-4 Dai	فلو[س دهلی ضرب	۴۲ الهی ماه دی Pl. VII. *PANJ. ARCH. SURV.* Æ ·45
283	Agrah	46 Abán [1009]	اکبر شاهی دو تانکی	ابان الهی ۴۶ اکره ضرب Pl. VII. (*Two tankas.*) *EDEN.* Æ ·65
284	,,	47 Ardi-bihist [1010]	,,	. . . . اردی الهی ۴۷ اکره ضرب (*Two tankas.*) *PANJ. ARCH. SURV.* Æ ·8

No.	Mint.	Year : Month	Obv.	Rev.
Æ 285	Agrah	47 Tír [1010]	اکبر شاهی یاك تانکی	تیر الهی ۴۷ اکره ضرب (*One tanka.*) Æ ·55
286	„	47 Abán [1010]	اکبر شاهی دو تانکی	„ but ابان (*Two tankas.*) *GRANT.* Æ ·6
287	„	4*x*	In centre, within ornamented border, ضرب اکره Margin obliterated.	. . . . . ۴ سنه PL. VII. *EDEN.* Æ ·6
287*a*	„	50 Shah-riwar [1013]	اکبر شاهی دو تانکی	شهرور الهی ۵۰ اکره ضرب (*Two tankas.*) *EDEN.* Æ ·7
287*b*	—	— Khúr-dád	ت]نکه اکبر شاهی شانزدهم حصه[ت	. . الهی خورداد (*Tanka.*) *EDEN.* Æ ·5

IV.—NÚR-AD-DÍN JAHÁNGÍR.

A.H. 1014—1037=A.D. 1605—1627.

No.	Mint.	Year: Month	Regnal year.	
				I.—AS GOVERNOR, WITH NAME SALÍM.
AR				SILVER.
288	Ahmad-ábád	Far-war-dín	2	Obv. مالك الملك [ك]سكه زد بر زر ضرب احمداباد Rev. سليم شاه سلطان ا]كبر شاه فروردين ٢ PL. VIII. *CUNNINGHAM.* AR ·75, Wt. 176
289	„	Khur-dád	2	Obv. as 288. Rev. as 288 : but خورداد ٢ *GIBBS.* AR ·75, Wt. 172

No.	Mint.	Year : Month.	Regnal year.	
				II.—AS EMPEROR. GOLD. I. — WITHOUT PORTRAITS, &c.
N				
290	Agrah	1015	—	Obv. مهر وماه نـــك ساحت نورا بر روى زرران ضرب ١٠١٩ اكره Rev. شـــاه ابن اكبر پـاد نـــكـــيـــر نور الدين جها شـــاه PL. VIII. *CUNNINGHAM.* N ·85, Wt. 202
291	Lahore	1015	1	Obv. الله لا اله الا مـــحـــمـــد رســـول الـــلـــه ضرب ١٠١٩ لاهور Rev. غـــازى جـهـانـكـيـر پـادشـاه مـــحـــمـــد نـــور الـــديـــن ١ سـنـه PL. VIII. *CUNNINGHAM.* N ·9, Wt. 202

No.	Mint.	Year; Month.	Regnal Year.	
AV 292	Lahore	1015	1	Obv. برنك مهر وماه نی زررا ساخت نورانی لاهور ضرب ١٠١٥ رو Rev. شاه ابن اكبر پاد نكير نور الدين جها شاه سنه ١ PL. VIII. *CUNNINGHAM.* AV ·9, Wt. 202
293 sq.	,,	,,	,,	As 292: but arrangement of obv. inscription slightly varied, and سنه omitted on rev. *CUNNINGHAM.* AV ·85, Wt. 201
294 sq.	,,	1016	3	As 293 : but ١٠١٦, and ٣ above اكبر PL. VIII. *BUSH.* AV ·9, Wt. 201
295	Agrah	1017	4	Obv. شاه كيتی اكره خسرو شهر سكه زد در ١٠١٧ Rev. as 292 : arrangement varied, year of reign at left side ٤ PL. VIII. *CUNNINGHAM.* AV 1·0, Wt. 211
296	,,	1018	5	As 295 : but ١٠١٨ and year of reign ٥ *STUBBS.* AV 1·0, Wt. 211

No.	Mint.	Year: Month.	Regnal Year.	
AV 297	Agrah	1020 Mihr	6	Obv., within scalloped border, ٦ مهر الهی ماه ۱۰۲۰ اکره ضرب Rev., within octagonal border, اکبر شاه نکیر شاه جها نور الدین PL. VIII. *CUNNINGHAM.* AV ·95, Wt. 168
298	,,	1021 Mihr	7	As 297: but eightfoil borders, and beneath obv., ۷ سنه ۱۰۲۱ AV ·95, Wt. 16
299	,,	1021 Dai	,,	Obv., within double dotted border, ماه دی الهی ضرب اکره ۱۰۲۱ ۷ شنه Rev. as 297, but leaf border. *GRANT.* AV ·9, Wt. 167
300	,,	1022 Ardi-bihist	,,	Obv., within double dotted border, ضرب اکره الهی ۸ بهست ۱۰۲۲ ماه اردی Rev. as 297, but double dotted border. PL. VIII. *CUNNINGHAM.* AV ·95, Wt. 168

No.	Mint.	Year: Month.	Regnal Year.	
AV 301	Agrah	1024 Ardibihist	10	As 300: but سنه ١٠ ١٠٢٤ *MARSDEN.* AV ·85, Wt. 168
302	Ajmír	1025	—	Obv. شاه دین پناه در اجمیر سکه ١٠٢٥ زد برز این Rev. نکیر ابن اکبر پادشاه جـهـا نـور الدین شاه PL. VIII. *CUNNINGHAM.* AV ·75, Wt. 168
303	Agrah	1025 Abán	11	Obv. ماه ابان الهی ضرب اکره سنه ١١ ١٠٢٤ Rev. as 297. AV ·75, Wt. 165
304	,,	1026 Mihr	12	Obv., within double dotted border, ماه مهر الهی ضرب اکره ١٢ سنه ١٠٢٦ Rev. as 297: but border of dots. AV ·9, Wt. 166

No.	Mint.	Year ; Month.	Regnal year.	
AV 305	Agrah	1028	14	Obv. بجهان بـــــت نـــشان زپنج نـــو تـــاهـــــست پنج مهر یش باد روان ســـکـــــه ایـــن ۱۴ Rev. جهانگیر ازشـــــاه بـــود دور زمان اوســـــــت در اکـــره زنـام فـــشـــــان زر نور ۱۰۲۸ PL. IX. (*Five mohrs.*) *I.O.C.* AV 1·45, Wt. 843
306	Ahmad-ábád	1028	,,	Obv. بــشرق وغـرب ۱۰۲۸ ۱۴ سنه جلوس سنه مهر احـمدابـاد Rev. الـهی تاجـهان جهانکیر شاه اکبر شاه باشـد روان بـاد PL. VIII. *MARSDEN.* AV ·85, Wt. 168
307	,,	1029	15	As 306 : but ۱۰۲۹ and ۱۵ *PRINSEP.* AV ·85, Wt. 168

No.	Mint.	Year : Month.	Regnal year.	
AV 308	Jahán-gírna-gar	[1033-4] Isfan-dár-miz	19	Obv. س]فندار[مز] الهٰ ماه ا جهانکیرنکر ١٩ ضرب Rev. as 297. Pl. VIII. *I.O.C.* AV ·6, Wt. 167
309	Patnah	1035 Bah-man	20	Obv. ماه بهمن الهٰ ١٠٣٥ ٢٠ پتنه ضرب Rev. as 297. *GRANT.* AV ·65, Wt. 167
310	Lahore	1036	22	Obv. سکه لاهور ی باد ابررو میمنت ٢٢ سنه Rev. شاه اکبر نور نکیر زنام شاه جها ١٠٣٦ Pl. VIII. AV ·85, Wt. 168
311	Burhán-púr	— Abán	—	Obv. ابان الهٰ برهانپور ب [ضر] Rev. as 297. Pl. VIII. *PRINSEP.* AV ·65, Wt. 167

No.	Mint.	Year.	Regnal year.	
N				**II.—With Portrait of Jahángír.**
312	—	1020	6	Obv. Bust of Jahángír, to left, radiate, wearing turban with egret (*jikkah*), and brocaded dress, and holding the Book in his hand: at left شبیه جهانکیر شاه اکبر شاه : at right, سنه ٦ جلوس Rev. Lion to left, surmounted by setting sun : beneath, ۱۰۲۰ سنه هجری Pl. IX. *MARSDEN.* *N* ·9, Wt. 168
313	—	„	„	Same : but lion to right. Pl. IX. *MARSDEN.* *N* ·9, Wt. 168
314	—	„	„	Same : but holding fruit in left hand in front of mouth, and resting right hand on left forearm ; lion to right. Pl. IX. *PAYNE KNIGHT.* *N* ·85, Wt. 168
315, 316	—	„	„	Same : but holding goblet in right hand in front of eyes, and the Book in left ; شش instead of ٦ ; lion to right. Pl. IX. *PAYNE KNIGHT.* *N* ·85, Wt. 169 (Ringed.) *MARSDEN.* *N* ·85
317 ¼	—	1021	7	Obv. Jahángír, nimbate, seated cross-legged on throne, head to left, and goblet in right hand. Rev., within ornamented eightfoil, نکیر شاه اکبر شاه جهـــــــا نور الدین ۱۰۲۱ ۷ Pl. IX. *N* ·45, Wt. 42

No.	Mint.	Year.	Regnal year.	
AV 318	Ajmír	1023	8	Obv. Jehángír, nimbate, seated cross-legged on throne, head to left, and goblet in right hand. بروی سکه زر داد چندین روز نو زینت شبیه شاه ۸ نور الدین جهانگیر ابن اکبر شاه Rev. In centre, lion to right surmounted by sun. Beneath, ۱۰۲۳ Around, زد بزر این سکه در اجمیر شاه دین پناه شاه نور الدین جهانگیر ابن اکبر پادشاه Pl. IX. *PAYNE KNIGHT.* AV ·75, Wt. 169
319, 320, 321	"	"	9	Obv. as 318, but At right : قضا بر سکه زر کرد تصویر شبیه حضرت شاه جهانگیر Rev. حروف جهانگیر والله اکبر اجمیر ۱۰۲۳ ضرب | Sun | معین یا ۹ سنه زروز ازل در عدد شد برابر Pl. IX. *I.O.C.* AV ·8, Wt. 168 *BIRD.* AV ·8, Wt. 169 *MARSDEN.* AV ·8, Wt. 168

No.	Mint.	Year.	Regnal year.	Zodiacal sign.	
					III.—WITH ZODIACAL SIGNS.
AV 322	Agrah	1028	14	Aries	Obv. Ram skipping, to left, surmounted by sun : beneath, ۱۴ سنه جلوس Rev. شاه اکبر از جهانگیر شاه یافت در اکره روی ۱۰۲۸ زر زیور PL. X. *MARSDEN.* AV ·85, Wt. 168
323	,,	1030	16	,,	As 322, but no inscription on obv. ; and ۱۰۳۰ and ۱۶ on rev. PL. X. *MARSDEN.* AV ·8, Wt. 168
324, 325, 326	,,	1028	14	Taurus	Obv. Humped bull, standing, to left, surrounded by solar rays. Rev. شاه اکبر از جهانگیر شاه سکه ۱۰۲۸ اکره داد زینت زر ۱۴ PL. X. *I.O.C.* AV ·85, Wt. 166 PL. X. *MARSDEN.* AV ·8, Wt. 168 AV ·85, Wt. 165

No.	Mint.	Year.	Regnal year.	Zodiacal sign.	
AV 327, 328	Agrah	1030	16	Taurus	Obv. as 324 : but bull to right. Rev. as 322 : but years ١٠٣٠ and ١٦ AV ·85, Wt. 168 Pl. X. *MARSDEN.* AV ·8, Wt. 163
329	„	1032	18	„	As 327 : but years ١٠٣٢ and ١٨ *PAYNE KNIGHT.* AV ·85, Wt. 168
330	„	1029	15	Gemini	Obv. Two naked male figures embracing, surrounded by solar rays. Rev. as 322, but ١٠٢٩ and ١٥ *PAYNE KNIGHT.* AV ·8, Wt. 168
331	„	1031	16	„	As 330 : but twins smaller, differently posed, and brandishing one a mace, the other a pair of weights (?) ; on reverse, ١٠٣١ and ١٦ Pl. X. *I.O.C.* AV ·8, Wt. 168
332	„	1032	18	„	As 330 : but ١٠٣٢ and ١٨ Pl. X. *GEORGE III. R.* AV ·8, Wt. 168
333	„	1033	19	„	As 330 : but ١٠٣٣ and ١٩ *MARSDEN.* AV ·8, Wt. 168
333*a* 333*b*	„	1029	15	Cancer	Obv. Crab, erect, surmounted by sun ; five stars in field, and six on back of crab ; beneath, ١٥ Rev. as 322 : but ١٠٢٩ Pl. X. *PAYNE KNIGHT* AV ·8, Wt. 168 *MARSDEN.* AV ·8, Wt. 168

No.	Mint.	Year.	Regnal year.	Zodiacal sign.	
AV 333c	Agrah	1030	16	Cancer	As 333*a*: but nothing beneath obv. and no pellets on back of crab; on rev., years ١٠٣٠ and ١٦; اكبر above شاه. (Rude work.*) Pl. X. AV ·8, Wt. 162
334	,,	1028	14	Leo	Obv. Lion passant to right, surrounded by solar rays; in front سنه ١٤ Rev. as 322: but ١٠٢٨ Pl. X. *MARSDEN.* AV ·85, Wt. 168
335	,,	1029	15	,,	As 334: but سنه ١٥, and [١]٠٢٩ *CUNNINGHAM.* AV .75, Wt. 168
336	,,	1031	17	,,	As 334: but inscription on obv. effaced, and ١٠٣١ and ١٧ on rev. *PAYNE KNIGHT.* AV ·8, Wt. 168
337	,,	1031	17	,,	As 334: but lion to *left*, no inscription on obv.; ١٠٣١ and ١٧ on rev. Pl. X. *PAYNE KNIGHT.* AV ·8, Wt. 168

* Three of these Zodiacal mohrs exhibit very rude workmanship, 333[c], 339 and 346[a]: all these are of the year 1030, and 16 of reign, and all arrange the top of reverse شاه اكبر instead of اكبر شاه

No.	Mint.	Year.	Regnal year.	Zodiacal sign.	
AV 338	Agrah	1028	14	Virgo	Obv. Winged woman, standing, back forwards, face to left, surrounded by solar rays, ear of corn in right hand, left arm raised: at left, ۱۴ سنه Rev. as 322: but ۱۰۲۸ *I.O.C.* AV ·8, Wt. 168
339	,,	1030	16	,,	Obv. Woman squatting, with long braid of hair hanging down her back; bud in right hand; solar rays on each side. Rev. as 322: but ۱۰۳۰ and ۱۶; and اکبر above شاه (Rude work.) Pl. X. *CRACHERODE.* AV ·8, Wt. 168
340	,,	1031	16	,,	Obv. Woman with pitcher on head supported by one hand, numerous dots in field, border of solar rays. Rev. as 322: but ۱۰۳۱ and ۱۶ Pl. X. *PAYNE KNIGHT.* AV ·85, Wt. 167
341	,,	1033	19	,,	As 339: but ۱۰۳۳ and ۱۹ Pl. X. *PAYNE KNIGHT.* AV ·8, Wt. 167
342	,,	1028	14	Libra	Obv. Scales and weights, with solar rays round beam. Rev. as 324. *I.O.C.* AV ·8, Wt. 167

No.	Mint.	Year.	Regnal year.	Zodiacal sign.	
AV 343	Agrah	1030	16	Libra	Obv. as 342 : Rev. as 322, but ١٠٣٠ and ١٦ Pl. X. *GEORGE III. R.* AV ·85, Wt. 169
344	,,	1032	18	,,	As 343 : but ١٠٣٢ and ١٨ *MARSDEN.* AV ·85, Wt. 169
345	,,	1033	19	,,	As 343 : but ١٠٣٣ and ١٩ *CUNNINGHAM.* AV ·8, Wt. 169
346	,,	1030	—	Scorpio	Obv. Scorpion surrounded by solar rays. Rev. as 322 : but ١٠٣٠ Pl. X. *PAYNE KNIGHT.* AV ·8, Wt. 169
346*a*	,,	,,	[1]6	,,	As 346 : but solar rays on back only, scorpion varied ; and on rev., اکبر above شاه, ١٠٣٠ and ١٦ (Rude work.) Pl. X. *MARSDEN.* AV ·8, Wt. 164
347	,,	1032	17	,,	As 346 : but ١٠٣٢ and ١٧ *GEORGE III. R.* AV ·8, Wt. 168
348	,,	1031	16	Sagittarius	Obv. Centaur with stretched bow, aiming backwards, surrounded by solar rays. Rev. as 322 : but ١٠٣١ and ١٦ Pl. X. *MARSDEN.* AV ·8, Wt. 168
349	,,	1032	17	,,	As 348 : but ١٠٣٢ and ١٧ *MARSDEN.* AV ·8, Wt. 167

No.	Mint.	Year.	Regnal year.	Zodiacal sign.	
AV 350	Agrah	1028	14	Capricornus	Obv. Mythical monster, with forepart of goat and tail of fish, surrounded by solar rays. Rev. as 324. Pl. X. *LADY FRERE.* AV ·85, Wt. 168
351	,,	1029	14	,,	Obv. as 350. Rev. as 322 : but ١٠٢٩ and ١٤ *CUNNINGHAM.* AV ·75, Wt. 168
352	,,	1030	—	,,	As 351 : but ١٠٣٠ *I.O.C.* AV ·8, Wt. 167
353	,,	1031	16	,,	As 351 : but ١٠٣١ and ١٦ Pl. X. *CUNNINGHAM.* AV ·85, Wt. 168
354	,,	1032	17	,,	As 351 : but ١٠٣٢ and ١٧ *MARSDEN.* AV ·8, Wt. 168
355	,,	1031	16	Aquarius	Obv. Man with pitcher on right shoulder, surrounded by solar rays. Rev. as 322 : but ١٠٣١ and ١٦ Pl. X. *MARSDEN.* AV ·85, Wt. 167
356	,,	1032	18	,,	Obv. Man seated, with pitcher over shoulder, whence pours a stream of water. Rev. as 322 : but ١٠٣٢ and ١٨ Pl. X. (Rude work.) *MARSDEN.* AV ·85, Wt. 169

No.	Mint.	Year.	Regnal year.	Zodiacal sign.	
AV 357	Ahmad-ábád	—	—	Aquarius	Obv. Water-bottle, surrounded by solar rays. Rev. پادشاه اکبر نور الدين جهانگير ابن شاه جنانك ۱۰۸ ؟ احمداباد سكه زد در PL. X. AV ·8, Wt. 167
358	Agrah	1028	13	Pisces	Obv. Two fish, heads to tails, surrounded by solar rays. Rev. as 322 : but ۱۰۲۸ and ۱۳ PL. X. AV ·85, Wt. 168
359	,,	1031	17	,,	As 358 : but ۱۰۳۱ and ۱۷ *I.O.C.* AV ·8, Wt. 168
360	,,	1033	18	,,	As 358 : but ۱۰۳۳ and ۱۸ *MARSDEN.* AV ·8, Wt. 168

SILVER.

I.—With Zodiacal Signs.

No.	Mint.	Year.	Regnal year.	Zodiacal sign.	
Æ 361- 363	Ahmad- ábád	1027	13	Aries	Obv. Ram as 322, but سنه جلوس ١٣ Rev. پادشاه اکبر ١٠٢٧ جهانگیر پادشاه ب ضر احمداباد *MARSDEN.* Æ ·8, Wt. 176 Pl. XI. *BANKS.* Æ ·8, Wt. 174 *MARSDEN.* Æ ·8, Wt. 175
364, 365	,,	,,	,,	Taurus	Obv. Forepart of bull to right, issuing from clouds, under sun; beneath, سنه جلوس ١٣ Rev. as 361. Pl. XI. *EDEN.* Æ ·8, Wt. 175 *MARSDEN.* Æ ·8, Wt. 174
366	Agrah	1029	15	,,	Obv. Humped bull, standing to left, as 324, surrounded by rays. Rev. as 322, but years ١٠٢٩ and ١٥ [Similar to mohr (as 324), but struck in silver.] Æ ·8, Wt. 175

No.	Mint.	Year.	Regnal year.	Zodiacal sign.	
Æ 367	Agrah	1033	19	Gemini	Obv. Twins as gold 330, rev. as 322; but ١٠٣٣ and ١٩. (A mohr struck in silver). Æ ·85. Wt. 172
368, 369	Ahmad-ábád	1027	13	,,	Obv. Twins embracing, seated, surrounded by solar rays (different design from gold); beneath, سنه ١٣ Rev. as 361. (Year obscure.) *MARSDEN.* Æ ·75, Wt. 174 Pl. XI. Æ ·8, Wt. 177
370, 371	,,	,,	,,	Cancer	Obv. Crab, surmounted by sun, as 333*a*; but no stars on back of crab. Beneath, سنه ١٣ Rev. اکبر شهنشاه نکیر شاه جها را داد زیور احمداباد زر ١٠٢٧ Pl. XI. *THOMAS.* Æ ·85, Wt. 176 *MARSDEN.* Æ ·85, Wt. 171
372, 373	,,	,,	,,	Leo	Obv. Lion passant to left, stars on body; behind, sun, as 337; beneath, سنه جلوس ١٣ Rev. as 370. *MARSDEN.* Æ ·85, Wt. 174 *PAYNE KNIGHT.* Æ ·85, Wt. 170

No.	Mint.	Year.	Regnal year.	Zodiacal sign.	
Æ 374	Ahmad-ábád	1027	—	Scorpio	Scorpion, no sun. Rev. as 370. Pl. XI. *MARSDEN.* Æ ·95. Wt. 168
375	Agrah	1029	14	Capricornus	Mythical goat, as 351. (A mohr struck in silver.) *THOMAS.* Æ ·8, Wt. 176

No.	Mint.	Year.	Regnal year.	Zodiacal sign.	
AV					**IMITATIONS OF ZODIACAL ISSUES.**
					GOLD.
376	Agrah	1028	—	Cancer	Obv. Crab surrounded by rays; no inscription. Rev. as 322: ١٠٢٨ PL. XI. *MARSDEN.* AV ·85, Wt. 168
377, 377*a*	„	1032	—	Leo	Obv. Lion, as 334; no inscription. Rev. as 322: but ١٠٣٢ PL. XI. *MARSDEN.* AV ·85, Wt. 165 *I.O.C.* AV ·85, Wt. 165
378	„	1028	14	Virgo	Obv. Winged woman, as 339: but سنه ١٤ Rev. as 322: but ١٠٢٨ PL. XI. *MARSDEN.* AV ·85, Wt. 167
379	„	1033	17	„	Obv. Winged woman dancing, holding flower in left hand. Rev. as 32 . ١٠٣٣ and ١٧ PL. XI. *MARSDEN.* AV ·85, Wt. 167

No.	Mint.	Year.	Regnal year.	Zodiacal sign.	
AV 380	Agrah	1028	12	Scorpio	Obv. Scorpion, as 346. Rev. as 322: ١٠٢٨ and ١٢ PL. XI. *PAYNE KNIGHT.* AV ·8, Wt. 168
381	„	1033	17	Sagittarius	Obv. Centaur, as 348. Rev. as 322: ١٠٣٣ and ١١٧ (*sic*) PL. XI. *PAYNE KNIGHT.* AV ·8, Wt. 169
382	„	1031	16	Capricornus	Obv. Mythical goat, as 350. Rev. as 322: ١٠٣١ and ١٦ PL. XI. *MARSDEN.* AV ·85, Wt. 168
383	„	1028	13	Aquarius	Obv. Man seated, as 356. Rev. as 322: ١٠٢٨ and ١٣ PL. XI. AV ·8, Wt. 168
384	„	„	„	Pisces	Obv. Two fish, as 358. Rev. as 322: ١٠٢٨ and ١٣ PL. XI. AV ·8, Wt. 168

SILVER.

No.	Mint.	Year.	Regnal year.	Zodiacal sign.	
AR 385	Ahmadábád	1027	13	Leo	As 372. PL. XI. *THOMAS.* AR ·85, Wt. 176

No.	Mint.	Year.	Regnal year.	Zodiacal sign.	
AR					**IMITATION HALF-RUPEES.** *(Struck from dies similar to, and often identical with, those of the imitation gold mohrs.)*
386	Agrah	1028	14	Aries	As 322. Pl. XI. *EDEN.* AR ·8, Wt. 89
387	,,	,,	,,	Taurus	As 324. Pl. XI. *THOMAS.* AR ·8, Wt. 89
388, 389	,,	1029	15	Gemini	As 330, but ١٠٢٩ and ١٥ Pl. XI. *CRACHERODE.* AR ·8, Wt. 89 *MARSDEN.* AR ·8, Wt. 89
390	,,	1031	17	Cancer	As 322: no inscr. on obv., but eleven stars; and years ١٠٣١ and ١٧ on rev. Pl. XI. *MARSDEN.* AR ·8, Wt. 89
391	,,	1029	16	Leo	As 334: but ١٦ and ١٠٢٩ Pl. XI. AR ·8, Wt. 89
392	,,	1033	—	,,	As 334: but no inscr. on obv., and ١٠٣٣ and ١٠١ on rev. *MARSDEN.* AR ·75, Wt. 75 (This is more ancient than the other half-rupees in this series.)

No.	Mint.	Year.	Regnal year.	Zodiacal sign.	
393, 394	Agrah	1033	17	Virgo	Dancing girl, as 379. Pl. XI. *MARSDEN.* Æ ·8, Wt. 89 Æ ·8, Wt. 89
395	„	1032	18	Libra	As 344. Pl. XI. Æ ·8, Wt. 89
396	„	1031	17	„	As 344: but ١٠٣١ and ١٧ (Struck in copper.) *FREUDENTHAL.* Æ ·85
397	„	1028	12	Scorpio	As 380. Pl. XI. *CRACHERODE.* Æ ·8, Wt. 89
398	„	1033	17	Sagittarius	As 381. Pl. XI. *CRACHERODE.* Æ ·8, Wt. 89
399	„	„	18	Capricornus	As 351: but ١٠٣٣ and ١٨ Pl. XI. *CRACHERODE.* Æ ·8, Wt. 89
400	„	1028	13	Aquarius	As 383. Pl. XI. *MARSDEN.* Æ ·8, Wt. 89
401	„	„	„	Pisces	As 384. Pl. XI. *MARSDEN.* Æ ·8, Wt. 89

No.	Mint.	Year.	Regnal year.	
				II.—WITHOUT ZODIACAL SIGNS.
Æ 402	Agrah	1014	1	Obv. نك مهر وماه ساخت نورا بر روی زررانی ۱۰۱۴ ضرب اکره Rev. شاه ابن اکبر پاد نکیر نور الدین جها شاه ۱ PL. XII. *CUNNINGHAM.* Æ ·85, Wt. 212
403	,,	,,	,,	Obv. الله لا اله الا محمد رسول الله ۱۰۱۴ ضرب اکره Rev. غازی جهانکیر پادشاه محمد نور الدین ۱ سنه PL. XII. *CUNNINGHAM.* Æ ·85, Wt. 210

No.	Mint.	Year; Month.	Regnal year.	
AR 404	Akbar-nagar	1014	—	As 402 : but ضرب اکبرنگر ١٠١٤, and no regnal year. Pl. XII. *PANJ. ARCH. SURV.* AR ·9, Wt. 212
405	Kábul	„	1	As 403 : but ضرب کابل ١٠١٤ Pl. XII. *CUNNINGHAM.* AR ·7, Wt. 105
406	„	1015	„	As 405 : but ١٠١٥ „ AR ·75, Wt. 106
407	„	1015 Amar-dád	1	As 403 : but ضرب کابل ١٠١٤ and نور الدین ١٠١٥ سنه ١ امرداد *CUNNINGHAM.* AR ·75, Wt. 105
408	Agrah	1015	1	As 403 : but ١٠١٥ (still سنه ١) *CUNNINGHAM.* AR ·8, Wt. 211
409	„	„	2	As 402 : but ١٠١٥ and ٢ *GRANT.* AR ·85, Wt. 211
410	Akbar-nagar	„	1	As 402 : but ضرب اکبرنگر ١٠١٥, regnal year, شاه *GRANT.* AR .85, Wt. 212
411	Ahmad-ábád	„	2	As 403 : but ضرب احمداباد ١٠١٥ ; and ٢ on rev. Pl. XII. *GRANT.* AR .8, Wt. 212
412	Akbar-nagar	„	—	As 402 : but ضرب اکبرنگر ١٠١٥, no regnal year. *CUNNINGHAM.* AR ·85, Wt. 212

No.	Mint.	Year: Month.	Regnal year.	
Æ 413	Patnah	1015 Isfandármiz	2	As 403 : but ضرب پتنه ۱۰۱۵ and ۲ Pl. XII. *CUNNINGHAM.* Æ ·85, Wt. 212
414	Lahore	1015	1	Obv. بونك مهر وماه نی زر را ساخت نورا نی ضرب لاهور ۱۰۱۵ رو Rev. as 402 : but ۱ سنه beneath شاه Pl. XII. *GRANT.* Æ ·95, Wt. 208
415 sq.	"	"	2	Obv. بونك مهر وماه نی ساخت نورا نی ۱۰۱۵ لاهور رو زر را ضرب Rev. as 402 : but ۲ over اکبر Pl. XII. *GRANT.* Æ ·9, Wt. 208
416 sq.	"	"	2	As 403 : but on obv. ضرب ۱۰۱۵ لاهور on rev. سنه ۲ next to غازی at top. *THOMAS.* Æ ·85, Wt. 210
417	Ahmad-ábád	1016	2	As 403 : but احمداباد ۱۰۱۶, and سنه ۲ *CUNNINGHAM.* Æ ·8, Wt. 210
418, 419	Akbar-nagar	"	—	As 402 : but ضرب اکبرنکر ۱۰۱۶, no regnal year. *GRANT.* Æ ·85, Wt. 212 " Æ ·85, Wt. 211

No.	Mint.	Year.	Regnal year.	
Æ 420 sq.	Lahore	1016	2	As 403 : but ١٠١٦ ضرب لاهور ; and in top line of rev. ٢ سنه *PANJ. ARCH. SURV.* Æ ·9, Wt. 211
421, 422 sq.	"	"	3	As 415 : but ١٠١٦ on obv., and ٣ over اكبر on rev. *GRANT.* Æ ·85, Wt. 205 Æ ·85, Wt. 209
423	Agrah	1017	4	Obv. پناه گیتی اکره خسرو شهر سکه زد در ١٠١٧ Rev. as 402, but differently divided ; regnal year, ۴ *CUNNINGHAM.* Æ 1·0, Wt. 216
424	Lahore	"	5	Obv. دور تا فلك بود در باد روان بدهر ٥ Rev. نگير جها بنام شاه ١٠١٧ سکه لاهور PL. XII. *GRANT.* Æ 1·0, Wt. 216

No.	Mint.	Year.	Regnal year.	
Æ 425	Ahmad-ábád	1018	5	Obv. الله دـــتـــب از عنایـا ابـاد ا]حـمـد سـكـه زد در ۱۰۱۸ Rev. as 402 : differently divided, regnal year ٥ Pl. XII. *CUNNINGHAM.* Æ ·9, Wt. 221
426, 427	Agrah	,,	,,	As 423 : but ۱۰۱۸ and ٩ *CUNNINGHAM.* Æ 1·1, Wt. 215 *PANJ. ARCH. SURV.* Æ 1·05, Wt. 220
428	Patnah	,,	,,	As 403 : but on obv. ضرب پتنه ۱۰۱۸ and on rev. سنه ٩ *I.O.C.* Æ ·85, Wt. 211
429	Lahore	,,	4	As 424 : but ۱۰۱۸ on rev.; regnal year ۴ on obv. *CUNNINGHAM.* Æ 1·0, Wt. 219
430, 431	,,	,,	5	,, ,, regnal year ٥ on obv. *GRANT.* Æ ·95, Wt. 217 *PANJ. ARCH. SURV.* Æ ·95, Wt. 220

No.	Mint.	Year: Month.	Regnal year.	
AR 432 sq.	Agrah	1019 Isfan-dár-miz	5	Obv., within highly ornamented borders. زد بر زر در اکــره را ایــن سکه در اسفنـدارمز ٥ Rev., within borders as obv., شاه نکیر ابن اکبر جـــهـــا زمـــان شـــاه شهنشاه ١٠١٩ Pl. XII. *THOMAS.* AR ·9, Wt. 220
433	Kash-mír	1019	—	As 402: but ضرب کشمیر ١٠١٩ Pl. XII. *GRANT.* AR ·85, Wt. 210
434	Lahore	,,	5	As 424: but ١٠١٩ and ٥ *GRANT.* AR ·9, Wt. 220
435, 436 sq.	,,	,,	,,	As 432: but لاهور and امر after شهنشاه ٥ *CUNNINGHAM.* AR ·8, Wt. 219 *PANJ. ARCH. SERV.* AR ·85, Wt. 220

No.	Mint.	Year: Month.	Regnal year.	
Æ 437, 438	Lahore	1019 Bahman	5	Obv. زر لاهور شـــــد چون مه انور ۵ در ماه بهمن Rev. ابن اکبر شاه نـــکـــیـــر نور الدین جها شـــــاه بدور ۱۰۱۹ Border of wreath on each side. *EDEN.* Æ 1·05, Wt. 216 Pl. XII. *PANJ. ARCH. SURV.* Æ 1·05, Wt. 220
438*a*	—	1019	,,	As 403 : but mint obliterated, year .. ۱۹ regnal year ۵ سنه *PANJ. ARCH. SURV.* Æ ·8, Wt. 208
439 sq.	Agrah	1020 Abán	6	Obv., within cruciform borders, ٦ ابان الهی اکره ماه ـــبـــ ضر ۱۰۲۰ Rev., within circle, اکبر شاه نکیر شاه جـــهـــا نور الدین Pl. XII. *THOMAS.* Æ ·85, Wt. 175

No.	Mint.	Year: Month.	Regnal year.	
Æ 440	Kanda- hár	1020	6	As 403 : but ... ۱۰۲۰ ضرب قند ; and on rev. ٦ over نور Pl. XIII. *GRANT.* Æ ·85, Wt. 211
441 sq.	Agrah	1021 Isfan- dár- miz	,,	Obv., within wavy border, مز ماه سفندار الهی ۱۰۲۱ ب سنه ٦ ضز اکره Rev. as 439, within octagon. Pl. XIII. *EDEN.* ·9, Wt. 173
442 sq.	,,	1021 Ardi- bihist	7	Obv., within wavy border, ٧ بهست ماه اردی الهی ضرب اکره ۱۰۲۱ سنه Rev. as 439. Pl. XIII. *THOMAS.* Æ ·8, Wt. 176
443	Patnah	1021 Shah- riwar	,,	Obv. ماه شهریور الهی ٧ پتنه ۱۰۲۱ ضرب Rev. as 439 : differently divided. Æ ·8, Wt. 175
444	Dehlí	1021 Mihr	,,	Obv. ماه مهر الهی ۱۰۲۱ ٧ ضرب دهلی سنه Rev. as 439. Pl. XIII. *GORDON.* Æ ·75, Wt. 174

No.	Mint.	Year: Month.	Regnal year.	
Æ 445, 446	Kanda-hár	1021	7	As 414 : but قندهار (with ١٠٢١ above) and ٧ over نور PL. XIII. *PANJ. ARCH. SURV.* Æ ·8, Wt. 209 „ „ Æ ·85, Wt. 209
447	Lahore	[„] Far-war-dín	„	Obv. ماه فروردین الهی لاهور ٧ ضرب Rev. as 439. PL. XIII. Æ ·9, Wt. 175
448	„	1021 Amar-dád	„	As 447 : but month امرداد *EDEN.* Æ ·9, Wt. 174
449	„	1021 Isfan-dár-miz	„	As 447 : but month اسفندارمز *PLAYFAIR.* Æ ·85, Wt. 175
450	Kanda-hár	1022	8	As 402 : but ضر[ب] قندهار (with ١٠٢٢ above) ; and ٨ over نور *GRANT.* Æ ·85, Wt. 210
451	„	1023 Ardi-bihist	„	Obv., within circle, بهشت ماه اردی الهی ضرب قندهار سنه ٨ ١٠٢٣ Rev. as 439. PL. XIII. *THOMAS.* Æ ·9, Wt. 175

No.	Mint.	Year: Month.	Regnal year.	
Æ 452	Lahore	— Dai	8	Obv. ماه دي الهی ضرب لاهور ۸ Rev. as 439. GRANT. Æ ·85, Wt. 175
453	Agrah	1023 Khúrdád	9	Obv. ماه خورداد الهی ضرب اکره ۹ سنه ۱۰۲۳ Rev. as 439. THOMAS. Æ ·9, Wt. 177
454	Kandahár	1023 Tír	,,	As 451 : but month تیر and regnal year ۹ EDEN. Æ ·85, Wt. 178
455	Lahore	— Ardibihist	,,	Obv. بهست ماه اردی الهی ضرب لاهور ۹ Rev. as 439. Pl. XIII. GRANT. Æ ·85, Wt. 176
456	,,	— Tír	,,	As 455 : but month تیر GRANT. Æ ·85, Wt. 176
457	,,	— Dai	10	As 455 : but month دی ; regnal year ۱۰ CUNNINGHAM. Æ ·75, Wt. 175

No.	Mint.	Year: Month.	Regnal year.	
Æ 458, 459 sq.	Agrah	1025 Shahriwar	11	Obv., within square border, ماه شهريور الهی ضرب اکره سنه ١١ ١٠٢٥ Rev. as 439, border as obv. *CUNNINGHAM.* Æ ·75, Wt. 174 *I.O.C.* Æ ·75, Wt. 176
460	Ajmír	1025	,,	Obv. جهان اجمير فيروز در كشت ١٠٢٥ سكه زر Rev. اكبر شاه نكير شاه جها زنور نام سنه ١١ Pl. XIII. *THEOBALD.* Æ ·9, Wt. 177
461	Ahmad-ábád	1025 Abán	—	Obv. م]اه ابان الهی مزين باد ا]حمد اباد ضرب Rev. . . . شا نور الدين جها ن]كير ١٠٢٥ Pl. XIII. *GRANT.* Æ ·3, Wt. 175

No.	Mint.	Year: Month.	Regnal year.	
AR 462	Kash- mír	1025	—	Obv. [بــر]نــك شاخت انور روی زر را نـ ضرب کشمیر ۱۰۲۵ Rev. as 402. *CUNNINGHAM.* AR ·85, Wt. 205
463	Lahore	,,	11	Obv. همیشه ل باد ابرو ۱۰۲۵ ســکــه لاهــور Rev. زنام شــــاه جهانگیر شاه اکــبــر ۱۱ نــور سنه PL. XIII. *CUNNINGHAM.* AR ·85, Wt. 174
464 sq.	Agrah	1026 Dai	11	Obv. ماه دی الهی ضرب اکره ۱۱ ســنــه ۱۰۲۶ Rev. as 439. *THOMAS.* AR ·75, Wt. 175
465 sq.	,,	1026 Tír	12	As 464 : but regnal year ۱۲, month تیر *EDEN.* AR ·75, Wt. 175
466	Ahmad- ábád	1026 Azur	—	As 461 : but month اذر and year ۱۰۲۶ *CUNNINGHAM* AR ·8, Wt. 177

No.	Mint.	Year: Month.	Regnal year.	
AR 467	Patnah	1026 Shahriwar	12	Obv. ماه شهریور الهی ۱۲ پتنه ۱۰۲۶ ضرب Rev. شاه اکبر شاه نکیر نور الدین جها Pl. XIII. AR ·7, Wt. 175
468	Tattah	1026 Khúrdád	,,	Obv. ۱۲ ماه خورداد الهی ضرب تته ۱۰۲۶ Pl. XIII. *PANJ. ARCH. SURV.* AR ·8, Wt. 176
469	Lahore	1026	,,	As 463 : but ۱۰۲۶ and ۱۲ *CUNNINGHAM.* AR ·85, Wt. 175
470, 471	Kandahár	,,	,,	Obv. ۱۰۲۶ سکه قندهار شد دلخواه Rev. شاه اکبر ۱۲ شاه سنه نکیر از جها *THOMAS.* AR ·8, Wt. 174 *GOVT. OF INDIA.* AR ·85, Wt. 175

No.	Mint.	Year: Month.	Regnal year.	
AR 472	Kanda- hár	1027	13	As 470: but ۱۰۲۷ and ۱۳ PL. XIII. *PRINSEP.* AR ·8, Wt. 174
473	Kábul	,, Shah- riwar	,,?	Obv. ماه شهرور الهی کابل ۱۲ (or ۱۳) Rev. پادشاه اکبر نکیر ابن ۱۰۲۷ جها نو]ر الدین شاه PL. XIII. *CUNNINGHAM.* AR ·85, Wt. 176
474 sq.	Agrah	1027 Abán	13	Obv. ماه ابان الهی ضرب اکره ۱۳ سنه ۱۰۲۷ Rev. as 439. *CUNNINGHAM,* AR ·75, Wt. 174
475	Ahmad- ábád	1027	,,	Obv. اله بت از عنایا احمداباد در زد سکه ۱۰۲۷ Rev. as 402: but ۱۳ سنه PL. XIV. *CUNNINGHAM.* AR ·85, Wt. 174

No.	Mint.	Year: Month.	Regnal year.	
AR 476	Patnah	1027 Abán	13	Obv. ماه ابان الهی ١٣ ضرب ١٠٢٧ پتنه Rev. as 439. *CUNNINGHAM.* AR ·8, Wt. 17
477	Lahore	1027	,,	As 463: but [١٠]٢٧ and ١٣ *GORDON.* AR ·85, Wt. 175
478	Ahmad-ábád	1028	—	As 475: but ١٠٢٨ and regnal year nearly obliterated [١٣] *GIBBS.* AR ·85, Wt. 175
479	Patnah	1028 Khúr-dád	14	Obv. ماه خورداد الهی ١٤ پتنه ١٠٢٨ ضرب Rev. as 439. *PRINSEP.* AR ·65, Wt. 175
480	,,	1028 Amar-dád	,,	Same as 479: but month امرداد AR ·65, Wt. 176
481, 482	Kanda-hár	1028	,,	As 470: but ١٠٢٨ and ١٤ *GRANT.* AR ·85, Wt. 174 AR ·8, Wt. 172
483	Ahmad-ábád	1029	,,	As 475: but ١٠٢٩ and ١٤ AR ·85, Wt. 176

No.	Mint.	Year: Month.	Regnal year.	
Æ 484	Ahmad-ábád	1029	15	As 475: but ١٠٢٩ and ١٥ *CUNNINGHAM.* Æ ·8, Wt. 174
485	Patnah	1029 Shah riwar	,,	Obv. ماه شهریور الهی ١٥ پتنه ١٠٢٩ ضرب Rev. as 439. Æ ·7, Wt. 175
486	Kanda-hár	1029	14	As 470: but ١٠٢٩ and سنه ١٤ *I.O.C.* Æ ·75, Wt. 171
487	,,	,,	15	,, ,, سنه ١٥ *GRANT.* Æ ·8, Wt. 176
488	Lahore	,,	,,	Obv. لاهور سکه بر روی میمنت باد ١٠٢٩ Rev. نور اکبر جهانگیر شاه شاه زنام ١٥ سنه Pl. XIV. Æ ·7, Wt. 175

No.	Mint.	Year: Month.	Regnal year.	
Æ 489	Patnah	1030 Shah-riwar	16	Obv. ماه شهریور الهی ١٦ پتنه ١٠٣٠ ضرب Rev. as 439. Æ ·75, Wt. 175
490	Kanda-hár	1030	15	As 470: but ١٠٣٠ and ١٥ سنه Æ ·75, Wt. 176
491	Lahore	,,	16	Obv. سکه لاهوری باد ابررو میمنت ١٦ سنه Rev. شاه اکبر نور نکیر زنام شاه جها ١٠٣٠ Pl. XIV. *GRANT.* Æ ·85, Wt. 174
492, 493	Ahmad-ábád	1031	16	As 475: but ١٠٣١ and ١٦ سنه *GRANT.* Æ ·85, Wt. 176 Æ ·85, Wt. 176
494	Lahore	,,	,,	As 491: but ١٠٣١ and ١٦ سنه *CUNNINGHAM.* Æ ·85, Wt. 176
495	,,	,,	17	As 491: but ١٠٣١ and ١٧ سنه *THOMAS.* Æ ·85, Wt. 176

No.	Mint.	Year: Month.	Regnal year.	
Æ 496	Lahore	1032	17	As 491 : but سنه (١٧) and ١٠٣٢ *GRANT.* Æ ·85, Wt. 176
497	Patnah	1033 Isfan-dár-miz	18	Obv. ماه اسفندارمز الهی ١٨ پتنه ١٠٣٣ ضرب Rev. as 439. *PRINSEP.* Æ ·75, Wt. 172
498	Súrat	1033	„	Obv. ما]ه ١٨ ر سورت ضرب Rev. ن]ور الدین جهـا نگیر پادشا[ه ١٠٣٣ Pl. XIV. *GRANT.* Æ ·8, Wt. 176
499	Lahore	1033	„	As 491 : but سنه (١٨) and ١٠٣٣ *CUNNINGHAM.* Æ ·8, Wt. 176
500	„	1034	19	As 491 : but سنه (١٩) and ١٠٣٤ *CUNNINGHAM.* Æ ·8, Wt. 176

No.	Mint.	Year: Month.	Regnal year.	
Æ 501	Jahán-gír-nagar	— Shah-riwar	19	Obv. ماه شهریور الهی ...انکیرنکر ۱۹ ضرب Rev. اکبر شاه نکیر شاه جہا نور الدین Pl. XIV. *PRINSEP.* Æ ·7, Wt. 175
502	Agrah	1035	21	Obv. زر زیور ی در اکره رو یافت ۱۰۳۵ Rev. شاه نکیر شاه اکبر جہا از ۲۱ *PRINSEP.* Æ ·85, Wt. 174
503	Ahmad-ábád	— Abán	,,	Obv. ماه] ابان الهی ا]حمداباد ۲۱ ... Rev. as 501. *MARSDEN.* Æ ·75, Wt. 173
504	Lahore	1035	21	As 491: but سنه ۲۱ and ۱۰۳۵ *CUNNINGHAM.* Æ ·85, Wt. 175
505	,,	1036	,,	As 491: but سنه ۲۱ and ۱۰۳۶ *PANJ. ARCH. SURV.* Æ ·85, Wt. 176

No.	Mint.	Year: Month.	Regnal year.	
AR 506	Lahore	1036	22	٢٢ As 491 : but سنه and ١٠٣٦ *EDEN.* AR ·9, Wt. 175
507	Patnah	1036 Far-war-dín	,,	Obv. ماه فروردين الهى ١٠٣٦ ٢٢ پتنه ضرب Rev. as 439: no borders; differently arranged. AR ·75, Wt. 175
508	Lahore	1037	,,	٢٢ As 491 : but سنه and ١٠٣٧ *GRANT.* AR ·85, Wt. 175
509	Akbar-nagar	— Far-war-dín	—	As 476 : but (*sic*) فروردى and اكبرنكر ; instead of year, a dagger. *EDEN.* AR ·75, Wt. 176
510	Jahán-gírna-gar	— Mihr	20?	Obv. ماه مهر الهى ٢٠ (؟) جهانكيرنكر سنه ضرب Rev. as 439. Pl. XIV. *I.O.C.* AR ·65, Wt. 170
511	Kanda-hár	10*xx* Far-war-dín	—	Obv. ماه فروردى (*sic*) الهى ضرب قندهار سنه ١٠٠ (?) Rev. as 439. *EDEN.* AR ·85, Wt. 174

No.	Mint.	Year.	Regnal year.	
				COPPER.
Æ 512	Agrah	1021	7	Obv. اکره ب ضر ۷ سنه Rev. روان ۱۰۲۱ سنه Pl. XIV. *PLAYFAIR.* Æ 1·0
				III.—WITH NAME OF NÚR-JAHÁN.
				GOLD.
AV 513	Súrat	1036	—	Obv. جهانگیر زحکم شا[ه صد زیو[ر یافت ضرب سورت Rev. شاه پاد جهان نور ز]نام بیگم زر ۱۰۳۶ ✠ [سنه] Pl. XIV. *CUNNINGHAM.* AV ·75, Wt. 166

No.	Mint.	Year.	Regnal year.	
				SILVER.
AR 514	Súrat	1033	19	As 513: but ۱۰۳۳ ۱۹ سنه *CUNNINGHAM.* AR ·75, Wt. 173
515	Ahmad-ábád	1034	—	As 513: but on obv. ضرب احمدابا[د], and year on rev. ۱۰۳۴ Pl. XIV. *THOMAS.* AR ·75, Wt. 174
516, 517	Lahore	,,	20	Obv. شاه جهانكير بحكم يافت صد زيور سنه ۲۰ جلوس Rev. زنام شاه ۱۰۳۴ نور جهان پاد بيكم زر ضرب لاهور Pl. XIV. *CUNNINGHAM.* AR ·8, Wt. 175 *PRINSEP.* AR ·8, Wt. 174

No.	Mint.	Year.	Regnal year.	
AR 518	Lahore	1034	—	Obv. as 516. Rev. زنام نو[ر جهان پادشاه زر بیگم ۱۰۳۴ ضرب لاهور Pl. XIV. *MARSDEN.* AR ·85, Wt. 176
519 ½	Súrat	,,	2[0]	As 513: but سنه ۱۰۳۴ ۲ Pl. XIV. *CUNNINGHAM.* AR ·65, Wt. 85
520	,,	1035	2[1]	As 513: but سنه ۱۰۳۵ ۲ *GRANT.* AR ·8, Wt. 173
521	,,	1036	—	As 513: but سنه ۱۰۳۶ *GRANT.* AR ·8, Wt. 176
522	Ahmad-ábád	1037	2[2]	As 513: but ضرب احمداباد ; and ۱۰۳۷ ۲ *CUNNINGHAM.* AR ·8, Wt. 174
523, 524	Agrah	,,	22	Obv. ۲۲ بحکم شاه جها نگیر یافت صد زیور سنه ۱۰۳۷ Rev. زنام شاه نورجهان پاد بیگم زر ضرب اگره Pl. XIV. *CUNNINGHAM.* AR ·85, Wt. 172 *EDEN.* AR ·8, Wt. 175

No.	Mint.	Year.	Regnal year.	
AR 525	Patnah	1037	22	As 523: but regnal year omitted on obv., and lowest lines of rev., ۲۲ ضرب پتنه Pl. XIV. *CUNNINGHAM.* AR ·75, Wt. 174
526 ½	„	—	„	As 525. Pl. XIV. AR ·65, Wt. 89

DÁWAR BAKHSH.

USURPER.

A.H. 1037 = A.D. 1627-8.

No.	Mint.	Year.	Regnal year.	
				SILVER.
Æ 527	Lahore	1037	1	Obv. الله لا اله الا محمد ١٠٣٧ رسول الله ضرب لاهور Rev. پادشاه بخش داور المظفر احد ابو سنه PL. XIV. *GIBBS.* Æ ·85, Wt. 169

V.—SHIHÁB-AD-DÍN SHÁH-JAHÁN.

A.H. 1037—1068 = A.D. 1628—1658.

No.	Mint.	Year: Month.	Regnal year.	
				GOLD.
AV 528	Ahmad-ábád	1038 Ardi-bihist	2	Obv. لا اله الا الله / محمد / رسول الله / ضرب / احمدآباد الهی سنه / اردی بهست ماه Rev. پادشاه غازی / شاه جهان ۱۰۳۸ / محمد / شهاب الدین ثانی / صاحب قران ثا *I.O.C.* AV ·95, Wt. 168
529	,,	1038 Khúr-dád	,,	As 528: but month خورداد PL. XV. AV ·9, Wt. 168

No.	Mint.	Year: Month.	Regnal year.	
AV 530	Dawlat-ábád	—	2	Obv. area, within ornamented diamond border, لا اله الا الله محمد رسول الله ٢ Margin, بصدق ابی بکر وعدل عمر بازرم عثمان وعلم علی Rev. area, within eightfoil, پادشاه غازی Margin, شها[ب] الدین | محمد صاحب | قران ثانی | ضر[ب] دوا[ت]اباد PL. XV. *DA CUNHA.* AV ·9, Wt. 167
531	Lahore	1039 Abán	,,	Obv. لا اله الا الله محمد رسول الله سنه ٢ ضرب لاهور الهی ابان ماه Rev. as 528: but ١٠٣٩ *MARSDEN.* AV ·85, Wt. 169
532	Ahmad-ábád	1040 Far-war-dín	4	As 528: but سنه ٤ and month فروردی (*sic*) on obv.; and on rev. ١٠٤٠ *I.O.C.* AV ·75, Wt. 169

No.	Mint.	Year: Month.	Regnal year.	
AV 533	Súrat	— Far-war-dín	4	As 528: but no Hijrah year; and lowest lines of obv., ضرب سنه ۴ سورت الهی ماه فروردی (*sic*) *I.O.C.* AV ·85, Wt. 169
534	Akbar-ábád	1042	—	Obv. Area, within lozenge border, as 530, but no regnal year. Rev. شهاب الدین م محمد صاحبقران ثا ی شاه جهان پادشاه غاز ضر]ب اکبراباد ۱۰۴۲ Pl. XV. AV ·95, Wt. 167
535	"	—	5	Obv. as 534. Rev. صاحب قران ثانی محمد شاه پادشاه غاز شهاب الدین جهان ی ضرب اکبراباد سنه ۵ (Pierced.) AV 1·05

No.	Mint.	Year.	Regnal year.	
AV 536	Lahore	1042	5	Obv. as 530: but area enclosed in circular border; no regnal year; and ١٠٤٢ in margin. Rev. پادشاه غازی الدین محمد شاه جهان ب صاحب قران ثانی شها ٥ ضرب سنه لاهور Pl. XV. *PRINSEP.* AV ·85, Wt. 169
537, 538	Akbar-ábád	1043	6	As 534: but ١٠٤٣, and regnal year ٦ on rev. *GRANT.* AV ·9, Wt. 164 *MARSDEN.* AV ·95, Wt. 167
539	,,	,,	,,	Obv. as 534. Rev. Area, within diamond border, پادشاه غازی ٦ شاه جهان ١٠٤٣ Margin, شهاب الدین | محمد صاحب | قران ثانی | ضرب اکبراباد *GRANT* AV ·95, Wt. 168
540	Burhán-púr	,,	,,	As 539: but square borders; ١٠٤٣ in obv. area, and mint برهانپور (Formerly ringed.) *PRINSEP.* AV ·9

No.	Mint.	Year.	Regnal year.	
AV 541	Akbar-ábád	1043	—	Obv. Area, within oval eightfoil border, لله لا اله الا ا محمد رسول الله Margin as 530. Rev. Area, within oval eightfoil border, پاد شاه غازی جهان شاه Margin as 539. Pl. XV. *PRINSEP.* AV ·85, Wt. 16
542 sq.	—	—	6	Obv. Area, within square, لا اله الا الله محمد رسول الله Margin obliterated. Rev. Area, within square, پادشاه غازی ٦ شاه جهان Margin obliterated. *DA CUNHA.* AV ·6, Wt. 166
543	—	1044	—	As 539: square borders, nearly obliterated; year [١٠]۴۴ in obv. area; mint obliterated. AV ·8, Wt. 169

No.	Mint.	Year.	Regnal year.	
AV				
544	Ahmad-ábád	1045	8	As 539 : square borders, ۱۰۴۵ in obv. area ; regnal year ۸ in rev. area, احمداباد, in rev. margin. Pl. XV. *GUTHRIE.* AV ·95, Wt. 169
545	Akbar-ábád	„	„	„ ۱۰۴۵ and ۸ in rev. area. *BURGESS.* AV ·9, Wt. 168
546	„	1046	9	„ square borders, ۱۰۴۶ in obv. area, ۹ in rev. area. *I.O.C.* AV ·85, Wt. 168
547	„	1047	11	„ ۱۰۴۷ and ۱۱ in rev. area. *BURGESS.* AV ·95, Wt. 168
548	„	1048	„	„ ۱۰۴۸ and ۱۱ in rev. area. (Formerly ringed.) *HAY.* AV ·9
549	—	1049	12	„ square borders, ۱۲ in obv. margin, ۴۹ and obscure mint (بهمار ؟) in rev. margin. Pl. XV. *GOVT. OF INDIA.* AV ·8, Wt. 169
550	Akbar-ábád	1050	13	„ ۰۵۰ and ۱۳ in rev. area. *HAY.* AV ·85, Wt. 167

No.	Mint.	Year.	Regnal year.	
AV 551	Akbar-ábád	1050	14	As 539: ١٠٥٠ and ١٤ in rev. area. PL. XV. *STUBBS.* *AV* ·9, Wt. 168
552	Dawlat-ábád	,,	—	,, ١٠٥٠ beneath rev. area; and دولتاباد in margin. *DA CUNHA.* *AV* ·8, Wt. 111
553	,,	1051	14	,, ١٠٥١ beneath rev. area; ١٤ and ضرب [د]ول[ت]ا[ب]اد in rev. margin. *AV* ·8, Wt. 168
554	Akbar-ábád	,,	15	,, ١٠٥١ and ١٥ in rev. area. *LADY FRERE.* *AV* ·85, Wt. 168
555	Burhán-púr	,,	—	,, square borders; ١٠٥١ in obv. area; margins obscure. *I.O.C.* *AV* ·85, Wt. 164
556	Akbar-ábád	1052	16	,, ١٠٥٢ and ١٦ in rev. area. *LADY FRERE.* *AV* ·85, Wt. 168
557	,,	1053	,,	,, ١٠٥٣ and ١٦ in rev. area. *AV* ·9, Wt. 166
558	,,	1056	19	,, square borders; ١٠٥٦ in obv. area, ١٩ in rev. area. *PRINSEP.* *AV* ·8, Wt. 168
559	,,	1057	21	,, ١٠٥٧ and ٢١, both in rev. area. (Barbarous.) *MARSDEN.* *AV* ·9, Wt. 167

No.	Mint.	Year.	Regnal year.	
AV 560 sq.	Akbar-ábád	1057	21	As 559. (Barbarous.) *MARSDEN.* AV ·85, Wt. 168
561	„	[1059]	23	As 539: no Hijrah year, but ٢٣ in rev. area. *YEAMES.* AV ·95, Wt. 165
562	Burhán-púr	1060	„	„ square borders; ١٠٦٠ in obv. area, برهانپور ٢٣ in rev. margin. *MARSDEN.* AV ·85, Wt. 169
563	„	1061	25	„ square borders; ١٠٦١ in obv. area, برهانپور ٢٥ in rev. margin. Pl. XV. AV ·85, Wt. 169
564	Akbar-ábád	„	„	„ ١٠٦١ and ٢٥ in rev. area. AV ·85, Wt. 168
565	„	1062	26	„ ١٠٦٢ in obv. area, ٢٦ in rev. area. *PROF. WILSON.* AV ·75, Wt. 168
566	Dawlat-ábád	1063	27	„ ١٦٣ (*sic*) and ٢٧ in obv. area, ٢٦ ضرب دولتاباد in rev. margin. Pl. XV. *LADY FRERE.* AV ·8, Wt. 169
567	Akbar-ábád	1064	28	„ ١٠٦٤ in obv. area and ٢٨ in rev. area. AV ·75, Wt. 168

No.	Mint.	Year.	Regnal year.	
AV 568	Sháh-jahán-ábád	1066	30	Obv. as 539 : within circle, in margin ١٠٦٦ Rev. Area, as 539 : within circle, regnal year ٣٠ Margin, سکه شاه جهان‌اباد رایج در جهان جاودان بادا بنام ثانی صاحب قران PL. XV. *MARSDEN.* AV 1·15, Wt. 168
569	Dawlat-ábád	1067	,,	As 539 : but in obv. area, ١٠٦٧ and ٣٠ mint in rev. margin, ضرب دولت‌اباد (Barbarous.) *MARSDEN.* AV ·85, Wt. 167
570	Multán	1068	31	,, square borders ; ١٠٦٨ in obv. area, ٣١ in rev. area ; ملتان in margin. *I.O.C.* AV ·75, Wt. 168
571	Dawlat-ábád	,,	,,	,, eightfoil borders ; ١٠٦٨ in obv. margin, ٣١ in rev. area ; دولت‌اباد in rev. margin. *MARSDEN.* AV ·85, Wt. 167
572	Akbar-ábád	,,	32	Obv. as 541 : eightfoil borders ; ١٠٦٨ in margin. Rev. as 539 : but regnal year ٣٢ in area ; margin differently divided, and mint ضرب دار الخلافه اکبراباد *PRINSEP.* AV ·9, Wt. 166

No.	Mint.	Year.	Regnal year.	
AV 573	Dawlat-ábád	1068	32	Obv. as 541 : eightfoil borders ; ١٠٦٨ in margin. Rev. as 539 : ٣٢ in area ; ضر[ب] دولتاباد in margin. AV ·8, Wt, 168
574	Multán	,,	,,	As 539 : square borders ; ١٠٦٨ in obv. area ; ٣٢ in rev. area ; ضرب ملتان in margin. *THEOBALD.* AV ·75, Wt. 168
575	Burhán-púr	,,	3[2]	,, square borders ; ١٠٦٨ in obv. area ; ٣x in rev. area ; [بر]هانپور in margin. *PRINSEP.* AV ·75, Wt. 169
576, 577 sq.	—	—	—	,, square borders with ornamented quatrefoil corners, mint and date obliterated. (Barbarous.) *LADY FRERE.* AV ·8, Wt. 169 PL. XV. (Barbarous.) *PANJ. ARCH. SURV.* AV ·9, Wt. 188

No.	Mint.	Year.	Regnal year.		
					SILVER.
					With name Kharram.
Æ 578	Lahore	1037	1	Obv.	لا الـه الا الـلـه مـحـمـد رسول الله ضرب لاهور سـنـه ا جـلـوس ١٠٣٧
				Rev.	بـادشـاه غـازى الدين محمد شاه جهان خرم صـر ابـو المظفر نـا
					PL. XVI. *CUNNINGHAM.* Æ ·85, Wt. 172
579	Agrah	,,	,,	Obv.	لا الـه الا الـلـه مـحـمـد رسـول الـلـه .٣٧ ضـر ب دار الـخـلافه اكـره
				Rev.	احد سـنـه غـازى شـاه جهان پادشـاه مـحـمـد شـهاب الـديـن نى صاحب قـران ثـا
					PRINSEP. Æ ·9, Wt. 168

No.	Mint.	Year.	Regnal year.	
ÆR 580	Burhán-púr	[10]37	1	Obv. as 579: but lower lines, ب ضر برهانپور ے ۳۷ هجر Rev. پادشاه غازی احد شاه جهان سنه محمد شهاب الدین ثانی صاحب قران ثا Pl. XVI. *PANJ. ARCH. SURV.* ÆR ·9, Wt. 174
581	Agrah	1038	„	Obv. as 579: but ۱۰۳۸ Rev. as 580. Pl. XVI. *GRANT.* ÆR ·85, Wt. 172
582 ¼	„	„	2	Obv. اکره ا]لخلافه دار ض]رب ۱۰۳۸ سنه Rev. پادشاه غازی شاه جهان نثار ۲ سنه Pl. XVI. (Nisár.) *PLAYFAIR.* ÆR ·7, Wt. 44

No.	Mint.	Year: Month.	Regnal year.	
Æ 583	Akbar-ábád	1038 Tír	2	Obv. لا اله الا الله محمد رسول الله ضرب دار الخلافه اكبراباد الهي سنه ٢ .. تير ماه Rev. as 580: but ١]٠٣٨ سنه (in place of احد سنه) Pl. XVI. *I.O.C.* Æ ·85, Wt. 172
584	Patnah	,,	,,	Obv. beneath Kalimah (as 579), ضرب پتنه الهي سنه ٢ تير ماه Rev. as 580: but ١٠٣٨ (in place of احد سنه) Pl. XVI. *THEOBALD.* Æ 1·0, Wt. 172
585, 586	Súrat	1038	1	Obv., beneath Kalimah (as 579), ضرب سورت ی ١٠٣٨ سنه هجر Rev. as 580: احد سنه Pl. XVI. *PRINSEP.* Æ ·9, Wt. 175 *GRANT.* Æ ·9, Wt. 174

No.	Mint.	Year.	Regnal year.	
Æ 587	Súrat	103*x*	—	As 585: but unit of date obliterated, and no regnal year. *CUNNINGHAM.* Æ ·85, Wt. 175
588	Akbar-ábád	1039	2	Obv. Area, within circle, لا اله الا الله محمد ١٠٣٩ رسول الله Margin, بصدق ابی بکر وعدل عمر | بازرم عثمان وعلم علی Rev. پادشاه غازی الدین محمد شاه جهان ب ٢ صاحب قران ثانی شها ضرب اکبراباد Pl. XVI. *EDEN.* Æ ·9, Wt. 177
589	Akbar-nagar	”	”	Obv., beneath Kalimah (as 583), ب ٢ ضر اکبرنگر الهی سنه . . . . . . Rev. as 580: but ١]٠٣٩ Pl. XVI. *EDEN.* Æ ·75, Wt. 125

No.	Mint.	Year: Month.	Regnal year.	
Æ 590	Patnah	1039 Azur	2	Obv., beneath Kalimah, ضرب ٢ پتنه الهی سنه اذر ماه Rev. as 580: but ١٠٣٩ *BANKS.* Æ 1·05, Wt. 175
591	Lahore	1039 Abán	,,	Obv., beneath Kalimah, ٢ سنه ضرب لاهور الهی ابان ماه Rev. as 580: but ١٠٣٩ *GRANT.* Æ ·95, Wt. 173
592	Multán	1039	3	As 588: but ١٠٣٩ above محمد on obv., and ٣ سنه above محمد on rev.; mint ملتان *CUNNINGHAM.* Æ ·86, Wt. 177
593	Akbar-ábád	1040	4	,, but ١٠٤٠ in obv. margin, and ٤ above صاحب on rev. Æ ·9, Wt. 176
594	,,	,,	,,	As 593: but obv. within sixfoil, and ٤ above ب of ضرب *I.O.C.* Æ ·85, Wt. 174

No.	Mint.	Year: Month.	Regnal year	
Æ 595	Burhán-pur	1040	—	As 588: but obv. area in diamond border, divided الا ا | لله ; year ١٠٤٠ ; mint برهانپور Æ 1·0, Wt. 177
596	Patnah	1040 Amar-dád	3	Obv., beneath Kalimah, ضرب پتنه السنه ٣ امرداد ماه Rev. as 580: but ١٠٤٠ *CUNNINGHAM.* Æ 1·0, Wt. 172
597	,,	1040 Bah-man	,,	As preceding: but بهمن Æ 1·0, Wt. 174
598	Súrat	1040	—	As 585: but ١٠٤٠ ; no regnal year. *BANKS.* Æ ·9, Wt. 176
599	Lahore	,,	3	As 588: but ١٠٤٠ in obv. margin, and ٣ above صاحب on rev. *CUNNINGHAM.* Æ ·9, Wt. 175
600	Multán	,,	,,	As 592: but ١٠٤٠. Æ ·85, Wt. 167
601	,,	,,	4	,, but ١٠٤٠ ; and سنه with ٤ above Æ ·85, Wt. 175
602	,,	,,	,,	,, unit of date obliterated; سنه with ٤ above *THOMAS.* Æ ·85, Wt. 177

No.	Mint.	Year: Month.	Regnal year.	
Æ 603	Dehlí	1040 Dai	3	Obv. لا اله الا الله محمد رسول الله الهی دی ماه هلی ضرب ۳ د Rev. as 580: but ۱۰۴۰, and پاد in second line. Pl. XVI. *GOVT. OF INDIA.* Æ ·95, Wt. 176
604	Akbar-ábád	1041	4	As 588: but ۱۰۴۱ in obv. margin, and ۴ over ضرب on rev. صا]حبقران joined. *GRANT.* Æ ·85, Wt. 174
605	,,	,,	5	Obv. as 588: but square border; ۱۰۴۱ at foot of area. Rev. Area, within square, بادشاه غازی ۵ شاه جهان Margin, | ش[هاب] الدين | محمد صاحب | قران ثانی | ...اکبرابا]د Pl. XVI. *EDEN.* Æ ·85, Wt. 176
606	Alláh-ábád	,, Azur	4	Obv., beneath Kalimah, ضرب الهاباد الهی ۴ اذر ماه Rev. as 580: but ۱۰۴۱ Pl. XVI. *CUNNINGHAM.* Æ 1·0, Wt. 174

No.	Mint.	Year: Month.	Regnal year.	
AR 607	Patnah	1041 Tír	4	Obv., beneath Kalimah, ضرب پتنه الهی ۴ تیر ماه Rev. as 580: but ۱۰۴۱ *MARSDEN.* AR ·95, Wt. 173
608	„	1041 Azur	„	As 607: but month اذر PL. XVI. *GRANT.* AR 1·0, Wt. 175
609	„	1041 Dai	„	„ but month دی *PRINSEP.* AR ·95, Wt. 176
610	Dehlí	1041	4	Obv. as 588: but ۱۰۴۱ in margin. Rev. پادشاه غازی قران ثانی شاه جهان حب شهاب الدین محمد صا ر ضرب دهلی ۴ *THEOBALD.* AR ·9, Wt. 174
611	Lahore	„	„	As 588: but ۱۰۴۱ in obv. margin; and ۴ over صاحب, and mint لاهور *MARSDEN.* AR ·85, Wt. 176
612	„	„	5	„ and ۵ over ضرب *I.O.C.* AR ·8, Wt. 173

No.	Mint.	Year.	Regnal year.	
Æ 613	Akbar-ábád	1042	5	As 605 : ١٠٤٢ in obv. area ; ٥ end of first line of rev. *THOMAS.* Æ ·85, Wt. 167
614	Multán	,,	,,	As 588 : ١٠٤٢ over محمد in obv. area ; ⊙ سنه over شاه on rev. ; mint ملتان *GRANT.* Æ ·85, 174
615	Akbar-ábád	,,	6	As 588 : ١٠٤٢ in obv. area ; ٦ and اکبراباد on rev. Æ ·9, Wt. 174
616	Burhán-púr	,,	,,	As 605 : ١٠٤٢ in obv. area ; ضرب برهانپور and ٦ in rev. margin. *CUNNINGHAM.* Æ ·9, Wt. 177
617	Patnah	,,	,,	,, ١٠٤٢ in obv. margin ; ضرب پتنه and ٦, in rev. margin. *CUNNINGHAM.* Æ ·95, Wt. 175
618	Súrat	,,	—	As 585 : ١٠٤٢ ; no regnal year on rev. Æ ·8, Wt. 176

No.	Mint.	Year.	Regnl year.	
Æ 619, 620 sq.	Multán	1042	6	As 605: ۱۰۴۲ in obv. area; ۶ above غازی on rev.; and ضرب ملتان *I.O.C.* Æ ·85, Wt. 175 *EDEN.* (sq.) Æ ·8, Wt. 170
621	Akbar-ábád	1043	„	Obv. Area, within ornamented diamond border, الله لا اله الا محمد رسول الله ۱۰۴۳ Margin, بصدق ابی بکر وعدل عمر بازرم عثمان وعلم علی Rev. شهاب الدین محمد صاحبقران ثانی ۶ شاه جهان پادشاه غازی ضرب اکبراباد Pl. XVI. *CUNNINGHAM.* Æ 1·0, Wt. 176
622	„	„	„	Obv. as 621. Rev. Area, within diamond border, پاد شاه جهان شاه ۶ Margin, شهاب الدین محمد صاحب قران ثانی ضرب اکبراباد Pl. XVI. *THEOBALD.* Æ ·9, Wt. 176

No.	Mint.	Year.	Regnal year.	
Æ 623	Alláh-ábád	[1043]	6	As 605: traces of date on obv.; ضرب الهاباد in rev. margin. Pl. XVII. *CUNNINGHAM.* Æ 1·0, Wt. 175
624	Patnah	[,,]	,,	As 605: no date on obv.; ٦ in rev. area, and ضرب پتنه in margin. *PRINSEP.* Æ ·85, Wt. 169
625	Bhakar	1043	,,	Obv. as 605: but circular border; date in margin ١٠٤٣ Rev. پادشاه غازی الدین محمد شاه جهان شهاب صاحبقران ثانی سنه ٦ ضرب بهکر Pl. XVII. *CUNNINGHAM.* Æ ·8, Wt. 177
626	Bhakar?	,,	,,	As 605: circular borders; ١٠٤٣ in obv. margin, and سنه ٦ ضرب بکر in rev. margin. Pl. XVII. *HAY.* Æ ·85, Wt. 176
627	Súrat	[,,]	,,	,, ٦ in obv. area; ضرب سورت in rev. margin. Æ ·85, Wt. 171
628	Multán	,,	,,	,, ١٠٤٣ in obv. area, ٦ in rev. area; mint ملتان *PLAYFAIR.* Æ ·85, Wt. 173

No.	Mint.	Year : Month.	Regnal year.	
Æ 629	Akbar-nagar	1043 Far-war-din	7	Obv., beneath Kalimah, ب ضر اکبرنگر ۷ الهی م]اه فروردی (*sic*) Rev. ...... مد] شاه جهان [مد ۱۰۴۳ شهاب الدین نی صاحب قران ثا Pl. XVII. *CUNNINGHAM.* Æ ·85, Wt. 176
630	Súrat	,,	,,	As 605 : ۷ in obv. area, ۱۰۴۳ in margin ; سورت in rev. margin. Æ ·85, Wt. 177
631	Ahmad-ábád	1044	,,	,, ۱۰۴۴ in obv. area ; ۷ in rev. area ; mint, احمداباد *PRINSEP.* Æ ·9, Wt. 174
632	Lahore	,,	,,	Obv. ۱۰۴۴ سنه لاهور ضرب Rev. پادشاه غازی نثار شاه جهان سنه ۷ Pl. XVII. (Nisár). *PANJ. ARCH. SURV.* Æ ·6, Wt. 43

No.	Mint.	Year.	Regnal year.	
AR 633	Akbar-ábád	1044	8	As 605: ١٠۴۴ in obv. area; ٨ in rev. area, mint اكـ.ا.ا. *MARSDEN.* AR ·85, Wt. 177
634	Bhakar	1045	,,	,, ١٠۴٥ in obv. margin; سنه in rev. margin; ضرب بهكر Pl. XVII. *CUNNINGHAM.* AR ·85, Wt. 176
635	Patnah	[10]45	,,	,, ۴٥ in obv. area; ۴ over علی ; ٨ in rev. area; ضر[ب] پتنه *GIBBS.* AR ·9, Wt. 170
636	Súrat	1045	,,	,, ٨ in obv. area; ١٠۴٥ in obv. margin; ضر[ب] سورت AR ·9, Wt. 177
637	Multán	,,	9	,, ١٠۴٥ in obv. area; ٩ in rev. area; [ضرب] ملتان *PLAYFAIR.* AR ·95, Wt. 173
638, 639	Súrat	1046	,,	,, ٩ in obv. area; ١٠۴٦ in obv. margin; [ضرب] سورت *GOVT. OF INDIA.* AR ·85, Wt. 176 *GRANT.* AR ·9, Wt. 175

No.	Mint.	Year: Month.	Regnal year.	
AR 640	Lahore	1046	9	As 605 : ۱۰۴۶ in obv. margin ; ۹ سنه ضرب لاهور in rev. margin. *GRANT.* AR ·9, Wt. 174
641	Jahán-gírna-gar	[104]6	,,	,, [۱۰]۴۶ in obv. area ; ۹ in rev. area ; mint جها . . . . نكر *MARSDEN.* AR ·9, Wt. 177
642	Akbar-ábád	1047	10	,, ۱۰۴۷ in obv. area ; ۱۰ in rev. area ; صرب اكبراباد *EDEN.* AR ·9, Wt. 175
643	Tattah	,, Khur-dád	,,	Obv. لا اله الا الله محمد رسول الله ب ضرب ۱۰ تته الهي خورداد ماه Rev. پادشاه غازي شاه جهان محمد ۱۰۴۷ شهاب الدين ن . . . . PL. XVII. *GRANT.* AR ·85, Wt. 177
644	,,	,, Tír	,,	Same as 643 : but month تير ماه *CUNNINGHAM.* AR ·85, Wt. 177

No.	Mint.	Year.	Regnal year.	
Æ 645	Lahore	1047	11	As 605: [۱۰]۴۷ in obv. margin; ۱۱ سنه ضرب لاهور in rev. margin. *I.O.C.* Æ ·85, Wt. 176
646	Jahán-gírna-gar	1048	12	,, ۱۰۴۸ in obv. area; ۱۲ in rev. area; ضر[ب] جهانگیرنگر in rev. margin. *CURETON.* Æ ·9, Wt. 176
647	Kanda-hár	,,	,,	,, but ضر[ب] قندهار *THEOBALD.* Æ ·85, Wt. 176
648	Multán	,,	11	,, ۱۰۴۸ in obv. area; ۱۱ in rev. area; ضرب ملتان in rev. margin. *THEOBALD.* Æ ·85, Wt. 175
649	—	,,	—	,, ۱۰۴۸ in obv. margin; mint and regnal year obliterated. Æ ·8, Wt. 163
650	Súrat	1049	12	,, ۱۰۴۹ in obv. margin; ۱۲ and سورت ... in rev. margin. Æ ·85, Wt. 177

No.	Mint.	Year.	Regnal year.	
Æ 651 $\frac{1}{4}$	Lahore	1049	13	Obv. لاهــــور ضــرب دار السلطنه ۱۰۴۹ ســـنـه Rev. پادشاه غازی ۱۳ شاه جهان رن نثـــا Pl. XVII. (Nisár). *CUNNINGHAM.* Æ ·65, Wt. 44
652	Súrat	1051	—	As 605: ۱۰۵۱ in obv. margin; سورت in rev. margin. ضرب *GRANT.* Æ ·85, Wt. 163
653 $\frac{1}{2}$	—	—	17	,, ۱۷ in rev. area; margins nearly obliterated. *GRANT.* Æ ·65, Wt. 88
654	—	1054	—	,, ۱۵۴ (*sic*) in obv. area; mint and regnal year obliterated. Æ ·85, Wt. 177
655	Akbar-nagar	1055	18	,, ۱۰۵۵ in obv. area; ۱۸ in rev. area; اک[بر]نکر... in rev. margin. *GRANT.* Æ ·8, Wt. 176
656	Akbar-ábád	1056	19	,, ۱۰۵۶ in obv. margin; ۱۹ ضرب کبراباد in rev. margin. Æ ·9, Wt. 174

No.	Mint.	Year: Month.	Regnal year.	
Æ 657	Dawlat-ábád	1056	19	As 605: ١٠٥٦ and ١٩ in obv. area; ضرب دولتاباد in rev. margin. Æ ·85, Wt. 176
658	Kanda-hár	—	,,	,, ١٩ in rev. area; قندهار... in rev. margin. Æ ·85, Wt. 174
659	Súrat	1057	20	,, but ornamented diamond borders; ١٠٥٧ in obv. margin, ٢٠ at foot of rev. area; ضر[ب] سورت in rev. margin. Pl. XVII. *EDEN*, Æ ·9, Wt. 175
660	,,	,,	21	As 659: but ١٠٥٧ and ٢١ *BURNES.* Æ ·85, Wt. 177
661 ½	—	—	,,	As 605: ٢١ in rev. area; margins partly obliterated. *GRANT.* Æ ·7, Wt. 88
662	Súrat	1058	—	,, ١٠٥٨ in obv. margin; ضرب سورت in rev. margin. *GRANT.* Æ ·85, Wt. 174
663	Tattah	,, Shah-riwar	22	As 643: but ٢٢ and month [شه]ريو[ر] on obv. and ١٠٥٨ on rev. Æ ·75, Wt. 177

No.	Mint.	Year.	Regnal year.	
Æ 664	Patnah	—	22	As 605 : ٢٢ in rev. area ; ضرب پتنه in rev. margin. *PRINSEP.* Æ ·8, Wt. 175
665	Akbar-ábád	1059	23	„ ١٠٥٩ in obv. margin ; ٢٣ ضرب اكبراباد in rev. margin. *GRANT.* Æ ·85, Wt. 171
666	Junah-garh	„	—	„ [١]٠٥٩ in obv. margin ; ضرب جوندك . . in rev. margin. Pl. XVII. *THOMAS.* Æ ·95, Wt. 177
667	„	1060	—	As preceding : but ١٠٦ in obv. margin. *EDEN.* Æ 1·0, Wt. 175
668	Dawlat-ábád ?	„	23	As 605 : [١٠]٦٠ in obv. area ; ٢٣ in rev. area ; (?) لتاباد ..... in rev. margin. Æ ·85, Wt. 171
669 ½	Sháhja-hánábád	„	24	Obv. دار الخلافه ضرب ١٠٦٠ شاهجهان ابا[د] هجری سنه ٢٤ سنه جلوس Rev. بادشاه غازی شاه جهان نی ت نثار صاحبقران ثا Pl. XVII. (Nisár. Thin.) Æ 1·15, Wt. 88

No.	Mint.	Year.	Regnal year.	
AR 670	Patnah	—	25	As 605 : ۲۵ in rev. area ; ضرب پتنه in rev. margin. AR ·8, Wt. 175
671 $\frac{1}{4}$	Kash- mír	1061	,,	Obv. کشمیر ضرب ۱۰۶۱ سنه Rev. ۲۵ ثانی قران حب نثار صا PL. XVII. (Nisár.) AR ·7, Wt. 41
672	—	—	,,	As 605 : mint obliterated, ۲8 in rev. area. *MARSDEN.* AR ·8, Wt. 177
673	Súrat	1064	28	,, ۱۰۶۴ in obv. margin ; ۲۸ in rev. area ; سورت in rev. margin. *MARSDEN.* AR ·8, Wt. 178
674	Multán	1066	29	,, ۱۰۶۶ in obv. area ; ۲۹ in rev. area ; ضر[ب] ملتان in rev. margin. *I.O.C.* AR ·8, Wt. 172
675	Súrat	—	30	,, ۳۰ in rev. area ; ض[رب] سورت in rev. margin. *I.O.C.* AR ·9, Wt. 178

No.	Mint.	Year.	Regnal year.	
AR 676, 677	Dawlat- ábád	1067	31	As 605: ١٠٦٧ and ٣١ in obv. area; ضرب دولت‌اباد in rev. margin. Pl. XVII. *GRANT.* AR ·9, Wt. 176 *PANJ. ARCH. SURV.* AR ·9, Wt. 176
678 ¼	Sháhja- hánábád	,,	,,	Obv. جهان‌اباد شاه دار الخلافه ضرب ١٠٦٧ Rev. ثانی قران ت حب نثار صا ٣١ Pl. XVII. (Nisár.) AR ·75, Wt. 44
679	Súrat	,,	,,	As 605: circular borders; ١٠٦٧ in obv. margin; ٣١ in rev. area; ضرب سورت in rev. margin. *GRANT.* AR ·95, Wt. 175
680	,,	1068	,,	As 679: but ١٦٨ (*sic*). *GRANT.* AR ·9, Wt. 176
681	Sháhja- hánábád	,,	32	As 605: eightfoil borders; ١٠٦٨ in obv. margin; شهاب الدين محمد صاحبقران ثانی ضرب دار ٣٢ الخلافه شاه‌جهان‌اباد in rev. margin. Pl. XVII. *MARSDEN.* AR 1·0, Wt. 175

No.	Mint.	Year.	Regnal year.	
Æ 682	Ahmad-ábád	—	32	As 605 : ضرب احمداباد ۳۲ in rev. margin. *GIBBS.* Æ ·8, Wt. 178
683, 684	Dawlat-ábád	1068	,,	,, eightfoil borders ; ۱۰۶۸ in obv. margin ; ۳۲ in rev. area ; ضرب دولتاباد in rev. margin. *GRANT.* Æ ·9, Wt. 176 *THEOBALD.* Æ ·9, Wt. 177
685	Súrat	(1059)	,,	,, ۱۰۵۹ in obv. margin (an old die) ; ۳۲ in rev. area ; سورت in rev. margin. *GRANT.* Æ ·9, Wt. 178
686	,,	—	,,	As 685 : but no Hijrah year legible. *PRINSEP.* Æ ·9, Wt. 176
687	—	1069	,,	As 605 : ۱۰۶۹ in obv. margin ; ۳۲ in rev. margin ; mint obliterated. Æ ·9, Wt. 178
688	Kábul	—	—	,, ضا[رب] کابل in rev. margin ; year obliterated. *CUNNINGHAM.* Æ ·85, Wt. 175

ANONYMOUS LARGESSE (NISÁR).

GOLD.

No.	Mint.	Year.	Regnal year.	
N 689	Sháhja-hánábád	1069	—	Obv. ثانی قران تـ حـب نثار صا Rev. جهان اباد شـاه دار الخلافه ضـرب ۱۰۶۹ Pl. XVII. *N* ·65, Wt. 43

SHÁH SHUJÁ'.

IN BENGAL, ETC.

A.H. 1068-1070 = A.D. 1658-1660.

No.	Mint.	Year.	Regnal year.	
				SILVER.
Æ 690	Akbar-ábád	1068	—	Obv. Area, within square, لا اله الا الله محمد رسول الله ١٠٦٨ Margin .... | بازرم عثمان | عمر.......... Rev. Area, within square, پادشاه غازی شجاع محمد شاه Margin, ...[ا]کبر[ا]باد | قران ثانی | .... | .... Pl. XVIII. *Cunningham.* Æ ·85, Wt. 177
691	Jalún-ábád?	,,	1	Obv. as 690 : but ١٠٦٨ above رسول Rev. Area, within square, محمد شجاع شاه احمد پادشاه غاز Margin, (؟) جلون اباد | ..صر الدين | .... | ...... Pl. XVIII. *Prinsep.* Æ ·85, Wt. 177

MURÁD BAKHSH.

IN GUJARÁT.

A.H. 1068 = A.D. 1658.

No.	Mint.	Year.	Regnal year.	
				GOLD.
AV 692	Ahmad-ábád	1068	1	Obv. Area, within square, لا اله الا الله محمد رسول الله Margin, | بصدق ابی بکر | وعدل عمر | بازرم عثمان | وعلم ١٠٦٨ علی Rev. Area, within square, پادشاه غازی محمد مراد بخش Margin, | ابو المظفر | مروج الدین | ضرب احمداباد | ...الہی احد Pl. XVIII. *Cunningham.* AV ·85, Wt. 170

No.	Mint.	Year.	Regnal year.	
				SILVER.
Æ 693- 695	Ahmad- ábád	1068	1	As 692 : but سنه احد in rev. margin. *GRANT.* Æ ·85, Wt. 177 Pl. XVIII. *THOMAS.* Æ ·95, Wt. 178 *CUNNINGHAM.* Æ ·95, Wt. 176
696- 698	Súrat	„	„	„ but سورت ضرب Pl. XVIII. *CUNNINGHAM.* Æ ·9, Wt. 178 *MARSDEN.* Æ ·9, Wt. 170 *EDEN.* Æ ·95, Wt. 176
699	„	—	„	Obv. لا] الـــه الا الـلـه مـــحــــمـــد رســـول الـــلـــه ضر ب ســـورت . . . Rev. مـــراد شـــا]ه غاز ی محـــمد سکندر ثانی ز صاحبقران جهانی یا] فـــــت ا[ر]ث احد سنه Pl. XVIII. *CUNNINGHAM.* Æ ·9, Wt. 174
700	Cambay (Khan- báyat)	—	1	As 692 : but no year in obv. margin ; in rev. margin, ضرب کهنبایت | احد Pl. XVIII. *PANJ. ARCH. SURV.* Æ ·9, Wt. 173

VI.—AURANGZÍB 'ÁLAMGÍR.

A.H. 1069—1118=A.D. 1659—1707.

No.	Mint.	Year.	Regnal year.	
				GOLD.
AV 701	Tattah	[10]72	5	Obv. مـــانــوس مـيـمـنـت سنه ٥ جلـوس ب ضـر تـتـه Rev. اورنك زيب عالمگير شـــاه زد چو مهر منير سـكـه در جـهـان ٧٢ PL. XVIII. AV ·85, Wt. 170
702	Aurang-ábád	1074	6	Obv. اورنك ابـــاد ب مـانـوس ضـر مـيـمـنـت سـنـه ٦ جلـوس Rev. as 701 : but ١٠٧٤ over نك PL. XVIII. I.O.C. AV ·85, Wt. 169

No.	Mint.	Year.	Regnal year.	
AV 703	Multán	1075	8	As 701: but ٨, ملتان ; ١٠٧٥ *I.O.C.* AV ·85, Wt. 169
704	,,	1077	9	,, but ٩, ملتان ; ١٠٧٧ *PROF. WILSON.* AV ·8, Wt. 169
705	Aurang-ábád	1079	11	As 702: but ١١, اورنك اباد ; ١٠٧٩ *I.O.C.* AV ·85, Wt. 169
706	Akbar-nagar	—	12	Obv. Area, within square, سنه ١٢ ضرب اكبرنكر Margin, س[كه] | جلوس | ميمنت | مانوس Rev. Area, within square, شاه غازى عالمكير پاد Margin nearly obliterated. Pl. XVIII. *MARSDEN.* AV ·75, Wt. 168
707	Súrat	[108]3	16	Obv. سنه ١٦ جلوس ميمنت مانوس سورت ... Rev. as 701 : but سكه ٣ AV ·85, Wt. 171
708	Golkon-dah	1086	20	,, but ٣٠ (for ٢٠), كلكنده ; ١٠٨٦ Pl. XVIII. *I.O.C.* AV ·8, Wt. 170

No.	Mint.	Year.	Regnal year.	
AV 709	Sháh-jahán-ábád	1091	24	Obv. دار الخلافه شاه جهان اباد ضرب جلوس میمنت مانوس ۲۴ سنه Rev. as 701 : but ۱۰۹۱ over نك PL. XVIII. *I.O.C.* AV ·85, Wt. 169
710	Ahmad-nagar	1097	29	As 701 : but on obv. ۱۰۹۷, احمدنكر; and ۲۹ on rev. over نك *LADY FRERE.* AV ·85, Wt. 169
711	Bíjápúr	1099	31	Obv. جلوس س میمنت مانو سنه ۳۱ الـ]ظفر دا]ر بیجاپور Rev. as 701 : but ۹۹ over ه of سکه PL. XVIII. *MARSDEN.* AV ·9, Wt. 171
712	Golkon-dah	—	,,	As 701 : but ۳۱ سنه, کلکنده (no Hijrah year). *MARSDEN.* AV ·8, Wt. 169
713	Sháh-jahán-ábád	1100	32	As 709 : but ۳۲ and ۱ . . AV ·9, Wt. 168
714	,,	1101	34	,, but ۳۴ and ۱۱۰۱ AV ·9, Wt. 168

No.	Mint.	Year.	Regnal year.	
AV 715 $\frac{1}{4}$	Chíná- patan (Madras)	1103	35	Obv. ٣٥ ضرب چيناپتن Rev. ١١٠٣ عالمگير (*sic*) شاه نثار پاد Pl. XVIII. (Nisár). AV ·5, Wt. 46
716	Sháh- jahán- ábád	1106	38	As 709: but ٣٨ and ١١٠٦ *MARSDEN.* AV ·8, Wt. 169
717	Bíjápúr	1107	40	Obv. جلـ]وس ميـ]منت ما]نوس دار الظفر ضر]ب ٤٠ بيـ]جاپو[ر Rev. as 709: but ١ ٠٧ *LADY FRERE.* AV ·85, Wt. 167
718	—	1109	41	As 701: but mint obliterated, ٤١; and ١١٠٩ over نك *PRINSEP.* AV ·85, Wt. 168
719	Khujis- tah- bunyád (Aurang- ábád)	,,	4*x*	,, but ٤x, خجسته بنياد; ١١٠٩ over نك Pl. XVIII. *GOVT. OF INDIA.* AV ·8, Wt. 169
720	Burhán- púr	1111	43	,, but ٤٣, [بر]هانپور; and ١١١١ over نك *MARSDEN.* AV ·85, Wt. 170

No.	Mint.	Year.	Regnal year.	
AV 721 $\frac{1}{4}$	[Chíná]- patan	1111	4[*x*]	Obv. ۴ ضـــرب ....پتـن Rev. ۱۱۱۱ عالمكـير شا[ه] ز]ثار پاد Pl. XVIII. (Nisár.) AV ·45, Wt. 46
722	Bíjápúr	1112	44	As 717 : but ۴۴; and ۱۱۱۲ *DA CUNHA.* AV ·9, Wt. 168
723	Burhán- púr	1115	47	As 701 : but ۴۷ برهانپور سنه; and ۱۱۱۵ over نك *BENG. AS. SOC.* AV ·85, Wt. 169
724	Etáwá	1118	50	Obv. جلوس ميـــمنت ۵۰ سنه مانوس ب ضـــر اتاوا Rev. as 701 : but ۱۱۱۸ over نك *I.O.C.* AV ·85, Wt. 168

No.	Mint.	Year.	Regnal year.		
					SILVER.
Æ 725	Akbar-ábád	—	1	Obv.	[سنه] جلوس مانوس میمنت مستقر الخلافه سنه احد ضرب ا]ک[بر]اباد
				Rev.	عالمگیر پا]دشاه غاز . . . .
					PL. XIX. *THOMAS.* Æ 1·0, Wt. 175
726	Calcutta	1069	1	Obv.	کلکته ضرب سنه احد جلوس میمنت مانوس
				Rev.	شاه غازی بادر (*sic*) عالمگیر ۱۰۶۹ زیـ[ب محمد اورنگ
					PL. XIX. *PRINSEP.* Æ ·85, Wt. 176

No.	Mint.	Year.	Regnal year.	
Æ 727	Kábul	—	1	Obv. سنه جلوس ١ میمنت ما]نوس دار الملك ضرب كابل Rev. as 701: بدر instead of مهر ; no Hijrah year. *CUNNINGHAM.* Æ ·85, Wt. 174
728	Patnah	1070	,,	Obv. پتنه ضرب مانوس میمنت جلوس احد سنه Rev. ابو الظفر محیی الدین محمد ١٠٧٠ ب]هادر [ا]ورنك‌زیب عالمكیر [پادشاه غاز] Pl. XIX. *CUNNINGHAM.* Æ ·95, Wt. 174
729	Multán	1070 (*sic*)	3	Obv. ملتا دار الامان ن ضرب میمنت مانوس جلوس[سن]ه ٣ Rev. as 701: but ١٠٧٠ (*sic*). Pl. XIX. *CUNNINGHAM.* Æ ·95, Wt. 176

No.	Mint.	Year.	Regnal year.	
Æ 730	Aurang-ábád	1071	3	As 728 : but ٣, اورنكاباد ; and ١٠٧١ *CUNNINGHAM.* Æ ·9, Wt. 176
731	Súrat	,,	,,	Obv. ٣ سنه جلوس میمنت مانوس ضرب سورت Rev. عالمگیر اورنکزیب شاه زد چو بدر منیر ١٠٧١ سکه در جهان *BOMBAY AS. SOC.* Æ ·85, Wt. 175
732 $\frac{1}{8}$	—	,,	4	Obv. مانوس میمنت ٤ سنه جلوس ..ب Rev. as 701 : but ١٠٧١, and بدر for مهر Pl. XIX. Æ ·45, Wt. 22
733	Akbar-ábád	,,	4	Obv. Area, within square, اکبراباد ضرب Margin, سنه ٤ | جلوس | میمنت | مانوس Rev. Area, within square, پادشاه غازی شاه عالمگیر Margin | ابو الظفر | محیی الدین محمد | اورنکزیب | بهادر سنه ١٠٧١ Pl. XIX. *PLAYFAIR.* Æ ·95, Wt. 175

No.	Mint.	Year.	Regnal year.	
Æ 734	Júnah-[garh]	1071	—	Obv. Area, within square, مانوس میمنت جلوس Margin, ... | ..... | جونه | ضرب Rev. Area, within square, عالم گیر زیب اورنگ شاه Margin, ... | منیر سنه ١٠٧١ | چو بدر | ..... Pl. XIX. *GIBBS.* Æ ·9, Wt. 179
735	Súrat?	[10]72	—	As 707: year ٧٢, mint and regnal year obscure; بدر for مهر *PRINSEP.* Æ ·85, Wt. 172
736	Multán	1073	5	" but سنه ٥, ملتان; بدر for مهر; and ١٠٧٣ above نك *CUNNINGHAM.* Æ ·9, Wt. 177
737	—	"	5	Obv. منیر چو مهر ١٠٧٣ زد در جهان سکه . . . . . . Rev. یب اورنگ ز شا[ه عالمگیر ٥ *GOVT. OF INDIA.* Æ ·8, Wt. 176

No.	Mint.	Year.	Regnal year.	
AR 738, 739	Júnah- garh	1074	6	As 734 : but Obv. margin | ضرب | جونه‌کر. | سنه ٦ | and ornaments. Rev. margin, | سکه زد | در جهان | چو بدر منیر | سنه ١٠٧٤ GRANT. AR ·9, Wt. 176 Pl. XIX. ,, AR ·9, Wt. 175
740	Súrat	[1]075	—	As 731: but [١]٠٧٥ ; regnal year obliterated, سورت above ضرب GRANT. AR ·9, Wt. 176
741	,,	[1]076	8	As preceding, but سنه, and [١]٠٧٦ AR 9, Wt. 177
742	Multán	1076	,,	As 701 : but ملتان ,سنه ; ١٠٧٦ over نك ,بدر for مهر GRANT. AR ·9, Wt. 176
742a ⅛	Akbar- nagar	107[6]	9	Obv. اکبرنکر ضرب ٩ سنه ؟ Rev. پاد شاه عالمکیر ١٠٧ Pl. XIX. MARSDEN. AR ·45, Wt. 22
743	Sháh- jahán- ábád	1076	,,	Obv. فه جهاباد دار الخلا شاه ن ضرب جلوس میمنت مانوس ٩ سنه Rev. as 701, but ١٠٧٦ over نك ; بدر for مهر Pl. XIX. AR ·9, Wt. 176

No.	Mint.	Year.	Regnal year.	
Æ 744	Súrat	1077	9	As 731 : but سنه (٩ above), and ١٠٧٧ ; سورت above ضرب *MARSDEN.* Æ ·9, Wt. 177
745 ¼	Akbar-ábád	,,	—	Obv. اکبراباد ضرب ١٠٧٧ سنه Rev. پادشاه غازی عالمگیر شا[ه] Pl. XIX. *MARSDEN.* Æ ·5, Wt. 41
746	Súrat	[1]081	—	As 731 : but ١]٠٨١ ; regnal year partly obliterated ; سورت above ضرب Æ ·9, Wt. 178
747	,,	[10]82	13	As preceding, but ١٢ (cut off) and ٨٢ Æ ·95, Wt. 177
748	Golkon-dah	1076 (*sic*)* [1083]	14	Obv. مانوس میمنت ١٤ سنه جلوس ب ضر کلکنده Rev. as 731 : but ١٠٧٦ at left of last line. Pl. XIX. *MARSDEN.* Æ ·9, Wt. 175

* An old reverse die has been used for the Golkonda coins, nos. 748, 751, 755.

No.	Mint.	Year.	Regnal year.	
Æ 749 ¼	Golkondah	—	15	As 748 : but سنه (١٥ above); rev. partly obliterated. PL. XIX. *MARSDEN*. Æ ·6, Wt. 44
750	Súrat	—	16	As 731 : but سنه (١٦ above); Hijrah year obliterated; سورت above ضرب *PRINSEP*. Æ ·9, Wt. 176
750*a*	,,	[10]84	—	As preceding : but سنه (١[above) on obv., and ٨٤ on rev. *GOVT. OF INDIA*. Æ 85, Wt. 176
751	Golkondah	1076 (*sic*)	16	As 748 : but ١٦, and ١٠٧٦ on rev. *CUNNINGHAM*. Æ ·95, Wt. 178
752	Júnah-[garh]	1085	—	As 734 : rev. differently arranged. Obv. margin, ... | .... | ... ضرب | جونه Rev margin, ١٠٨٥ | ...... | .... سكه زد | چ *GRANT*. Æ ·95, Wt. 176
753	Aurangábád	1088	20	Obv. اورنـــك‌اباد / ر‌ــب / مانوس ضر / ميمــنت / ٢٠ / سنه جلوس Rev. as 731 : but ١٠٨٨ over نك *THEOBALD*. Æ ·9, Wt. 172
754	Súrat	1089	21	As 731 : but سنه (٢١ above), and ٨٩ ; سورت above ضرب Æ 1·0, Wt. 178
755 ⅛	Golkondah	1076 (*sic*)	,,	As 748 : but سنه (٢١ above), and ٧٦ *MARSDEN*. Æ ·45, Wt. 22

No.	Mint.	Year.	Regnal year.	
Æ 756	—	[10]89	22	As 748: but ۲۲ سنه, and ۸۹; mint obliterated. *GIBBS.* Æ ·95, Wt. 178
757	Júnah-garh	1090	—	As 734: but Obv. margin .... | ..... | ..ضرب | جونه‌ک Rev. margin, سکه زد | در جهان | چو بدر | منیر سنه ۱۰۹۰ Æ 1·0, Wt. 173
758	Súrat	,,	22	Obv. ۲۲ سنه مانوس میمنت جلوس ضرب سورت Rev. as 731: but ۱۰۹۰ over نك *I.O.C.* Æ ·95, Wt. 178
759	,,	,,	23	As 758: but ۲۳ سنه, and ۱۰۹۰ *BENG. AS. SOC.* Æ ·95, Wt. 178
760	Patnah?	,,	,,	,, but ؟..ضرپتة [ب], ۲۳ سنه, and ۱۰۹۰ *BOMBAY AS. SOC.* Æ ·85, Wt. 178
761	Súrat	1091	,,	,, but ۲۳, and ۱۰۹۱ *PRINSEP.* Æ 1·0, Wt. 177
762 ½	,,	,,	24	,, but ۲۴, and ۱۰۹۱ Pl. XIX. Æ ·8, Wt. 88
763	Bíjápúr	,,	,,	,, but بیجاپور, ۲۴ سنه, and ۱۹۱ (*sic*) Æ ·85, Wt. 177

No.	Mint.	Year.	Regnal year.	
AR 764	—	1092	24	As 758: mint obliterated, سنه ٢٤, and ١٠٩٢ *I.O.C.* AR ·85, Wt. 175
765, 766	Súrat	1093	25	,, but سنه ٢٥, and ١٠٩٣ *BOMBAY AS. SOC.* AR ·95, Wt. 176 *BANKS.* AR ·9, Wt. 174
767 ½	—	109[3]	,,	,, but mint obliterated, سنه ٢٥, and ١٠٩ (unit of date obliterated.) *GIBBS.* AR ·75, Wt. 88
768	Súrat	1094	27	,, but سنه ٢٧, and ١٠٩٤ *MARSDEN.* AR ·85, Wt. 177
769	,,	1095	,,	,, but سنه ٢٧, and ١٠٩٥ AR ·9, Wt. 178
770	[Júnah-garh]	1096	28	Areas as 734: but سنه ٢٨ on obv. end, r., and ١٠٩٦ on rev. over يب; differently arranged. Obv. margin nearly obliterated. Rev. margin, ... | سكه | زد در | جهان *GRANT.* AR ·95, Wt. 177
771	Súrat	,,	29	As 758: but سنه ٢٩, and ١٠٩٦ AR ·95, Wt. 178
772	'Alam-gírpúr	,,	—	,, but المگيرپور, regnal year obliterated; on rev. ١٠٩٦ PL. XIX. AR ·9, Wt. 176

No.	Mint.	Year.	Regnal year.	
Æ 773	Súrat	1097	29	As 758 : but ٢٩ سنه, and ١٠٩٧ Æ ·95, Wt. 178
774	Burhán-púr	1098	30	,, but ٣[٠] سنه ,برهانپور, and ١٠٩٨ Æ ·85, Wt. 178
775	Súrat	1098	,,	,, but ٣٠ سنه, and ١٠٩٨ *MARSDEN.* Æ ·95, Wt. 176
776	La[hore]	,,	,,	Obv. لا ... دار السلطنه ضرب جلوس ميمنت مانوس ٣٠ سنه Rev. as 731 : but ١٠٩٨ over نك *PRINSEP.* Æ ·85, Wt. 178
777	Narnól	,,	[3?1]	As 758 : but نول.., ٣ سنه, and ١٠٩٨ Pl. XIX. *BENGAL AS. SOC.* Æ ·86, Wt. 177
778	Golkon-dah	,,	[3]1	,, but گلكنده, [٣]١ سنه at left, and ١٠٩٨ *BENGAL AS. SOC.* Æ ·9, Wt. 177
779	Jahán-gírna-gar	1099	32	,, but جهانگيرنگر, ٣٢ سنه, and ١٠٩٩ at left. Æ ·85, Wt. 179
779a	Súrat	,,	,,	,, but ٣٢ سنه, and ١٠٩٩ *BENGAL AS. SOC.* Æ ·1, Wt. 177
780	,,	1100	,,	,, but ٣٢ سنه, and ١١٠٠ *MARSDEN.* Æ ·95, Wt. 177

No.	Mint.	Year.	Regnal year.	
Æ 781	Zafar-púr	1100	32	As 758: but ظفرپور, سنه ٣٢, and ١١٠٠ PL. XIX. Æ ·95, Wt. 178
782	Kábul	[1100]	„	Obv. ما]نوس منـ]منت جلـ]وس دار الملك ضرب كابل ٣٢ Rev. as 731: no year. PL. XIX. Æ ·9, Wt. 178
783	Etáwah	1100	33	As 758: but اتاوه, سنه ٣٣, and ١١٠٠ *PRINSEP.* Æ 1·0, Wt. 175
783*a* ⅛	Gol-kondah	—	—	„ but ... ضرب كلكـ *MARSDEN.* Æ ·45, Wt. 21
784	Súrat	1101	34	„ but سنه ٣٤, and ١١٠١ *BOMBAY. AS. SOC.* Æ 1·0, Wt. 177
785	Cambay	1102	„	„ but كنبايت, سنه ٣٤, and ١١٠٢ over جهان *BENGAL AS. SOC.* Æ ·9, Wt. 178
786	Nárnól	„	„	„ but نارنول, سنه ٣٤, and ١١٠٢ *THOMAS.* Æ ·95, Wt. 177
787	Etáwah	„	35	„ but اتاوه, سنه ٣٥, and ١١٠٢ *EDEN.* Æ 1·05, Wt. 175

No.	Mint.	Year.	Regnal year.	
Æ 788	Chíná- patan	—	35	Obv. مانوس میمنت سنه ٣٥ جلوس ب ضر چیناپتن Rev. as 731 : no Hijrah year. PL. XX. *GIBBS.* Æ 1·0, Wt. 180
789	Akbár- ábád	1103	,,	Obv. اکبراباد ضرب مستقر الخلافه میمنت جلوس مانوس ٣٥ Rev. as 731 : but year ١١٠٣ after جهان *PRINSEP.* Æ 1·05, Wt. 175
790	Súrat	,,	,,	As 758 : but ٣٥ سنه, and ١١٠٣ *PRINSEP.* Æ 1·0, Wt. 179
791	Luck- now	—	,,	,, but لکهنو, ٣٥ سنه; no Hijrah year. *PRINSEP.* Æ 1·0, Wt. 176
792, 792*a*	Etáwah	1104	36	,, but اتاوه, ٣٦ سنه, and ١١٠٤ *PLAYFAIR.* Æ 1·05, Wt. 177 *I.O.C.* Æ 1·0, Wt. 171
793	Luck- now	,,	,,	,, but لکهنو, ٣٦ سنه, and ١١٠٤ after جهان (Zigzag border to reverse.) *PLAYFAIR.* Æ 1·0, Wt. 177

No.	Mint.	Year.	Regnal year.	
AR 794	Súrat	1104	36	As 731 : but سنه (٣٦ above), and ١١٠٤ over نك *GOVT. OF INDIA.* AR 1·0, Wt. 179
795	Bíjápúr	1105	37	,, but ٣٧, at left ; دار الظف[ر] بیجاپور, and ١١٠٥ over نك AR ·9, Wt. 177
796, 796*a*	Súrat	,,	,,	,, but ٣٧ and ١١٠٥ (Counterstruck with galloping horseman.) PL. XX. AR 1·0, 178 *BANKS.* AR 1·0, Wt. 173
797	Etáwah	,,	38	,, but اتاوه, سنه (٣٨ above), and ١١٠٥ *MARSDEN.* AR 1·1, Wt. 174
798	Ajmír	,,	,,	Obv. دار الخیر اجمیر ضرب ج]لوس میمنت مانوس ٣٨ [سنه] Rev. as 731 : but ١١٠٥ over نك PL. XX. AR ·9, Wt. 178
799	Lahore	,,	,,	Obv. لاهور دار السلطنه ضرب جلوس میمنت مانوس ٣٨ سنه Rev. as 731 : but ١١٠٥ over نك *THOMAS.* AR ·95, Wt. 174

No.	Mint.	Year.	Regnal year.	
Æ 800	Etáwah	1106	38	As 731 : but اتاوه, سنه (٣٨ above), and ١١٠٦ over نك *PLAYFAIR.* Æ 1·05, Wt. 178
801	Patnah	,,	,,	,, but .. پتة, سنه (٣٨ above), and ١١٠٦ Æ ·9, Wt. 172
802	[Lahore]	,,	,,	As 799 : but no mint name legible beyond دار السلطنه, and date سنه (٣٨ above) and ١١٠٦ *GOVT. OF INDIA.* Æ ·95, Wt. 174
803	Etáwah	1107	39	As 758 : but اتاوه, سنه (٣٩ above), and ١١٠٧ *MARSDEN.* Æ 1·0, Wt. 175
804	Barailí	,,	,,	,, but بريلى, سنه (٣٩ above), and ١١٠٧ under نك Pl. XX. Æ ·95, Wt. 177
805	Nasrat-ábád	—	3*x*	Obv. مانوس میمنت سنه (٣ above) جلوس ابا[د ضرب نصرت Rev. as 731 : year obliterated. Pl. XX. Æ ·9, Wt. 178
806	Bíjápúr	1107	40	As 758 : but دار الظفر بیجاپور ; ۴۰ over ب of ضرب ; and ١١٠٧ Æ ·9, Wt. 177
807	Barailí	,,	40	,, but بريلى, ۴۰ سنه, and ١١٠٧ under نك Æ ·95, Wt. 177

No.	Mint.	Year.	Regnal year.	
AR 808	Zafar-ábád	1107	40	As 758 : but ظفراباد, ۴۰ سنه, and ۱۱۰۷ Pl. XX. AR ·9, Wt. 178
809	Ahmad-nagar	1108	„	„ but احمدنگر, ۴۰ سنه, and ۱۱۰۸ over منير Pl. XX. AR ·95, Wt. 178
810	Súrat	„	„	„ but ۴۰ سنه, and ۱۱۰۸ *GEORGE III. R.* AR ·9, Wt. 178
811	Etáwah	„	41	„ but اتاوه, ۴۱ سنه, and ۱۱۰۸ Pl. XX. *GRANT.* AR 1·1, Wt. 174
812	Khujis-tah-bunyád (Aurang-ábád)	„	„	„ but خجسته بنياد, ۴۱ سنه, and ۱۱۰۸ AR ·95, Wt. 178
813	Ajmír	„	„	As 798 : but ۴۱, and ۱۱۰۸ *CUNNINGHAM.* AR ·95, Wt. 178
814	Lahore	„	„	As 799 : but ۴۱ سنه (above ت of ميمنت), and ۱۱۰۸ Pl. XX. *GRANT.* AR ·95, Wt. 176
815	Chíná-patan	—	„	As 758: but چيناپتن, ۴۱ سنه; no Hijrah year AR ·9, Wt. 180
816	Cambay	1109	4*x*	„ but ك[نب]ايت, ۴[سنه, and ۱۱۰۹ in last line AR ·95, Wt. 178
817, 818	Akbar-ábád	„	42	As 789 : but ۴۲, and [۱]۱۰۹ *EDEN.* AR ·95, Wt. 177 *GIBBS.* AR ·95, Wt. 177

No.	Mint.	Year.	Regnal year.	
AR 819	Júnah-ga[rh]	1109	$4\frac{1}{2}$	As 758: but .. جونه‌ک, سنه ۴۲, and ۱۱۰۹ Pl. XX. AR ·9, Wt. 177
820	Barailí	1111	43	„ but بریلی, سنه ۴۳, and ۱۱۱۱ *CUNNINGHAM.* AR ·95, Wt. 176
821	Cambay	„	„	„ but کنبایت, سنه ۴۳, and ۱۱۱۱ over جهان Pl. XX. *EDEN.* AR 1·0, Wt. 179
822	Masuli-patan	„	44	As 731: but مچهلی پتن, سنه ۴۴ at left, and ۱۱۱۱ beneath نک Pl. XX. AR ·95, Wt. 178
823	Akbar-ábád	[11]12	„	As 789: but ۴۴, and [۱۱]۱۲ *PRINSEP.* AR ·9, Wt. 177
824	Etáwá	1112	45	As 758: but اتاوا, سنه ۴۵, and ۱۱۱۲ *I.O.C.* AR ·9, Wt. 175
825	Burhán-púr	1113	„	„ but برهانپو[ر], سنه ۴۵, and ۱۱۱۳ AR ·9, Wt. 178
826	Barailí	„	„	„ but بریلی, سنه ۴۵, and ۱۱۱۳ AR ·9, Wt. 177
827	Ajmír	1114	46	As 798: but ۴۶, and ۱۱۱۴ AR ·9, Wt. 178

No.	Mint.	Year.	Regnal year.	
Æ 828, 828*a*	Akbar- ábád	111[4]	46	As 789 : but ۴۶, and [۱۱۱]۴ *EDEN.* Æ ·95, Wt. 175 *PRINSEP.* Æ ·95, Wt. 176
829	Etáwah	1114	47	As 758 : but اتاوه, ۴۷ سنه, and ۱۱۱۴ *GOVT. OF INDIA.* Æ ·95, Wt. 176
830	Lahore	,,	,,	Obv. لاهور دار السلطنه سنه ۴۷ میمنت جلو]س مانوس Rev. as 799 : but ۱۱۱۴ *PRINSEP.* Æ ·9, Wt. 177
831	Etáwah	1115	,,	As 758 : but اتاوه, ۴۷ سنه, and ۱۱۱۵ Æ ·9, Wt. 177
832	Súrat	,,	,,	,, but ۴۷ سنه, and ۱۱۱۵ Æ ·95, Wt. 177
833	Sháh- jahán- ábád	,,	48	Obv. [فه جها اباد] دا]ر [ال]خلا شا ن ضرب ج]لوس میمنت مانوس ۴۸ سنه Rev. as 731 : but year ۱۱۱۵ over نك *PRINSEP.* Æ ·8, Wt. 176
834	Akbar- ábád	[11]16	,,	As 789 : but ۴۸, and ۱۶ *EDEN.* Æ ·9, Wt. 175

No.	Mint.	Year.	Regnal year.	
AR 835	Etáwá	1116	49	As 758 : but اتاوا, سنه ۴۹, and ۱۱۱۶ AR ·9, Wt. 176
836	Barailí	,,	,,	,, but بریلی, سنه ۴۹, and ۱۱۱۶ *THOMAS.* AR ·95, Wt. 176
837	Súrat	,,	,,	,, but سنه ۴۹, and ۱۱۱۶ *MARSDEN.* AR 1·0, Wt. 173
838	Akbar-ábád	1117	,,	As 789 : but ۴۹, and ۱۱۱۷ *PRINSEP.* AR ·9, Wt. 176
839	Súrat	,,	,,	As 758 : but ۴۹, and ۱۱۱۷ AR ·9, Wt. 178
840 ½	,,	11xx	4x	,, but ۴ and ۱۱ (unit of regnal year, and unit and decade of Hijrah year, cut off). *I.O.C.* AR ·75, Wt. 90
841	Etáwá	1117	50	,, but سنه ۵۰, اتاوا, and ۱۱۱۷ AR ·9, Wt. 175
842	,,	1118	,,	As preceding : but ۱۱۱۸ AR ·9, Wt. 176

No.	Mint.	Year	Regnal year.	
AR 843	[Akbar-ábád]	—	51	As 789: but ٥١; اكبراباد and Hijrah year obliterated. *CUNNINGHAM.* AR ·9, Wt. 176
844	Sháh-jahán-ábád	1118	„	As 833: but mint entirely legible; and ٥١, and ١١١٨ *CUNNINGHAM.* AR ·9, Wt. 176
845	„	1119	„	As preceding: but ١١١٩ *PLAYFAIR.* AR ·85, Wt. 177
846	Luck-now	—	„	As 758: but لكهنو, سنه ٥١; no Hijrah year. *BENGAL AS. SOC.* AR ·95, Wt. 177

A'ZAM SHÁH.

A.H. 1118-1119 = A.D. 1707.

No.	Mint.	Year.	Regnal year.	
				GOLD.
AV 847	Khujistah-bunyád (Aurang-ábád)	1118	1	Obv. جلوس ا[شر ف سنه احد ضرب خجسته بنیاد Rev. ممالك اعظم شاه شـــا]ه ۱۱۱۸ ب[دولت و جاه پاد سکـ]ه زد د]ر ج[ہ]ان PL. XX. *MARSDEN.* AV 8, Wt. 169
848	—	,,	,,	Obv. . . . . . . ب ضر جلوس ف احد اشر سنه Rev. as 847 ; lowest two lines obliterated. *CUNNINGHAM.* AV 85, Wt. 168

No.	Mint.	Year.	Regnal year.	
AV 849	Burhán-púr	1119	1	As 847 : but بر]هانپور, and ١١١٩. (Last line of reverse wanting.) PL. XX. *MARSDEN.* AV ·8, Wt. 170
				SILVER.
AR 850	Ahmad-ábád	"	"	Obv. جلوس اشر ف سنه احد ضرب احمداباد Rev. as 847, but ١١١٩ PL. XX. *CUNNINGHAM.* AR ·9, Wt. 176
851	Burhán-púr	"	"	As 850 : but برهانپور PL. XX. *MARSDEN.* AR ·9, Wt. 178

KÁM BAKHSH.

A.H. 1119—1120 = A.D. 1708.

No.	Mint.	Year.	Regnal year.	
				GOLD.
AV 852	Haidar-ábád	1120	2	Obv. مانـ]ـوس ميـ]ـمنت ٢ جلـ]ـوس حيدرابا[د ضرب د]ار الخلا[فه Rev. . . . . پاد كام بخش شا[ه ١١٢٠ ب]ر خورشيد و ماه سكـ[ه دكن[زد Pl. XXI. *GIBBS.* AV ·9. Wt. 170

No.	Mint.	Year.	Regnal year.	
				SILVER.
Æ 853	Bíjápúr	1120	2	Obv. جلوس س میمنت مانو سنه ۲ الظف[ر دار بیجاپور ب ضر
				Rev. . . . . کام بخش شاه بر خو]رشید و ماه که ۱۱۲ دکن زد
				Pl. XXI. *CUNNINGHAM.* Æ ·95, Wt. 176

VII.—SHÁH-'ÁLAM BAHÁDUR.

A.H. 1119—1124=A.D. 1707—1712.

No.	Mint.	Year.	Regnal year.	
				GOLD.
AV 854	Pesh-áwar	1120	2	Obv. مانوس / میمنت / جلوس / ضرب ۲ / پشاور Rev. پادشاه غا[ز]ی / ۱۱۲۰ / عالم بهادر / شا[ه / سکه مبارك PL. XXI. DA CUNHA. AV ·8, Wt. 169
855	Khujis-tah-bunyád (Aurang ábád)	,,	,,	Obv. مانوس / میمنت / سنه جلوس ۲ / ضرب / خج[سته] بنیاد Rev. as 854. I.O.C. AV ·85, Wt. 169

No.	Mint.	Year.	Regnal year.		
AV 856	Sháh-jahán-ábád	1120	2	Obv.	جهان‌اباد شـــــا[ه دار الخـلافـــه ضــــربـــــ سـكـه ۲ مـبـارك
				Rev.	غازى شـــــــاه عــالـم پـاد شـــــــاه سكه سنه ۱۱۲۰
					PL. XXI. AV ·8, Wt. 167
857	Bur-hánpúr	,,	,,	Obv.	جلوس مـــيــمـــنـــت ما]نوس دار السرو[ر سنه ۲ ضــــربـــــ بر]هانپور
				Rev.	۱۱[۲]۰ غازى پادشاه بـهــــا[در شـاه عــالـم س]كـه [مـبـار[ك
					MARSDEN AV ·8, Wt. 167

No.	Mint.	Year.	Regnal year.	
AV 858	Lahore	1120	2	Obv. لاهـو[ر دار السلـطنه ضـرب سنه ۲ مـيـمـنـت جلو]س مانوس Rev. غازى شا[ه شاه عالم بـاد سـكـ[ه ١١٢٠ . . . . Pl. XXI. *I.O.C.* AV ·8, Wt. 170
859	—	,,	,,	Obv. . . ضرب سنه۲ مانوس مـيـمـنـت جـلـوس Rev. as 854. *I.O.C.* AV ·9, Wt. 169
860	Sholá-púr	1121	—	As 854: but no year on rev., and lowest lines of obv. سنه] جلوس ١٢١[١ ض]ـرب ش]لاپور AV ·8, Wt. 169

No.	Mint.	Year.	Regnal year.	
AV 861	Khujistah-bunyád (Aurangábád)	1121	4	Obv. مانوس میمنت ۴ سنه جلوس ضرب خجسته بنیاد Rev. as 854, but ۱۱۲۱ Pl. XXI. *MARSDEN.* AV ·85, Wt. 169
862	Ujjain	1122	—	As 854 : but ۱]۱۲۲ after مبارك on rev., and lowest lines of obv. ضرب دار الفتح اوجين Pl. XXI. *GIBBS.* AV ·85, Wt. 168
863	Akbarábád	1123	5	Obv. جلوس مانوس میمنت مستقر الملك سنه ۵ ضرب اکبراباد Rev. ۱۱۲۳ غازی پادشاه بها در شا عالم ی سکه مبار Pl. XXI. AV 1·25, Wt. 184

No.	Mint.	Year.	Regnal year.	
AV 864	Khujis-tah-bunyád (Aurang-ábád)	1123	5	As 855 : but ١١٢٣, and سنه ٥ PRINSEP. AV ·85, Wt. 169
865	Sháh-jahán-ábád	—	—	Obv. شاه جهان[اباد ب ضر دار الخلافه ميمنت جلوس مانوس Rev. as 854 : but no year. MARSDEN. AV ·85, Wt. 169

No.	Mint.	Year.	Regnal year.	
				SILVER.
Æ 866	Ajmír	1119	1	Obv. اجمیر مستقر الخلاف[ه ضرب جلوس میمنت مانوس احد [سنه] Rev. غازی شاه عا]لم بهادر پاد شاه سکه ا] مبارك ۱۱۱۹ PL. XXI. *THOMAS.* Æ ·9, Wt. 178
867	Sháh-jahán-ábád	,,	,,	Obv. جهان‌ابا[د دار الخلافه .شاه ضرب احد سنه مبارك Rev. غازی شاه شاه عالم پاد سکه سنه ۱۱۱۹ PL. XXI. *THOMAS.* Æ ·9, Wt. 176

No.	Mint.	Year.	Regnal year.		
Æ 868	'Azím-ábád (Patnah)	1120	2	Obv.	عظي[م]اباد ٢ سنه جلوس ضرب
				Rev.	عالم شاه پ]ادشاه غازى سكه ١١٢٠
					Pl. XXI. *CUNNINGHAM.* Æ 1·05, Wt. 174
869, 870	Akbar-ábád	,,	,,	Obv.	جلوس مانوس ميمنت مستقر الملك سنه٢ ضرب سكه] اكبراباد
				Rev.	١١٢٠ غازى پادشاه بها در شاه عالم ك سكه مبار
					EDEN. Æ ·9, Wt. 176
					Pl. XXI. *EDEN.* Æ ·85, Wt. 177

No.	Mint.	Year.	Regnal year.	
AR 871	Lahore	1120	2	Obv. لاه[ور دار السلطنه ضرب سنه ۲ میمنت جلو]س مانوس Rev. غازی شا]ه شاه عالم پاد سکه ۱۱۲۰ *THEOBALD.* AR ·8, Wt. 176
872	Sháh-jahán-ábád	1121	3	As 856 : but سنه ۳ and ۱۱۲۱ *I.O.C.* AR ·8, Wt. 176
873	Burhán-púr	,,	4	Obv. جلوس مانوس میمنت سنه ۴ دار السرور ضرب برهانپور Rev. as 869 : but ۱۱۲۱ Pl. XXI. *I.O.C.* AR ·9, Wt. 176

No.	Mint.	Year.	Regnal year.	
Æ 874	Sholá- púr	1122	4	Obv. مانوس میمنت جلوس ۴ سنه ضرب شلاپور Rev. پادشاه غازی ۱۱۲۲ شاه عالم بهادر لک سکه مبار Pl. XXI. *CUNNINGHAM.* Æ ·95, Wt. 175
875	Súrat	1123	6	Obv. مانو ۶ جلوس س سنه میمنت ضرب سورت Rev. as 869 : but ۱۱۲۳ Pl. XXI. *GRANT.* Æ ·95, Wt. 174
876 ½	—	11*xx*	—	Obv. مانو ۱ سنه جلوس س میمنت ضرب Rev. as 869 : year partly obliterated (۱۱) *GOVT. OF INDIA.* Æ ·75, Wt. 89

VIII.—JAHÁNDÁR.

A.H. 1124 = A.D. 1712.

No.	Mint.	Year.	Regnal year.	
				GOLD.
AV 877	Khujistah-bunyád (Aurangábád)	1124	1	Obv. مانوس / میمنت / سنه احد جلوس / ضرب / خجسته بنیاد
				Rev. پادشاه جهان / شا[ه / قران جهاندا[ر ۱۱۲۴ / حب / زد سکه بر زر چو[ن مهر] صا[
				PL. XXII. CUNNINGHAM AV ·9, Wt. 169

No.	Mint.	Year.	Regnal year.	
AV 878	Khujistah-bunyád	1124	1	Obv. as 877. Rev. جـــهـــانـــدار شـــاه چون مهر و ماه ابو الفتح ۱۱۲۴ حـــــــــــــــب ؟ . . . . Pl. XXII. *DA CUNHA.* AV ·8, Wt. 170
879	Súrat	[11]24	,,	Obv. as 877 : but mint سورت Rev. [ابـ]و[الـ]فتح غازی جهاندار شـ]ـــــــا[ه چو]ن مــهــر و ماه ۲۴ ســـکـــه در] افاق زد *DA CUNHA.* AV ·85, Wt. 170
880	Sháh-jahán-ábád	1124	,,	Obv. جـــهـــان ابـــاد دار الـخـــلافـه شـــاه ضـــرب مـــانـــوس احد سنه مـــیـــمـــنـــت جلوس Rev. غازی جـــهـــاندار[ه شـــــا ۱۱۲۴ برمهرو ماه ابو الفتح ســـکـ[ـه در افاق زد Pl. XXII. *MARSDEN.* AV ·85 Wt. 169

No.	Mint.	Year.	Regnal year.	
AV 881, 882, 883	[Akbar-ábád]	112[4]	1	Obv. ج]لـوس مـانوس مـ]يـمـنـت م]سـتـقـر الملك سنه] احد ضـر]ب .... Rev. ابـو الـفـ]تح غـازى ١١٢ شـاه مـهـ]ر و مـاه جهاندار سـكـه در اقـاق زد چـون *MARSDEN.* *AV* ·75, Wt. 169 *DA CUNHA.* *AV* ·75, Wt. 169 *PRINSEP.* *AV* ·7, Wt. 168
884	—	—	,,	Obv. as 877 : mint obliterated. Rev. غا[ز]ى شـا[ه ما]ه جهاندار سنه (؟) سـ[كه ... چ[ون] ... *I.O.C.* *AV* ·8, Wt. 170

No.	Mint.	Year.	Regnal year.	
				SILVER.
Æ 885	Sháh- jahán- ábád	1124	1	Obv. ا]حد مبارك سنه جهان اباد شاه ضر دار الخلافه ب Rev. جهاندار شاه ١١٢٤ ا]بو الفتح غازی بر مهر و ماه سکه در] افاق زد PL. XXII. *GRANT.* Æ ·85, Wt. 177
886	,,	,,	,,	As 880. *THOMAS.* Æ ·9, Wt. 173
887, 888	[Akbar- ábád]	,,	,,	As 881: mint obliterated; ١١٢٤ fully legible on 887. PL. XXII. *EDEN.* Æ ·9, Wt. 177 *THOMAS.* Æ ·85, Wt. 176
889	Sháh- jahán- ábád	,,	—	Obv. سنه جهان اباد شا]ه دار الخلافه ضرب Rev. ١١٢٤ پادشاه غازی جهاندار شاه نثا]ر PL. XXII. (Nisár.) *THOMAS.* Æ ·6, Wt. 45

IX.—FARRUKH-SIYAR.

A.H. 1124—1131 = A.D. 1713—1719.

No.	Mint.	Year.	Regnal year.	
				GOLD.
AV 890	Mur-shid-ábád	[1124]	1	Obv. مـــانـــو]س مـــيـمـنـت احـــد جلوس سنه ضـ]ـرب . ا . ا . ش . . .
				Rev. ز]د از[ف]ضل حق بر سيم سـ[كه و ز]ر فـرخ سـيـر PL. XXII. *DA CUNHA.* AV ·75, Wt. 170
891	Sháh-jahán-ábád	1127	4	Obv. [فه جهاباد دا]ر الخلا شاه ن ضرب جلوس ميمنت مانوس ۴ سـنه
				Rev. بہ]ر وبر فرخ [سي]ر پـادشـاه حق بر سيم و زر از] فـضـل سـكـه زد ۱۱۲۷ PL. XXII. *GIBBS.* AV ·85, Wt. 169

No.	Mint.	Year.	Regnal year.		
AV 892	Lahore	1129	5	Obv.	لاهور دار السلطنه ضرب سنه ۵ میمنت جلوس مانوس
				Rev.	بحر وبر فرخ سیر پادشاه حق بر سیم و زر ۱۱۲۹ فضل سکه زد از
					Pl. XXII. *PRINSEP.* AV ·9, Wt. 169
893	Barailí?	—	,,	Obv.	مانوس میمنت ۵ سنه جلوس ضرب بر سمد..
				Rev.	حق بحر و بر فرخ[سیر ش[اه ب]ر سیم و زر پاد سک[ه زد از فضل
					Pl. XXII. (Barbarous.) *I.O.C.* AV 1·0, Wt. 168

No.	Mint.	Year	Regnal year.	
AV 894	Burhán-púr	—	6	Obv. جلـــوس مانو[س مـــيـــمـــنـــت ٦ ســـنـــه دار الـسرو[ر ضـــرب بـــرهـــانـــپـــور Rev. as 892 : but no Hijrah year. PL. XXII. *GIBBS.* AV ·85, Wt. 169
895	Patnah	1130	7	Obv. مانوس مـــي]ـــمـــنـــت سـنـه جلـوس ـــب ضر پتنه Rev. as 892 : but ١١٣٠ *MARSDEN.* AV ·8, Wt. 169
896	Sháh-jahán-ábád	,,	,,	Obv. as 891 : but regnal year ٧ Rev. حـــق فـــرخ ســـيـــر شـــ١١٣٠ـــا]ه ا]ز فضل پاد بحر و بر ســـكـ]ـه ز]د بـــر سيم و [زر AV ·8, Wt. 169

No.	Mint.	Year.	Regnal year.	
AV 897	Multán	1130	7	Obv. مانوس ميمنت ٧ سنه جلوس ب ضر ملتان Rev. as 892 : but ۱۱۳۰ Pl. XXII. *HAY.* AV ·8, Wt. 169
898	Bíjápúr	—	,,	Obv. جلوس س ميمنت مانو سنه ٧ [ا]ظفر دار بيجاپور ب ضر Rev. as 892. Pl. XXII. *I.O.C.* AV ·85, Wt. 169
899	Lahore	[1]131	8	As 892 : but سنه (٨ above) on obv., and [۱]۱۳۱ on rev. *I.O.C.* AV ·8, Wt. 169

No.	Mint.	Year.	Regnal year.	
				SMALL ISSUE.
AV 900	—	1125	—	Obv. .. ربری ضـــرب Rev. ١١٢٥ ســـيـــر محمد فرخ Pl. XXII. AV ·35, Wt. 22
900*a*	Karrah	—	3	Obv. امتـــياز ضـــرب ٣ كره سنه Rev. ف]ـرخ سير شـــا پـــاد ه Pl. XXII. *I.O.C.* AV ·45, Wt. 53
901	Gútí	1128	5	Obv. ٥ كوتی ضـــرب Rev. as 900 : but ١١٢٨ Pl. XXII. AV ·35, Wt. 44
902	Gang-púr	,,	,,	Obv. 8 كنكپور ضـرب Rev. as 900 : but year obliterated. Pl. XXII. AV ·3, Wt. 22

No.	Mint.	Year.	Regnal year.	
				SILVER.
Æ 903	Jahán-gírna-gar	1124	1	Obv. as 890 : but mint ج]هانكيرنكر Rev. پرور عظيم دين شا]ه ابوا]لفتح وظفر پاد سكه ۱۱۲۴ . . . Pl. XXIII. *MARSDEN.* Æ ·9, Wt. 187
904	Multán	1125	,,	Obv. as 890 : but mint ملتان Rev. پ]اد شاه غاز ی ۱۱۲۵ سكه فرخ سير *CUNNINGHAM.* Æ ·9, Wt. 175
905	Akbar-ábád	—	2	Obv. جلوس مانوس ميمنت مستقر الملك سنه ۲ ضرب ا]كبرابا[د Rev. as 896 : but no Hijrah year. *PRINSEP.* Æ ·9, Wt. 176

No.	Mint.	Year.	Regnal year.	
Æ 906	Súrat	—	2	Obv. مانوس میمنت ۲ سنه جلوس ضرب سورت Rev. بحر و بر فرخ [سیر] شا[ه] ا]ز فضل حق پاد سکه زد بر سیم و زر *BOMBAY AS. SOC.* Æ ·95, Wt. 179
907, 908	Katak	1125	,,	Obv. as 906 : but mint كتك Rev. حق بحر و بر فرخ [سير شا[ه] زد از فضل پاد ۱۱۲۵ سکه .... (On 908, حق transferred to end of first line.) Pl. XXIII. *MARSDEN.* Æ ·9, Wt. 187 *MARSDEN.* Æ ·9, Wt. 187
909	Sháh-jahán-ábád	,,	,,	As 891 : but ۲ سنه, and no Hijrah year. *THOMAS.* Æ ·85, Wt. 177
910	Lahore	1125	,,	Obv. as 892 : but سنه ۲ Rev. ا]ز فضل حق ۱۱۲۵ پادشا[ه] بحر و بر فرخ سیر سک[ه] ز[د [بر] سیم و]زر *GOVT. OF INDIA.* Æ ·9, Wt. 175

No.	Mint.	Year.	Regnal year.	
AR 911	Multán	—	2	Obv. مانوس میمنت سنه ۲ جلوس ضرب م]لتان Rev. از فضل [حق شا[ه پاد بحر و بر فرخ سیر سکه] زد بر سیم[و زر AR ·9, Wt. 176
912	Akbar-ábád	—	3	As 905 : but سنه ۳ *GIBBS.* AR ·9, Wt. 176
913	'Azím-ábád (Patnah)	[11]26	,,	Obv. مانوس میمنت سنه ۳ جلوس عظیم ضرب اباد Rev. زد از فضل حق بر سیم[وزر شا[ه بحر و بر فرخ سیر سکه] پاد ۲۶ *CUNNINGHAM.* AR ·95, Wt. 176
914	Katak	1126	,,	Obv. as 913 : but ضرب کتك Rev. as 892, varied ; ۱۱۲۶ below فضل *MARSDEN.* AR ·9, Wt. 187

No.	Mint.	Year.	Regnal year.	
Æ 915, 916	Sháh-jahán-ábád	1127	4	As 891 : but Hijrah year ١١٢٧ (obliterated on 915). *EDEN.* Æ ·9, Wt. 174 *PLAYFAIR.* Æ ·85, Wt. 173
917	Súrat	[11]27	„	As 906 : but سنه (with ٤ above) ; mint obliterated except ت and the vowel ُ ; and ٢٧ legible at left of rev. Æ ·9, Wt. 177
918	Etáwá	1128	5	Obv. مانوس میمنت سنه ٥ جلوس ضرب اتاوا Rev. as 892 : but year ١١٢٨ Pl. XXIII. *THOMAS.* Æ 1·05, Wt. 176
919	Akbar-ábád	1128	„	As 905 : but ٥ سنه, and ١١٢٨ above rev. *PRINSEP.* Æ ·9, Wt. 177
920	Chíná-patan	„	„	Obv. مان]و[س میـ]ـمنت سنه جلوس ضرب چیناپتن Rev. as 906 : with year ١١٢٨ Pl. XXIII. *I.O.C.* Æ ·9, Wt. 179

No.	Mint.	Year.	Regnal year.	
Æ 921	Súrat	—	5	As 906 : but سنه ٥ *MARSDEN.* Æ ·9, Wt. 178
922	Sháh-jahán-ábád	1128	,,	As 891 : but سنه ٥, and ١١٢٨ over فضل, and از in last line of rev. *GOVT. OF INDIA.* Æ 1·1, Wt. 178
923	,,	,,	,,	As 922 : but [از] before فضل and ١١٢٨ at end of rev. Æ ·85, Wt. 177
924	Akbar-ábád	[11]29	,,	Obv. as 905 : but سنه ٥, مستقر الخلافه Rev. as 892. Pl. XXIII. *MARSDEN.* Æ ·95, Wt. 176
925	Sháh-jahán-ábád	1129	,,	As 891 : but سنه ٥, and ١١٢٩ over فضل ; از in last line. Pl. XXIII. *THOMAS.* Æ 1·0, Wt. 177
926	,,	,,	6	As 925 : but سنه ٦ *GRANT.* Æ 1·05, Wt. 175
927	Gwálior	1129	,,	Obv. مانوس میمنت سنه ٦ جلوس ضرب گوالیار Rev. as 892. Pl. XXIII. *I.O.C.* Æ ·95, Wt 175

No.	Mint.	Year.	Regnal year.	
Æ 928, 929	Lahore	1129	6	As 892: but ٦ سنه Pl. XXIII. *THOMAS.* Æ 1·1, Wt. 172 *BENGAL AS. SOC.* Æ ·9, Wt. 178
930, 931	Mur-shid-ábád	—	,,	Obv. مانوس میمنت ٦ سنه جلوس ض]رب مر]شداباد Rev. زد از فضل حق بر سی]م[و زر] پـاد]شـ[اه بـ]حر و بر فرخ سیر سـکـ[ه . . . . *GOVT. OF INDIA.* Æ ·85, Wt. 180 Pl. XXIII. *MARSDEN.* Æ ·8, Wt. 179
932	Akbar-ábád	[11]30	7	Obv. as 905: but سنه ٧ مستقر الخلافه Rev. as 892: [١١]٣٠ *THEOBALD.* Æ ·95, Wt. 177
933	Arkát	,,	,,	Obv. مانوس می]منت سنه ٧ جلوس ضرب ارکات Rev. حق فرخ [سیر ١١٣٠ شـ[اه و زر پاد بحر و بر سـ[که زد از فضل بر[سیم Pl. XXIII. *EDEN.* Æ ·9, Wt. 177

No.	Mint.	Year.	Regnal year.	
Æ 934	Súrat	—	7	As 906 : but سنه. No Hijrah year. *BOMBAY AS. SOC.* Æ 1·0, Wt. 179
935	Multán	1130	,,	Obv. as 904 : but سنه Rev. as 892 : but ۱۱۳۰ Pl. XXIII. *CUNNINGHAM.* Æ ·95, Wt. 177
936	A'zam-nagar	—	—	Obv. مانوس مـ]يـمـنـت سنه جـ]لوس اعظم نكر ب ضـر Rev. بحر [و] بر فرخ [سير شـ]اه حق بر سيم و زر پا]د فـضـل سكه زد از Pl. XXIII. *GIBBS.* Æ ·9, Wt. 177

X.—RAFÍ'-AD-DARAJÁT.

A.H. 1131 = A.D. 1719.

No.	Mint.	Year.	Regnal year.	
				GOLD.
AV 937	Sháh-jahán-ábád	1131	1	Obv. فه جها ابا[د / ه / دار الخلا شا ن / ضرب / ج]لوس ميمنت مانوس / احد / سنه Rev. رفيع الدرجا / ١١٣١ / ب]ركا شاهنشه بحر و بر / ز]د با هراران / س]كه [بهند] PL. XXIII. *I.O.C.* AV ·85, Wt. 169
937*a*	Mu'az-zam-ábád	„	„	Obv. مانوس / م]يمنت / احد جلوس سنه / ضرب / م]عظماباد Rev. As preceding, partly obliterated; ١١٣١ under شاهنشه PL. XXIII. *GRANT.* AV ·8, Wt. 168

No.	Mint.	Year.	Regnal year.	
				SILVER.
Æ 938, 939	Akbar-ábád	1131	1	Obv. اکبراباد مستقر الخلافه ضرب جلوس میمنت مانوس احد سنه Rev. as 937. Pl. XXIII. *CUNNINGHAM.* Æ 1·0, Wt. 172 *EDEN.* Æ ·85, Wt. 173
940, 941	Sháh-jahán-ábád	,,	,,	As 937: but ١١٣١ at left top of rev. *CUNNINGHAM.* Æ ·9, Wt. 175 Pl. XXIII. *GRANT.* Æ ·95, Wt. 173
942	Kúrá	,,	,,	Obv. مانوس میمنت جلوس احد سنه ضرب کورا Rev. as 937. Pl. XXIII. *CUNNINGHAM.* Æ ·9, Wt. 175

No.	Mint.	Year.	Regnal year.	
Æ 943	Lahore	1131	1	Obv. جلوس مانوس میمنت احد دار السلطنه لاهور ضرب Rev. رفیع الدرجا ت شاهنشه بحر و بر ت با]هزاران برکا١١٣١ سک]ه زد [بهند Pl. XXIII. *EDEN.* Æ ·95, Wt. 177
944	Patnah?	,,	,,	Obv. as 942 : but ضرب تـه.. Rev. as 937. *THOMAS.* Æ ·95, Wt. 179

XI.—RAFÍ'-AD-DAULAH SHÁH-JAHÁN II.

A.H. 1131 = A.D. 1719.

No.	Mint	Year.	Regnal year.		
					GOLD.
AV 945	Sháh-jahán-ábád	1131	1	Obv.	[فـــه جها اباد] دا]رالـــخـــلا شـــاه ن ضـــرب جلوس ميمنت مانوس ســـنه احد
				Rev.	شاه جهان ى پادشاه غاز ١١٣١ ء ك سكه مبار
					PL. XXIV. *GRANT.* AV ·9, Wt. 167
946	Khujis-tah-bunyád (Aurang-ábád)	„	—	Obv.	بدر م]يـــمـــنـــت جلوس مـــانوس ضـــرب خ]جسته بنيا[د
				Rev.	شا[ا[ه] جهان ى شـــاه غـــاز ســـكه ١١٣١ مـــبـــ]ارك سنه
					PL. XXIV. *CUNNINGHAM.* AV ·8, Wt. 169

No.	Mint.	Year.	Regnal year.	
				SILVER.
AR 947	Akbar-ábád	1131	1	Obv. اکبراباد مستقر الخلافه ضرب جلوس میمنت مانوس احد . . . Rev. as 945, but ١١٣١ at top. PL. XXIV. AR ·95, Wt. 176
948	Barailí	,,	,,	Obv. مانوس میمنت احد سنه جلوس ضرب بریلی Rev. as 945, but ١١٣١ over مبارک PL. XXIV. *GRANT.* AR 1·0, Wt. 175
949	Súrat	—	,,	As 948: but mint ت . . . and no Hijrah year visible. *I.O.C.* AR ·95, Wt. 177
950	'Azím-ábád (Patnah)	1131	,,	Obv. عظیم اباد ضرب جلوس میمنت مانوس احد سنه Rev. پادشاه غازی شاه جهان سکه مبارک ١١٣١ PL. XXIV. *THEOBALD.* AR ·95, Wt. 178

No.	Mint.	Year.	Regnal year.	
Æ 951	Lahore	1131	1	Obv. as 943. Rev. as 945 : ١١٣١ over مبارك PL. XXIV. *CUNNINGHAM.* Æ ·9, Wt. 175
952	Mur-shid-ábád	,,	,,	Obv. as 948, but mint مرشدابا[د Rev. شاه جهان ی ١١٣١ پا]دشاه غا[ز PL. XXIV. *GOVT. OF INDIA.* Æ ·8, Wt. 180

NIKU-SIYAR.

A.H. 1131 = A.D. 1719.

No.	Mint.	Year.	Regnal year.	
				GOLD.
AV 953	Súrat	—	1	Obv. مانوس / ميمنت / سنه احد جلوس / ضرب / سورت Rev. ب]لطف اله محمد / شا[ه / پا]دشاه زمان / سکه / زد]د[ر] جهان PL. XXIV. *I.O.C.* AV ·95, Wt. 171

IBRÁHÍM.

A.H. 1132 = A.D. 1720.

No.	Mint.	Year.	Regnal year.	
				GOLD.
AV 954, 955	Sháh-jahán-ábád	1132	1	Obv. as 945. Rev. ب]ر[سي]م محمد ابراهيم شـــــاه شـــاهـــان ۱۱۳۲ ب]ـــفـــضـــل سـكـه زد در جـهـان *CUNNINGHAM.* AV ·8, Wt. 167 PL. XXIV. *GIBBS.* AV ·75, Wt. 168
				SILVER.
AR 956, 957	,,	,,	,,	As 954: but ۱۱۳۲ at right of rev. (Date effaced on 957.) PL. XXIV. *CUNNINGHAM.* AR ·9, Wt. 175 *GIBBS.* AR ·8, Wt. 172

XII.—MUHAMMAD SHÁH.

A.H. 1131—1161=A.D. 1719—1748.

No.	Mint.	Year.	Regnal year.		
					GOLD.
AV 958	Khujistah-bunyád (Aurangábád)	1131	1	Obv.	مانوس میمنت احد جلوس سنه ضرب خجسته بنیاد
				Rev.	۱۱۳۱ محمد شاه ی پادشاه غاز ی سکه مبار Pl. XXV. *I.O.C.* AV ·65, Wt. 169
959	Sháh-jahán-ábád	1134	3	Obv.	فه جها اباد دار الخلا شاه ن ضرب جلوس میمنت مانوس ۳ سنه
				Rev.	محمد شاه پادشاه غازی ۱۱۳۴ صاحب قران ثانی سکه مبارک Pl. XXV. (Formerly ringed.) AV 1·0

No.	Mint.	Year.	Regnal year.	
AV 960	Sháh-jahán-ábád	113[7]	7	As 959 : but سنه [٧], and ١١٣ (unit cut off). *MARSDEN.* AV ·8, Wt. 168
961	Etáwá	1139	9	As 958 : but سنه [٩], اتاوا; and ١١٣٩ AV 1·1, Wt. 168
961*a*	——	1*xxx*	,,	As preceding : but mint and Hijrah date effaced. (Súrat fabric.) *BANKS.* AV ·75, Wt. 169
962, 963	Sháh-jahán-ábád	11*xx*	11	As 959 : but سنه [١١], and ١١ AV ·8, Wt. 168 *I.O.C.* AV ·75, Wt. 168
964	,,	114*x*	14	As 959 : but سنه [١٤], and ١١٤ (unit cut off). *MARSDEN.* AV ·75, Wt. 167
965	,,	114[5]	15	As 959 : but سنه [١٥], and ١١٤ (unit cut off). AV ·8, Wt. 168
966	,,	114[6]	16	As 959 : but سنه [١٦], and ١١٤ (unit cut off). AV ·8, Wt. 168
967	Akbar-ábád	1147	17	Obv. جلوس مانوس ميمنت مستقر الخلافه سنه ١٧ ضرب اكبراباد Rev. as 958 : but ١١٤٧ PL. XXV. AV ·85, Wt. 168
967*a*	Súrat	11*xx*		As 958 : but regnal year cut off ; mint [س]ورت ; and ١١ (decimal and unit cut off). *BANK COLL.* AV ·85, Wt. 171

No.	Mint.	Year.	Regnal year.	
AV 968	Etáwá	1150	20	As 958 : but ٢٠ سنه, اتاوا ; and ١١٥٠ PL. XXV. *PRINSEP.* AV ·9, Wt. 169
969	Khujis-tah-bunyád	11[50]	,,	As 958 : but ٢٠ سنه, and ١١ (unit and decade cut off). *I.O.C.* AV ·8, Wt. 169
970, 971	Sháh-jahán-ábád	1152	22	As 959 : but ٢٢ سنه, and ١١٥٢ (١١٥*x* on 971) *I.O.C.* AV ·95, Wt. 168 *MARSDEN.* AV ·9, Wt. 168
972	,,	1153	23	As 959 : but ٢٣ سنه, and ١١٥٣ AV ·85, Wt. 169
973	Kash-mír	1154	24	Obv., in centre, within triple circle, ٢٤ سنه جلوس Around, in four ovals with ornamented borders, ميمنت | مانوس | ضرب | كشمير Rev., interlaced, ٥٥ محمد شاه شا غاز مبارك پاد سكه ١١٥٤ PL. XXV. *CUNNINGHAM.* AV ·85, Wt. 168

No.	Mint.	Year.	Regnal year.	
AV 974	Lahore	1155	25	Obv. لاهور دار السلطنه ضرب سنه ۲۵ میمنت جلوس مانوس Rev. as 958 : but ۱۱۵۵ PL. XXV. AV ·8, Wt. 168
975	Sháh-jahán-ábád	1157	26	As 959 : but ۲٦ سنه, and ۱۱۵۷ *MARSDEN.* AV 1·15, Wt. 166
975a	Ahmad-nagar Far-rukh-[ábád]	—	31	Obv. مانوس میمنت سنه ۳۱ جلوس ضرب احمدنکر فرخ Rev. ا]لله محمد شا[ه] غازی ی زد ز تایید حامی سکه مبا[ر PL. XXV. AV ·95, Wt. 167

No.	Mint.	Year.	Regnal year.	
				SMALL ISSUE.
AV 976	Karrah	1161	—	Obv. کــره ضــرب Rev. محمد شـــاه پـــا]دشاه ۱۱۶۱ Pl. XXV. *I.O.C.* *AV* ·4, Wt. 52
977	,,	—	—	Obv. کــر[ه ضــرب امتــیاز Rev. محمد شاه ش]ـــــ[ا پاد ه Pl. XXV. *I.O.C.* *AV* ·5, Wt. 51

No.	Mint.	Year.	Regnal year.	
				SILVER.
AR 978	Akbar-ábád	1132	1	Obv. اکبراباد م]ستقر الخلافه ضرب ج]لوس میمنت مانوس احد سنه Rev. as 958 : but ۱۱۳۲ *CUNNINGHAM.* AR ·9, Wt. 176
979	Súrat	113[2-33]	2	Obv. مانوس میمنت ۲ سنه جلوس ضرب سورت Rev. as 958 : but ۱۱۳ (unit cut off). *BOMBAY AS. SOC.* AR 1·05, Wt. 176
980	Mur-shid-ábád	11[32-33]	„	Obv. مانو]س میمنت ۲ سنه جلوس ضرب مرشدابا]د Rev. as 958: but ۱۱ (unit and decade cut off). *BENGAL AS. SOC.* AR ·85, Wt. 180

No.	Mint.	Year.	Regnal year.	
AR 981	Súrat	113[3-34]	3	As 979: but سنه ٣, and ١١٣ (unit cut off). *BOMBAY AS. SOC.* AR 1·0, Wt. 178
982	„	„	4	As 979: but سنه ٤, and ١١٣ (unit cut off). AR 1·0, Wt. 178
983	Sháh-jahán-ábád	1134	„	As 959: but سنه ٤, and ١١٣٤ (over صاحب). *GOVT. OF INDIA.* AR ·9, Wt. 174
984	„	1135	5	„ but سنه 9, and ١١٣٥ (over صاحب) *MARSDEN.* AR ·85, Wt. 175
985	Akbar-nagar Oudh	„	„	Obv. اكبرنگر اود ضرب ٥ سنه جلوس ميمنت مانوس Rev. as 958: but ١١٣٥ PL. XXV. *CUNNINGHAM.* AR 1·0, Wt. 174

No.	Mint.	Year.	Regnal year.	
Æ 986	Akbar-ábád ?	11[36-37]	6	Obv. مانوس / ميمنت / ٦ سنه جلوس / ضرب / ا]ك[براباد (؟) Rev. as 958: unit and decade cut off. Æ ·9, Wt. 175
987	Súrat	—	,,	As 979: but ٦ سنه; Hijrah year cut off. *BOMBAY AS. SOC.* Æ ·95, Wt. 178
988	Lahore	—	,,	As 974: but ٦ سنه; Hijrah year cut off. Æ ·85, Wt. 176
989	Tattah	1137	,,	Obv. مانوس / ميمنت / ٦ سنه جلوس / ب / ضر تته (تته pointed.) Rev. as 958: but ١١٣٧ over ميا *MARSDEN.* Æ ·8, Wt. 177

No.	Mint.	Year.	Regnal year.	
Æ 990	'Azím-ábád*	11[36-37]	6	Obv. ....يم.. ضرب جلوس ميمنت مانوس ٦ سنه Rev. as 958 : but ۱۱۱ (unit cut off). *BENGAL AS. SOC.* Æ ·85, Wt. 178
991	Sháh-jahán-ábád	1137	7	As 959 : but سنه (with ٧ above), and ۱۱۳۷ (over صاحب). *I.O.C.* Æ ·85, Wt. 175
992	'Azím-ábád	,,	,,	Obv. عظ]يم اباد ضرب جلوس ميمنت مانوس ٧ سنه Rev. ۱۱۳۷ محمد شاه ے پاد شاه غاز سک]ه مبارك *BENGAL AS. SOC.* Æ ·85, Wt. 180

* The م thus dotted, compared with no. 992, identifies the mint.

No.	Mint.	Year.	Regnal year.	
Æ 993	Etáwá	1139	9	As 958 : but ٩ سنه, اتاوا ; and ١١٣٩ Æ 1·0, Wt. 177
994	„	1140	„	As preceding, but ١١٤٠. *PLAYFAIR.* Æ 1·0, Wt. 173
995	[Lahore]	11[3 - 40]	„	As 974 : but ٩ سنه, mint and Hijrah year partly obliterated. *GOVT. OF INDIA.* Æ ·85, Wt. 175
996	Sháh-jahán-ábád	„	„	As 959 : but ٩ سنه, and ١١ (unit and decade cut off). Æ ·85, Wt. 175
997	Akbar-ábád	11[40-41]	10	As 967 : but ١٠ سنه, and ١١ (unit and decade cut off). *GOVT. OF INDIA.* Æ ·9, Wt. 175
998	Kúrá	1141	11	Obv. مانوس ميمنت سنه ١١ جلوس ضرب كورا Rev. as 958 : but ١١٤١ Pl. XXV. *MARSDEN,* Æ ·95, Wt. 174

No.	Mint.	Year.	Regnal year.	
Æ 999	Sháh-jahán-ábád	1142	11	١١ As 959 : but سنه, and ١١٤٢ (over صاحب) *GOVT. OF INDIA.* Æ ·85, Wt. 176
1000	,,	,,	12	١٢ ,, but سنه, and ١١٤٢ *GOVT. OF INDIA.* Æ ·9, Wt. 175
1001	,,	1143	13	١٣ ,, but سنه, and ١١٤٣ *I.O.C.* Æ ·85, Wt. 175
1002	Etáwá	11[43-44]	,,	١٣ As 958 : but سنه, اتاوا; and ١١١ (unit and decade cut off). *GRANT.* Æ 1·0, Wt. 175
1003	Lahore	11[44-45]	14	As 974 : but ١٤ سنه, and ١١٢ (unit and decade cut off). *I.O.C.* Æ ·85, Wt. 175
1004	Sháh-jahán-ábád	1145	15	١٥ As 959 : but سنه, and ١١٤٥ (over صاحب) *DE BODE.* Æ ·8, Wt. 174
1005	Súrat	11[45-46]	,,	١٥ As 979 : but سنه ; ١١ (unit and decade cut off). *I.O.C.* Æ ·95, Wt. 175

No.	Mint.	Year.	Regnal year.	
Æ 1006	Sháh-jahán-ábád	114[6-47]	16	As 959 : but ١٦ سنه, and ١١٤ (unit cut off). *MARSDEN.* Æ ·85, Wt. 174
1007	Lahore	11[46-47]	,,	As 974 : but ١٦ سنه, and ١١ (unit and decade cut off). *I.O.C.* Æ ·8, Wt. 175
1008	Sháh-jahán-ábád	1147	17	As 959 : but ١٧ سنه, and ١١٤٧ *I.O.C.* Æ ·9, Wt. 175
1009	,,	[,,]	,,	As preceding ; but Hijrah year obliterated. Æ ·85, Wt. 171
1010	,,	,,	,,	As preceding : but Hijrah year ١١٤٧ over صاحب *BENGAL AS. SOC.* Æ ·85, Wt. 176
1011	Ajáyúr ?	1148	1x	Obv. مانوس میمنت ١[سنه جلوس ضرب اجایور Rev. as 958 : but ١١٤٨ PL. XXV. Æ ·95, Wt. 179

No.	Mint.	Year.	Regnal year.	
Æ 1012	Sháh-jahán-ábád	11[48-49]	18	As 959 : but سنه with ۱۸ above, Hijrah year partly cut off. *GOVT. OF INDIA.* Æ ·85, Wt. 171
1013	Súrat	"	19	As 979: but سنه with ۱۹ above, and ۱۱ (unit and decade cut off). *GOVT. OF INDIA.* Æ ·95, Wt. 178
1014	Sháh-jahán-ábád	114[9]	"	As 959 : but سنه with ۱۹ above, and ۱۱۴ (over صاحب). *DE BODE.* Æ ·85, Wt. 176
1015	(Lahore)	11[49-50]	"	As 974 : but ۱۹ سنه, mint and Hijrah year partly obliterated. *I.O.C.* Æ ·8, Wt. 171
1016	Islám-ábád (Chitta-gong)	1150	"	Obv. اسلام اباد ضرب میمنت مانوس جلوس ۱۹ سنه Rev. as 958: but ۱۱۵۰ *PRINSEP.* Æ ·9, Wt. 174
1017	Benáres	"	20	Obv. محمد ابا[د میمنت سنه (۲ above) جلوس مانوس ضرب بنارس Rev. as 958 : but ۱۱۵۰ *EDEN.* Æ ·9, Wt. 175

No.	Mint.	Year.	Regnal year.	
AR 1018	Lahore	115[0]	20	As 974 : but ۲۰ سنه, mint partly obliterated, and unit of Hijrah year cut off. *THEOBALD.* AR ·75, Wt. 177
1019	Sháh-ábád	1151	21	Obv. مانوس میمنت ۲۱ سنه جلوس ضرب شاه اباد فنوج ر Rev. as 958 : but ۱۱۵۱ PL. XXV. AR 1·0, Wt. 174
1020	Sháh-jahán-ábád	1152	22	As 959 : but ۲۲ سنه, and ۱۱۵۲ *THOMAS.* AR ·9, Wt. 175
1021	,,	—	,,	As preceding, but Hijrah year cut off. AR ·85, Wt. 171
1022	'Azím-ábád	1152	,,	Obv. عظیم اباد ضرب میمنت مانوس جلوس ۲۲ سنه Rev. as 958 : but ۱۱۵۲, and سکه above مبارك *MARSDEN.* AR 1·1, Wt. 179

No.	Mint.	Year.	Regnal year.	
Æ 1023	'Azím-ábád	1152	22	As preceding, mint partly obliterated. *I.O.C.* Æ ·9, Wt. 177
1024	Sháh-jahán-ábád	1153	23	As 959 : but ٢٣ سنه and ١١٥٣ *THOMAS.* Æ 1·0, Wt. 175
1025	„	„	„	As preceding, unit of Hijrah year cut off. *DE BODE.* Æ ·85, Wt. 170
1026	„	1154	24	As 959 : but ٢٤ سنه and ١١٥٤ *GRANT.* Æ ·9, Wt. 172
1027	„	1155	25	„ but ٢٥ سنه, and ١١٥٥ *GRANT.* Æ ·95, Wt. 172
1028	„	„	„	As preceding, but unit of Hijrah year effaced. *GRANT.* Æ 1·05, Wt. 160
1029	Far-rukh-ábád	115[5]	„	Obv. مانوس میمنت سنه ٢٥ جلوس ضرب فرخ اباد Rev. as 959 : but ١١٥٥ (over صاحب) Pl. XXV. *EDEN.* Æ 1·05, Wt. 174

No.	Mint.	Year.	Regnal year.	
AR 1030	Mur-shid-ábád	115[5]	25	Obv. مانوس ميمنت ٢٥ سنه جلوس ضرب مرشد ا[باد Rev. as 958 : but ١١٥ (unit cut off). *GOVT. OF INDIA.* AR ·85, Wt. 179
1031	Etáwá	1156	26	Obv. as 958 : but ٢٦ سنه, اتاوا ; and ١١٥٦ *THEOBALD.* AR 1·0, Wt. 175
1032	Siwái-Jaipúr	,,	,,	Obv. مانوس ميمنت ٢٦ سنه جلوس ضرب سواي جي پور Rev. as 958 : but ١١٥٦ Pl. XXV. *I.O.C.* AR ·9, Wt. 175
1033 1034	Sháh-jahán-ábád	1157	,,	As 959 : but ٢٦ سنه and ١١٥٧ *THOMAS.* AR 1·05, Wt. 176 *PRINSEP.* AR ·9, Wt. 172
1035	Barailí	115[7]	,,	Obv. مانوس م]يمنت ٢٧ جلوس سنه يلى ضرب بر Rev. as 958 : but ١١٥ (unit cut off.) Pl. XXV. AR ·85, Wt. 174

No.	Mint.	Year.	Regnal year.	
Æ 1036	Sháh- jahán- ábád	11[58]	28	As 959 : but سنه (۲۸ above) and ۱۱ (unit and decade cut off.) Æ ·9, Wt. 175
1037	Akbar- ábád	1158	29	Obv. جلوس مانوس میمنت مستقر الخلافه سنه ۲۹ ضرب اکبراباد Rev. as 958 : but ۱۱۵۸ *CUNNINGHAM.* Æ 1·05, Wt. 169
1038	Sháh- jahán- ábád	1159	,,	As 959 : but سنه (۲۹ above), and ۱۱۵۹ *BENG. AS. SOC.* Æ ·9, Wt. 176

XIII.—AHMAD SHÁH.

A.H. 1161—1167=A.D. 1748—1754.

No.	Mint.	Year.	Regnal year.	
				GOLD.
AV 1039	Sháh- jahán- ábád	[11]61	1	Obv. [فــه جهــا ابــاد] دا]ر[اا]خــلا شــان ضــرب جلوس ميمنت مانوس احد ســنه Rev. احــمــد شــاه بـهـاد[ر ی پـــادشـــاه غاز ا ٦١ ی س]ـكـ[ه] مبار PL. XXVI. *CUNNINGHAM.* AV ·8, Wt. 168
1040	Benáres	1162	2	Obv. مـحـ]مد[اباد مـيـمـنـت ٢ جلو سنه س مانوس ضـرب بنـارس Rev. as 1039, partly obliterated ; year ١١٦٢ PL. XXVI. *YEAMES.* AV ·75, Wt. 168

No.	Mint.	Year.	Regnal year.	
AV 1041 1042	Sháh-jahán-ábád	[11]66	6	As 1039 : but سنه with ٦ above, and ٦٦ MARSDEN. AV ·85. Wt. 168 AV ·75, Wt. 167
1043	,,	[11]67	7	As 1039 : but سنه with ٧ above, and ٦٧ PROF. WILSON. AV ·95, Wt. 168
1044	—	—	—	Obv. ا]حمد شا Reverse plain. PL. XXVI. AV ·25, Wt. 3

No.	Mint.	Year.	Regnal year.	
				SILVER.
Æ 1045	'Azím-ábád	1161	1	Obv. مانوس میمنت احد سنه جلوس عظیماباد ضرب Rev. احمد شاه بهادر پادشاه غازی ۱۱۶۱ سکه مبارک Pl. XXVI. *EDEN.* Æ ·95, Wt. 178
1046	Sháh-jahán-ábád	,,	,,	As 1039. *PRINSEP.* Æ ·9, Wt. 175
1047	Far-rukh-ábád	,,	,,	Obv. as 1045 : but ضرب فرخاباد Rev. as 1039. Pl. XXVI. *CUNNINGHAM.* Æ ·95, Wt. 171
1048	Akbar-ábád	—	2	Obv. جلوس مانوس میمنت مستقر الخلافه سنه ۲ ضرب اکبراباد Æ ·9, Wt. 175

No.	Mint.	Year.	Regnal year.	
Æ 1049	Sháh-jahán-ábád	[1]162	2	As 1039 : but ٢ سنه and ١٦٢ *GRANT.* Æ ·95, Wt. 174
1050	,,	[1]164	3	As 1039 : but ٣ سنه and ١٦٤ *BENG. AS. SOC.* Æ ·95, Wt. 176
1051	,,	,,	4	As preceding : but ٤ سنه *THOMAS.* Æ ·95, Wt. 175
1052	Benáres	,,	,,	As 1040, but ٤ سنه, محمدابا[د] distinct, and ١١٦٤ *EDEN.* Æ ·85, Wt. 176
1053 1054	Sháh-jahán-ábád	1165	5	As 1039, but ٥ سنه and ١١٦٥ *BENG. AS. SOC.* Æ ·9. Wt. 176 *THOMAS.* Æ ·95, Wt. 175
1055	Mur-shid-ábád	—	,,	Obv. مانو[س میمنت ٥ سنه جلوس ضرب مر]شد ابا[د Rev. as 1039 : partly obliterated, no Hijrah year. *GOVT. OF INDIA.* Æ ·85, Wt. 179
1056	Sháh-jahán-ábád	—	6	As 1039 : but ٦ سنه ; Hijrah year obliterated. *THOMAS.* Æ 9, Wt. 175

No.	Mint.	Year	Regnal year.	
Æ 1057	Murád-ábád	1167	6	Obv. مانوس میمنت جلوس سنه ٦ ضرب مراداباد Rev. as 1039 : but ١١٦٧ PL. XXVI. *CUNNINGHAM.* Æ ·95, Wt. 174
1058	Mur-shid-ábád	—	,,	As 1055 : but سنه ٦ Æ 1·0, Wt. 179

XIV.—'ÁLAMGÍR II.

A.H. 1167—1173=A.D. 1754—1759.

No.	Mint.	Year.	Regnal year.	
				GOLD.
AV 1059	Sháh- jahán- ábád	—	1	Obv. [فـه]جـهـا[ابـاد] د[ا]ر[اا]خـلا شـاه ن ضـرب جلوس ميمنت مانوس احد سـنـه Rev. اا عالمگير پـاد شـاه غـاز ى س]كه مبار PL. XXVI. *MARSDEN.* AV ·85, Wt. 159
1060	„	1168	2	Obv., within looped square, الله الرسول الله محمد ١١٦٨ لا اله الا In segments, outside, | عدل عمر | (*sic*) بـ]الصدق ابو بكر حلـ[ـم] عثمان | علم على Rev., within looped square, محمد عالمگير عزيز الدين پادشاه غاز ى مبار سكه ابو العدل In segments, outside, | جلوس ميمنت | مان[و]س ضرب د]ار الخلافه | شاهجهان‌اباد سنه ٢ PL. XXVI. *MARSDEN.* AV ·8, Wt. 168

No.	Mint.	Year.	Regnal year.		
AV 1061	Sháh- jahán- ábád	—	2	Obv.	جـــهـــا]ن ابـــاد شـــــاه ٢ دار ا]لخلافه سنه ب مـــانـــوس ضـــر [جـلـوس ميمنت]
				Rev.	خلد] الله ملكه و سلطا[نه محـــــمـــد عـالـم]كير پـادشـاه غـازي ابو ا]لـعـدل عزيـز الدين [سكه مبار]
					MARSDEN. AV :75, Wt. 168
1062	Indra- púr	11[70]	4	Obv.	مـــهـــر انـدرپـور ضرب جلوس ميمنت مانوس ٤ ســـنـه
				Rev.	١١ عـالـمگـيـر پا]دشـاه غاز سكه م]بارك ه
					Pl. XXVI. *LADY FRERE.* AV ·9, Wt. 168

No.	Mint.	Year.	Regnal year.	
AV 1063 1064*	Sháh-jahán-ábád	1170	4	Obv. as 1059: but سنه ۴ Rev. عا]لمگیر غاز پادشاه ی عزیز الدین ۱۱۷۰ شاه ...وچو تابان مهر و ماه شـــــکـه زد بر]هفت کـشـور *I.O.C.* AV ·85, Wt. 167 AV ·8, Wt. 167
1065	Lahore	1171	5	Obv. لاهور دار السلطنه ضرب سنه ۵ میمنت جلوس مانوس Rev. ۱۱۷۱ عالمگیر ی پادشاه غاز ی سکه مبار Borders of wreaths. Pl. XXVI. *I.O.C.* AV ·8, Wt. 168

* The inscription being too large for the flan is only completely legible by a comparison of the two specimens.

No.	Mint.	Year.	Regnal year.	
AV 1066	Ahmad-nagar Far-rukh-ábád	1171	6	Obv. مانوس ميمنت ٦ سنه جلوس ضرب احمدنكر فرخ اباد Rev. as 1065. PL. XXVI. *GRANT.* AV ·9, Wt. 168
1067	Indra-púr	11*xx*	6	As 1062 : but ٦ سنه ; at right, above rev., ١١ (unit and decade cut off.) (No ه after مبارك.) *MARSDEN.* AV ·8, Wt. 168

SMALL ISSUE.

No.	Mint.	Year.	Regnal year.	
1068 1069 1070 1070*a*	Karrah	1170	—	Obv. كره ضرب ا]متياز Rev. عالمكير ياد ١١٧٠ شاه سنه (Date partly obliterated on all but 1068.) *I.O.C.* AV ·45, Wt. 52 PL. XXVI. *MARSDEN.* AV ·4, Wt. 51 ,, AV ·46, Wt. 52 ,, AV ·45, Wt. 51

No.	Mint.	Year.	Regnal year.	
				SILVER.
Æ 1071	Sháh-jahán-ábád	116x	1	As 1059: but ١١٦ (unit cut off) above rev. *EDEN.* Æ ·9, Wt. 175
1072	Mur-shid-ábád	[11]68	,,	Obv. مانو]س میمنت احد سنه جلوس ضرب مر]شداباد Rev. as 1059: but ٦٨ after مبار Æ 1·0, Wt. 179
1073	Sháh-jahán-ábád	—	2	As 1061. *BENGAL AS. SOC.* Æ ·8, Wt. 176
1074 1074a	,,	1168	,,	As 1060. *MARSDEN.* Æ ·8, Wt. 176 *THOMAS.* Æ ·95, Wt. 175
1075	—	1169	,,	Obv. مانوس میمنت جلو]س ٢ [symbol] سنه Rev. ...... ی پاد شاه غا]ز ک ١١٦٩ س]که مبار *GOVT. OF INDIA.* Æ ·8, Wt. 176

No.	Mint.	Year.	Regnal year.	
Æ 1076	Sháh-jahán-ábád	—	3	As 1061 : but سنه ۳ Æ ·9, Wt. 175
1077	Akbar-ábád	1171	4	Obv. اکبراباد ضرب ۱۱۷۱ سنه Rev. عالمگیر ۴ نثار سنه Pl. XXVI. (Nisár.) Æ ·45, Wt. 20
1078	Indra-púr	1168 (*sic*)	„	As 1062 : but سنه ۴ ; and ۱۱۶۸ (*sic*) above rev. (An old reverse die.) *CUNNINGHAM.* Æ ·95, Wt. 175
1079	Sháh-jahán-ábád	—	„	As 1059 : but سنه ۴ ; no date on rev. *CUNNINGHAM.* Æ ·9, Wt. 170
1080	„	1170	„	As 1063. *THOMAS.* Æ ·9, Wt. 175
1081	Mur-shid-ábád	[11]71	„	As 1072 : but سنه ۴ ; and ۷۱ after مبار *PRINSEP.* Æ ·95, Wt. 180
1082	Sháh-jahán-ábád	1172	5	As 1063 : but سنه ۵ and ۱۱۷۲ Pl. XXVI. *CUNNINGHAM.* Æ ·85, Wt. 175

No.	Mint.	Year.	Regnal year.	
AR 1083	Azím-ábád	1172	5	As 1059 : but سنه ٥ ; عظ]يم اباد ; and ١١٧٢ (Formerly ringed.) *PRINSEP.* AR ·8, Wt. 178
1084	Ahmad-nagar Far-rukh-ábád	,,	6	Obv. as 1072 ; but نكر فرحاباد . . . . ; سنه ٦ Rev. as 1059, but ١١٧٢ (Formerly ringed.) *I.O.C.* AR 1·15
1085	Lahore	,,	,,	As 1065 : but سنه ٦ ; and ١١٧٢ *GOVT. OF INDIA.* AR ·88, Wt. 173
1035*a*	Mur-shid-ábád	—	,,	As 1072 : but سنه ٦ ; Hijrah year obliterated. *GOVT. OF INDIA.* AR 1·0, Wt. 180
1035*b*	Karrah	—	—	Obv. ضر] سنه ب . . تياز كره Rev. . . . مكير . . . . شـــــاه] سكه زد عزيز ا]لدين *I.O.C.* AR ·7, Wt. 175

SHÁH-JAHÁN [III].

A.H. 1173-74 = A.D. 1759-60.

No.	Mint.	Year.	Regnal year		
					GOLD.
AV 1086	Islám-ábád	1173	1	Obv.	اسلام ابا[د ضرب میمنت مانوس جلوس احد سنه
				Rev.	۱۱۷۳ شاهجهان ی پادشاه غاز ك [سکه مبا]ر
					PL. XXVI. *GRANT.* AV ·85, Wt. 168
1087	Ahmad-nagar Far-rukh-ábád	,,	,,	Obv.	مانوس میمنت احد سنه جلوس ضرب ا]حمدنکر فرخ اباد
				Rev.	شا]ه جهان پادشاه غازی س]که ۱۱ ۷۳ مبارك
					PL. XXVI. *CUNNINGHAM.* AV 1·0, Wt. 167

No.	Mint.	Year.	Regnal year.	
				SILVER.
AV 1088	Ahmad-nagar Far-rukh-ábád	1173	1	As 1087. *EDEN.* Æ 1·1, Wt. 166
1089	Ahmad-ábád	"	"	Obv. as 1087 : but ا[حمد]اباد Rev. as 1086 : but unit of date obscure. *GOVT. OF INDIA.* Æ ·9, Wt. 179
1090	Indra-púr	"	"	Obv. مهر اندرپور ضرب جلوس میمنت مانوس احد سنه Rev. ۱۱۷۳ شاهجهان پادشاه غاز سکه مبارك PL. XXVI. *PLAYFAIR.* Æ 1·0, Wt. 173

No.	Mint.	Year.	Regnal year.	
AV 1091	Sháh-jahán-ábád	1174	1	Obv. فه جها اباد دار الخلا شا ن ضرب جلوس میمنت مانوس سنه احد Rev. شاه جهان ۱۱۷۴ پادشاه غاز سکه مبار (Formerly ringed.) AR 1·15
1092	Ahmad-nagar Far-rukh-ábád	„	„	As 1087 : but ۱۱۷۴ CUNNINGHAM. AR 1·0, Wt. 174

XV.—SHÁH-'ÁLAM.

A.H. 1173—1221 = A.D. 1759—1806.

No.	Year.	Regnal year.		
				SHÁHJAHÁNÁBÁD.
				I. PLAIN TYPE.
				GOLD.
AV 1093	[11]76	3	Obv.	[فه جها] ابا[د دا]ر الـخلا شـاه ن ضـرب جلوس ميمنت مانوس سـنه ۳
			Rev.	اله محمد شاه عالم پا[د شـ[اه سايه فضل حامى دين سـ]ـكـه[زد در هف[ت كشور
				PL. XXVII. AV ·8, Wt. 168

No.	Year.	Regnal year.	
AV 1094	1205	32	Obv. as 1093: but ۳۲; flower in loop of جلوس Rev. [شاه] شاه اله دين محمد عالم پا[د م سکه صاحب قرا حا ۱۲۰۵ ن زد ز تایید Imperial umbrella over حب. Pl. XXVII. AV ·8, Wt. 165
1095	1206	34	As 1094: but ۳۴ and ۱۲۰۶ *PRINSEP.* AV ·8, Wt. 165

No.	Year.	Regnal year.	
			SILVER.
Æ 1096	1198	25	Obv. as 1093 : but ۲۵ Rev. اله محمد شاه عالم باد شـــــــاه سا]یه [ف]ضل حامی دین ۱]۱۹۸ ســـــــکـ[ـه زد در]هفت کش[ور Umbrella over می. *PRINSEP.* Æ ·85, Wt. 173
1097	1199	26	As preceding : but ۲۶ and ۹۹ *PRINSEP.* Æ ·9, Wt. 174
1098	1202	30	Obv. as 1093 : but ۳۰ ; flower in loop of جلوس Rev. اله محمد شاه عالم باد شـــــــاه زد ز تایید حامی دین ۱۲۰۲ نـــــــی سکه صاحب قرا Umbrella over می. *GRANT.* Æ 1·0, Wt. 171

No.	Year.	Regnal year.	
Æ 1099-1101	1218	46	As 1094: but ۴۶ and ۱۲۱۸ Lion rampant to right of umbrella.* Pl. XXVII. Æ 1·05, Wt. 172 Pl. XXVII. (Lion debased.) Æ 1·05, Wt. 172 " *PRINSEP.* Æ ·9, Wt. 172
1102	"	"	As preceding: but company's cinquefoil substituted for lion. *PRINSEP.* Æ ·9, Wt. 172
1103	1219	"	As preceding: but ۱۲۱۹ *THOMAS.* Æ ·9, Wt. 172

* Issued on the occasion of the restoration of Sháh-'Álam to liberty by the British after Gen. Lord Lake's victory over the Maráthas in 1803. According to Marsden, Sháh-'Álam was prejudiced by his courtiers against the lion on these pieces, which they described as an unclean animal, and the cinquefoil of the Company was substituted. These, and the following coins of this mint, are of native workmanship, but issued under British influence.

No.	Year.	Regnal year.	
			2. LARGE TYPE.
			(Probably Nisárs.)
			GOLD.
AV 1104	1218	46	As 1094 : but ٤٦ ; ١٢١٨ ; and tree to right of umbrella. PL. XXVII. *MARSDEN.* AV 1·35, Wt. 166
			SILVER.
AR 1105	1174	2	As 1094 : but ٢ ; ١١٧٤ ; no tree or umbrella. *MARSDEN.* AR 1·3, Wt. 176
1106	1217	45	„ but ٤٥ ; ١٢١٧ ; tree and umbrella. AR 1·3, Wt. 172
1107	1218	„	„ but ٤٥ ; ١٢١٨ ; tree and umbrella. *GRANT.* AR 1·2, Wt. 172
1108	„	46	„ but ٤٦ ; ١٢١٨ ; tree and umbrella. AR 1·4, Wt. 174
1109	„	„	„ but ٤٦ ; ١٢١٨ ; cinquefoil and umbrella. AR 1·25, Wt. 172

No.	Year.	Regnal year.	
			3. Wreath Type.
			Obv. and Rev. enclosed in wreath of roses, thistles, and shamrocks.
			GOLD.
AV 1110	1219	47	As 1094: but ٤٧ ; ١٢١٩ ; cinquefoil and umbrella. AV 1·0, Wt. 166
1111	1221	48	„ but ٤٨ ; ١٢٢١ ; cinquefoil and umbrella. Pl. XXVII. AV 1·05, Wt. 166
			SILVER.
AR 1112	1219	47	As 1110. AR 1·1, Wt. 173
1113	1220	„	„ but ١٢٢٠. AR 1·05, Wt. 172
1114	„	48	„ but ٤٨, and ١٢٢٠. THOMAS. AR 1·0, Wt. 172
1115	„	„	„ „ „ EDEN. AR 1·0, Wt. 172
			4. Dotted Border Type.
			SILVER.
AR 1116 1117	1221	49	As 1094: but ٤٩ ; ١٢٢١ ; cinquefoil and umbrella. THOMAS. AR 1·0, Wt. 173 Pl. XXVII. EDEN. AR ·95, Wt. 172

No.	Year.	Regnal year.	
			ETÁWÁ.
			SILVER.
Æ 1118	—	18	Obv. مانوس میمنت سنه جلوس ۱۸ ضرب اتاوا ۷ Rev. شاه عالم ی پادشاه غاز ک سکه مبار Umbrella above عا of عالم Flag after شاه Pl. XXVII. *MARSDEN.* Æ 1·1, Wt. 174
1119	1194	22	As 1118: but ۲۲; and ۱۱۹۴; and fish instead of flag. *I.O.C.* Æ 1·05, Wt. 168
1120	—	23	„ but ۲۳; year obscure; and fish instead of flag. *MARSDEN.* Æ 1·05, Wt. 174

No.	Year.	Regnal year.		
				AHMADÁBÁD.
				SILVER.
Æ 1121	118[8-9]	16	Obv.	مانوس
				میمنت
				سنه ١٦ جلوس
				ضرب
				احمداباد
				Mint-mark [illegible] in loop of جلوس
			Rev.	١١٨ شاه عالم
				پادشاه غازی
				سکه مبارک
				PL. XXVII. *GOVT. OF INDIA.* Æ 1·0, Wt. 180

ARKÁT.

SILVER.

No.	Year.	Regnal year.	
Æ 1122	119*x*	12 ?	Obv. مـــانوس مـيـمـنت (۱۲(? سنـــه جلوس ضـــرب اركـــات Rev. اله حامی دین محمد شـــــــاه سایه فضل شاه عالم پاد سـكه ۱۱۹ زد بر هفت كـشـــور Pl. XXVII. *I.O.C.* Æ ·8, Wt. 175
1123	1191	18	Same: but ۱۸ and ۱۱۹۱ *I.O.C.* Æ ·85, Wt. 176
1124	12[00]	27	„ but ۲۷ and ۱۲ *I.O.C.* Æ 1·0, Wt. 176
1125	1201	28	„ but ۲۸ and ۱۲۰۱ *I.O.C.* Æ 1·0, Wt. 176
1126	1213	—	„ but ۱۲۱۳, -:- instead of regnal year. *BANK COLL.* Æ ·9, Wt. 176
1127	1214	—	„ but ۱۲۱۴, -:- instead of regnal year. *BANK COLL.* Æ ·9, Wt. 173

No.	Year.	Regnal year.	
			AKBARÁBÁD. **SILVER.**
AR 1128	1175	3	Obv. جلوس مانوس میمنت مستقر الخلا[فه سنه ۳ ضرب اکبراباد Rev. فضل اله س]ایه ۱۱۷۵ شاه محمد شاه لم حامی دین عا باد سکه هفـ[ت] کشـ[و]ر *PLAYFAIR.* AR 1·1, Wt. 174
1129	1198	26	Same: but ۲۶ and ۱۱۹۸ Fish to right on obv. (حامیدین in one word.) PL. XXVII. *PRINSEP.* AR ·9, Wt. 172
1130	1218	45	As preceding: but ۴۵ and ۱۲۱۸ *PRINSEP.* AR ·9, Wt. 171

No.	Year.	Regnal year.	
Æ 1131	121[9]	47	Obv. as preceding : but ۴۷ Rev. ......ن محمد...عا..پانی ۱۲۱ صاحب قرانی . . . . . . *PLAYFAIR.* Æ ·85, Wt. 170
1132	1220	,,	As preceding : year ۱۲۲۰ ; flower over قر *I.O.C.* Æ ·8, Wt. 172

No.	Year.	Regnal year.	
			BENÁRES. SILVER.
Æ 1133	1183	10	Obv. محمداباد میمنت ١٠ جلوس سنه مانوس ضرب بنا[ر]س in loop of جلوس Rev. اله حامی [د]ین محمد فضـ[ـل شاه عالم پادشـ[ـاه س]ـکه ١١٨٣ زدبـر هفت کشـ[ـور Æ ·9, Wt. 175
1134	—	13	Same : but ١٣ ; no Hijrah year. (Reverse differently arranged) in loop of جلوس ; on reverse. Æ ·95, Wt. 174
1135	1189	17	Same : but ١٧ and ١١٨٩ Umbrella in loop of جلوس Stars on reverse. Pl. XXVIII. Æ ·95, Wt. 174
1136	—	18	Same as 1135 : but ١٨ ; no Hijrah year. Flag in loop of جلوس Æ ·9, Wt. 174
1137	—	19	Same as 1136 : but ١٩ ; fish to left of flag. Pl. XXVIII. Æ ·85, Wt. 173

No.	Year.	Regnal year.	
Æ 1138-1141	1196	23	Same as 1133 : but ٢٣ and ١١٩٦ Umbrella and fish on obv. Rev. inscription differently arranged and partly cut off. (Four sizes, half, quarter, eighth, and sixteenth of a rupee, from the same die.) Pl. XXVIII. *MARSDEN.* Æ ·75, Wt. 87 ,, Æ ·65, Wt. 43 ,, Æ ·66, Wt. 22 ,, Æ ·45, Wt. 11
			FOUR-PETAL FLOWER TYPE.
			GOLD.
AV 1142	1209	37	Same as 1133 ; but ٣٧ and ١٢٠٩ Four-petal flower in loop of جلوس Fish on reverse. AV ·8, Wt. 168
			SILVER.
Æ 1143	1203	30	Same as 1142 : but ١٧ سنه ٣٠ and ١٢٠٣ Pl. XXVIII. Æ ·9, Wt. 174
1144 ¼	[,,]	,,	,, inscriptions partly cut off. *MARSDEN.* Æ ·7, Wt. 44
1145	1207	35	,, but ١٧ سنه ٣٥, and ١٢٠٧ (Thin.) *MARSDEN.* Æ 1·25, Wt. 175

No.	Year.	Regnal year.	
Æ 1146	—	35	Same as 1145, but Hijrah year obliterated. *BENGAL AS. SOC.* Æ ·85, Wt. 174
1147	121[3]	41	Same as 1142 : but ا ك سنه ۴١ and ١٢١ (unit cut off). *I.O.C.* Æ ·9, Wt. 174
1148, 1149	1217	45	,, but ا ك سنه ۴۵ and ١٢١٧ (Thin.) Pl. XXVIII. *MARSDEN.* Æ 1·15, Wt. 176 *BENGAL AS. SOC.* Æ ·85, Wt. 176
1150	1222	49	,, but ا ك سنه ۴٩ and ١٢٢٢ *I.O.C.* Æ ·9, Wt. 175
1151	1224	,,	Same as 1150 : but ١٢٢۴ Æ ·85, Wt. 174
1152 ¼	1225	,,	,, but ١٢٢٥ *I.O.C.* Æ ·65, Wt. 44

No.	Year.	Regnal year.	
			BAHÁDURPATAN.
			GOLD.
AV 1153	119*x*	14	Obv. مــانــوس مـيـمـنت ١٣ ح سـنه جلوس ضـر]ب بهادرپـتـن Rev. اله حامی دیـن س[ایه ش[اه ف]ضل شاه عالم پ[اد ١١٩ زد]بـر هـفت کشور *MARSDEN.* *AV* ·85, Wt. 170
1154	1197	20	As preceding: but ٢٠ and ١١٩٧ *AV* ·9, Wt. 160

No.	Year.	Regnal year.	
			DILSHÁDÁBÁD. SILVER.
Æ 1155	1186	—	Obv. جلوس میـــمـنـت ۱۱۸۶ ضرب دل شاداباد بـــــ م]انوس Rev. . . . عا . . . . ے پادشاه غـــاز شا]ه سـ]كه ۱۱۸۱ مـبـارك (An old reverse.) *PRINSEP.* Æ ·8, Wt. 173
1156	12*xx*	—	As preceding : but on obv. ۱۲۵۱ ल No year on rev. *PRINSEP.* Æ ·7, Wt. 172

No.	Year.	Regnal year.	
			JAHÁNGÍRNAGAR.
			SILVER.
Æ 1157	1183	10	Obv. جلـــوس مانوس مـــيـــمـــنـــت ١٠ سنه سکه مبـــار ک ضرب جهانكيرنكر Cinquefoil over سنه. Rev. اله حامی دین محمد شـــــــــــاه سایه فضل شاه عالم باد ســـــــــــکه ١١٨٣ زد بر هـــفـــت کشور Pl. XXVIII. Æ 1·1, Wt. 179

No.	Year.	Regnal year.	
			SRÍNAGAR.
			SILVER.
Æ 1158	—	1	Obv. سری نکر / ضرب / جلوس میمنت مانوس / احد سنه Rev. عالم / شاه / پادشاه غازی / سکه مبارك Æ ·65, Wt. 31
1159	—	2	As preceding: but ۲ سنه Pl. XXVIII. *I.O.C.* Æ ·65, Wt. 35

No.	Year.	Regnal year.	
			SÚRAT.
			SILVER.
Æ 1160 $\frac{1}{8}$	—	4	Obv. مانوس میمنت ۴ سنه جلوس ضرب سورت Rev. شاه عالم پادشاه غاز ی سکه مبار The flan is so small that only a small part of the inscription is visible. Æ ·45, Wt. 22
1161 1162	—	5	Same: but ٥ Pl. XXVIII. Æ ·8, Wt. 168 *I.O.C.* Æ ·8, Wt. 168
1163 $\frac{1}{2}$	—	6	,, but ٦ Pl. XXVIII. Æ ·7, Wt. 88
1164 $\frac{1}{2}$	—	22	,, but ٢٢ *MARSDEN.* Æ ·65, Wt. 89
1165	—	32	,, but ٣٢ *BANK COLL.* Æ ·85, Wt. 179

No.	Year.	Regnal year.	
			'AZÍMÁBÁD. (PATNAH.) GOLD.
AV 1166	1174	2	Obv. عظیم اباد ضرب میمنت مانوس جلوس ۲ سنه Rev. اله محمد شاه عالم پاد شاه سایه فضل حامی دین سکه ۱۱۷۴ زد بر هفت کشور PL. XXVIII. *MARSDEN.* AV 1·05, Wt. 171
1167 $\frac{1}{16}$	1182	10	Obv. ۱۰ سنه ضرب عظیم اباد Rev. ۱۱۸۲ شاه عالم سکه پادشاه PL. XXVIII. *MARSDEN.* AV ·45, Wt. 12
			SILVER.
AR 1168	1174	2	As 1166 : same die. *MARSDEN.* AR 1·15, Wt. 179
1169	—	5	„ but ۵ ; Hijrah year obliterated. *PRINSEP.* AR ·9, Wt. 179

No.	Year.	Regnal year.	
			AHMADNAGAR FARRUKHÁBÁD.
			GOLD.
AV 1170	[11]94	21	Obv. ما]نوس / میمنت / ٢١ سنه جلوس / ضرب / احمدنگر فرخ اباد
			Rev. اله محمد شاه عالم پاد / شاه / ٩٣ سایه فـ]ضل حامی دین / سکه / [زد بر هفت کشور]
			PRINSEP. AV ·95, Wt. 167
1171	[11]96	23	Same : but ٢٣ and ٩٦
			Pl. XXIX. *PROF. WILSON.* AV ·95, Wt. 167
1171*a*	—	31	Obv. same : but ٣١
			Rev. ا]له محمد شاه‌عالم [پاد / شاه / زد ز تایید حامی د]ین / ن / سکه صا]حب قرا
			AV ·95, Wt. 166

No.	Year.	Regnal year.	
			SILVER.
Æ 1172	[11]79	6	Same as 1170 : but ٦ and ٧٩ Pl. XXIX. *MARSDEN.* Æ 1·1, Wt. 174
1173	[11]87	15	„ but ١٥ and ٨٧ *I.O.C.* Æ 1·1, Wt. 170
1174	[11]89	17	„ but ١٧ and ٨٩ *MARSDEN.* Æ 1·05, Wt. 175
1175	[11]92	19	„ but ١٩ and ٩٢ *MARSDEN.* Æ 1·1, Wt. 175
1176	[11]95	21	„ but ٢١ and ٩٥ *PLAYFAIR.* Æ 1·2, Wt. 168
1177	[11]96	23	„ but ٢٣ and ٩٦ *MARSDEN.* Æ 1·1, Wt. 174
1178	[11]99	27	„ but ٢٧ and ٩٩ Æ 1·05, Wt. 173
1179	—	31	„ 1171*a*. (Ringed.) *GRANT.* Æ 1·05
1180	[1]216	39	„ 1171*a*: but ٣٩ and ٢١٦ *I.O.C.* Æ 1·0, Wt. 171
1181	[1]217	„	„ but ٣٩ and ٢١٧ *GRANT.* Æ 1·0, Wt. 160

No.	Year.	Regnal year.	
			Large Issue.
Æ 1182	1218	39	Same as 1171*a*: but ٣٩ and ١٢١٨ Pl. XXIX. *MARSDEN.* Æ 1·45, Wt. 341
1183	,,	,,	,, ,, (Thin.) *MARSDEN.* Æ 1·4, Wt. 172

LUCKNOW.

SILVER.

No.	Year.	Regnal year.	
1184	—	1	Obv. مانوس میـــمـــنت احد سنه جلوس ضـرب لکهنو
			Rev. غـــازی شـــــــاه شاه عالم پاد ســـکـ[ـه . . . . *PRINSEP.* Æ ·95, Wt. 176

No.	Year.	Regnal year.	
			MURSHIDÁBÁD.
			GOLD.
AV 1185	1181	—	Obv. مانوس م]ـيمنـت س]نه جلوس ضرب مر]شـ[دابـ]ا[د Rev. شاه عا[لم] ١١٨١ پادشاه غا[ز ی [سكه مبار] Pl. XXIX. *MARSDEN.* AV ·8, Wt. 164
			SILVER.
AR 1186	11[74]	2	Same as 1185 : but ٢ سنه on obv. ; ١١ before عا[لم] on rev., and traces of سكه مبار beneath. AR ·85, Wt. 168

No.	Year.	Regnal year.	
Æ 1187	—	7	Obv. as 1185 : but سنه, and cinquefoil. Rev. [اله حامی دین محمد / شـــه] / سا]یه فضل شاه عالم ... / [سـکـه] / [زد بر هفت کشور] *GOVT. OF INDIA.* Æ ·9, Wt. 166
1188	1180	8	As preceding : but ٨ on obv., and ١١٨٠ above هفت on rev. Pl. XXIX. *I.O.C.* Æ ·9, Wt. 179
1189	1184	11	,, but ١١ and ١١٨٤ *I.O.C.* Æ ·9, Wt. 180
1190	1186	12	Same : but ١٢ and ١١٨٦ *I.O.C.* Æ ·9, Wt. 177
1191	—	,,	,, Hijrah year obliterated. *MARSDEN.* Æ ·9, Wt. 179
1192	119*x*	19	,, but ١٩ and ١١٩ *GOVT. OF INDIA.* Æ ·9, Wt. 179

No.	Year.	Regnal year.	
Æ 1193	—	19	Same as 1187 : but Hijrah year obliterated. Pl. XXIX. *MARSDEN.* Æ ·9, Wt. 179
1194 ½	—	25	,, 1185 : but ٢٥ ; Hijrah year obliterated. *MARSDEN.* Æ ·75, Wt. 79
1195	—	28	,, but ٢٨ ; Hijrah year obliterated. Æ ·9, Wt. 178
1196 ⅛	—	9	Fragment of inscription as 1185, but ٩ سنه ; sun on rev. ; Hijrah year obliterated. *I.O.C.* Æ ·45, Wt. 22
1197 1/16	—	15	Same as 1196 : but ١٥, no sun. *I.O.C.* Æ ·35, Wt. 11
1198 1/16	—	19	,, but ١٩, no sun. *I.O.C.* Æ ·4, Wt. 11
1198*a* ⅛	—	,,	,, but ١٩, no sun ; cinquefoil on obv. *I.O.C.* Æ ·55, Wt. 22

No.	Year.	Regnal year.	
			NAJÍBÁBÁD. SILVER.
AR 1199	—	12	Obv. نـــجـــيـــب ابـــاد ضـــرب جلوس ميمنت مانوس ١٢ سـنـه Rev. ا]له محمد شاه عالم[پاد شـــا]ه سایه فضل حامی دین ســـ]که زد]بـــر هفـــت کشور AR ·9, Wt. 175
1200 *Double*	1195	22	Same: but ٢٢ and ١١٩٥ PL. XXIX. *MARSDEN.* AR 1·05, Wt. 348
1201	[11]99	26	,, but ٢٦ and ٩٩ *PRINSEP.* AR ·95, Wt. 173
1202	[1]210	36	,, but ٣٦ and ٢١٠ *PRINSEP.* AR ·85, Wt. 172
1203	[12]14	41	,, but ۴۱ and ۱۴ *PRINSEP.* AR ·85, Wt. 170
1204, 1205	[1]215	42	,, but ۴۲ and ۲۱۵ *PRINSEP.* AR ·85, Wt. 169 *PRINSEP.* AR ·85, Wt. 169

NO MINT.

GOLD.

No.	Year.	Regnal year.		
Æ 1205a	1183	—	Obv. ۱۱۸۳ سنه ❖] ⁘ ❖	Rev. عالم شاه
				Pl. XXIX. MARSDEN. $\mathcal{N}$ ·2, Wt. 25

For distribution (*Nisár.*)

BÍDÁR-BAKHT.

PRETENDER.

A.H. 1202–3 = A.D. 1788.

No.	Mint.	Year.	Regnal year.	
				GOLD.
AV 1206	Sháh- jahán- ábád	1202	1	Obv. [اباد] [فه] د[ا]ر الخلا شـــا[جهان ضـــرب جلوس میمنت مانوس احد ســـنه Rev. بیدار بخت شـــاه ۱۲۰۲ تاج و محمد جهان تـــخـــت بزر سـ]کـ[ـه]زد وا[ر]ث PL. XXIX. *CUNNINGHAM.* AV ·8, Wt. 166
1207 1208	Ahmad- ábád	1203	,,	Obv. as preceding: but احمداباد Rev. م]حمد [ب]یدار [ب]خت شـــاه ۱۲۰۳ تاج و تخت جهان ســـ[ـه بزر زد وارث (Hijrah year obliterated on 1208.) PL. XXIX. *GIBBS.* AV ·75, Wt. 166 *CUNNINGHAM.* AV ·75, Wt. 166
				SILVER.
AR 1209	Sháh- jahán- ábád	1202	,,	As 1206. *GIBBS.* AR ·85, Wt. 174

XVI.—MUHAMMAD AKBAR II.

A.H. 1221—53 = A.D. 1806—1837.

No.	Year.	Regnal year.	
			SHÁHJAHÁNÁBÁD.
			SILVER.
Æ 1210	1221	1	Obv. جهان اباد دار الخلافه شاه ضرب جلوس میمنت مانوس احد سنه Rev. محمد اکبر شاه پادشاه غازی ۱۲۲۱ صاحب قران ثانی سکه مبارك Umbrella over حب ; cinquefoil after ثا PL. XXIX. *EDEN.* Æ ·9, Wt. 171
1211	1222	,,	Same: but ۱۲۲۲ *THOMAS.* Æ ·9, Wt. 172
1212	1223	3	,, but ۳ and ۱۲۲۳ *THOMAS.* Æ 1·05, Wt. 172
1213	1224	,,	,, but ۳ and ۱۲۲۴ *PRINSEP.* Æ 1·1, Wt. 173
1214	12*xx*	6	,, but ٦ and ۱۱ *THOMAS.* Æ 1·0, Wt. 174
1215, 1216	1251	31	,, but ۳۱ and ۱۲۵۱ *THOMAS.* Æ 1·05, Wt. 171 *HAY.* Æ 1·15, Wt. 172

XVII.—BAHÁDUR SHÁH II.

A.H. 1253—75 = A.D. 1837—1857.

No.	Year.	Regnal year.	
			SHÁHJAHÁNÁBÁD.
			SILVER.
Æ 1217	1257	5	Obv. as 1210 : but ٥
			Rev. شاه ١٢٥٧ محمد بهادر پادشاه غازی سراج الدین لمظفر ابو ا Umbrella and cinquefoil after الدین PL. XXIX. Æ 1·15, Wt. 172
1218	1258	6	Same : but ٦ and ١٢٥٨ *CUNNINGHAM.* Æ 1·15, Wt. 171

EARLY COPPER LOCAL ISSUES.*

No.	Year.	Obv.	Rev.
		AGRAH.	
Æ 1219	936	٩٣٦ فی تاریخ سنة Fleuron above and beneath.	الضرب دار قلع اكره Æ ·7
1220	,,	,,	,, but قلعة Æ ·75
1221, 1222	937	,, ٩٣٧	دار الخلا فة ضرب اک[ره Æ ·75 Æ ·7
1223	938	,, ٩٣٨	,, Æ ·7
1224, 1225	939	,, ٩٣٩	,, Æ ·7 Æ ·7
1226	940	,, ٩٤٥	,, Æ ·65
1227	942	,, ٩٤٢	,, Æ ·65
1228	94*x*	,, ٩٤ above سنة	Within oval, ضرب اكره Margin illegible. Æ ·6

* These coins have already been described in this Catalogue of the Coins of the *Muhammadan States*, pp. 159 – 163, and illustrated in Plate XII. of the same. They belong, however, to the period of Bábar and Humayún, though they do not bear their names; and they are repeated here for convenience of reference.

No.	Year.	Obv.	Rev.	
		JAUNPÚR.		
Æ 1229 1230	939	٩٣٩ فی تاریخ سنة Fleuron above and beneath.	دار الضرب ممه (؟) چونپور خطة	Æ ·7 Æ ·7
1231	940	٩٤٠ ,,	,,	Æ ·7
		CHAMPANÍR.		
1232	942	ضرب شهر الزمان	چنپانیار سنة ٩٤٢	Æ ·65
		LAHORE.		
1233	938	٩٣٨ فی تاریخ سنة	دار الخ[ـلا فـ[ـة لاهور ضرب	Æ ·7
		MANDÚ.		
1234, 1235	942	فی تاریخ ٩٤٢ سنة ꕥ	ضرب مندو	Æ ·7 Æ ·7

APPENDIX.

COINAGE

OF THE HONOURABLE

THE EAST INDIA COMPANY

IN THE NAME OF THE

MOGHUL EMPERORS.

EAST INDIA COMPANY'S ISSUES.

I.—MURSHIDÁBÁD,

(In the Name of Sháh-'Álam.)

(i.) Early Issues, between Annexation of Bengal, in 1765, and 19-san Regulation of 1793.

1. Issue of Regnal Year 10 of Sháh-'Álam, A.H. 1182–3 (1768).

No milling. Dotted rim.

No.	Denomination.	Obv.	Rev.
		GOLD.	
AV 1	½-Mohr	مانوس میمنت ١٠ سنه جلوس ضرب مرشداباد Over سنه, a cinquefoil.	اله حامی دین محمد شاه سایه فضل شاه عالم پاد سکه ١١٨٢ زد بر هفت کشور Pl. XXX. *Bank Coll.* AV 7, Wt. 95
2	¼-Mohr	Same.	*Bank Coll.* AV 6, Wt. 48

No.	Denomination.	Obv.	Rev.
AV 3	⅛-Mohr	١٠ سنه ضـــرب مرشـدابـاد No cinquefoil.	١١٨٣ شـــــاه عالم ســـكـــه پادشاه Pl. XXX. *BANKS.* AV ·5, Wt. 24
4	$\frac{1}{16}$-Mohr	,, No cinquefoil.	,, *BANK COLL.* AV ·5, Wt. 12

SILVER.

No.	Denomination.	Obv.	Rev.
AR 5	4 Annas	As 1. Cinquefoil	As 1. Pl. XXX. *BANKS.* AR ·65, Wt. 45
6	2 Annas	As 3.	As 3: but ١١٨٢ *BANKS.* AR ·55, Wt. 23
7	1 Anna	As 3.	As 3: but ١١٨٢ *BANKS.* AR ·45, Wt. 11

No.	Denomination.	Obv.	Rev.
		2. Issue of Regnal Year 11, A.H. 1183-4 (1769-70). *No milling. Dotted rim.*	
AV		GOLD.	
8	Mohr	As 1: but ١١ Cinquefoil.	As 1: but ١١٨٤ Pl. XXX. *BANK COLL.* AV 1·0, Wt. 192
AR		SILVER.	
9	Rupee	As 1: but ١١ Cinquefoil.	As 1: but ١١٨٣ *MARSDEN.* AR 1·05, Wt. 180
10	"	"	" but ١١٨٤ *BANK COLL.* AR 1·0. Wt. 180
11	½-Rupee	"	" but ١١٨٤ *BANK COLL.* AR ·85, Wt. 90
12	4 Annas	"	" Hijrah year cut off. *BANK COLL.* AR ·6, Wt. 45
13	2 Annas	"	" Hijrah year cut off. *BANK COLL.* AR ·5, Wt. 23
14*	Anna	"	" Hijrah year cut off. Pl. XXX. *BANK COLL.* AR ·35, Wt. 11

* The smaller coins of the preceding series are struck from the same die as the larger, and therefore show only a part of the inscription.

No.	Denomination.	Obv.	Rev.
		3. Issues of Regnal Years 12—19, A.H. 1185—1203 (*sic*).	
		No milling. Dotted rim.	
		GOLD.—Year 12.	
AV 15	Mohr	As 1: but ۱۲ Cinquefoil.	As 1: but ۱۱۸۵ AV ·9, Wt. 191
		SILVER.—Year 13.	
AR 16	Rupee	As 1: but ۱۳ Cinquefoil.	As 1: but ۱۱۸۵ *I.O.C.* AR 1·0, Wt. 180
		GOLD.—Years 15, 19.	
AV 17	Mohr	As 1: but ۱۵ Cinquefoil.	As 1: but ۱۱۸۷ Pl. XXX. AV ·9, Wt. 191
18	,,	,, but ۱۹	,, but ۱۱۹۶ *MARSDEN.* AV ·9, Wt. 191
19	,,	,, ,,	,, but ۱۱۹۷ Pl. XXX. *MARSDEN.* AV ·9, Wt. 191
20	,,	,, ,,	,, but ۱۱۹۸ *MARSDEN.* AV ·9, Wt. 191
21	,,	,, ,,	,, but ۱۲۰۱ *MARSDEN.* AV ·9, Wt. 190
22	$\frac{1}{4}$-Mohr	,, ,,	,, but ۱۲۰۳ Pl. XXX. *MARSDEN.* AV ·6, Wt. 48

No.	Denomination.	Obv.	Rev.
AV 23	$\frac{1}{8}$-Mohr	As 3: but ١٩ No cinquefoil.	As 3: but ١٢٠٢ *I.O.C.* AV ·5, Wt. 24
24	,,	,, ,,	,, but ١٢٠٣ *MARSDEN.* AV ·5, Wt. 24
25	$\frac{1}{16}$-Mohr	,, ,,	,, but ١٢٠٢ *YEAMES.* AV ·4, Wt. 12
26	,,	,, ,,	,, but ١٢٠٣ *BANKS.* AV ·4, Wt. 12
27	,,	,, ,,	,, but ١٢٠٣ *MARSDEN.* AV ·4, Wt. 12

4. Trial-piece of Regnal Year 26 A.H. 1198 (1784).

Milled rims.

SILVER.

No.	Denomination.	Obv.	Rev.
AR 28	Rupee	As 1: but ٢٦ Cinquefoil.	As 1: but ١١٩٨

Round the edge,

UNITED * EAST * INDIA * COMPANY * J784 *

Pl. XXX. *BANK COLL.* AR 1·05, Wt. 180

(ii.) Issue of "old 19-san Sikkah" 1793—1818.

Oblique milling ////////

GOLD.

No.	Denomination.	Obv.	Rev.
AV 29, 30	Mohr	As 1 : but ١٩ Cinquefoil.	As 1 : but ١٢٠٢ PL. XXX. AV 1·05, Wt. 191 *MARSDEN.* AV 1·0
31, 32	½-Mohr	,, ,,	,, ,, AV ·85, Wt. 95 *MARSDEN.* AV ·85
33, 34	¼-Mohr	As 3 : but ١٩ Cinquefoil.	As 3 : but ١٢٠٣ PL. XXX. AV ·65, Wt. 47 *MARSDEN.* AV ·65

SILVER.

No.	Denomination.	Obv.	Rev.
AR 35, 36*	Rupee	As 1 : but ١٩ Cinquefoil.	As 1 : but ١٢٠٢ PL. XXX. *BANK COLL.* AR 1·2, Wt. 180 *MARSDEN.* AR 1·2
37, 38	,,	,, ,,	As 1 : but no Hijrah year. PL. XXX. *BANK COLL.* AR 1·05, Wt. 180 *MARSDEN.* AR 1·05
39, 40	½-Rupee	,, ,,	As preceding. *MARSDEN.* AR ·85, Wt. 90 AR ·85
41, 42	4 Annas	As 3 : but ١٩ Cinquefoil.	As 3 : but ١٢٠٣ *MARSDEN.* AR ·65, Wt. 45 AR ·65

* On 35 and 36 the milling extends some distance over the edge on to the faces of the coin.

No.	Denomination.	Obv.	Rev.
		(iii.) Issue of "new 19-san Sikkah" 1818—1832. *Straight milling* ||||||||||||	
		GOLD.	
AV 43	¼-Mohr	As 3 : but ١٩ Cinquefoil.	As 3 : but ١٢٠٤ Pl. XXX. *EDEN.* AV ·75, Wt. 51
		SILVER.	
AR 44, 45	Rupee	As 1 : but ١٩ Cinquefoil.	As 1 : but no Hijrah year. *I.O.C.* AR 1·05, Wt. 190 *I.O.C.* AR 1·05, Wt. 192
46	½-Rupee	,, ,,	,, ,, AR ·9, Wt. 96
		(iv.) Latest issue of "19-san" 1832-5. *Plain edge. Serrated rim.*	
		SILVER.	
AR 47, 48	Rupee	As 1 : but ١٩ Cinquefoil.	As 1 : but no Hijrah year. Pl. XXX. *BANKS.* AR 1·05, Wt. 185 *I.O.C.* AR 1·05, Wt. 193
49	½-Rupee	,, ,,	,, ,, *I.O.C.* AR ·9, Wt. 96

No.	Denomination.	Obv.	Rev.
		II. FARRUKHÁBÁD. (In name of Sháh-'Álam.) (i.) Issue of old Farrukhábád or "old 45-san Lucknow Rupee," 1803—1819. *Oblique milling.* SILVER.	
Æ 50	Rupee	مانوس ميمنت ۴۵ جلوس ضرب فرخ اباد Cinquefoil.	As 1 : but no Hijrah year. Pl. XXXI. Æ 1·05, Wt. 174
		(ii.) Issue of new Farrukhábád or "new 45-san Lucknow Rupee," 1819—1833. *Straight milling.* SILVER.	
Æ 51	Rupee	As 50. Cinquefoil.	As 1, but no Hijrah year. Below زد small ٨ Æ 1·05, Wt. 179

No.	Denomination.	Obv.	Rev.
		(iii.) LATEST ISSUE OF FARRUKHÁBÁD, 1833—35. *Plain edge: plain rim.* SILVER.	
Æ 52	Rupee.	As 50. Cinquefoil.	As 1, but no Hijrah year. PL. XXXI. *I.O.C.* Æ 1·05, Wt. 180
53	½-Rupee	,, ,,	,, *I.O.C.* Æ ·9, Wt. 89
54	¼-Rupee	۴۵ سنه ضرب فرخاباد Cinquefoil.	۱۲۰۳ شاه عالم سکه پادشاه PL. XXXI. Æ ·65, Wt. 45

No.	Denomination.	Obv.	Rev.
		III. BENÁRES. (IN NAME OF SHÁH-'ÁLAM.) (i.) NATIVE STYLE, A.H. 1212—33. GOLD.	
AV 55	Mohr	... محمد اباد ميمنت ٢٦ جلوس سنه مانوس ب ضر بنارس	پاد اله محمد حـ]امی دین شاه فـ]ضل عـ]ـالم ١٢١٤ سایه کشور زد بر هفت [سـ]كـ[ـه AV ·85, Wt. 166
56	,,	,,	,, but ١٢٣٥ *YEAMES.* AV ·75 Wt. 165
		SILVER.	
AR 57	Rupee	Same.	Same : but ١٢١٢ *CURETON.* AR ·9, Wt. 173
58	,,	,,	,, ,, ١٢١٨ *MARSDEN.* AR ·9, Wt. 172
59	,,	,,	,, ,, ١٢٢١ AR ·85, Wt. 173
60	,,	,,	,, ,, ١٢٢٢ AR ·95, Wt. 172
61	,,	,,	,, ,, ١٢٢٤ PL. XXXI. AR ·95, Wt. 172
62	,,	,,	,, ,, ١٢٢٧ AR ·95, Wt. 172
63	,,	,,	,, ,, ١٢٢٩ AR ·8, Wt. 172
64	,,	,,	,, ,, ١٢٣١ AR ·9, Wt. 172
65	,,	,,	,, ,, ١٢٣٣ AR ·85, Wt. 172

No.	Denomination.	Obv.	Rev.
		(ii.) OLD* BENARES RUPEE, 1806—1819. *Oblique milling.* SILVER.	
Æ 66	Rupee	محمداباد میمنت ١٢ جلوس سنه مانوس ۴٩ ب ضرب بنارس Flower in loop of جلوس	اله حامی دین محمد فضل شاه عالم پادشاه سکه ١٢٢٩ زد بر هفت کشور سایه PL. XXXI. Æ 1·05, Wt. 176

IV. CALCUTTA.

(IN NAME OF SHÁH-ÁLAM.)

ISSUE OF REGNAL YEAR 4 : A.H. 1176 (1763).

SILVER.

No.	Denomination.	Obv.	Rev.
Æ 67	Rupee	As 1 : but ۴ and کلکته	As 1 : but ١١٧٦ PL. XXXI. *MARSDEN.* Æ 1·1, Wt. 180

* The Benáres issues from 1819 to 1830, when the mint was abolished, were similar to those of Farrukhábád, which name they displayed.

V. BOMBAY.

(MUNBAI.)

(i. In name of the Sháh [Muhammad.])

Issue of Regnal Year 1 : a.h. 1131 (1719).

SILVER.

No.	Denomination.	Obv.	Rev.
Æ 68, 69, 70	¼-Rupee	مانوس میمنت احد سنه جلوس ضرب منبی	غازی شا۵ن سکه مبارک ۱۱۳۱ Pl. XXXI. Æ ·6, Wt. 37 *Banks.* Æ ·65, Wt. 37 Æ ·55, Wt. 37

Issue of Regnal Year 1*x* : a.h. 1143 (1730).

SILVER.

No.	Denomination.	Obv.	Rev.
71	„	Same : but ۱	Same : but ۱۴۳ Pl. XXXI. Æ ·6, Wt 37

No.	Denomination.	Obv.	Rev.
		(ii. In name of Muhammad Sháh.) Issue of Regnal Year 7 = a.h. 1137 (1725). SILVER.	
Æ 72	Rupee	مانوس میمنت ٧ سنه جلوس ضرب منبی	١١ محمد شاه ی پادشاه غاز ی سکه مبار Pl. XXXI. *Bombay As. Soc.* Æ 1·0, Wt. 178
		Issue of Regnal Year 18 : a.h. 1148 (1735). SILVER.	
Æ 73	Rupee	As 72 : but ١٨ سنه Counterstamp over mint, ⊥	As 72 : but ١١٤٨ Æ ·95, Wt. 177
74	,,	,, Unit of year obliterated. No counterstamp.	,, Unit of Hijrah year obliterated. Æ ·95, Wt. 179
		(iii. In the name of Sháh-'Álam.) Issue of Regnal Year 9=a.h. 1182 (1768). GOLD.	
AV 75, 76	Mohr	مانوس میمنت ٩ سنه جلوس ضرب منبی Star in س of جلوس	١١٨ عالم . . . ی پادشاه غاز ی سکه مبار (Top line blundered.) *Marsden.* AV ·8, Wt. 178 Pl. XXXI. *Banks.* AV ·85, Wt. 178

No.	Denomination.	Obv.	Rev.
		SILVER.	
		A.H. 1188 (1774).	
Æ 77	¼-Rupee	Same as 75 : regnal year ۹	Same as 75 : but ۱۱۸۸ Pl. XXXI. *MARSDEN.* Æ ·5, Wt. 34
		No year.	
78	Rupee	Same as 75 : regnal year obliterated.	Same as 75. *I.O.C.* Æ ·85, Wt. 178
79,* 79*a*.	"	"	" Pl. XXXI. *PRINSEP.* Æ 1·0, Wt. 179 " Æ 1·0, Wt. 179

MUMBAI-SÚRAT.

(In the name of Sháh-'Álam.)

Issue of Regnal Year 45 (1802).

No.	Denomination.	Obv.	Rev.
		SILVER.	
Æ 80	¼-Rupee	مانوس میـ]ـمنت ۴۵ سنه جلوس ت ممبی سور	.... حامی دین فضل شاه غا]ز .... Pl. XXXI. *GIBBS.* Æ ·55, Wt. 43

* These two rupees, 79, 79*a*, have a very modern appearance, and the inaccuracy of the letters shows that the engraver must have been ignorant of the Persian characters. According to Atkins, *Coins of British Possessions and Colonies*, 1889, p. 139, they were struck at Calcutta for Bombay in 1800.

No.	Denomination.	Obv.	Rev.

VI. SÚRAT.

(In the name of Sháh-'Álam.)

(i.) With Crowned Head, 1802.

GOLD.

No.	Denomination.	Obv.	Rev.
AV 81	¼-Mohr ?	. . . . جلوس . . . . Crowned head over و ; traces of the Súrat star in loop of س .	. . . . شاه غا . . . . Over شا 1802, incuse, on oval label. Pl. XXXII. AV ·5, Wt. 59

(ii.) 46-san issue, 1825.

with crown.*

GOLD.

No.	Denomination.	Obv.	Rev.
AV 82, 83	Mohr	مانو]س مـيـمنت ۴٦ سنه جلوس Star in س .	شا]ه عالم پادشاه غا]ز ی س]ك[ه] مبـ]ار Crown over پا]دشاه Pl. XXXII. *BANK COLL.* AV ·7, Wt. 180 „ „ AV ·7, Wt. 179
84	¼-Mohr ?	Portion of same inscr., and star.	Portion of same inscr. Crown inverted. *BANK COLL.* AV ·45, Wt. 59

* In place of the upper point over شاه.

No.	Denomination.	Obv.	Rev.
		SILVER.	
Æ 85	Rupee	Portion of same inscr. as 82, and star. [1825] incuse on raised label.	Portion of same inscr. Crown, as 82. PL. XXXII. Æ 1·05, Wt. 180
86	½-Rupee	Same: [1825]	Same. Æ ·6, Wt. 90
		(iii.) 46-SAN ISSUE, WITHOUT CROWN.	
		GOLD.	
AV 87-89	Mohr	As 82.	As 82: no crown. PL. XXXII. *BANK COLL.* AV ·75, Wt. 179 *MARSDEN.* AV ·75 *BANK COLL.* AV ·7
90, 91	¼-Mohr?	" only partly legible.	*BANK COLL.* AV ·55, Wt. 60 *BANK COLL.* AV ·55
92, 93	$\frac{1}{16}$-Mohr?	" "	*MARSDEN.* AV ·3, Wt. 12 *MARSDEN.* AV ·25, Wt. 9
		SILVER.	
94, 95	Rupee	As 82: only partly legible.	Æ ·75, Wt. 179 Æ ·8, Wt. 179

No.	Denomination.	Obv.	Rev.
		(iv.) 46-SAN ISSUE. *Straight milling : line round rim.* SILVER.	
Æ 96, 97	Rupee	Same as 82.	Same as 82 : but above, ۱۲۱۵ ; no crown. PL. XXXII. Æ 1·05, Wt. 180 *I.O.C.* Æ 1·05
		(v.) 46-SAN ISSUE. *Plain edge : serrated rim.* SILVER.	
Æ 98	Rupee	Same as 82.	Same as 82 : above, ۱۲۱۵ ; ♓ over پادشاه ; no crown. PL. XXXII. Æ 1·1, Wt. 180
99	½-Rupee	"	" Æ ·9, Wt. 90
100	¼-Rupee	"	" Æ ·65, Wt. 45

VII. ARKĀT.

(In name of 'Ālamgír II.)

(i.) Issued at Fort St. George, Madras.

Native style.

SILVER.

No.	Denomination.	Obv.	Rev.
Æ			
101-105	Rupee	مانوس مـــيمنت Ψ ٦ سنه جلوس ضــرب اركــات	عزيز الدين عالمگير ـــــــــــــــے پـــادشـــاه غـــاز ی سـكــه مــبــار *BANK COLL.* Æ ·8, Wt. 176 Æ ·8, Wt. 172 Pl. XXXII. Æ ·8, Wt. 174 (Hijrah year ١١٧٣) *BANK COLL.* Æ ·8, Wt. 174 *I.O.C.* Æ ·9, Wt. 185
106	,,	,, No regnal year	,, but ١٣١٤ *BANK COLL.* Æ ·8, Wt. 174
107	,,	,, but ٣	,, Hijrah year illegible. *BANK COLL.* Æ ·85, Wt. 172
108	¼-Rupee	Portion of same inscr.	Portion of same inscr. *MARSDEN.* Æ ·5, Wt. 44

(ii.) LATER MILLED COINS

ISSUED AT MADRAS AND CALCUTTA.*

1. MADRAS ISSUE.

GOLD.

Oblique milling in centre of edge: raised rim.

No.	Denomination.	Obv.	Rev.
AV 109	½-Mohr	مانوس میمنت ٦ سنه ψ جلوس ضرب ارکات	محمد ١١٧٢ عزیز الدین عالمگیر ی پادشاه غاز سکه مبار PL. XXXII. *I.O.C.* AV ·85, Wt. 90
110	¼-Mohr	ψ ٦ سنه ضرب ارکات	١١٧٢ شاه پاد سکه عالمگیر *I.O.C.* AV ·65, Wt. 45

* The Calcutta issues are distinguished by the mint-mark of a rose from those of Fort St. George (Madras), which bear a trísúl ψ. Those of Calcutta here described have a straight milling, whilst the Madras issues have an oblique milling or cable-pattern in the centre of the edge. The use of a straight milling prevailed at Calcutta from 1818 to 1833 on Bengal issues, and it is probable that the same period may be assigned for the rose rupees of Arkát.

SILVER.

Oblique milling in centre of edge; raised rim.

No.	Denomination.	
Æ 111	Double rupee	As 109: but ۲ by error for ۶ (Very coarse work.) PL. XXXII. *I.O.C.* Æ 1·5, Wt. 373
112	,,	As preceding; Hijrah year obliterated. (Better work. Struck over Dollar.) *I.O.C.* Æ 1·5, Wt. 372
113, 114	Rupee	As 109. *BANKS.* Æ 1·1, Wt. 185 *I.O.C.* Æ 1·1, Wt. 180
115	,,	,, but ۱۱۷۶ by error for ۱۱۷۲ *PRINSEP.* Æ 1·1, Wt. 180
116	,,	,, *BANK COLLECTION.* Æ 1·1, Wt. 179
117, 118	½-Rupee	,, *MARSDEN.* Æ ·85, Wt. 90 Æ ·85
119	¼-Rupee	As 110 Æ ·65, Wt. 45
120	Anna	,, *I.O.C.* Æ ·4, Wt. 11

No.	Denomination.	
		2. Calcutta issue.
		Straight milling.
Æ 121	Rupee	As 109 : but rose instead of trisúl. THOMAS. Æ 1·05, Wt. 179
122	½-Rupee	,, ,, ,, Pl. XXXII. Æ ·85, Wt. 90
123, 124	¼-Rupee	As 110 ,, ,, Æ ·65, Wt. 45 Æ ·65
125	2 Annas	,, ,, ,, Æ ·5, Wt. 22
126	Anna	,, ,, ,, Æ ·4, Wt. 11

No.	Denomination.	Obv.	Rev.
		(iii.) ISSUED AT PONDICHERRY BY THE FRENCH COMPAGNIE DES INDES. (*Native style.*)	
		(A. IN NAME OF 'ÁLAMGÍR II.)	
		SILVER.	
Æ 127	Rupee	Same as 109 : but O instead of ♆. Regnal year ٢	Same as 109. Hijrah year obliterated. PL. XXXII. *BANK COLL.* Æ ·95, Wt. 176
		(B. IN NAME OF SHÁH-'ÁLAM.)	
		SILVER.	
Æ 128	"	Same as 127. Regnal year ۵	حامی دین الله محمد شـــــاه سـ]ایه فضل شاه عالم پاد ســـــ]کـه [زد بر هفت کشور] No Hijrah year. PL. XXXII. *BANKS.* Æ ·9, Wt. 172
129	"	" Regnal year ٦	" *I.O.C.* Æ ·9, Wt. 174
130	"	" Regnal year ١٠	" year ١١٨٥ *BANKS.* Æ ·95, Wt. 176
131	"	" Regnal year ١٣	" year ١٨٨ *I.O.C.* Æ ·95, Wt. 177
132	"	" Regnal year ١٦	" year ١٩١ *BANK COLL.* Æ ·9, Wt. 177
133	"	" Regnal year ١٧	" year ١١٩٢ *BANK COLL.* Æ ·9, Wt. 175

No.	Denomination.	Obv.	Rev.
AR 134	Rupee	Same as 127; Regnal year ٢٢	Same as 128; but year ١٩٧ *I.O.C.* AR ·95, Wt. 177
135	„	„ Regnal year ٢٣	„ year ١٩٩ *MARSDEN.* AR ·9, Wt. 175
136, 137	„	„ Regnal year ٢٥	„ year ١٢٠٠ (obliterated on 137). AR ·9, Wt. 176 *MARSDEN.* AR ·9, Wt. 176
138	„	„ Regnal year ٢٨	„ year obliterated. (Clipped.) *PRINSEP.* AR ·9, Wt. 160
139	„	„ Regnal year ٢٩	„ year ١٢ *MARSDEN.* AR ·9, Wt. 176
140	„	„ Regnal year ٣٠	„ year obliterated. *MARSDEN.* AR ·9, Wt. 174
141	„	„ Regnal year ٣٢ (for 22?)	„ year ١١٩٨ (Thin.) *BANKS.* AR 1·05, Wt. 177
142	„	„ Regnal year ٣٢ (for 22?)	„ year ١١٩٨ *MARSDEN.* AR ·9, Wt. 173
143	„	„ Regnal year ٣٢	„ year ٠٧ *THEOBALD.* AR ·9, Wt. 172
144	„	„ Regnal year ٢٣	„ year ١٨ AR ·95, Wt. 174

VIII. MASULIPATAN.

IN NAME OF 'ÁLAMGÍR II (*sic*).

SILVER.

No.	Denomination.	Obv.	Rev.
Æ 145	Double Rupee	مانوس میمنت ۳۱ ψ سنه جلوس ضرب مچهلی پتن	عالمگیر غازی ۱۱۹۴ پادشاه ک سکه مبارک Pl. XXXII. *MARSDEN.* Æ 1·25, Wt. 348
146	Rupee	,, Partly cut off.	,, but ۱۱۹۷ *I.O.C.* Æ ·85, Wt. 174
147	½-Rupee	,, ,,	,, but ۱۱۹۸ *I O.C.* Æ ·65, Wt. 87

IN NAME OF SHÁH-'ÁLAM.

SILVER.

No.	Denomination.	Obv.	Rev.
148	Rupee	Same as 145 : but ٥۳۹	Same as 128 : but year ۲۱۲ Pl. XXXII. *MARSDEN.* Æ ·95, Wt. 175
149	,,	,,	,, but ۱۲ *MARSDEN.* Æ ·95, Wt. 175

COPPER ISSUES OF THE EAST INDIA COMPANY.

CALCUTTA.

(In name of Sháh-'Álam.)

No.	Denomination.	Obv.	Rev.
Æ 150, 151	4 Páis	م]يمنت ١١ سنه ضرب كلكته	١١٧٧* شاه عالم پادشاهی غاز *BANKS.* Æ 1·05, Wt. 425 *MARSDEN.* Æ 1·05, Wt. 446
152	,,	,,	,, but ٨٨ *MARSDEN.* Æ 1·05, Wt. 442
153	2 Páis	Same : but . . ر٠ اپمد (?)	,, but ١١٨٨ *BANKS.* Æ ·9, Wt. 223

* For ١١٨٨, probably.

(BENGAL PROVINCE.)

NO MINT.

(In name of Sháh-'Álam.)

Issue of Regnal Year 22: A.H. 1195.

No.	Denomination.	Obv.	Rev.
Æ 154-156	2 Páis	س جلو ۲۲ سنه Five stars.	شاه عالم شاه پاد ۱۱۹۵ Two stars. *FREUDENTHAL.* Æ 1·15, Wt. 204 * Æ 1·05, Wt. 239 *FREUDENTHAL.* Æ 1·1, Wt. 213
157-159	1 Pái	,, (No. 159 has only two stars.)	,, *FREUDENTHAL.* Æ ·9, Wt. 113 † Æ ·85, Wt. 110 Æ ·9, Wt. 111
160, 161	½-Pái	,,	,, Æ ·7, Wt. 50 ‡ Æ ·7, Wt. 57
162, 163	¼-Pái	,,	,, Æ ·6, Wt. 29 § Æ ·65, Wt. 28

* Duplicates of this in the Museum weigh 224, 228, 220, and 218 grs.
† ,, ,, ,, ,, 101, 109, and 112 grs.
‡ ,, ,, ,, ,, 54, 55, 57, and 58 grs.
§ ,, ,, ,, ,, 24, 25, 28, and 31 grs.

No.	Denomination.	Obv.	Rev.
		ISSUE OF REGNAL YEAR 37 (NO HIJRAH YEAR).	
		*a. Persian and Nágarí.**	
164-168	1 Pái	سکه ψ یک پای एक पाई सीका	شاه عالم پاد شاه جلوس ψ ۳۷ سنه
		(Different dies, slightly varied.)	
			FREUDENTHAL. Æ ·95, Wt. 100 *FREUDENTHAL.* Æ 1·0, Wt. 99 *FREUDENTHAL.* Æ ·85, Wt. 100 (Worn.) Æ ·9, Wt. 79 (Nágarí not debased.) Æ ·95, Wt. 100
169	2 Páis	سکه دو پای द्वौ पाई सीका	As 164: without trisúl. *FREUDENTHAL.* Æ 1·15, Wt. 188
170	½-Pái	سکه آد پای आधि पाई सीका	As 169. *FREUDENTHAL.* Æ ·65, Wt. 47

* The Nágarí is generally debased.

No.	Denomination.	Obv.	Rev.
		Persian, Bengálí and Nágarí.	
Æ 171- 174	1 Pái	এক পাই সিক্কা يك پای سكه एक पाई सीका	As 169. *FREUDENTHAL* Æ 1·1, Wt. 136 *FREUDENTHAL.* Æ 1·0, Wt. 103 *FREUDENTHAL.* Æ ·9, Wt. 100 (Milled rim.) *BANKS.* Æ 1·2, Wt. 221
175	½-Pái	আদ পাই সিক কা نيم پای سكه आर्ध पाई सीका	As 169. *FREUDENTHAL.* Æ ·95, Wt. 59
		ISSUE OF REGNAL YEAR 45 (NO HIJRAH YEAR).	
		Persian and Nágarí.	
176- 179	1 Pái	As 164.	As 164: but ۴۵ Æ ·9, Wt. 92 Æ ·9. Wt. 99 (With trisúl on obv., and star on rev.) Æ ·9, Wt. 100 („ star varied.) Æ ·85, Wt. 99
		Persian, Bengálí and Nágarí.	
180	1 Pái	As 171.	As 171 : but ۴۵ *FREUDENTHAL.* Æ 2·0, Wt. 92

BENÁRES.

No.	Denomination.	Obv.	Rev.
Æ 181	[2 Páis]	ضرب بنارس ٢٨ Ψ	عالم شاه فلوس Ψ ١٢٢١ Fish above date. Æ 1·2, Wt. 240
182	„	٢٩ سنه ضرب بنارس Ψ	Same: but ١٢٢٨ below فلوس Æ 1·05, Wt 200
183	[½-Pái]	Same as 181.	Same as 181. Æ ·6, Wt. 30

No.	Denomination.	Obv.	Rev.
		ARKÁT.	
Æ 184	2 Páis	جلوس ٢٧ سنه ضرب ارکات	والا هجر ١٢٠٠ سنه Pl. XXXIII. *FREUDENTHAL.* Æ ·9, Wt. 207
185	,,	جلوس دت ضر ارکا سنه ب	Same: but ١٢٠٨ *FREUDENTHAL.* Æ ·9, Wt. 207
186	,,	,, but ٣٩	Same: but ١٢١ (unit cut off). *FREUDENTHAL.* Æ ·95, Wt. 205
187	1 Pái	,, but ٣٩	Same: but ١٢ (unit and decade cut off). *FREUDENTHAL.* Æ ·7, Wt. 105

INDEXES.

I. INDEX OF YEARS.

*** Hijrah years in brackets [ ] are calculated by means of the *regnal* years.

Year A.H.	Regnal year.	MONTH.	Metal.	MINT.	EMPEROR.	NO.	Page.
933	—	—	AR	—	Bábar*	1	5
935	—	—	„	—	„	2	6
936	—	—	„	Lahore	„	3	7
„	—	—	„	—	„	4	7
942	—	—	„	—	Humáyún*	18	10
962	—	—	„	—	„	11	9
963	—	—	„	—	Akbar	84	21
„	—	—	Æ	Nárnól	„	255	49
964	—	—	AR	—	„	85	21
965	—	—	Æ	Nárnól	„	256	49
966	—	—	„	—	„	257	49
967	—	—	AR	Agrah	„	86	22
„	—	—	„	—	„	87	22
96*x*	—	—	„	Jaunpúr	„	88, 88*a*	22, 23
970	—	—	„	—	„	89, 90	23
„	—	—	„	Agrah	„	91	23
971	—	—	AV	„	„	23	11
„	—	—	„	„ ?	„	24	12
„	—	—	„	Lahore	„	25	12
„	—	—	„	—	„	26-28	12
„	—	—	AR	—	„	92, 93	23
„	—	—	„	Dehlí	„	94	24
972	—	—	AV	—	„	29	12
„	—	—	„	Agrah	„	30	12
„	—	—	„	Sárangpúr	„	31	13
973	—	—	„	—	„	32	13
„	—	—	AR	—	„	95	24
974	—	—	AV	Lahore	„	33	13
„	—	—	AR	Jaunpúr	„	96	24
975	—	—	AV	—	„	34-37	13
„	—	—	„	Dehlí	„	38	13
„	—	—	AR	„	„	97	25
„	—	—	„	Jaunpúr	„	98	25
„	—	—	„	—	„	99	25
976	—	—	AV	—	„	39	14

* See also Early Local Copper, A.H. 936-942, on pp. 262-3.

Year A.H.	Regnal year.	MONTH.	Metal.	MINT.	EMPEROR.	NO.	Page.
976	—	——	AV	Agrah	Akbar	40	14
”	—	——	AR	——	”	100	25
977	—	——	AV	Jaunpúr	”	41	14
”	—	——	”	Dehlí	”	42	14
”	—	——	”	Lahore	”	43	14
”	—	——	”	——	”	44	15
”	—	——	AR	Agrah	”	101	25
978	—	——	AV	”	”	45	15
”	—	——	”	Jaunpúr	”	46	15
”	—	——	AR	——	”	102	25
97x	—	——	AV	Jaunpúr	”	47	15
”	—	——	Æ	Lahore	”	258	49
980	—	——	AV	Ahmadábád	”	48	15
”	—	——	”	Agrah	”	49	15
”	—	——	AR	——	”	103	25
”	—	——	Æ	Nárnól	”	259	49
”	—	——	”	——	”	260	49
981	—	——	AV	Agrah	”	50, 51	16
”	—	——	AR	——	”	104	26
982	—	——	AV	Agrah	”	52,53,54	16, 17
”	—	——	”	Ahmadábád	”	55, 56	17
”	—	——	AR	”	”	105, 106	26
”	—	——	Æ	”	”	261	50
”	—	——	”	Nárnól	”	262	50
983	—	——	AV	Ahmadábád	”	57	17
”	—	——	”	Jaunpúr	”	58	17
”	—	——	”	Lahore	”	59, 60	17
”	—	——	AR	——	”	107, 112	26
”	—	——	”	Jaunpúr	”	108-10	26
”	—	——	”	Ahmadábád	”	111	26
”	—	——	Æ	Dógám	”	263	50
984	—	——	AV	Sirhind	”	61	17
”	—	——	”	——	”	62, 64	17, 18
”	—	——	”	Muhammad-ábád Udaipúr	”	63	17
”	—	——	AR	——	”	113	26
985	—	——	AV	——	”	65	18
”	—	——	AR	Dehlí	”	114	26
”	—	——	”	——	”	115-17	27
”	—	——	Æ	Málpúr	”	264	50
986	—	——	AV	Fathpúr	”	66	19
”	—	——	AR	——	”	118, 119	27
”	—	——	”	——	”	120	27
”	—	——	”	Lahore	”	122, 123	28
”	—	——	”	Fathpúr	”	124	28
987	—	——	AV	”	”	67	19
”	—	——	”	Lahore	”	68	19
”	—	——	AR	——	”	121, 132	27, 29

Year A.H.	Regnal year.	MONTH.	Metal.	MINT.	EMPEROR.	NO.	Page
987	—	——	Æ	Fathpúr	Akbar	125, 125*a*, 126	28
,,	—	——	,,	Ahmadábád	,,	127	28
,,	—	——	,,	Urdú	,,	128	29
,,	—	——	,,	Lahore	,,	129, 130	29
,,	—	——	,,	Patnah	,,	131	29
,,	—	——	Æ	——	,,	265, 267	50, 51
,,	—	——	,,	Fathpúr	,,	266	51
988	—	——	AV	,,	,,	69	19
,,	—	——	,,	Lahore	,,	70	20
,,	—	——	,,	——	,,	71, 72	20
,,	—	——	Æ	Lahore	,,	133	29
,,	—	——	,,	Fathpúr	,,	134, 135	29
,,	—	——	,,	——	,,	136	30
,,	—	——	Æ	Fathpúr	,,	268	51
989	—	——	Æ	Lahore	,,	137	30
,,	—	——	,,	Fathpúr	,,	138, 139	30
98*x*	—	——	Æ	Ahmadábád	,,	269	51
,,	—	——	,,	Jaunpúr	,,	270	51
990	—	——	Æ	——	,,	140	30
[991]	28	——	,,	Peshawar?	,,	177	35
992	—	——	,,	——	,,	141	30
,,	—	——	,,	——	,,	252*a*	47
993	—	——	,,	——	,,	142	30
[,,]	30	Dai	,,	Ahmadábád	,,	178	35
[,,]	,,	Mardád	,,	,,	,,	179	35
994	—	——	,,	——	,,	143	30
,,	—	——	Æ	Dógám	,,	271	52
[,,]	31	Mihr	,,	Alláhábád	,,	273	53
995	—	——	Æ	——	,,	144, 145	30
[,,]	32	——	AV	——	,,	163	32
[,,]	,,	——	Æ	——	,,	180	35
[,,]	,,	——	Æ	Kábul	,,	274	53
[996]	33	——	Æ	——	,,	181	35
[,,]	,,	——	Æ	Kábul	,,	274*a*	53
997	—	——	Æ	——	,,	146, 147 252*b*	30 47
[,,]	34	——	,,	——	,,	182-84	35
998	—	——	,,	——	,,	148, 149	31
[,,]	35	Ardibihist	,,	——	,,	185	35
[,,]	,,	Amardád	,,	——	,,	186	36
999	—	——	,,	——	,,	150	31
[,,]	36	Abán	,,	Lahore	,,	187	36
[,,]	,,	Bahman	,,	,,	,,	188	36
[,,]	,,	——	,,	Tattah	,,	189	36
[,,]	,,	Dai	Æ	Lahore	,,	275	53
[,,]	,,	——	,,	Nárnól ?	,,	276	53
9*xx*	—	——	,,	Gwálior	,,	272	52

Year A.H.	Regnal year.	MONTH.	Metal.	MINT.	EMPEROR.	NO.	Page.
1000	—	——	AV	Urdú-Zafar-Karín	Akbar	73-82	20
,,	—	——	AR	,,	,,	151-59	31
,,	—	——	Æ	,,	,,	273	52
[,,]	37	——	AR	——	,,	190	36
[,,]	,,	——	,,	Ahmadábád	,,	191	36
[,,]	,,	Dai	Æ	Multán	,,	277	53
[1001]	38	——	AR	Ahmadábád	,,	192	36
[,,]	,,	Bahman	,,	,,	,,	193	36
[,,]	,,	Tír	,,	Lahore	,,	194	37
[,,]	,,	Farwardín	,,	,,	,,	195	37
[,,]	,,	Ardibihist	,,	,,	,,	196	37
[,,]	,,	Shahriwar	Æ	Gwálior	,,	278	53
[1002]	39	Azur	AR	Lahore	,,	198	37
[,,]	,,	Farwardín	Æ	,,	,,	279	54
[1003]	40	Khúrdád	AR	Tattah	,,	199	37
[,,]	,,	Bahman	,,	,,	,,	200	38
[,,]	,,	,,	,,	——	,,	201	38
[,,]	,,	——	,,	——	,,	202	38
[1004]	41	Khúrdád	,,	Ahmadábád	,,	203	38
[,,]	,,	Isfandármiz	,,	Lahore	,,	204	38
[,,]	,,	——	,,	——	,,	205	38
[1005]	42	Bahman	AV	Agrah	,,	164	32
,,	,,	Khúrdád	AR	Ahmadábád	,,	206	39
,,	,,	Tír	,,	,,	,,	207	39
,,	,,	Abán	,,	,,	,,	208	39
,,	,,	Shahriwar	,,	Patnah	,,	209	39
,,	,,	——	,,	,,	,,	210	39
,,	,,	Tír	,,	Lahore	,,	211	39
,,	,,	Bahman	,,	,,	,,	212	39
,,	,,	Tír	,,	Dehlí ?	,,	213	40
,,	,,	——	,,	——	,,	214	40
[1006]	43	Khúrdád	,,	Patnah	,,	215	40
,,	,,	Bahman	,,	,,	,,	216	40
,,	,,	——	,,	——	,,	217	40
,,	,,	Shahriwar	,,	——	,,	218	40
,,	,,	Tír	Æ	Lahore	,,	279*a*	54
[1007]	44	Ardibihist	AV	Agrah	,,	165	32
,,	,,	Amardád	AR	Ahmadábád	,,	219	40
,,	,,	Shahriwar	,,	Patnah	,,	220	41
,,	,,	Abán	,,	Kábul	,,	221	41
,,	,,	Ardibihist	,,	Lahore	,,	222	41
,,	,,	Shahriwar	,,	,,	,,	223	41
,,	,,	Abán	,,	,,	,,	224	41
,,	,,	Azur	,,	,,	,,	225	41
,,	,,	Amardád	Æ	Bairátah	,,	280-81*a*	54
[1005-7]	42-4	Dai	,,	Dehlí	,,	282	54
[1008]	45	Isfandármiz	AV	Asír	,,	166	33

Year A.H.	Regnal year.	MONTH.	Metal.	MINT.	EMPEROR.	NO.	Page.
[1008]	45	Dai	Æ	Kábul	Akbar	226	41
,,	,,	,,	,,	Lahore	,,	227	42
,,	,,	Bahman	,,	,,	,,	228	42
[1009]	46	Tír	,,	Ahmadábád	,,	229	42
,,	,,	Azur	,,	Patnah	,,	230	42
,,	,,	Dai	,,	Kábul	,,	231	42
,,	,,	Khúrdád	,,	Lahore	,,	232	42
,,	,,	Azur	,,	,,	,,	233	43
,,	,,	Dai	,,	,,	,,	234	43
,,	,,	Abán	Æ	Agrah	,,	283	54
[1010]	47	Bahman	Æ	Ahmadábád	,,	235	43
,,	,,	Mihr	,,	,,	,,	236	43
,,	,,	Azur	,,	Kábul	,,	237	43
,,	,,	Khúrdád	,,	Lahore	,,	238	44
,,	,,	Abán	,,	,,	,,	239	44
,,	,,	Dai	,,	,,	,,	240	44
,,	,,	Ardibihist	Æ	Agrah	,,	284	54
,,	,,	Tír	,,	,,	,,	285	55
,,	,,	Abán	,,	,,	,,	286	55
[1011]	48	Mihr	Æ	Burhánpúr	,,	241	44
,,	,,	Dai	,,	,,	,,	197	37
,,	,,	Amardád	,,	Lahore	,,	242	44
,,	,,	Abán	,,	,,	,,	243-44*a*	44, 45
[1012]	49	Farwardín	AV	Agrah	,,	167	33
,,	,,	Amardád	,,	,,	,,	168	33
,,	,,	Azur	,,	,,	,,	169	33
,,	,,	Abán	Æ	Kábul	,,	245	45
,,	,,	Dai	,,	,,	,,	246	45
,,	,,	Ardibihist	,,	Lahore	,,	247	45
,,	,,	Abán	,,	,,	,,	248	45
,,	,,	Farwardín	,,	Patnah ?	,,	249	45
[10*xx*]	4*x*	——	Æ	Agrah	,,	287	55
[1013]	50	Amardád	AV	,,	,,	170	33
,,	,,	Khúrdád	,,	,,	,,	173-74	34
,,	,,	Amardád	,,	Lahore	,,	171	34
,,	,,	Farwardín	,,	——	,,	172	34
,,	,,	Amardád	Æ	Agrah	,,	250	46
,,	,,	Farwardín	,,	Lahore	,,	251	46
,,	,,	Shahriwar	Æ	Agrah	,,	287*a*	55
[1014]	51	——	AV	,,	,,	175	34
x	2	Farwardín	Æ	Ahmadábád	Salím [Jahángír] as Governor	288	56
x	,,	Khúrdád	,,	,,	,,	289	56
1014	1	——	,,	Agrah	Jahángír	402, 403	79
,,	—	——	,,	Akbarnagar	,,	404	80
,,	1	——	,,	Kábul	,,	405	80
1015	—	——	AV	Agrah	,,	290	57

Year A.H.	Regnal year.	MONTH.	Metal.	MINT.	EMPEROR.	NO.	Page.
1015	1	——	AV	Lahore	Jahángír	291-93	57-58
,,	1	——	AR	Kábul	,,	406	80
,,	,,	Amardád	,,	,,	,,	407	80
,,	,,	——	,,	Agrah	,,	408	80
,,	1	——	,,	Akbarnagar	,,	410	80
,,	——	——	,,	,,	,,	412	80
,,	1	——	,,	Lahore	,,	414	81
,,	2	——	,,	Agrah	,,	409	80
,,	,,	——	,,	Ahmadábád	,,	411	80
,,	,,	Isfandármiz	,,	Patnah	,,	413	81
,,	,,	——	,,	Lahore	,,	415, 416	81
1016	,,	——	,,	Ahmadábád	,,	417	81
,,	,,	——	,,	Lahore	,,	420	82
,,	3	——	AV	,,	,,	294	58
,,	,,	——	AR	,,	,,	421, 422	82
,,	——	——	,,	Akbarnagar	,,	418, 419	81
1017	4	——	AV	Agrah	,,	295	58
,,	,,	——	AR	,,	,,	423	82
,,	5	——	,,	Lahore	,,	424	82
1018	,,	——	AV	Agrah	,,	296	58
,,	,,	——	AR	Ahmadábád	,,	425	83
,,	,,	——	,,	Agrah	,,	426, 427	83
,,	,,	——	,,	Patnah	,,	428	83
,,	(4 *sic*)	——	,,	Lahore	,,	429	83
,,	5	——	,,	,,	,,	430, 431	83
1019	,,	Isfandármiz	,,	Agrah	,,	432	84
,,	——	——	,,	Kashmír	,,	433	84
,,	5	——	,,	Lahore	,,	434-36	84
,,	,,	Bahman	,,	,,	,,	437, 438	85
,,	,,	——	,,	——	,,	438*a*	85
1020	6	Mihr	AV	Agrah	,,	297	59
,,	,,	——	,,	——	,,	312-16	63
,,	,,	Abán	AR	Agrah	,,	439	85
,,	,,	——	,,	Kandahár	,,	440	86
1021	,,	Isfandármiz	,,	Agrah	,,	441	86
,,	7	Mihr	AV	,,	,,	298	59
,,	,,	Dai	,,	,,	,,	299	59
,,	,,	——	,,	——	,,	317	63
,,	,,	Ardibihist	AR	Agrah	,,	442	86
,,	,,	Shahriwar	,,	Patnah	,,	443	86
,,	,,	Mihr	,,	Dehlí	,,	444	86
,,	,,	——	,,	Kandahár	,,	445, 446	87
[,,]	,,	Farwardín	,,	Lahore	,,	447	87
,,	,,	Amardád	,,	,,	,,	448	87
,,	,,	Isfandármiz	,,	,,	,,	449	87
,,	,,	——	Æ	Agrah	,,	512	99
1022	8	Ardibihist	AV	,,	,,	300	59
,,	,,	——	AR	Kandahár	,,	450	87

Year A.H.	Regnal year.	MONTH.	ZODIACAL SIGN.	Metal.	MINT.	EMPEROR.	NO.	Page.
1023	8	——		AV	Ajmír	Jahángír	318	64
,,	,,	Ardibihist		AR	Kandahár	,,	451	87
[,,]	,,	Dai		,,	Lahore	,,	452	88
,,	9	——		AV	Ajmír	,,	319-21	64
,,	,,	Khúrdád		AR	Agrah	,,	453	88
,,	,,	Tír		,,	Kandahár	,,	454	88
[,,]	,,	Ardibihist		,,	Lahore	,,	455	88
[,,]	,,	Tír		,,	,,	,,	456	88
[1024]	10	Dai		,,	,,	,,	457	88
1024	,,	Ardibihist		AV	Agrah	,,	301	60
1025	—	——		,,	Ajmír	,,	302	60
,,	11	Abán		,,	Agrah	,,	303	60
,,	,,	Shahriwar		AR	,,	,,	458, 459	89
,,	,,	——		,,	Ajmír	,,	460	89
,,	—	Abán		,,	Ahmadábád	,,	461	89
,,	—	——		,,	Kashmír	,,	462	90
,,	11	——		,,	Lahore	,,	463	90
1026	,,	Dai		,,	Agrah	,,	464	90
,,	12	Mihr		AV	,,	,,	304	60
,,	,,	Tír		AR	,,	,,	465	90
,,	—	Azur		,,	Ahmadábád	,,	466	90
,,	12	Shahriwar		,,	Patnah	,,	467	91
,,	,,	Khúrdád		,,	Tattah	,,	468	91
,,	,,	——		,,	Lahore	,,	469	91
,,	,,	——		,,	Kandahár	,,	470, 471	91
1027	,,	Shahriwar		,,	Kábul	,,	473	92
,,	13	——		,,	Kandahár	,,	472	92
,,	,,	Abán		,,	Agrah	,,	474	92
,,	,,	——		,,	Ahmadábád	,,	475	92
,,	,,	Abán		,,	Patnah	,,	476	93
,,	,,	——		,,	Lahore	,,	477	93
,,	,,	——	Aries	,,	Ahmadábád	,,	361-63	72
,,	,,	——	Taurus	,,	,,	,,	364, 365	72
,,	,,	——	Gemini	,,	,,	,,	368, 369	73
,,	,,	——	Cancer	,,	,,	,,	370, 371	73
,,	,,	——	Leo	,,	,,	,,	372, 373	73
,,	,,	——	,,	,,	,,	,,	385	76
,,	—	——	Scorpio	,,	,,	,,	374	74
1028	13	——	Pisces	AV	Agrah	,,	358	71
,,	14	——	——	,,	,,	,,	305	61
,,	,,	——	——	,,	Ahmadábád	,,	306	61
,,	—	——	——	AR	,,	,,	478	93
,,	14	Khúrdád	——	,,	Patnah	,,	479	93
,,	,,	Amardád	——	,,	,,	,,	480	93
,,	,,	——	——	,,	Kandahár	,,	481, 482	93
,,	,,	——	Aries	AV	Agrah	,,	322	65
,,	,,	——	,,	AR	,,	,,	386	77
,,	,,	——	Taurus	AV	,,	,,	324-26	65

Year. A.H.	Regnal year.	MONTH.	ZODIACAL SIGN.	Metal.	MINT.	EMPEROR.	NO.	Page.
1028	14	——	Taurus	AR	Agrah	Jahángír	387	77
,,	—	——	Cancer	AV	,,	,,	376	75
,,	14	——	Leo	,,	,,	,,	334	67
,,	,,	——	Virgo	,,	,,	,,	338	68
,,	,,	——	,,	,,	,,	,,	378	75
,,	,,	——	Libra	,,	,,	,,	342	68
,,	12	——	Scorpio	,,	,,	,,	380	76
,,	,,	——	,,	AR	,,	,,	397	78
,,	14	——	Capricornus	AV	,,	,,	350	70
,,	13	——	Aquarius	,,	,,	,,	383	76
,,	,,	——	,,	AR	,,	,,	400	78
,,	,,	——	Pisces	AV	,,	,,	384	76
,,	,,	——	,,	AR	,,	,,	401	78
1029	14	——	——	,,	Ahmadábád	,,	483	93
,,	,,	——	——	,,	Kandahár	,,	486	94
,,	,,	——	Capricornus	AV	Agrah	,,	351	70
,,	,,	——	,,	AR	,,	,,	375	74
,,	15	——	Taurus	,,	,,	,,	366	72
,,	,,	——	Gemini	AV	,,	,,	330	66
,,	,,	——	Cancer	,,	,,	,,	333*a*, *b*	66
,,	,,	——	Gemini	AR	,,	,,	388, 389	77
,,	,,	——	Leo	AV	,,	,,	335	67
,,	16	——	,,	AR	,,	,,	391	77
,,	15	——	——	AV	Ahmadábád	,,	307	61
,,	,,	——	——	AR	,,	,,	484	94
,,	,,	Shahriwar	——	,,	Patnah	,,	485	94
,,	,,	——	——	,,	Kandahár	,,	487	94
,,	,,	——	——	,,	Lahore	,,	488	94
1030	,,	——	——	,,	Kandahár	,,	490	95
,,	16	Shahriwar	——	,,	Patnah	,,	489	95
,,	,,	——	——	,,	Lahore	,,	491	95
,,	,,	——	Aries	AV	Agrah	,,	323	65
,,	,,	——	Taurus	,,	,,	,,	327, 328	66
,,	,,	——	Cancer	,,	,,	,,	333*c*	67
,,	,,	——	Virgo	,,	,,	,,	339	68
,,	,,	——	Libra	,,	,,	,,	343	69
,,	—	——	Scorpio	,,	,,	,,	346	69
,,	16	——	,,	,,	,,	,,	346*a*	69
,,	—	——	Capricornus	,,	,,	,,	352	70
1031	16	——	——	AR	Ahmadábád	,,	492, 493	95
,,	,,	——	——	,,	Lahore	,,	494	95
,,	,,	——	Gemini	AV	Agrah	,,	331	66
,,	,,	——	Virgo	,,	,,	,,	340	68
,,	,,	——	Sagittarius	,,	,,	,,	348	69
,,	,,	——	Capricornus	,,	,,	,,	{ 353 { 382	70 76
,,	,,	——	Aquarius	,,	,,	,,	355	70
,,	17	——	Cancer	AR	,,	,,	390	77

Years. A.H.	Regnal year.	MONTH.	ZODIACAL SIGN.	Metal.	MINT.	EMPEROR.	NO.	Page.
1031	17	—	Leo	AV	Agrah	Jahángír	336, 337	67
,,	,,	—	Libra	AR	,,	,,	396	78
,,	,,	—	Pisces	AV	,,	,,	359	71
,,	,,	—	—	AR	Lahore	,,	495	95
1032	,,	—	—	,,	,,	,,	496	96
,,	—	—	Leo	AV	Agrah	,,	377	75
,,	17	—	Scorpio	,,	,,	,,	347	69
,,	18	—	Libra	AR	,,	,,	395	78
,,	17	—	Capricornus	AV	,,	,,	354	70
,,	,,	—	Sagittarius	,,	,,	,,	349	69
,,	18	—	Taurus	,,	,,	,,	329	66
,,	,,	—	Gemini	,,	,,	,,	332	66
,,	,,	—	Libra	,,	,,	,,	344	69
,,	,,	—	Aquarius	,,	,,	,,	356	70
1033	,,	Isfandármiz	—	AR	Patnah	,,	497	96
,,	,,	—	—	,,	Súrat	,,	498	96
,,	,,	—	—	,,	Lahore	,,	499	96
,,	19	—	—	,,	Súrat	Jahángír & Núr-Jahán	514	100
,,	,,	—	Gemini	AV	Agrah	Jahángír	333	66
,,	,,	—	,,	AR	,,	,,	367	73
,,	—	—	Leo	,,	,,	,,	392	77
,,	19	—	Virgo	AV	,,	,,	341	68
,,	17	—	,,	,,	,,	,,	379	75
,,	,,	—	,,	AR	,,	,,	393, 394	78
,,	19	—	Libra	AV	,,	,,	345	69
,,	18	—	Capricornus	AR	,,	,,	399	78
,,	17	—	Sagittarius	AV	,,	,,	381	76
,,	,,	—	,,	AR	,,	,,	398	78
,,	18	—	Pisces	AV	,,	,,	360	71
[1033-4]	,,	Isfandármiz	—	,,	Jahángírnagar	,,	308	62
,,	,,	Shahriwar	—	AR	,,	,,	501	97
1034	,,	—	—	,,	Lahore	,,	500	96
,,	—	—	—	,,	Ahmadábád	Jahángír & Núr-Jahán	515	100
,,	—	—	—	,,	Lahore	,, ,,	518	101
,,	20	—		,,	,,	,, ,,	516, 517	100
,,	,,	—		,,	Súrat	,, ,,	519	101
1035	,,	Bahman		AV	Patnah	Jahángír	309	62
,,	21	—		AR	Agrah	,,	502	97
[,,]	,,	Abán		,,	Ahmadábád	,,	503	97
,,	,,	—		,,	Lahore	,,	504	97
,,	,,	—		,,	Súrat	Jahángír & Núr-Jahán	520	101
1036	,,	—		AR	Lahore	Jahángír	505	97
,,	22	—		AV	,,	,,	310	62
,,	,,	—		AR	,,	,,	506	98
,,	,,	Farwardín		,,	Patnah	,,	507	98

Years. A.H.	Regnal year.	MONTH.	Metal.	MINT.	EMPEROR.	NO.	Page.
1036	—	——	AV	Súrat	Jahángír & Núr-Jahán	513	99
„	—	——	AR	„	„ „	521	101
1037	22	——	„	Ahmadábád	„ „	522	101
„	„	——	„	Agrah	„ „	523, 524	101
[„]	„	——	„	Patnah	„ „	525, 526	102
„	„	——	„	Lahore	Jahángír	508	98
10*xx*	—	Farwardín	„	Kandahár	„	511	98
1037	1	——	„	Lahore	Dáwar Bakhsh	527	103
„	1	——	„	„	Sháh-Jáhan	578	114
„	„	——	„	Agrah	„	579	114
„	„	——	„	Burhánpúr	„	580	115
1038	„	——	„	Agrah	„	581	115
„	„	——	„	Súrat	„	585, 586	116
„	2	Ardibihist	AV	Ahmadábád	„	528	104
„	„	Khúrdád	„	„	„	529	104
[„]	„	——	„	Daulatábád	„	530	105
„	„	——	AR	Agrah	„	582	115
„	„	Tír	„	Akbarábád	„	583	116
„	„	„	„	Patnah	„	584	116
1039	„	Abán	AV	Lahore	„	531	105
„	„	——	AR	Akbarábád	„	588	117
„	„	——	„	Akbarnagar	„	589	117
„	„	Azur	„	Patnah	„	590	118
„	„	Abán	„	Lahore	„	591	118
„	3	——	„	Multán	„	592	118
1040	„	Amardád	„	Patnah	„	596	119
„	„	Bahman	„	„	„	597	119
„	„	——	„	Lahore	„	599	119
„	„	——	„	Multán	„	600	119
„	„	Dai	„	Dehlí	„	603	120
„	—	——	„	Burhánpúr	„	595	119
„	—	——	„	Súrat	„	598	119
„	4	Farwardín	AV	Ahmadábád	„	532	105
[„]	„	„	„	Súrat	„	533	106
„	„	——	AR	Akbarábád	„	593-94	118
„	„	——	„	Multán	„	601-2	119
1041	„	——	„	Akbarábád	„	604	120
„	„	Azur	„	Alláhábád	„	606	120
„	„	Tír	„	Patnah	„	607	121
„	„	Azur	„	„	„	608	121
„	„	Dai	„	„	„	609	121
„	„	——	„	Dehlí	„	610	121
„	„	——	„	Lahore	„	611	121
„	5	——	AR	Akbarábád	„	605	120
„	„	——	„	Lahore	„	612	121
1042	—	——	AV	Akbarábád	„	534	106
[„]	5	——	„	„	„	535	106

Years. A.H.	Regnal year.	MONTH.	Metal.	MINT.	EMPEROR.	NO.	Page.
1042	5	——	AV	Lahore	Sháh-Jahán	536	107
"	"	——	AR	Akbarábád	"	613	122
"	"	——	"	Multán	"	614	122
"	"	——	"	"	"	619, 620	123
"	6	——	"	Akbarábád	"	615	122
"	"	——	"	Burhánpúr	"	616	122
"	"	——	"	Patnah	"	617	122
"	—	——	"	Súrat	"	618	122
1043	6	——	AV	Akbarábád	"	537-39	107
"	"	——	"	Burhánpúr	"	540	107
"	—	——	"	Akbarábád	"	541	108
["]	6	——	"	——	"	542	108
"	"	——	AR	Akbarábád	"	621-22	123
["]	"	——	"	Alláhábád	"	623	124
["]	"	——	"	Patnah	"	624	124
"	"	——	"	Bhakar	"	625-26	124
["]	"	——	"	Súrat	"	627	124
"	"	——	"	Multán	"	628	124
"	7	Farwardín	"	Akbarnagar	"	629	125
"	"	——	"	Súrat	"	630	125
1044	—	——	AV	——	"	543	108
"	7	——	AR	Ahmadábád	"	631	125
"	"	——	"	Lahore	"	632	125
"	8	——	"	Akbarábád	"	633	126
1045	"	——	AV	Ahmadábád	"	544	109
"	"	——	"	Akbarábád	"	545	109
"	"	——	AR	Bhakar	"	634	126
"	"	——	"	Patnah	"	635	126
"	"	——	"	Súrat	"	636	126
"	9	——	"	Multán	"	637	126
1046	"	——	AV	Akbarábád	"	546	109
"	"	——	AR	Súrat	"	638-39	126
"	"	——	"	Lahore	"	640	127
"	"	——	"	Jahángírnagar	"	641	127
1047	10	——	"	Akbarábád	"	642	127
"	"	Khúrdád	"	Tattah	"	643	127
"	"	Tír	"	"	"	644	127
"	11	——	"	Lahore	"	645	128
"	"	——	AV	Akbarábád	"	547	109
1048	"	——	"	"	"	543	109
"	"	——	AR	Multán	"	648	128
"	12	——	"	Jahángírnagar	"	646	128
"	"	——	"	Kandahár	"	647	128
"	—	——	"	——	"	649	128
1049	12	——	AV	——	"	549	109
"	"	——	AR	Súrat	"	650	128
"	13	——	"	Lahore	"	651	129
1050	"	——	AV	Akbarábád	"	550	109

Years. A.H.	Regnal year.	MONTH.	Metal.	MINT.	EMPEROR.	NO.	Page.
1050	14	——	AV	Akbarábád	Sháh-Jahán	551	110
,,	—	——	,,	Daulatábád	,,	552	110
1051	14	——	,,	,,	,,	553	110
,,	15	——	,,	Akbarábád	,,	554	110
,,	—	——	,,	Burhánpúr	,,	555	110
,,	—	——	AR	Súrat	,,	652	129
1052	16	——	AV	Akbarábád	,,	556	110
1053	,,	——	,,	,,	,,	557	110
[1054]	17	——	AR	——	,,	653	129
1054	—	——	,,	——	,,	654	129
1055	18	——	,,	Akbarnagar	,,	655	129
1056	19	——	AV	Akbarábád	,,	558	110
,,	,,	——	AR	,,	,,	656	129
,,	,,	——	,,	Daulatábád	,,	657	130
[,,]	,,	——	,,	Kandahár	,,	658	130
1057	20	——	,,	Súrat	,,	659	130
,,	21	——	AV	Akbarábád	,,	559, 560	110-11
,,	,,	——	AR	Súrat	,,	660	130
[,,]	,,	——	,,	——	,,	661	130
1058	22	Shahriwar	,,	Tattah	,,	663	130
,,	—	(*Months are*	,,	Súrat	,,	662	130
[,,]	22	*not recorded*	,,	Patnah	,,	664	131
[1059]	23	*after this.*)	AV	Akbarábád	,,	561	111
1059	,,		AR	,,	,,	665	131
,,	—		,,	Junahgarh	,,	666	131
1060	23		AV	Burhánpúr	,,	562	111
,,	—		AR	Junahgarh	,,	667	131
,,	23		,,	Daulatábád ?	,,	668	131
,,	24		,,	Sháhjahánábád	,,	669	131
1061	25		AV	Burhánpúr	,,	563	111
,,	,,		,,	Akbarábád	,,	564	111
[,,]	,,		AR	Patnah	,,	670	132
,,	,,		,,	Kashmír	,,	671	132
[,,]	,,		,,	——	,,	672	132
1062	26		AV	Akbarábád	,,	565	111
1063	27		,,	Daulatábád	,,	566	111
1064	28		AR	Súrat	,,	673	132
,,	,,		AV	Akbarábád	,,	567	111
1066	29		AR	Multán	,,	674	132
,,	30		AV	Sháhjahánábád	,,	568	112
[,,]	,,		AR	Súrat	,,	675	132
1067	,,		AV	Daulatábád	,,	569	112
,,	31		AR	,,	,,	676, 677	133
,,	,,		,,	Sháhjahánábád	,,	678	133
,,	,,		,,	Súrat	,,	679	133
1068	,,		AV	Multán	,,	570	112
,,	,,		,,	Daulatábád	,,	571	112
,,	,,		AR	Súrat	,,	680	133

Year. A.H.	Regnal year.	Metal.	MINT.	EMPEROR.	NO.	Page.
1068	32	AV	Akbarábád	Sháh-Jahán	572	112
"	"	"	Daulatábád	"	573	113
"	"	"	Multán	"	574	113
"	3[2]	"	Burhánpúr	"	575	113
"	32	AR	Sháhjahánábád	"	681	133
["]	"	"	Ahmadábád	"	682	134
"	"	"	Daulatábád	"	683, 684	134
["]	"	"	Súrat	"	685	134
["]	"	"	"	"	686	134
1068	—	"	Akbarábád	Shujá'	690	135
"	1	"	Jalúnábád ?	"	691	135
"	"	AV	Ahmadábád	Murád Bakhsh	692	136
"	"	AR	"	"	693-95	137
"	"	"	Súrat	"	696-99	137
["]	"	"	Cambay	"	700	137
1069	32	"	——	Sháh-Jahán	687	134
"	—	AV	Sháhjahánábád	Anonymous	689	134
"	1	AR	Golkondah	Aurangzíb	726	143
["]	"	"	Akbarábád	"	725	143
["]	"	"	Kábul	"	727	144
1070	"	"	Patnah	"	728	144
" (*sic*)	3	"	Multán	"	729	144
1071	"	"	Aurangábád	"	730	145
"	"	"	Súrat	"	731	145
"	4	"	——	"	732	145
"	"	"	Akbarábád	"	733	145
"	—	"	Júnahgarh	"	734	146
1072	5	AV	Tattah	"	701	138
"	—	AR	Súrat ?	"	735	146
1073	5	"	Multán	"	736	146
"	"	"	——	"	737	146
1074	6	AV	Aurangábád	"	702	138
"	"	AR	Júnahgarh	"	738-39	147
1075	8	AV	Multán	"	703	139
"	—	AR	Súrat	"	740	147
1076	8	"	"	"	741	147
"	"	"	Multán	"	742	147
["]	9	"	Akbarnagar	"	742*a*	147
"	"	"	Sháhjahánábád	"	743	147
1077	"	AV	Multán	"	704	139
"	"	AR	Súrat	"	744	148
"	—	"	Akbarábád	"	745	148
1079	11	AV	Aurangábád	"	705	139
[1080]	12	"	Akbarnagar	"	706	139
1081	—	AR	Súrat	"	746	148
1082	13	"	"	"	747	148
(1076 *sic*)	14	"	Golkondah	"	748	148
[1083]	15	"	"	"	749	149

Years. A.H.	Regnal year.	Metal.	MINT.	EMPEROR.	NO.	Page.
[1083]	16	AV	Súrat	Aurangzíb	707	139
(1076 *sic*)	,,	AR	Golkondah	,,	751	149
[1084]	,,	,,	Súrat	,,	750	149
,,	—	,,	,,	,,	750*a*	149
1085	—	,,	Júnahgarh	,,	752	149
1086	20	AV	Golkondah	,,	708	139
1088	,,	AR	Aurangábád	,,	753	149
1089	21	,,	Súrat	,,	754	149
(1076 *sic*)	,,	,,	Golkondah	,,	755	149
1089	22	,,	——	,,	756	150
1090	—	,,	Júnahgarh	,,	757	150
,,	22	,,	Súrat	,,	758	150
,,	23	,,	,,	,,	759	150
,,	,,	,,	Patnah ?	,,	760	150
1091	,,	,,	Súrat	,,	761	150
,,	24	,,	,,	,,	762	150
,,	,,	,,	Bíjápúr	,,	763	150
,,	,,	AV	Sháhjahánábád	,,	709	140
1092	,,	AR	——	,,	764	151
1093	25	,,	Súrat	,,	765-66	151
[,,]	,,	,,	——	,,	767	151
1094	27	,,	Súrat	,,	768	151
1095	,,	,,	,,	,,	769	151
1096	28	,,	[Júnahgarh]	,,	770	151
,,	29	,,	Súrat	,,	771	151
,,	—	,,	'Alamgírpúr	,,	772	151
1097	29	AV	Ahmadnagar	,,	710	140
,,	,,	AR	Súrat	,,	773	152
1098	30	,,	Burhánpúr	,,	774	152
,,	,,	,,	Súrat	,,	775	152
,,	,,	,,	Lahore	,,	776	152
,,	30	,,	Nárnól	,,	777	152
,,	31	,,	Golkondah	,,	778	152
1099	,,	AV	Bíjápúr	,,	711	140
[,,]	,,	,,	Golkondah	,,	712	140
,,	32	AR	Jahángírnagar	,,	779	152
,,	,,	,,	Súrat	,,	779*a*	152
1100	,,	AV	Sháhjahánábád	,,	713	140
,,	,,	AR	Súrat	,,	780	152
,,	,,	,,	Zafarpúr	,,	781	153
[,,]	,,	,,	Kábul	,,	782	153
,,	33	,,	Etáwah	,,	783	153
1101	34	AV	Sháhjahánábád	,,	714	140
,,	,,	AR	Súrat	,,	784	153
1102	,,	,,	Cambay	,,	785	153
,,	,,	,,	Nárnól	,,	786	153
,,	35	,,	Etáwah	,,	787	153

Year. A.H.	Regnal year.	Metal.	MINT.	EMPEROR.	NO.	Page.
1103	35	AV	Chínápatan	Aurangzíb	715	141
[„]	„	AR	„	„	788	154
„	„	„	Akbarábád	„	789	154
„	„	„	Súrat	„	790	154
[„]	„	„	Lucknow	„	791	154
1104	36	„	Etáwah	„	792, 792a	154
„	„	„	Lucknow	„	793	154
„	„	„	Súrat	„	794	155
1105	37	„	Bíjápúr	„	795	155
„	„	„	Súrat	„	796, 796a	155
„	38	„	Etáwah	„	797	155
„	„	„	Ajmír	„	798	155
„	„	„	Lahore	„	799	155
1106	„	AV	Sháhjahánábád	„	716	141
„	„	AR	Etáwah	„	800	156
„	„	„	Patnah	„	801	156
„	„	„	Lahore	„	802	156
1107	39	„	Etáwah	„	803	156
„	„	„	Barailí	„	804	156
„	40	„	Bíjápúr	„	806	156
„	„	AV	„	„	717	141
„	„	AR	Barailí	„	807	156
„	„	„	Zafarábád	„	808	157
1108	„	„	Ahmadnagar	„	809	157
„	„	„	Súrat	„	810	157
„	41	„	Etáwah	„	811	157
„	„	„	Khujistah-bunyád	„	812	157
„	„	„	Ajmír	„	813	157
„	„	„	Lahore	„	814	157
[„]	„	„	Chínápatan	„	815	157
1109	„	AV	——	„	718	141
„	4½	„	Khujistah-bunyád	„	719	141
„	„	AR	Cambay	„	816	157
„	42	„	Akbarábád	„	817, 818	157
„	4½	„	Júnahgarh	„	819	158
1111	43	AV	Burhánpúr	„	720	141
„	4[3]	„	[Chíná]patan	„	721	142
„	43	AR	Barailí	„	820	158
„	„	„	Cambay	„	821	158
„	44	„	Masulipatan	„	822	158
1112	„	AV	Bíjápúr	„	722	142
„	„	AR	Akbarábád	„	823	158
„	45	„	Etáwá	„	824	158
1113	„	„	Burhánpúr	„	825	158
„	„	„	Barailí	„	826	158
1114	46	„	Ajmír	„	827	158
[„]	„	„	Akbarábád	„	828, 828a	159
„	47	„	Etáwah	„	829	159

Year. A.H.	Regnal year.	Metal.	MINT.	EMPEROR.	NO.	Page.
1114	47	Æ	Lahore	Aurangzíb	830	159
1115	,,	AV	Burhánpúr	,,	723	142
,,	,,	Æ	Etáwah	,,	831	159
,,	,,	,,	Súrat	,,	832	159
,,	48	,,	Sháhjahánábád	,,	833	159
1116	,,	,,	Akbarábád	,,	834	159
,,	49	,,	Etáwá	,,	835	160
,,	,,	,,	Barailí	,,	836	160
,,	,,	,,	Súrat	,,	837	160
1117	,,	,,	Akbarábád	,,	838	160
,,	,,	,,	Súrat	,,	839	160
,,	50	,,	Etáwá	,,	841	160
1118	,,	AV	,,	,,	724	142
,,	,,	Æ	,,	,,	842	160
[,,]	51	,,	Akbarábád	,,	843	161
,,	,,	,,	Sháhjahánábád	,,	844	161
[,,]	,,	,,	Lucknow	,,	846	161
,,	1	AV	Khujistah-bunyád	A'zam	847	162
,,	,,	,,	——	,,	848	162
1119	51	Æ	Sháhjahánábád	Aurangzíb	845	161
,,	1	AV	Burhánpúr	A'zam	849	163
,,	,,	Æ	,,	,,	851	163
,,	,,	,,	Ahmadábád	,,	850	163
,,	,,	,,	Ajmír	Bahádur	866	171
,,	,,	,,	Sháhjahánábád	,,	867	171
1120	2	AV	Haidarábád	Kám Bakhsh	852	164
,,	,,	Æ	Bijápúr	,,	853	165
,,	,,	AV	Peshawar	Bahádur	854	166
,,	,,	,,	Khujistah-bunyád	,,	855	166
,,	,,	,,	Sháhjahánábád	,,	856	167
,,	,,	,,	Burhánpúr	,,	857	167
,,	,,	,,	Lahore	,,	858	168
,,	,,	,,	——	,,	859	168
,,	,,	Æ	'Azímábád	,,	868	172
,,	,,	,,	Akbarábád	,,	869-70	172
,,	,,	,,	Lahore	,,	871	173
1121	—	AV	Sholápúr	,,	860	168
,,	3	Æ	Sháhjahánábád	,,	872	173
,,	4	AV	Khujistah-bunyád	,,	861	169
,,	,,	Æ	Burhánpúr	,,	873	173
,,	,,	,,	Sholápúr	,,	874	174
1122	—	AV	Ujjain	,,	862	169
1123	5	,,	Akbarábád	,,	863	169
,,	,,	,,	Khujistah-bunyád	,,	864	170
,,	6	Æ	Súrat	,,	876	174
1124	1	AV	Khujistah-bunyád	Jahándár	877-78	175-6
,,	,,	,,	Súrat	,,	879	176
,,	,,	,,	Sháhjahánábád	,,	880	176

Year. A.H.	Regnal year.	Metal.	MINT.	EMPEROR.	NO.	Page.
1124	1	Æ	Sháhjahánábád	Jahándár	885-86	178
"	"	"	[Akbarábád]	"	887	178
["]	"	Ꜳ	"	"	881-83	177
"	—	Æ	Sháhjahánábád	"	889	178
"	1	"	Jahángírnagar	Farrukh-siyar	903	184
["]	"	Ꜳ	Murshidábád	"	890	179
1125	—	"	——	"	900	183
"	1	Æ	Multán	"	904	184
"	2	"	Katak	"	907-8	185
"	"	"	Sháhjahánábád	"	909	185
"	"	"	Lahore	"	910	185
["]	"	"	Akbarábád	"	905	184
["]	"	"	Súrat	"	906	185
["]	"	"	Multán	"	911	186
[1126]	3	Ꜳ	Imtiyázgarh	"	900*a*	183
"	"	Æ	Katak	"	914	186
["]	"	"	Akbarábád	"	912	186
"	"	"	'Azímábád	"	913	186
1127	4	Ꜳ	Sháhjahánábád	"	891	179
"	"	Æ	"	"	915-16	187
"	"	"	Súrat	"	917	187
1128	5	Ꜳ	Gútí	"	901	183
"	"	"	Gangpúr	"	902	183
"	"	Æ	Etáwá	"	918	187
"	"	"	Akbarábád	"	919	187
"	"	"	Chínápatan	"	920	187
["]	"	"	Súrat	"	921	188
"	"	"	Sháhjahánábád	"	922-23	188
1129	"	Ꜳ	Lahore	"	892	180
["]	"	"	Barailí	"	893	180
"	"	Æ	Akbarábád	"	924	188
"	"	"	Sháhjahánábád	"	925	188
"	6	"	"	"	926	188
"	"	"	Gwálior	"	927	188
"	"	"	Lahore	"	928-29	189
["]	"	"	Murshidábád	"	930-31	189
["]	"	Ꜳ	Burhánpúr	"	894	181
1130	7	"	Patnah	"	895	181
"	"	"	Sháhjahánábád	"	896	181
"	"	"	Multán	"	897	182
["]	"	"	Bíjápúr	"	898	182
"	"	Æ	Akbarábád	"	932	189
"	"	"	Arkát	"	933	189
["]	"	"	Súrat	"	934	190
"	"	"	Multán	"	935	190
1131	8	Ꜳ	Lahore	"	899	182
"	1	"	Sháhjahánábád	Rafí'-ad-daraját	937	191
"	"	"	Mu'azzamábád	"	937*a*	191

Year. A.H.	Regnal year.	Metal.	MINT.	EMPEROR.	NO.	Page.
1131	1	Æ	Akbarábád	Rafí'-ad-daraját	938-39	192
,,	,,	,,	Sháhjahánábád	,,	940-41	192
,,	,,	,,	Kúrá	,,	942	192
,,	,,	,,	Lahore	,,	943	193
,,	,,	,,	Patnah ?	,,	944	193
,,	,,	AV	Sháhjahánábád	Rafí'-ad-daulah	945	194
,,	—	,,	Khujistah-bunyád	,,	946	194
,,	1	Æ	Akbarábád	,,	947	195
,,	,,	,,	Baraili	,,	948	195
,,	—	,,	Súrat	,,	949	195
,,	1	,,	'Azímábád	,,	950	195
,,	,,	,,	Lahore	,,	951	196
,,	,,	,,	Murshidábád	,,	952	196
[,,]	,,	AV	Súrat	Niku-siyar	953	197
,,	,,	Æ	Munbai	East India Company	App. 68-70	278
,,	,,	AV	Khujistah-bunyád	Muhammad	958	199
1132	,,	,,	Sháhjahánábád	Ibráhím	954-55	198
,,	,,	Æ	,,	,,	956-57	198
,,	,,	,,	Akbarábád	Muhammad	978	204
[1133]	2	,,	Súrat	,,	979	204
[,,]	,,	,,	Murshidábád	,,	980	204
1134	3	AV	Sháhjahánábád	,,	959	199
[,,]	,,	Æ	Súrat	,,	981	205
[,,]	4	,,	,,	,,	982	205
,,	,,	,,	Sháhjahánábád	,,	983	205
1135	5	,,	,,	,,	984	205
,,	,,	,,	Akbarnagar Oudh	,,	985	205
[113$\frac{6}{7}$]	6	,,	Akbarábád ?	,,	986	206
[,,]	,,	,,	Súrat	,,	987	206
[,,]	,,	,,	Lahore	,,	988	206
1137	,,	,,	Tattah	,,	989	206
[,,]	,,	,,	'Azímábád	,,	990	207
,,	7	,,	Sháhjahánábad	,,	991	207
[,,]	,,	AV	,,	,,	960	200
[,,]	,,	Æ	Munbai	E. I. C.	App. 72	278
,,	,,	,,	'Azímábád	Muhammad	992	208
1139	9	AV	Etáwá	,,	961	200
,,	,,	Æ	,,	,,	993	208
1140	,,	,,	,,	,,	994	208
[,,]	,,	,,	Lahore	,,	995	208
[,,]	,,	,,	Sháhjahánábád	,,	996	208
[1141]	10	,,	Akbarábád	,,	997	209
[,,]	11	AV	Sháhjahánábád	,,	962-63	200
,,	,,	Æ	Kúrá	,,	998	209
1142	,,	,,	Sháhjahánábád	,,	999	209
,,	12	,,	,,	,,	1000	209
1143	13	,,	,,	,,	1001	209

Year A.H.	Regnal Year.	Metal.	MINT.	EMPEROR.	NO.	Page.
[1143]	13	AR	Etáwá	Muhammad	1002	209
„	1x	„	Munbai	E. I. C.	App. 71	278
[1144]	14	AV	Sháhjahánábád	Muhammad	964	200
[„]	„	AR	Lahore	„	1003	210
114[5]	15	AV	Sháhjahánábad	„	965	200
„	„	AR	„	„	1004	210
„	„	„	Súrat	„	1005	210
114[6]	16	AV	Sháhjahánábád	„	966	200
[„]	„	AR	„	„	1006	210
[„]	„	„	Lahore	„	1007	210
1147	17	AV	Akbarábád	„	967	200
„	„	AR	Sháhjahánábád	„	1008-10	210
1148	1e	„	Ajáyúr ?	„	1011	211
„	18	„	Munbai	E. I. C.	App. 73	279
[„]	„	„	Sháhjahánábád	Muhammad	1012	211
[1149]	19	„	„	„	1014	211
[„]	„	„	Súrat	„	1013	211
[„]	„	„	Lahore	„	1015	211
1150	19	„	Islámábád	„	1016	212
„	20	AV	Etáwá	„	968	201
[„]	„	„	Khujistah-bunyád	„	969	201
„	„	AR	Benáres	„	1017	212
[„]	„	„	Lahore	„	1018	212
1151	21	„	Sháhábád	„	1019	212
1152	22	AV	Sháhjahánábád	„	970-71	201
„	„	AR	„	„	1020-21	212
„	„	„	'Azímábád	„	1022-23	212-13
1153	23	AV	Sháhjahánábád	„	972	201
„	„	AR	„	„	1024-25	213
1154	24	„	„	„	1026	213
„	„	AV	Kashmír	„	973	201
1155	25	AR	Sháhjahánábád	„	1027-28	213
„	„	AV	Lahore	„	974	202
[„]	„	AR	Farrukhábád	„	1029	213
[„]	„	„	Murshidábád	„	1030	214
1156	26	AR	Etáwá	„	1031	214
„	„	„	Siwáï-Jaipúr	„	1032	214
1157	„	AV	Sháhjahánábád	„	975	202
„	„	AR	„	„	1033-34	214
[„]	27	„	Barailí	„	1035	214
[1158]	28	„	Sháhjahánábád	„	1036	215
1158	29	„	Akbarábád	„	1037	215
1159	„	„	Sháhjahánábád	„	1038	215
1161	—	AV	Imtiyázgarh	„	976-77	203
„	1	„	Sháhjahánábád	Ahmad	1039	216
„	„	AR	„	„	1046	218
„	„	„	'Azímábád	„	1045	218

Year. A.H.	Regnal Year.	Metal.	MINT.	EMPEROR.	NO.	Page.
1161	1	AR	Farrukhábád	Ahmad	1047	218
1162	2	AV	Benáres	,,	1040	216
[,,]	,,	AR	Akbarábád	,,	1048	218
,,	,,	,,	Sháhjahánábád	,,	1049	219
1164	3	,,	,,	,,	1050	219
,,	4	,,	,,	,,	1051	219
,,	,,	,,	Benáres	,,	1052	219
1165	5	,,	Sháhjahánábád	,,	1053-54	219
[,,]	,,	,,	Murshidábád	,,	1055	219
1166	6	AV	Sháhjahánábád	,,	1041-42	217
[,,]	,,	AR	,,	,,	1056	219
1167	,,	,,	Murádábád	,,	1057	220
[,,]	,,	,,	Murshidábád	,,	1058	220
,,	7	AV	Sháhjahánábád	,,	1043	217
[,,]	1	,,	,,	'A'lamgír II.	1059	221
[,,]	,,	AR	,,	,,	1071	225
1068	,,	,,	Murshidábád	,,	1072	225
,,	2	AV	Sháhjahánábád	,,	1060-61	221-22
,,	,,	AR	,,	,,	1073-74*a*	225
1169	,,	,,	——	,,	1075	225
[,,]	,,	,,	Arkát	French East India Company	App. 127	288
[1170]	3	,,	Sháhjahánábád	'A'lamgír II.	1076	226
,,	—	AV	Imtiyázgarh	,,	1068-70*a*	224
,,	4	,,	Sháhjahánábád	,,	1063-64	223
,,	,,	AR	,,	,,	1079-80	226
[,,]	,,	AV	Indrapúr	,,	1062	222
1171	,,	,,	Farrukhábád	,,	1066	224
,,	,,	AR	Akbarábád	,,	1077	226
1168 [,,]	,,	,,	Indrapúr	,,	1078	226
,,	,,	,,	Murshidábád	,,	1081	226
,,	5	AV	Lahore	,,	1065	223
1172	,,	AR	Sháhjahánbád	,,	1082	226
,,	,,	,,	'Azimábád	,,	1083	227
[,,]	6	AV	Indrapúr	,,	1067	224
,,	,,	AR	Farrukhábád	,,	1084	227
,,	,,	,,	Lahore	,,	1085	227
[,,]	,,	,,	Murshidábád	,,	1085*a*	227
,,	,,	AV	Arkát	E. I. C.	App. 109-10	285
,,	,,	AR	,,	,,	,, 111-126	286-87
1173	1	AV	Islámábád	Sháh-Jahán III.	1086	228
,,	,,	,,	Farrukhábád	,,	1087	228
,,	,,	AR	,,	,,	1088	229
,,	,,	,,	Ahmadábád	,,	1089	229
,,	,,	,,	Indrapúr	,,	1090	229
1174	,,	,,	Sháhjahánábád	,,	1091	230
,,	,,	,,	Farrukhábád	,,	1092	230

Year. A.H.	Regnal year	Metal.	MINT.	EMPERORS.	NO.	Page.
[1174]	1	AR	Srínagar	Sháh-'Álam *	1158	248
[„]	„	„	Lucknow	„	1184	255
„	2	„	Sháhjahánábád	„	1105	235
[„]	„	„	Srínagar	„	1159	248
„	„	AV	'Azímábád	„	1166	250
„	„	AR	„	„	1168	250
[„]	„	„	Murshidábád	„	1186	254
1175	3	„	Akbarábád	„	1128	240
1176	„	AV	Sháhjahánábád	„	1093	231
„	4	AR	Calcutta	E. I. C.	App. 67	277
[1177]	„	„	Súrat	Sháh-'Álam	1160	249
[1178]	5	„	„	„	1161-62	249
[„]	„	„	'Azímábád	„	1169	250
[„]	„	„	Arkát	French E. I. C.	App. 128	288
1179	6	„	Farrukhábád	Sháh-'Álam	1172	252
[„]	„	„	Súrat	„	1163	249
[„]	„	„	Arkát	French E. I. C.	App. 129	288
[1180]	7	„	Murshidábád	Sháh-'Álam	1187	255
„	8	„	„	„	1188	255
1181	—	AV	„	„	1185	254
[„]	9	AR	„	„	1196	256
118[2]	„	AV	Munbai	E. I. C.	App. 75, 76	279
1182	10	„	'Azímábád	Sháh-'Álam	1167	250
„	„	„	Murshidábád	E. I. C.	App. 1, 2	267
„	„	AR	„	„	App. 5-7	268
1183	„	AV	„	„	App. 3, 4	268
„	„	AR	Benáres	Sháh-'Álam	1133	242
„	„	„	Jahángírnagar	„	1157	247
„	11	„	Murshidábád	E. I. C.	App. 9	269
1184	„	AV	„	„	„ 8	269
„	„	AR	„	„	„ 10, 11	269
„	„	„	„	Sháh-'Álam	1189	255
1185	10	„	Arkát	French E. I. C.	App. 130	288
„	12	AV	Murshidábád	E. I. C.	„ 15	270
„	13	AR	„	„	„ 16	270
1186	12	„	„	Sháh-'Álam	1190-91	255
„	—	„	Dilshádábád	„	1155	246
„	12	„	Najíbábád	„	1199	257
„	13	„	Benáres	„	1134	242
1187	15	AV	Murshidábád	E. I. C.	App. 17	270
[„]	„	AR	„	Sháh-'Álam	1197	256
„	„	„	Farrukhábád	„	1173	252
1188	11	Æ	Calcutta	E. I. C.	App. 150-3	291
„	9	AR	Munbai	„	„ 77	280
„	13	„	Arkát	French E. I. C.	„ 131	288
[„]	16	„	Ahmadábád	Sháh-'Álam	1121	238
1189	17	„	Farrukhábád	„	1174	252
„	„	„	Benáres	„	1135	242

* A large number of the coins with Sháh-Álam's name, chiefly those issued by the East India Company, present fictitious dates.

Year. A. H.	Regnal year	Metal.	MINT.	EMPEROR.	NO.	Page.
1202	1	AV	Sháhjahánábád	Bídár-Bakht	1206	259
,,	,,	AR	,,	,,	1209	259
1203	,,	AV	,,	,,	1207-8	259
,,	30	AR	Benáres	Sháh-'Álam	1143-44	243
,,	29	,,	Arkát	French E. I. C.	App. 139	289
[,, ?]	30	,,	,,	,,	,, 140	289
,,	19	AV	Murshidábád	E. I. C.	App. 24, 26-27	271
1204	,,	,,	,,	,,	,, 33-34, 43	272-73
,,	,,	AR	,,	,,	,, 41-42	272
[,,]	31	,,	Farrukhábád	Sháh-'Álam	1179	252
,,	45	,,	,,	E. I. C.	App. 54	275
1205	32	AV	Sháhjahánábád	Sháh-'Álam	1094	232
[,,]	,,	AR	Súrat	,,	1165	249
1206	34	AV	Sháhjahánábád	,,	1095	232
1207	35	AR	Benáres	,,	1145-46	243
,,	32	,,	Arkát	French E. I. C.	App. 143	289
1208	[3]5	Æ	,,	E. I. C.	,, 186	296
1209	37	AV	Benáres	Sháh-'Álam	1142	243
—	,,	Æ	—	E. I. C.	App. 164-75	293-4
1210	36	AR	Najíbábád	Sháh-'Álam	1202	257
1212	26	,,	Benáres	E. I. C.	App. 57	276
,,	39	,,	Masulipatan	,,	,, 148	290
1213	6	,,	Arkát	,,	,, 104	284
1214	,,	,,	,,	,,	,, 106	284
—	,,	,,	,,	,,	,, 101-5, 107-8	284
1214	26	AV	Benáres	,,	,, 55	276
,,	39	AR	Masulipatan	,,	,, 149	290
,,	41	,,	Najíbábád	Sháh-'Álam	1203	257
1215	—	,,	—	Akbar (posth.)	252*c-e*	47
,,	42	,,	Najíbábád	Sháh-'Álam	1204	257
,,	26	,,	Benáres	E. I. C.	App. 58	276
,,	46	,,	Súrat	,,	,, 96-100	282
1216	39	,,	Farrukhábád	Sháh-'Álam	1180	253
1217	,,	,,	,,	,,	1181	253
,,	45	,,	Sháhjahánábád	,,	1106	235
1218	,,	,,	,,	,,	1107	235
,,	39	,,	Farrukhábád	,,	1182-83	253
,,	45	,,	Akbarábád	,,	1130	240
,,	46	AV	Sháhjahánábád	,,	1104	235
,,	,,	AR	,,	,,	1099-1102, 1108-9	234-5
,,	43	,,	Arkát	French E. I. C.	App. 144	289
—	45	,,	Farrukhábád	E. I. C.	,, 50-53	274-5
—	,,	,,	Mumbai-Súrat	,,	,, 80	280
—	,,	Æ	—	,,	,, 176-80	294

Year. A.H.	Regnal year.	Metal.	MINT.	EMPEROR.	NO.	Page.
—	46	AV	Súrat	E. I. C.	App. 82-83, 87-93	281-2
—	,,	AR	,,	,,	,, 85-86, 94-95	282-3
1219	,,	,,	Sháhjahánábád	Sháh-'Álam	1103	234
,,	47	AV	,,	,,	1110	236
,,	,,	AR	,,	,,	1112	236
[,,]	,,	,,	Akbarábád	,,	1131	241
1220	,,	,,	,,	,,	1132	241
,,	,,	,,	Sháhjahánábád	,,	1113	236
,,	48	,,	,,	,,	1114-15	236
1221	,,	AV	,,	,,	1111	236
,,	26	AR	Benáres	E. I. C.	App. 59	276
,,	48	Æ	,,	,,	,, 181, 183	295
,,	49	AR	Sháhjahánábád	Sháh-'Álam	1116-17	236
[,,]	,,	Æ	Arkát	E. I. C.	App. 186-87	296
,,	1	AR	Sháhjahánábád	Muh. Akbar II.	1210	260
1222	,,	,,	,,	,,	1211	260
,,	49	,,	Benáres	Sháh-'Álam	1150	244
,,	26	,,	,,	E. I. C.	App. 60	276
1223	3	,,	Sháhjahánábád	Muh. Akbar II.	1212	260
1224	,,	,,	,,	,,	1213	260
,,	49	,,	Benáres	Sháh-'Álam	1151	244
1225	,,	,,	,,	,,	1152	244
[1226]	6	,,	Sháhjahánábád	Muh. Akbar II.	1214	260
,,	26	,,	Benáres	E. I. C.	App. 61	276
1227	,,	,,	,,	,,	,, 62	276
1228	49	Æ	,,	,,	,, 182	295
1229	26	AR	,,	,,	,, 63	276
,,	49	,,	,,	,,	,, 66	277
1231	26	,,	,,	,,	,, 64	276
1233	,,	,,	,,	,,	,, 65	276
1235	,,	AV	,,	,,	,, 56	276
1257	5	AR	Sháhjahánábád	Bahádur II.	1217	261
1258	6	,,	,,	,,	1218	261

ANNI DOMINI.

A.D.	A.H.	MINT.	COMPANY.	NO.	Page.
1784	1198	Murshidábád	E. I. C.	App. 28	271
1802	—	Súrat	,,	,, 81	281
1825	—	,,	,,	,, 85-6	282

II.—INDEX OF MINTS.

*** The Mints are arranged in the order of the Arabic alphabet. For those who are unaccustomed to this, the following index to the mints, arranged in the ordinary English alphabetical order, is prefixed.

MINT.	Metal.	YEAR A.H.	EMPEROR.	NO.	Page.
اتاوا (اتاوه) Etáwá (Etáwah) *	AR	1100	Aurangzíb	783	153
	,,	1102	,,	787	153
	,,	1104	,,	792, 792*a*	154
	,,	1105	,,	797	155
	,,	1106	,,	800	156
	,,	1107	,,	803	156
	,,	1108	,,	811	157
	,,	1112	,,	824	158
	,,	1114	,,	829	159
	,,	1115	,,	831	159
	,,	1116	,,	835	160
	,,	1117	,,	841	160
	,,	1118	,,	842	160
	AV	,,	,,	724	142
	AR	1128	Farrukh-siyar	918	187
	AV	1139	Muhammad	961	200
	AR	,,	,,	993	208
	,,	1140	,,	994	208
	,,	11[43]	,,	1002	209
	AV	1150	,,	968	201
	AR	1156	,,	1031	214
	,,	[1190]	Sháh-'Álam	1118	237
	,,	1194	,,	1119-20	237
اجايور Ajáyúr ?	AR	1148	Muhammad	1011	210
اجمير Ajmír	AV	1023	Jahángír	318-21	64
	,,	1025	,,	302	60
	AR	,,	,,	460	89
	,,	1105	Aurangzíb	798	155
	,,	1108	,,	813	157
	,,	1114	,,	827	158
	,,	1119	Bahádur	866	171

* The name is spelt both ways.

MINT.	Metal.	YEAR A.H.	EMPEROR.	NO.	Page.
اكره Agrah (*continued*)	AR	1033	Jahángír	367, 392-4, 398-9,	73, 77, 78
	,,	1035	,,	502	97
	,,	1037	Jahángír and Núr-Jahán	523-4	101
	,,	,,	Sháh-Jahán	579	114
	,,	1038	,,	581-2	115

Henceforward called اكبراباد *Akbarábád, q.v.*

MINT.	Metal.	YEAR A.H.	EMPEROR.	NO.	Page.
الداباد * Iláhábád (*Allahabad*)	Æ	[994]	Akbar	273*a*	53
	AR	—	,,	254-254*b*	48
	,,	1041	Sháh-Jahán	606	120
	,,	[1043]	,,	623	124
امتيازكره Imtiyázgarh (*Adoni*)	AV	[1125]	Farrukh-siyar	900*a*	183
	,,	1161	Muhammad	976	203
	,,	—	,,	977	203
	,,	1170	'Álamgír II.	1068-70*a*	224
	AR	—	,,	1085*b*	227
اندرپور Indrapúr (*Indore*)	AR	[1170]	'Álamgír II.	1078	226
	AV	,,	,,	1062	222
	,,	[1171]	,,	1067	224
	AR	1173	Sháh-Jahán III.	1090	229
اوجين Ujjain	AV	1122	Bahádur	862	169

اوذ Oudh — *See* اكبرنكر اوذ *Akbarnagar Oudh*

* The original form الداباس *Iláhábás* is preserved on 273*a*.

MINT.	Metal.	YEAR A.H.	EMPEROR.	NO.	Page.
اورنك اباد	†AR	1071	Aurangzíb	730	145
خجسته بنياد	†AV	1074	,,	702	138
Aurangábád	† ,,	1079	,,	705	139
Khujistah-bunyád*	†AR	1088	,,	753	149
	* ,,	1108	,,	812	157
	*AV	1109	,,	719	141
	* ,,	1118	A'zam	847	162
	* ,,	1120	Bahádur	855	166
	* ,,	1121	,,	861	169
	* ,,	1123	,,	864	170
	* ,,	1124	Jahándár	877-78	175-76
	* ,,	1131	Rafí'-ad-daulah	946	194
	* ,,	,,	Muhammad	958	199
	* ,,	11[50]	,,	969	201
برهانپور	AR	[1011]	Akbar	197, 241	37, 44
Burhánpúr	AV	—	Jahángír	311	62
	AR	1037	Sháh-Jahán	580	115
	,,	1040	,,	595	119
	,,	1042	,,	616	122
	AV	1043	,,	540	107
	,,	1051	,,	555	110
	,,	1060	,,	562	111
	,,	1061	,,	563	111
	,,	1068	,,	575	113
	AR	1098	Aurangzíb	774	152
	AV	1111	,,	720	141
	AR	1113	,,	825	158
	AV	1115	,,	723	142
	,,	1119	A'zam	849	163
	AR	,,	,,	851	163
	AV	1120	Bahádur	857	167
	AR	1121	,,	873	173
	AV	[1129]	Farrukh-siyar	894	181

* An asterisk (*) is affixed to those coins which bear only the name خجسته بنياد ; an obelus (†) to those which bear only اورنك اباد.

* Omits second name, Muhammadábád.

* Better سیتاپور *Sítápúr.*

† See note, p. 37.

خجسته بنیاد Khujistah-bunyád — *See* اورنكاباد *Aurangábád*

Henceforward called شاهجهاناباد *Sháhjahánábád, q.v.*

MINT.	Metal.	YEAR A.H.	EMPEROR.	NO.	Page.
دوگام Dógám	Æ	983	Akbar	263	50
	,,	994	,,	271	52
دولت اباد Daulatábád (*Deogír*)	AV	[1038]	Sháh-Jahán	530	105
	,,	1050	,,	552	110
	,,	1051	,,	553	110
	AR	1056	,,	657	130
?	,,	1060	,,	668	131
	AV	1063	,,	566	111
	,,	1067	,,	569	112
	AR	,,	,,	676-77	133
	AV	1068	,,	571, 573	112,113
	AR	,,	,,	683-84	134
سار[نك]پور Sárangpúr	AV	972	Akbar	31	13
سرهند Sirhind	AV	984	Akbar	61	17
سری نکر Srínagar	AR	[1173]	Sháh-'Álam	1158	248
	,,	[1174]	,,	1159	248
سوای جی پور Siwái-Jaipúr	AR	1156	Muhammad	1032	214

See ممبی سورت *Mumbai-Súrat*

MINT.	Metal.	YEAR A.H.	EMPEROR.	NO.	Page.
شاهجهان اباد Sháhjahánábád (*New Dehlí*)	AR	1060	Sháh-Jahán	669	131
	AV	1066	,,	568	112
	AR	1067	,,	678	133
	,,	1068	,,	681	133
	AV	1069	Anonymous	689	134
	AR	1076	Aurangzíb	743	147
	AV	1091	,,	709	140
	,,	1100	,,	713	140
	,,	1101	,,	714	140
	,,	1106	,,	716	141
	AR	1115	,,	833	159
	,,	1118	,,	844	161
	,,	1119	,,	845	161
	,,	,,	Bahádur	867	171
	AV	1120	,,	856	167
	AR	1121	,,	872	173
	AV	—	,,	865	170
	,,	1124	Jahándár	880	176
	AR	,,	,,	885, 889	178
	,,	[1125]	Farrukh-siyar	909	185
	AV	1127	,,	891	179
	AR	,,	,,	915-16	187
	,,	1128	,,	922-23	188
	,,	1129	,,	925-26	188
	AV	1130	,,	896	181
	,,	1131	Rafí'-ad-daraját	937	191
	AR	,,	,,	940-41	192
	AV	,,	Rafí'-ad-daulah	945	194
	,,	1132	Ibráhím	954-55	198
	AR	,,	,,	956-57	198
	AV	1134	Muhammad	959	199
	AR	,,	,,	983	205
	,,	1135	,,	984	205
	AV	113[7]	,,	960	200
	AR	,,	,,	991	207
	,,	[1139]	,,	996	208
	AV	[1141]	,,	962-3	200
	AR	1142	,,	999-1000	209
	,,	1143	,,	1001	209
	AV	114[4]	,,	964	200
	,,	114[5]	,,	965	200
	AR	,,	,,	1004	209
	AV	114[6]	,,	966	200
	AR	,,	,,	1006	210
	,,	1147	,,	1008-10	210
	,,	11[48]	,,	1012	211
	,,	114[9]	,,	1014	211
	AV	1152	,,	970-1	201

* These coins omit the first name احمدنگر.

MINT.	Metal.	YEAR. A.H.	EMPEROR.	NO.	Page.
قندهار Kandahár (*continued*)	AR	1023	Jahángír	451, 454	87-88
	,,	1026	,,	470-71	91
	,,	1027	,,	472	92
	,,	1028	,,	481-82	93
	,,	1029	,,	486-87	94
	,,	1030	,,	490	95
	,,	10*xx*	,,	511	98
	,,	1048	Sháh-Jahán	647	128
	,,	[1056]	,,	658	130
کابل Kábul	Æ	[995]	Akbar	274	53
	,,	[996]	,,	274*a*	53
	AR	[1007]	,,	221	41
	,,	[1008]	,,	226	41
	,,	[1009]	,,	231	42
	,,	[1010]	,,	237	43
	,,	[1012]	,,	245-46	45
	,,	1014	Jahángír	405	80
	,,	1015	,,	406-7	80
	,,	1027	,,	473	91
	,,	—	Sháh-Jahán	688	134
	,,	[1069]	Aurangzíb	727	144
	,,	[1100]	,,	782	153
کتك Katak (*Cuttack*)	AR	1125	Farrukh-siyar	907-8	185
	,,	1126	,,	914	186

کره Karrah — *An error for* امتياز کره *Imtiyázgarh, q.v.*

* Written کهنبایت on this coin (no. 700).

MINT.	Metal.	YEAR A.H.	EMPEROR.	NO.	Page.
لاهور Lahore (*continued*)	Æ	1016	Jahángír	420-22	82
	,,	1017	,,	424	82
	,,	1018	,,	429-31	83
	,,	1019	,,	434-38	84-85
	,,	1021	,,	447-49	87
	,,	[1023]	,,	452, 455-7	88
	,,	1025	,,	463	90
	,,	1026	,,	469	91
	,,	1027	,,	477	93
	,,	1029	,,	488	94
	,,	1030	,,	491	95
	,,	1031	,,	494-95	95
	,,	1032	,,	496	96
	,,	1033	,,	499	96
	,,	1034	,,	500	96
	,,	,,	Jahángír and Núr-Jahán	518	101
	,,	1035	Jahángír	504	96
	AV	1036	,,	310	62
	Æ	,,	,,	505-6	97-98
	,,	1037	,,	508	98
	,,	,,	Dáwar Bakhsh	527	103
	,,	,,	Sháh-Jahán	578	114
	AV	1039	,,	531	105
	Æ	,,	,,	591	118
	,,	1040	,,	599	119
	,,	1041	,,	611-12	121
	AV	1042	,,	536	107
	Æ	1044	,,	632	125
	,,	1046	,,	640	127
	,,	1047	,,	645	128
	,,	1049	,,	651	129
	,,	1098	Aurangzíb	776	152
	,,	1105	,,	799	155
	,,	1106	,,	802	156
	,,	1108	,,	814	157
	,,	1114	,,	830	159
	AV	1120	Bahádur	858	168
	Æ	,,	,,	871	173
	,,	1125	Farrukh-siyar	910	185
	AV	1129	,,	892	180
	Æ	,,	,,	928-29	189
	AV	1131	,,	899	182
	Æ	,,	Rafí'-ad-daraját	943	193
	,,	,,	Rafí'-ad-daulah	951	196
	,,	[1136]	Muhammad	988	206
	,,	[1139]	,,	995	208
	,,	11[44]	,,	1003	209
	,,	11[46]	,,	1007	210

MINT.	Metal.	YEAR A.H.	EMPEROR.	NO.	Page.
نارنول Nárnól	Æ	963	Akbar	255	49
	,,	965	,,	256	49
	,,	980	,,	259	49
	,,	982	,,	262	50
?	,,	[999]	,,	276	53
	AR	1098	Aurangzíb	777	152
	,,	1102	,,	786	153
نجيب اباد Najíbábád	AR	[1184]	Sháh-'Álam	1199	257
	,,	1195	,,	1200	257
	,,	1199	,,	1201	257
	,,	1210	,,	1202	257
	,,	1214	,,	1203	257
	,,	1215	,,	1204-5	257
Nasratábád نصرت اباد	AR	—	Aurangzíb	806	156

II. A. HONORIFIC EPITHETS OF MINTS.

Epithet.	Mint.	Emperors.
بلدة	Agrah	Akbar
حضرت	Dehlí	Akbar
خجسته بنياد	Aurangábád	Aurangzíb, &c.
شهر اكره خسرو پناه	Agrah	Jahángír
دار الاسلام	Dógám	Akbar
دار الامان	Multán	Aurangzíb
دار الخلافه	Agrah	Akbar, Sháh-Jahán
,, ,,	Ahmadábád	Akbar
,, ,,	Gwálior	Akbar
,, ,,	Jaunpúr	Akbar
,, ,,	Lahore	Akbar
,, ,,	Akbarábád (Agrah)	Sháh-Jahán
,, ,,	Sháhjahánábád (Dehlí)	Sháh-Jahán, Aurangzíb, &c.
دار الخير	Ajmír	Aurangzíb
دار السرور	Burhánpúr	Bahádur, Farrukh-siyar
دار السلطنه	Ahmadábád	Akbar
,, ,,	Fathpúr	Akbar
,, ,,	Lahore	Akbar, Sháh-Jahán, Aurangzíb, Bahádur, &c.
دار الظفر	Bíjápúr	Aurangzíb, Bahádur, &c.
دار الفتح	Ujjain	Bahádur
دار الملك	Kábul	Aurangzíb
مستقر الخلافه	Akbarábád (Agrah)	Aurangzíb, Farrukh-siyar, &c.
,, ,,	Ajmír	Bahádur
,, الملك	Akbarábád (Agrah)	Bahádur, Jahándár, Farrukh-siyar.

III. INDEX OF NAMES.

ا

پ

ج

د

ر

ز

س

ش

غ

ف

ك

م

IV. INDEX OF DENOMINATIONS, ETC.

V. INDEX OF FIGURES, ETC.

VI. INDEX OF PERSIAN DISTICHS.

AKBAR.

مهر مهر شاه اکبر ابروی این زر است
تا زمین و اسمان را مهر انور زیور است

The sun of the seal of Sháh Akbar is the glory of this gold
Whilst earth and sky are illumined by the shining sun.

AV 169, 174

زر ست از مهر اکبر پادشاه نور
بر ان زر نام شه نور علی نور

By the seal of Akbar Pádisháh gold becomes bright :
On this gold the Sháh's name is "light upon light."

AV 157

همیشه همچو زر مهر وماه رائج باد
بغرب وشرق جهان سکهء اله اباد

Like the golden orb of sun and moon, may ever pass
In the world's West and East the stamp of Alláhábád.

AR 254-254b

JAHÁNGÍR.

مالك الملك سکه زد بر زر
شاه سلطان سلیم شاه اکبر

The lord of the realm struck money of gold,
Sháh Sultán Salím, Akbar Sháh's [son].

AR 288-9

روی زررا ساخت نورانی برنك مهر و ماه
شاه نور الدین جهانکیر ابن اکبر پادشاه

Made the face of gold to shine like the sun and moon
Sháh Núr-ad-dín Jahángír, son of Akbar Pádisháh.

AV 290, 292-4. AR 402, 404, 409-10, 412, 414-15, 418, 421-2, 433, 445-6, 450, 462

سکه زد در شهر اگره خسرو گیتی پناه
شاه نور الدین جهانگیر ابن اکبر پادشاه

Money struck in the city of Agrah the Cæsar, refuge of the world,
Sháh Núr-ad-dín Jahángír, son of Akbar Pádisháh

AV 295-6. AR 423, 426-7

زد بزر این سکه در اجمیر شاه دین پناه
شاه نور الدین جهانگیر ابن اکبر پاد شاه

The Sháh, refuge of the faith, put this stamp on gold at Ajmír
Sháh Núr-ad-dín Jahángír, son of Akbar Pádisháh.

AV 302

از شاه جهانگیر بود دور زمان
در اگره زنام اوست زر نور فشان
تا هست نشان زپنج نوبت بجهان
این سکهٔ پنج مهر یش باد روان

To Sháh Jahángír belongs the whirligig of Time;
In Agrah by his name gold shines brightly:
So long as the pomp of the Five Guards * lasts in the world,
May the stamp of his Five-Mohrs be current.

AV 305

بشرق وغرب مهر احمد اباد
الهی تا جهان باشد روان باد

In East and West may the stamp of Ahmadábád,
O God, while the world lasts, be current.

AV 306-7

همیشه باد ابرروی سکهٔ لاهور
زنام شاه جهانگیر شاه اکبر نور

On the money of Lahore may there ever be
Light, by the name of Sháh Jahángír, Sháh Akbar's [son].

AV 310. AR 463, 469, 477, 483, 491, 494-6, 499-500, 504-6, 508

---

* *i.e.* The five daily prayers.

بروی سکهٔ زر داد چندین زیب وزیور
شبیه شاه نور الدین جهانکیر ابن شاه اکبر
زد بزر این سکه در اجمیر شاه دین پناه
شاه نور الدین جهانکیر ابن اکبر پادشاه

On the face of the golden coin, ornament and grace gave
The picture of Sháh Núr-ad-dín Jahángír, son of Akbar Sháh.
The Sháh, refuge of the faith, struck this coin of gold at
Ajmír,
Sháh Núr-ad-dín Jahángír, son of Akbar Pádisháh.

AV 318

قضا بر سکه زر کرد تصویر
شبیه حضرت شاه جهانکیر
حروف جهانکیر و الله اکبر
ز روز ازل در عدد شد برابر

Destiny has drawn on money of gold
The portrait of his Majesty Sháh Jahángír.
The letters of Jahángír and Alláhu Akbar
Are equal in value from the beginning of time.

AV 319-21

یافت در اکره روی زر زیور
از جهانکیر شاه شاه اکبر

The face of gold was decorated at Agrah
By Jahángír Sháh, Sháh Akbar's [son].

AV 322-3, &c., AR 502

سکهٔ اکره داد زینت زر
از جهانکیر شاه شاه اکبر

The money of Agrah gave ornament to gold
By Jahángír Sháh, Sháh Akbar's [son].

AV 324-6, &c.

سکه زد در احمداباد جنانات اله
شاه نور الدین جهانکیر ابن اکبر پادشاه

Money struck at Ahmadábád, God's Paradise,
Sháh Núr-ad-dín Jahángír, son of Akbar Pádisháh.

AV 327

زر احمداباد را داد زیور
جهانگیر شاه شهنشاه اکبر

To the gold of Ahmadábád gave adornment
Jahángír Sháh, Sháhánsháh Akbar's [son].

AR 370-4

بدهر باد روان تا فلك بود در دور
بنام شاه جهانگیر سکهٔ لاهور

So long as the heavens revolve, current be
In the name of Sháh Jahángír the money of Lahore.

AR 424, 429-31, 443

سکه زد در احمداباد از عنایات اله
شاه نور الدین جهانگیر ابن اکبر پادشاه

Money struck at Ahmadábád by the blessings of God
Sháh Núr-ad-dín Jahángír, son of Akbar Pádisháh.

AR 425, 475, 478, 483, 484, 492-3

در اسفندارمز این سکه را در اکره زد برزر
شهنشاه زمان شاه جهانگیر ابن شاه اکبر

In Isfandármiz at Agrah this stamp struck on gold
The Sháh of Sháhs of the world, Sháh Jahángír, son of
Sháh Akbar.

AR 432, 435-6

زر لاهور شد در ماه بهمن چون مه انور
بدور شاه نور الدین جهانگیر ابن شاه اکبر

The gold of Lahore in the month Bahman became like the
shining moon,
In the reign of Sháh Núr-ad-dín Jahángír, son of Sháh Akbar.

AR 437-8

جهان فیروز در اجمیر گشت سکهٔ زر
ز نور نام جهانگیر شاه شاه اکبر

The light of the world at Ajmír became the money of gold
By the light of the name of Jahángír, Sháb, Sháh Akbar's [son].

AR 461

سکهٔ قندهار شد دلخواه
از جهانگیر شاه اکبر شاه

The money of Kandahár became beauteous
By Jahángír Sháh, Akbar Sháh's [son].

Æ 470-2, 481-2, 486 7, 490

JAHÁNGIR AND NÚR-JAHÁN.

زحکم شاه جهانگیر یافت صد زیور (or بحکم)
زنام نور جهان پادشاه بیگم زر

By order of Sháh Jahángír a hundred beauties gained
Gold by the name of Núr-Jahán Pádisháh Bégam.

N 513. Æ 514-526

SHÁH-JAHÁN.

سکهٔ شاهجهان‌اباد رائج در جهان
جاودان بادا بنام ثانی صاحب قران

Be the money of Sháhjahánábád current through the world
For ever by the name of the other "Lord of the Conjunction."

N 586

MURÁD BAKHSH.

کر]فت ارث زصاحبقران شاه جهانی
مراد بخش شه محمد سکندر ثانی

Took the heritage of the "Lord of the Conjunction," Sháh Jahán,
Murád Bakhsh Muhammad Sháh, Second Alexander.

Æ 609

AURANGZÍB 'ÁLAMGÍR.

سکه زد در جهان چو مهر منیر
شاه اورنک زیب عالم کیر

Struck money through the world like the shining sun
Sháh Aurangzíb 'Álamgír.

N 701, &c.

سکه زد در جهان چو بدر منیر
شاه اورنگزیب عالم گیر

Struck money through the world like the shining moon
Sháh Aurangzíb 'Álamgír.

Æ 731, &c.

A'ZAM SHÁH.

سکه زد در جهان بدولت وجاه
پادشاه ممالك اعظم شاه

Struck money through the world with might and majesty
Pádishâh of the realms A'zam Sháh.

AV 847-9, Æ 860-1

KÁM BAKHSH.

سکه زد بر خورشید وماه
شاه دکن کام بخش پاد[شاه]

Struck money on sun and moon [*i.e.* gold and silver]
The Sháh of the Deccan Kám Bakhsh Pádisháh.

AV 852?, Æ 853

JAHÁNDÁR.

زد سکه بر زر چون مهر صاحب قران
جهاندار شاه پادشاه جهان

Struck money of gold like the sun the "Lord of the Conjunction"
Jahándár Sháh, Pádisháh of the world.

AV 877

در آفاق زد سکه چون مهر وماه
ابو الفتح غازی جهاندار شاه

In the horizons struck money like sun and moon
Abu-l-Fath Victorious Jahándár Sháh.

AV 879-884, Æ 885-8

FARRUKH-SIYAR.

سکه زد از فضل حق بر سیم و زر
پادشاه بحر و بر فرخ سیر

Struck money of gold and silver by grace of The Truth
The Pádisháh of sea and land Farrukh-siyar.

N 890-99, R 905-936

RAFÍ'-AD-DARAJÁT.

زد سکه بهند با هزاران برکات
شاهنشه بحر و بر رفیع الدرجات

Struck money in India, with a thousand blessings,
Sháh of Sháhs by sea and land Rafí'-ad-daraját.

N 937, R 938-44

NIKU-SIYAR.

سکه زد درجهان بلطف اله
پادشاه زمان محمد شاه

Struck money through the world by grace of God
Muhammad Sháh Pádisháh of the Age.

N 953

IBRÁHÍM.

سکه بر سیم زد در جهان
بفضل محمد ابرهیم شاه شاهان

Money of silver struck through the world,
By favour of Muhammad, Ibráhím Sháh of Sháhs.

N 954-5, R 956-7

'ÁLAMGÍR II.

سکه زد بر هفت کشور همچو تابان مهر وماه
شاه عزیز الدین عالمگیر غازی پادشاه

Struck money in the seven climates shining like the sun and moon
Sháh 'Azíz-ad-dín 'Álamgír Victorious Pádisháh.

N 1063, 1064, R 1080

VII. MISCELLANEOUS INDEX.

VIII. GENERAL INDEX.

[*Cross references are in square brackets.*]

COMPARATIVE TABLE OF HIJRAH AND CHRISTIAN YEARS AND MONTHS.*

A.H.	A.D.	Muharram	Safar	Rabí' I	Rabí' II	Jumádá I	Jumádá II	Rajab	Sha'bán	Ramadán	Shawwál	Zú-l-Ka'dah	Zú-l-Hijjah
932	1525	18. x. D	17. xi. F	16. xii. G	**26.** 15. i. B	13. ii. C	15. iii. E	13. iv. F	13. v. A	11. vi. B	11. vii. D	9. viii. E	8. ix. G
933	1526	8. x. B	7. xi. D	6. xii. E	**27.** 5. i. G	3. ii. A	5. iii. C	3. iv. D	3. v. F	1. vi. G	1. vii. B	30. vii. C	29. viii. E
934	1527	27. ix. F	27. x. A	25. xi. B	25. xii. D	**28.** 23. i. E	22. ii. G	22. iii. A	21. iv. C	20. v. D	19. vi. F	18. vii. G	17. viii. B
935	1528	15. ix. C	15. x. E	13. xi. F	13. xii. A	**29.** 11. i B	10. ii. D	11. iii. E	10. iv. G	9. v. A	8. vi. C	7. vii. D	6. viii. F
936	1529	5. ix. A	5. x. C	3. xi. D	3. xii. F	**30.** 1. i. G	31. i. B	1. iii. C	31. iii. E	29. iv. F	29. v. A	27. vi. B	27. vii. D
937	1530	25. viii. E	24. ix. G	23. x. A	22. xi. C	21. xii. D	**31.** 20. i. F	18. ii. G	20. iii. B	18. iv. C	18. v. E	16. vi. F	16. vii. A
938	1531	15. viii. C	14. ix. E	13. x. F	12. xi. A	11. xii. B	**32.** 10. i. D	8. ii. E	9. iii. G	7. iv. A	7. v. C	5. vi. D	5. vii. F
939	1532	3. viii. G	2. ix. B	1. x. C	31. x. E	29. xi. F	29. xii. A	**33.** 27. i. B	26. ii. D	27. iii. E	26. iv. G	25. v. A	24. vi. C
940	1533	23. vii. D	22. viii. F	20. ix. G	20. x. B	18. xi. C	18. xii. E	**34.** 16. i. F	15. ii. A	16. iii. B	15. iv. D	14. v. E	13. vi. G
941	1534	13. vii. B	12. viii. D	10. ix. E	10. x. G	8. xi. A	8. xii. C	**35.** 6. i. D	5. ii. F	6. iii. G	5. iv. B	4. v. C	3. vi. E
942	1535	2. vii. F	1. viii. A	30. viii. B	29. ix. D	28. x. E	27. xi. G	26. xii. A	**36.** 25. i. C	23. ii. D	24. iii. F	22. iv. G	22. v. B
943	1536	20. vi. C	20. vii. E	18. viii. F	17. ix. A	16. x. B	15. xi. D	14. xii. E	**37.** 13. i. G	11. ii. A	13. iii. C	11. iv. D	11. v. F
944	1537	10. vi. A	10. vii. C	8. viii. D	7. ix. F	6. x. G	5. xi. B	4. xii. C	**38.** 3. i. E	1. ii. F	3. iii. A	1. iv. B	1. v. D
945	1538	30. v. E	29. vi. G	28. vii. A	27. viii. C	25. ix. D	25. x. F	23. xi. G	23. xii. B	**39.** 21. i. C	20. ii. E	21. iii. F	20. iv. A
946	1539	19. v. B	18. vi. D	17. vii. E	16. viii. G	14. ix. A	14. x. C	12. xi. D	12. xii. F	**40.** 10. i. G	9. ii. B	9. iii. C	8. iv. E
947	1540	8. v. G	7. vi. B	6. vii. C	5. viii. E	3. ix. F	3. x. A	1. xi. B	1. xii. D	30. xii. E	**41.** 29. i. G	27. ii. A	29. iii. C
948	1541	27. iv. D	27. v. F	25. vi. G	25. vii. B	23. viii. C	22. ix. E	21. x. F	20. xi. A	19. xii. B	**42.** 18. i. D	16. ii. E	18. iii. G
949	1542	17. iv. B	17. v. D	15. vi. E	15. vii. G	13. viii. A	12. ix. C	11. x. D	10. xi. F	9. xii. G	**43.** 8. i. B	6. ii. C	8. iii. E
950	1543	6. iv. F	6. v. A	4. vi. B	4. vii. D	2. viii. E	1. ix. G	30. ix. A	30. x. C	28. xi. D	28. xii. F	**44.** 26. i. G	25. ii. B

* The month, day, and day of the week of the Christian year are placed under each Muhammadan month, and correspond to the first of that month. The week-days are lettered A (for Sunday), B (Monday), C (Tuesday), D (Wednesday), E (Thursday), F (Friday), G (Saturday). The months are indicated by Roman numerals. Thus 17. xi. F in the first line of the table shows that the month Safar of A.H. 932 began on Friday the 17th of November, 1525. The table is adapted from Wüstenfeld's well-known *Vergleichungs-Tabellen*, Leipzig, 1854.

A.H.	A.D.	Muharram	Safar	Rabí' I	Rabí' II	Jumádá I	Jumádá II	Rajab	Sha'bán	Ramadán	Shawwál	Zú-l-Ka'dah	Zú-l-Hijjah
951	1544	25. iii. C	21. iv. E	23. v. F	22. vi. A	21. vii. B	20. viii. D	18. ix. E	18. x. G	16. xi. A	16. xii. C	45. 14. i. D	13. ii. F
952	1545	15. iii. A	14. iv. C	13. v. D	12. vi. F	11. vii. G	10. viii. B	8. ix. C	8. x. E	6. xi. F	6. xii. A	46. 4. i. B	3. ii. D
953	1546	4. iii. E	3. iv. G	2. v. A	1. vi. C	30. vi. D	30. vii. F	28. viii. G	27. ix. B	26. x. C	25. xi. E	24. xii. F	47. 23. i. A
954	1547	21. ii. B	23. iii. D	21. iv. E	21. v. G	19. vi. A	19. vii. C	17. viii. D	16. ix. F	15. x. G	14. xi. B	13. xii. C	48. 12. i. E
935	1548	11. ii. G	12. iii. B	10. iv. C	10. v. E	8. vi. F	8. vii. A	6. viii. B	5. ix. D	4. x. E	3. xi. G	2. xii. A	49. 1. i. C
956	1549	30. i. D	1. iii. F	30. iii. G	29. iv. B	28. v. C	27. vi. E	26. vii. F	25. viii. A	23. ix. B	23. x. D	21. xi. E	21. xii. G
957	1550	20. i. B	19. ii. D	20. iii. E	19. iv. G	18. v. A	17. vi. C	16. vii. D	15. viii. F	13. ix. G	13. x. B	11. xi. C	11. xii. E
958	1551	9 i. F	8. ii. A	9. iii. B	8. iv. D	7. v. E	6. vi. G	5. vii. A	4. viii. C	2. ix. D	2. x. F	31. x. G	30. xi. B
959	1551	29. xii. C	52. 28. i. E	26. ii. F	27. iii. A	25. iv. B	25. v. D	23. vi. E	23. vii. G	21. viii. A	20. ix. C	19. x. D	18. xi. F
960	1552	18. xii. A	53. 17. i. C	15. ii. D	17. iii. F	15. iv. G	15. v. B	13. vi. C	13. vii. E	11. viii. F	10. ix. A	9. x. B	8. xi. D
961	1553	7. xii. E	54. 6. i. G	4. ii. A	6. iii. C	4. iv. D	4. v. F	2. vi. G	2. vii. B	31. vii. C	30. viii. E	28. ix. F	28. x. A
962	1554	26. xi. B	26. xii. D	55. 24. i. E	23. ii. G	24. iii. A	23. iv. C	22. v. D	21. vi. F	20. vii. G	19. viii. B	17. ix. C	17. x. E
963	1555	16. xi. G	16. xii B	56. 14. i. C	13. ii. E	13. iii. F	12. iv. A	11. v. B	10. vi. D	9. vii. E	8. viii. G	6. ix. A	6. x. C
964	1556	4. xi. D	4. xii. F	57. 2. i. G	1. ii. B	2. iii. C	1. iv. E	30. iv. F	30. v. A	28. vi. B	28. vii. D	26. viii. E	25. ix. G
965	1557	24 x. A	23. xi. C	22. xii. D	58. 21. i. F	19. ii. G	21. iii. B	19. iv. C	19. v. E	17. vi. F	17. vii. A	15. viii. B	14. ix. D
966	1558	14. x. F	13. xi. A	12. xii. B	59. 11. i. D	9. ii. E	11. iii. G	9. iv. A	9. v. C	7. vi. D	7. vii. F	5. viii. G	4. ix. B
967	1559	3. x. C	2. xi. E	1. xii. F	31. xii. A	60. 29. i. B	28. ii. D	28. iii. E	27. iv. G	26. v. A	25. vi. C	24. vii. D	23. viii. F
968	1560	22. ix. A	22. x. C	20. xi. D	20. xii. F	61. 18. i. G	17. ii. B	18. iii. C	17. iv. E	16. v. F	15. vi. A	14. vii. B	13. viii. D
969	1561	11. ix. E	11. x. G	9. xi. A	9. xii. C	62. 7. i. D	6. ii. F	7. iii. G	6. iv. B	5. v. C	4. vi. E	3. vii. F	2. viii. A
970	1562	31. viii. B	30. ix. D	29. x. E	28. xi. G	27. xii. A	63. 26. i. C	24. ii. D	26. iii. F	24. iv. G	24. v. B	22. vi. C	22. vii. E
971	1563	21. viii. G	20. ix. B	19. x. C	18. xi. E	17. xii. F	64. 16. i. A	14. ii. B	15. iii. D	13. iv. E	13. v. G	11. vi. A	11. vii. C
972	1564	9. viii. D	8. ix. F	7. x. G	6. xi. B	5. xii. C	65. 4. i. E	2. ii. F	4. iii. A	2. iv. B	2. v. D	31. v. E	30. vi. G
973	1565	29. vii. A	28 viii. C	26. ix. D	26. x. F	24. xi. G	24. xii. B	66. 22. i. C	21. ii. E	22. iii. F	21. iv. A	20. v. B	19. vi. D
974	1566	19. vii. F	18. viii. A	16. ix. B	16. x. D	14. xi. E	14. xii. G	67. 12. i. A	11. ii. C	12. iii. D	11. iv. F	10. v. G	9. vi. B

975	1567	8. vii. C	7. viii. E	5. ix. F	5. x. A	3. xi. B	3. xii. D	68. 1. i. E	31. i. G	29. ii. A	30. iii. C	28. iv. D	28. v. F
976	1568	26. vi. G	26. vii. B	24. viii. C	23. ix. E	22. x. F	21. xi. A	20. xii. B	69. 19. i. D	17. ii. E	19. iii. G	17. iv. A	17. v. C
977	1569	16. vi. E	16. vii. G	14. viii. A	13. ix. C	12. x. D	11. xi. F	10. xii. G	70. 9. i. B	7. ii. C	9. iii. E	7. iv. F	7. v. A
978	1570	5. vi. B	5. vii. D	3. viii. E	2. ix. G	1. x. A	31. x. C	29. xi. D	29. xii. F	71. 27. i. G	26. ii. B	27. iii. C	26. iv. E
979	1571	26. v. G	25. vi. B	24. vii. C	23. viii. E	21. ix. F	21. x. A	19. xi. B	19. xii. D	72. 17. i. E	16. ii. G	16. iii. A	15. iv. C
980	1572	14. v. D	13. vi. F	12. vii. G	11. viii. B	9. ix. C	9. x. E	7. xi. F	7. xii. A	73. 5. i. B	4. ii. D	5. iii. E	4. iv. G
981	1573	3. v. A	2. vi. C	1. vii. D	31. vii. F	29. viii. G	28. ix. B	27. x. C	26. xi. E	25. xii. F	74. 24. i. A	22. ii. B	24. iii. D
982	1574	23. iv. F	23. v. A	21. vi. B	21. vii. D	19. viii. E	18. ix. G	17. x. A	16. xi. C	15. xii. D	75. 14. i. F	12. ii. G	14. iii. A
983	1575	12. iv. C	12. v. E	10. vi. F	10. vii. A	8. viii. B	7. ix. D	6. x. E	5. xi. G	4. xii. A	76. 3. i. C	1. ii. D	2. iii. F
984	1576	31. iii. G	30. iv. B	29. v. C	28. vi. E	27. vii. F	26. viii. A	24. ix. B	24. x. D	22. xi. E	22. xii. G	77. 20. i. A	19. ii. C
985	1577	21. iii. E	20. iv. G	19. v. A	18. vi. C	17. vii. D	16. viii. F	14. ix. G	14. x. B	12. xi. C	12. xii. E	78. 10. i. F	9. ii. A
986	1578	10. iii. B	9. iv. D	8. v. E	7. vi. G	6. vii. A	5. viii. C	3. ix. D	3. x. F	1. xi. G	1. xii. B	30. xii. C	79. 29. i. E
987	1579	28. ii. G	30. iii. B	28. iv. C	28. v. E	26. vi. F	26. vii. A	24. viii. B	23. ix. D	22. x. E	21. xi. G	20. xii. A	80. 19. i. C
988	1580	17. ii. D	18. iii. F	16. iv. G	16. v. B	14. vi. C	14. vii. E	12. viii. F	11. ix. A	10. x. B	9. xi. D	8. xii. E	81. 7. i. G
989	1581	5. ii. A	7. iii. C	5. iv. D	5. v. F	3. vi. G	3. vii. B	1. viii. C	31. viii. E	29. ix. F	29. x. A	27. xi. B	27. xii. D
990	1582	26. i. F	25. ii. A	26. iii. B	25. iv. D	24. v. E	23. vi. G	22. vii. A	21. viii. C	19. ix. D	29. x. F	27. xi. G	27. xii. B
991	1583	25. i. C	24. ii. E	25. iii. F	24. iv. A	23. v. B	22. vi. D	21. vii. E	20. viii. G	18. ix. A	18. x. C	16. xi. D	16. xii. F
992	1584	14. i. G	13. ii. B	13. iii. C	12. iv. E	11. v. F	10. vi. A	9. vii. B	8. viii. D	6. ix. E	6. x. G	4. xi. A	4. xii. C
993	1585	3. i. E	2. ii. G	3. iii. A	2. iv. C	1. v. D	31. v. F	29. vi. G	29. vii. B	27. viii. C	26. ix. E	25. x. F	24. xi. A
994	1585	23. xii. B	86. 22. i. D	20. ii. E	22. iii. G	20. iv. A	20. v. C	18. vi. D	18. vii. F	16. viii. G	15. ix. B	14. x. C	13. xi. E
995	1586	12. xii. F	87. 11. i. A	9. ii. B	11. iii. D	9 iv. E	9. v. G	7. vi. A	7. vii. C	5. viii. D	4. ix. F	3. x. G	2. xi. B
996	1587	2. xii. D	88. 1. i. F	30. i. G	29. ii. B	29. iii. C	28. iv. E	27. v. F	26. vi. A	25. vii. B	24. viii. D	22. ix. E	22. x. G
997	1588	20. xi. A	20. xii. C	89. 18. i. D	17. ii. F	18. iii. G	17. iv. B	16. v. C	15. vi. E	14. vii. F	13. viii. A	11. ix. B	11. x. D
998	1589	10. xi. F	10. xii. A	90. 8. i. B	7. ii. D	8. iii. E	7. iv. G	6. v. A	5. vi. C	4. vii. D	3. viii. F	1. ix. G	1. x. B
999	1590	30. x. C	29. xi. E	28. xii. F	91. 27. i. A	25. ii. B	27. iii. D	15. iv. E	25. v. G	23. vi. A	23. vii. C	21. viii. D	20. ix. F
1000	1591	19. x. G	18. xi. B	17. xii. C	92. 16. i. E	14. ii. F	15. iii. A	13. iv B	13. v. D	11. vi. E	11. vii. G	9. viii. A	8. ix. C

A.H.	A.D.	Muharram	Safar	Rabí' I	Rabí' II	Jumádá I	Jumádá II	Rajab	Sha'bán	Ramadán	Shawwál	Zú-l-Ka'dah	Zú-l Hijjah
1001	1592	8. x. E	7. xi. G	6. xii. A	93. 5. i. C	3. ii. D	5. iii. F	3. iv. G	3. v. B	1. vi. C	1. vii. E	30. vii. F	29. viii. A
1002	1593	27. ix. B	27. x. D	25. xi. E	25. xii. G	94. 23. i. A	22. ii. C	23. iii. D	22. iv. F	21. v. G	20. vi. B	19. vii. C	18. viii. E
1003	1594	16. ix. F	16. x. A	14. xi. B	14. xii. D	95. 12. i. E	11. ii. G	12. iii. A	11. iv. C	10. v. D	9. vi. F	8. vii. G	7. viii. B
1004	1595	6. ix. D	6. x. F	4. xi. G	4. xii. B	96. 2. i. C	1. ii. E	1. iii. F	31. iii. A	29. iv. B	29. v. D	27. vi. E	27. vii. G
1005	1596	25. viii. A	24. ix. C	23. x. D	22. xi. F	21. xii. G	97. 20. i. B	18. ii. C	20. iii. E	18. iv. F	18. v. A	16. vi. B	16. vii. D
1006	1597	14. viii. E	13. ix. G	12. x. A	11. xi. C	10. xii. D	98. 9. i. F	7. ii. G	9. iii. B	7. iv. C	7. v. E	5. vi. F	5. vii. A
1007	1598	4. viii. C	3. ix. E	2. x. F	1. xi. A	30. xi. B	30. xii. D	1599. 28. i. E	27. ii. G	28. iii. A	27. iv. C	26. v. D	25. vi. F
1008	1599	24. vii. G	23. viii. B	21. ix. C	21. x. E	19. xi. F	19. xii. A	1600. 17. i. B	16. ii. D	16. iii. E	15. iv. G	14. v. A	13. vi. C
1009	1600	13. vii. E	12. viii. G	10. ix. A	10. x. C	8. xi. D	8. xii. F	1601. 6. i. G	5. ii. B	6. iii. C	5. iv. E	4. v. F	3. vi. A
1010	1601	2. vii. B	1. viii. D	30. viii. E	29. ix. G	28. x. A	27. xi. C	26. xii. D	2. 25. i. F	23. ii. G	25. iii. B	23. iv. C	23. v. E
1011	1602	21. vi. F	21. vii. A	19. viii. B	18. ix. D	17. x. E	16. xi. G	25. xii. A	3. 14. i. C	12. ii. D	14. iii. F	12. iv. G	12. v. B
1012	1603	11. vi. D	11. vii. F	9. viii. G	8. ix. B	7. x. C	6. xi. E	5. xii. F	4. 4. i. A	2. ii. B	3. iii. D	1. iv. E	1. v. G
1013	1604	30. v. A	29. vi. C	28. vii. D	27. viii. F	25. ix. G	25. x. B	23. xi. C	23. xii. E	5. 21. i. F	20. ii. A	21. iii. B	20. iv. D
1014	1605	19. v. E	18. vi. G	17. vii. A	16. viii. C	14. ix. D	14. x. F	12. xi. G	12. xii. B	6. 10. i. C	9. ii. E	10. iii. F	9. iv. A
1015	1606	9. v. C	8. vi. E	7. vii. F	6. viii. A	4. ix. B	4. x. D	2. xi. E	2. xii. G	31. xii. A	7. 30. i. C	28. ii. D	30. iii. F
1016	1607	28. iv. G	28. v. B	26. vi. C	26. vii. E	24. viii. F	23. ix. A	22. x. B	21. xi. D	20. xii. E	8. 19. i. G	17. ii. A	18. iii. C
1017	1608	17. iv. E	17. v. G	15. vi. A	15. vii. C	13. viii. D	12. ix. F	11. x. G	10. xi. B	9. xii. C	9. 8. i. E	6. ii. F	8. iii. A
1018	1609	6. iv. B	6. v. D	4. vi. E	4. vii. G	2. viii. A	1. ix. C	30. ix. D	30. x. F	28. xi. G	28. xii. B	10. 26. i. C	25. ii. E
1019	1610	26. iii. F	25. iv. A	24. v. B	23. vi. D	22. vii. E	21. viii. G	19. ix. A	19. x. C	17. xi. D	17. xii. F	11. 15. i. G	14. ii. B
1020	1611	16. iii. D	15. iv. F	14. v. G	13. vi. B	12. vii. C	11. viii. E	9. ix. F	9. x. A	7. xi. B	7. xii. D	12. 5. i. E	4. ii. G
1021	1612	4. iii. A	3. iv. C	2. v. D	1. vi. F	30. vi. G	30. vii. B	28. viii. C	27. ix. E	26. x. F	25. xi. A	24. xii. B	13. 23. i. D
1022	1613	21. ii. E	23. iii. G	21. iv. A	21. v. C	19. vi. D	19. vii. F	17. viii. G	16. ix. B	15. x. C	14. xi. E	13. xii. F	14. 12. i. A
1023	1614	11. ii. C	13. iii. E	11. iv. F	11. v. A	9. vi. B	9. vii. D	7. viii. E	6. ix. G	5. x. A	4. xi. C	3. xii. D	15. 2. i. F
1024	1615	31. . G	2. iii. B	31. iii. C	30. iv. E	29. v. F	28. vi. A	27. vii. B	26. viii. D	24. ix. E	24. x. G	22. xi. A	22. xii. C

1025	1616	20. i. D	19. ii. F	19. iii. G	18. iv. B	17. v. C	16. vi. E	15. vii. F	14. viii. A	12. ix. B	12. x. D	10. xi. E	10. xii. G
1026	1617	9. i. B	8. ii. D	9. iii. E	8. iv. G	7. v. A	6. vi. C	5. vii. D	4. viii. F	2. ix. G	2. x. B	31. x. C	30. xi. E
1027	1617	29. xii. D	**18.** 28. i. A	26. ii. B	28. iii. D	26. iv. E	26. v. G	24. vi. A	24. vii. C	22. viii. D	21. ix. F	20. x. G	19. xi. B
1028	1618	19. xii. E	**19.** 18. i. F	16. ii. G	18. iii. B	16. iv. C	16. v. E	14. vi. F	14. vii. A	12. viii. B	11. ix. D	10. x. E	9. xi. G
1029	1619	8. xii. A	**20.** 7. i. C	5. ii. D	6. iii. F	4. iv. G	4. v. B	2. vi. C	2. vii. E	31. vii. F	30. viii. A	28. ix. B	28. x. D
1030	1620	26. xi. E	26. xii. G	**21.** 24. i. A	23. ii. C	24. iii. D	23. iv. F	22. v. G	21. vi. B	20. vii. C	19. viii. E	17. ix. F	17. x. A
1031	1621	16. xi. C	16. xii. E	**22.** 14. i. F	13. ii. A	14. iii. B	13. iv. D	12. v. E	11. vi. G	10. vii. A	9. viii. C	7. ix. D	7. x. F
1032	1622	5. xi. G	5. xii. B	**23.** 3. i. C	2. ii. E	3. iii. F	2. iv. A	1. v. B	31. v. D	29. vi. E	29. vii. G	27. viii. A	26. ix. C
1033	1623	25. x. D	24. xi. F	23. xii. G	**24.** 22. i. B	20. ii. C	21. iii. E	19. iv. F	19. v. A	17. vi. B	17. vii. D	15. viii. E	14. ix. G
1034	1624	14. x. B	13. xi. D	12. xii. E	**25.** 11. i. G	9. ii. A	11. iii. C	9. iv. D	9. v. F	7. vi. G	7. vii. B	5. viii. C	4. ix. E
1035	1625	3. x. F	2. xi. A	1. xii. B	31. xii. D	**26.** 29. i. E	28. ii. G	29. iii. A	28. iv. C	27. v. D	26. vi. F	25. vii. G	24. viii. B
1036	1626	22. ix. C	22. x. E	20. xi. F	20. xii. A	**27.** 18. i. B	17. ii. D	18. iii. E	17. iv. G	16. v. A	15. vi. C	14. vii. D	13. viii. F
1037	1627	12. ix. A	12. x. C	10. xi. D	10. xii. F	**28.** 8. i. G	7. ii. B	7. iii. C	6. iv. E	5. v. F	4. vi. A	3. vii. B	2. viii. D
1038	1628	31. viii. E	30. ix. G	29. x. A	28. xi. C	27. xii. D	**29.** 26. i. F	24. ii. G	26. iii. B	24. iv. C	24. v. E	22. vi. F	22. vii. A
1039	1629	21. viii. C	20. ix. E	19. x. F	18. xi. A	17. xii. B	**30.** 16. i. D	14. ii. E	16. iii. G	14. iv. A	14. v. C	12. vi. D	12. vii. F
1040	1630	10. viii. G	9. ix. B	8. x. C	7. xi. E	6. xii. F	**31.** 5. i. A	3. ii. B	5. iii. D	3. iv. E	3. v. G	1. vi. A	1. vii. C
1041	1631	30. vii. D	29. viii. F	27. ix. G	27. x. B	25. xi. C	25. xii. E	**32.** 23. i. F	22. ii. A	22. iii. B	21. iv. D	20. v. E	19. vi. G
1042	1632	19. vii. B	18. viii. D	16. ix. E	16. x. G	14. xi. A	14. xii. C	**33.** 12. i. D	11. ii. F	12. iii. G	11. iv. B	10. v. C	9. vi. E
1043	1633	8. vii. F	7. viii. A	5. ix. B	5. x. D	3. xi. E	3. xii. G	**34.** 1. i. A	31. i. C	1. iii. D	31. iii. F	29. iv. G	29. v. B
1044	1634	27. vi. C	27. vii. E	25. viii. F	24. ix. A	23. x. B	22. xi. D	21. xii. E	**35.** 20. i. G	18. ii. A	20. iii. C	18. iv. D	18. v. F
1045	1635	17. vi. A	17. vii. C	15. viii. D	14. ix. F	13. x. G	12. xi. B	11. xii. C	**36.** 10. i. E	8. ii. F	9. iii. A	7. iv. B	7. v. D
1046	1636	5. vi. E	5. vii. G	3. viii. A	2. ix. C	1. x. D	31. x. F	29. xi. G	29. xii. B	**37.** 27. i. C	26. ii. E	27. iii. F	26. iv. A
1047	1637	26. v. C	25. vi. E	24. vii. F	23. viii. A	21. ix. B	21. x. D	19. xi. E	19. xii. G	**38.** 17. i. A	16. ii. C	17. iii. D	16. iv. F
1048	1638	15. v. G	14. vi. B	13. vii. C	12. viii. E	10. ix. F	10. x. A	8. xi. B	8. xii. D	**39.** 6. i. E	5. ii. G	6. iii. A	5. iv. C
1049	1639	4. v. D	3. vi. F	2. vii. G	1. viii. B	30. viii. C	29. ix. E	28. x. F	27. xi. A	26. xii. B	**40.** 25. i. D	23. ii. E	24. iii. G
1050	1640	23. iv. B	23. v. D	21. vi. E	21. vii. G	19. viii. A	18. ix. C	17. x. D	16. xi. F	15. xii. G	**41.** 14. i. B	12. ii. C	14. iii. E

A.H.	A.D.	Muharram	Safar	Rabí' I	Rabí' II	Jumádá I	Jumádá II	Rajab	Sha'bán	Ramadán	Shawwál	Zú-l-Ka'dah	Zú-l-Hijjah
1051	1641	12. iv. F	12. v. A	10. vi. B	10. vii. D	8. viii. E	7. ix. G	6. x. A	5. xi. C	4. xii. D	42. 3. i. F	1. ii. G	3. iii. B
1052	1642	1. iv. C	1. v. E	30. v. F	29. vi. A	28. vii. B	27. viii. D	25. ix. E	25. x. G	23. xi. A	23. xii. C	43. 21. i. D	20. ii. F
1053	1643	22. iii. A	21. iv. C	20. v. D	19. vi. F	18. vii. G	17. viii. B	15. ix. C	15. x. E	13. xi. F	13. xii. A	44. 11. i. B	10. ii. D
1054	1644	10. iii. E	9. iv. G	8. v. A	7. vi. C	6. vii. D	5. viii. F	3. ix. G	3. x. B	1. xi. C	1. xii. E	30. xii. F	45. 20. i. A
1055	1645	27. ii. B	29. iii. D	27. iv. E	27. v. G	25. vi. A	25. vii. C	23. viii. D	22. ix. F	21. x. G	20. xi. B	19. xii. C	46. 18. i. E
1056	1646	17. ii. G	19. iii. B	17. iv. C	17. v. E	15. vi. F	15. vii. A	13. viii. B	12. ix. D	11. x. E	10. xi. G	9. xii. A	47. 8. i. C
1057	1647	6. ii. D	8. iii. F	6. iv. G	6. v. B	4. vi. C	4. vii. E	2. viii. F	1. ix. A	30. ix. B	30. x. D	28. xi. E	28. xii. G
1058	1648	27. i. B	26. ii. D	26. iii. E	25. iv. G	24. v. A	23. vi. C	22. vii. D	21. viii. F	19. ix. G	19. x. B	17. xi. C	17. xii. E
1059	1649	15. i. F	14. ii. A	15. iii. B	14. iv. D	13. v. E	12. vi. G	11. vii. A	10. viii. C	8. ix. D	8. x. F	6. xi. G	6. xii. B
1060	1650	4. i. C	3. ii. E	4. iii. F	3. iv. A	2. v. B	1. vi. D	30. vi. E	30. vii. G	28. viii. A	27. ix. C	26. x. D	25. xi. F
1061	1650	25. xii. A	51. 24. i. C	22. ii. D	24. iii. F	22. iv. G	22. v. B	20. vi. C	20. vii. E	18. viii. F	17. ix. A	16. x. B	15. xi. D
1062	1651	14. xii. E	52. 13. i. G	11. ii. A	12. iii. C	10. iv. D	10. v. F	8. vi. G	8. vii. B	6. viii. C	5. ix. E	4. x. F	3. xi. A
1063	1652	2. xii. B	53. 1. i. D	30. i. E	1. iii. G	30. iii. A	29. iv. C	28. v. D	27. vi. F	26. vii. G	25. viii. B	23. ix. C	23. x. E
1064	1653	22. xi. G	22. xii. B	54. 20. i. C	19. ii. E	20. iii. F	19. iv. A	18. v. B	17. vi. D	16. vii. E	15. viii. G	13. ix. A	13. x. C
1065	1654	11. xi. D	11. xii. F	55. 9. i. G	8. ii. B	9. iii. C	8. iv. E	7. v. F	6. vi. A	5. vii. B	4. viii. D	2. ix. E	2. x. G
1066	1655	31. x. A	30. xi. C	29. xii. D	56. 28. i. F	26. ii. G	27. iii. B	25. iv. C	25. v. E	23. vi. F	23. vii. A	21. viii. B	20. ix. D
1067	1656	20. x. F	19. xi. A	18. xii. B	57. 17. i. D	15. ii. E	17. iii. G	15. iv. A	15. v. C	13. vi. D	13. vii. F	11. viii. G	10. ix. B
1068	1657	9. x. C	8. xi. E	7. xii. F	58. 6. i. A	4. ii. B	6. iii. D	4. iv. E	4. v. G	2. vi. A	2. vii. C	31. vii. D	30. viii. F
1069	1658	29. ix. A	29. x. C	27. xi. D	27. xii. F	59. 25. i. G	24. ii. B	25. iii. C	24. iv. E	23. v. F	22. vi. A	21. vii. B	20. viii. D
1070	1659	18. ix. E	18. x. G	16. xi. A	16. xii. C	60. 14. i. D	13. ii. F	13. iii. G	12. iv. B	11. v. C	10. vi. E	9. vii. F	8. viii. A
1071	1660	6. ix. B	6. x. D	4. xi. E	4. xii. G	61. 2. i. A	1. ii. C	2. iii. D	1. iv. F	30. iv. G	30. v. B	28. vi. C	28. vii. E
1072	1661	27. viii. G	26. ix. B	25. x. C	24. xi. E	23. xii. F	62. 22. i. A	20. ii. B	22. iii. D	20. iv. E	20. v. G	18. vi. A	18. vii. C
1073	1662	16. viii. D	15. ix. F	14. x. G	13. xi. B	12. xii. C	63. 11. i. E	9. ii. F	11. iii. A	9. iv. B	9. v. D	7. vi. E	7. vii. G
1074	1663	5. viii. A	4. ix. C	3. x. D	2. xi. F	1. xii. G	31. xii. B	64. 29. i. C	28. ii. E	28. iii. F	27. iv. A	26. v. B	25. vi. D

1075	1664	25. vii. F	24. viii. A	22. ix. B	22. x. D	20. xi. E	20. xii. G	65. 18. i. A	17. ii. C	18. iii. D	17. iv. F	16. v. G	15. vi. B
1076	1665	14. vii. C	13. viii. E	11. ix. F	11. x. A	9. xi. B	9. xii. D	66. 7. i. E	6. ii. G	7. iii. A	6. iv. C	5. v. D	4. vi. F
1077	1666	4. vii. A	3. viii. C	1. ix. D	1. x. F	30. x. G	29. xi. B	28. xii. C	67. 27. i. E	25. ii. F	27. iii. A	25. iv. B	25. v. D
1078	1667	23. vi. E	23. vii. G	21. viii. A	20. ix. C	19. x. D	18. xi. F	17. xii. G	68. 16. i. B	14. ii. C	15. iii. E	13. iv. F	13. v. A
1079	1668	11. vi. B	11. vii. D	9. viii. E	8. ix. G	7. x. A	6. xi. C	5. xii. D	69. 4. i. F	2. ii. G	4. iii. B	2. iv. C	2. v. E
1080	1669	1. vi. G	1. vii. B	30. vii. C	29. viii. E	27. ix. F	27. x. A	25. xi. B	25. xii. D	70. 23. i. E	22. ii. G	23. iii. A	22. iv. C
1081	1670	21. v. D	20. vi. F	19. vii. G	18. viii. B	16. ix. C	16. x. E	14. xi. F	14. xii. A	71. 12. i. B	11. ii. D	12. iii. E	11. iv. G
1082	1671	10. v. A	9. vi. C	8. vii. D	7. viii. F	5. ix. G	5. x. B	3. xi. C	3. xii. E	72. 1. i. F	31. i. A	29. ii. B	30. iii. D
1083	1672	29. iv. F	29. v. A	27. vi. B	27. vii. D	25. viii. E	24. ix. G	23. x. A	22. xi. C	21. xii. D	73. 20. i. F	18. ii. G	20. iii. B
1084	1673	18. iv. C	18. v. E	16. vi. F	16. vii. A	14. viii. B	13. ix. D	12. x. E	11. xi. G	10. xii. A	74. 9. i. C	7. ii. D	9. iii. F
1085	1674	7. iv. G	7. v. B	5. vi. C	5. vii. E	3. viii. F	2. ix. A	1. x. B	31. x. D	29. xi. E	29. xii. G	75. 27. i. A	26. ii. C
1086	1675	28. iii. E	27. iv. G	26. v. A	25. vi. C	24. vii. D	23. viii. F	21. ix. G	21. x. B	19. xi. C	19. xii. E	76. 17. i. F	16. ii. A
1087	1676	16. iii. B	15. iv. D	14. v. E	13. vi. G	12. vii. A	11. viii. C	9. ix. D	9. x. F	7. xi. G	7. xii. B	77. 5. i. C	4. ii. E
1088	1677	6. iii. G	5. iv. B	4. v. C	3. vi. E	2. vii. F	1. viii. A	30. viii. B	29. ix. D	28. x. E	27. xi. G	26. xii. A	78. 25. i. C
1089	1678	23. ii. D	25. iii. F	23. iv. G	23. v. B	21. vi. C	21. vii. E	19. viii. F	18. ix. A	17. x. B	16. xi. D	15. xii. E	79. 14. i. G
1090	1679	12. ii. A	14. iii. C	12. iv. D	12. v. F	10. vi. G	10. vii. B	8. viii. C	7. ix. E	6. x. F	5. xi. A	4. xii. B	80. 3. i. D
1091	1680	2. ii. F	3. iii. A	1. iv. B	1. v. D	30. v. E	29. vi. G	28. vii. A	27. viii. C	25. ix. D	25. x. F	23. xi. G	23. xii. B
1092	1681	21. i. C	20. ii. E	21. iii. F	20. iv. A	19. v. B	18. vi. D	17. vii. E	16. viii. G	14. ix. A	14. x. C	12. xi. D	12. xii. F
1093	1682	10. i. G	9. ii. B	10. iii. C	9. iv. E	8. v. F	7. vi. A	6. vii. B	5. viii. D	3. ix. E	3. x. G	1. xi. A	1. xii. C
1094	1682	31. xii. E	83. 30. i. G	28. ii. A	30. iii. C	28. iv. D	28. v. F	26. vi. G	26. vii. B	24. viii. C	23. ix. E	22. x. F	21. xi. A
1095	1683	20. xii. B	84. 19. i. D	17. ii. E	18. iii. G	16. iv. A	16. v. C	14. vi. D	14. vii. F	12. viii. G	11. ix. B	10. x. C	9. xi. E
1096	1684	8. xii. F	85. 7. i. A	5. ii. B	7. iii. D	5. iv. E	5. v. G	3. vi. A	3. vii. C	1. viii. D	31. viii. F	29. ix. G	29. x. B
1097	1685	28. xi. D	28. xii. F	86. 26. i. G	25. ii. B	26. iii. C	25. iv. E	24. v. F	23. vi. A	22. vii. B	21. viii. D	19. ix. E	19. x. G
1098	1686	17. xi. A	17. xii. C	87. 15. i. D	14. ii. F	15. iii. G	14. iv. B	13. v. C	12. vi. E	11. vii. F	10. viii. A	8. ix. B	8. x. D
1099	1687	7. xi. F	7. xii. A	88. 5. i. B	4. ii. D	4. iii. E	3. iv. G	2. v. A	1. vi. C	30. vi. D	30. vii. F	28. viii. G	27. ix. B
1100	1688	26. x. C	25. xi. E	21. xii. F	89. 23. i. A	21. ii. B	23. iii. D	21. v. E	21. v. G	19. vi. A	19. vii. C	17. viii. D	16. ix. F

A.H.	A.D.	Muharram	Safar	Rabí' I	Rabí' II	Jumádá I	Jumádá II	Rajab	Sha'bán	Ramadán	Shawwál	Zú-l-Ka'dah	Zú-l-Hijjah
1101	1689	15. x. G	14. xi. B	13. xii. C	**90.** 12. i. E	10. ii. F	12. iii. A	10. iv. B	10. v. D	8. vi. E	8. vii. G	6. viii. A	5. ix. C
1102	1690	5. x. E	4. xi. G	3. xii. A	**91.** 2. i. C	31. i. D	2. iii. F	31. iii. G	30. iv. B	29. v. C	28. vi. E	27. vii. F	26. viii. A
1103	1691	24. ix. B	24. x. D	22. xi. E	22. xii. G	**92.** 20. i. A	19. ii. C	19. iii. D	18. iv. F	17. v. G	16. vi. B	15. vii. C	14. viii. E
1104	1692	12. ix. F	12. x. A	10. xi. B	10. xii. D	**93.** 8. i. E	7. ii. G	8. iii. A	7. iv. C	6. v. D	5. vi. F	4. vii. G	3. viii. B
1105	1693	2. ix. D	2. x. F	31. x. G	30. xi. B	29. xii. C	**94.** 28. i. E	26. ii. F	28. iii. A	26. iv. B	26. v. D	24. vi. E	24. vii. G
1106	1694	22. viii. A	21. ix. C	20. x. D	19. xi. F	18. xii. G	**95.** 17. i. B	15. ii. C	17. iii. E	15. iv. F	15. v. A	13. vi. B	13. vii. D
1107	1695	12. viii. F	11. ix. A	10. x. B	9. xi. D	8. xii. E	**96.** 7. i. G	5. ii. A	6. iii. C	4. iv. D	4. v. F	2. vi. G	2. vii. B
1108	1696	31. vii. C	30. viii. E	28. ix. F	28. x. A	26. xi. B	26. xii. D	**97.** 24. i. E	23. ii. G	24. iii. A	23. iv. C	22. v. D	21. vi. F
1109	1697	20. vii. G	19. viii. B	17. ix. C	17. x. E	15. xi. F	15. xii. A	**98.** 13. i. B	12. ii. D	13. iii. E	12. iv. G	11. v. A	10. vi. C
1110	1698	10. vii. E	9. viii. G	7. ix. A	7. x. C	5. xi. D	5. xii. F	**99.** 3. i. G	2. ii. B	3. iii. C	2. iv. E	1. v. F	31. v. A
1111	1699	29. vi. B	29. vii. D	27. viii. E	26. ix. G	25. x. A	24. xi. C	23. xii. D	**1700.** 22. i. F	20. ii. G	22. iii. B	20. iv. C	20. v. E
1112	1700	18. vi. F	18. vii. A	16. viii. B	15. ix. D	14. x. E	13. xi. G	12. xii. A	**1701.** 11. i. C	9. ii. D	11. iii. F	9. iv. G	9. v. B
1113	1701	8. vi. D	8. vii. F	6. viii. G	5. ix. B	4. x. C	3. xi. E	2. xii. F	**1702.** 1. i. A	30. i. B	1. iii. D	30. iii. E	29. iv. G
1114	1702	28. v. A	27. vi. C	26. vii. D	25. viii. F	23. ix. G	23. x. B	21. xi. C	21. xii. E	**3.** 19. i. F	18. ii. A	19. iii. B	18. iv. D
1115	1703	17. v. E	16. vi. G	15. vii. A	14. viii. C	12. ix. D	12. x. F	10. xi. G	10. xii. B	**4.** 8. i. C	7. ii. E	7. iii. F	6. iv. A
1116	1704	6. v. C	5. vi. E	4. vii. F	3. viii. A	1. ix. B	1. x. D	30. x. E	29. xi. G	28. xii. A	**5.** 27. i. C	25. ii. D	27. iii. F
1117	1705	25. iv. G	25. v. B	23. vi. C	23. vii. E	21. viii. F	20. ix. A	19. x. B	18. xi. D	17. xii. E	**6.** 16. i. G	14. ii. A	16. iii. C
1118	1706	15. iv. E	15. v. G	13. vi. A	13. vii. C	11. viii. D	10. ix. F	9. x. G	8. xi. B	7. xii. C	**7.** 6. i. E	4. ii. F	6. iii. A
1119	1707	4. iv. B	4. v. D	2. vi. E	2. vii. G	31. vii. A	30. viii. C	28. ix. D	28. x. F	26. xi. G	26. xii. B	**8.** 24. i. C	23. ii. E
1120	1708	23. iii. F	22. iv. A	21. v. B	20. vi. D	19. vii. E	18. viii. G	16. ix. A	16. x. C	14. xi. D	14. xii. F	**9.** 12. i. G	11. ii. B
1121	1709	13. iii. D	12. iv. F	11. v. G	10. vi. B	9. vii. C	8. viii. E	6. ix. F	6. x. A	4. xi. B	4. xii. D	**10.** 2. i. E	1. ii. G
1122	1710	2. iii. A	1. iv. C	30. iv. D	30. v. F	28. vi. G	28. vii. B	26. viii. C	25. ix. E	24. x. F	23. xi. A	22. xii. B	**11.** 21. i. D
1123	1711	19. ii. E	21. iii. G	19. iv. A	19. v. C	17. vi. D	17. vii. F	15. viii. G	14. ix. B	13. x. C	12. xi. E	11. xii. F	**12.** 10. i. A
1124	1712	9. ii. C	10. iii. E	8. iv. F	8. v. A	6. vi. B	6. vii D	4. viii. E	3. ix. G	2. x. A	1. xi. C	30. xi. D	30. xii. F

1125	1713	28. i. G	27. ii. B	28. iii. C	27. iv. E	26. v. F	25. vi. A	24. vii. B	23. viii. D	21. ix. E	21. x. G	19. xi. A	19. xii. C
1126	1714	17. i. D	16. ii. F	17. iii. G	16. iv. B	15. v. C	14. vi. E	13. vii. F	12. viii. A	10. ix. B	10. x. D	8. xi. E	8. xii. G
1127	1715	7. i. B	6. ii. D	7. iii. E	6. iv. G	5. v. A	4. vi. C	3. vii. D	2. viii. F	31. viii. G	30. ix. B	29. x. C	28. xi. E
1128	1715	27. xii. F	16. 26. i. A	24. ii. B	25. iii. D	23. iv. E	23. v. G	21. vi. A	21. vii. C	19. viii. D	18. ix. F	17. x. G	16. xi. B
1129	1716	16. xii. D	17. 15. i. F	13. ii. G	15. iii. B	13. iv. C	13. v. E	11. vi. F	11. vii. A	9. viii. B	8. ix. D	7. x. E	6. xi. G
1130	1717	5. xii. A	18. 4. i. C	2. ii. D	4. iii. F	2. iv. G	2. v. B	31. v. C	30. vi. E	29. vii. F	28. viii. A	26. ix. B	26. x. D
1131	1718	24. xi. E	24. xii. G	19. 22. i. A	21. ii. C	22. iii. D	21. iv. F	20. v. G	19. vi. B	18. vii. C	17. viii. E	16. ix. F	15. x. A
1132	1719	14. xi. C	14. xii. E	20. 12. i. F	11. ii. A	11. iii. B	10. iv. D	9. v. E	8. vi. G	7. vii. A	6. viii. C	4. ix. D	4. x. F
1133	1720	2. xi. G	2. xii. B	31. xii. C	21. 30. i. E	28. ii. F	30. iii. A	28. iv. B	28. v. D	26. vi. E	26. vii. G	24. viii. A	23. ix. C
1134	1721	22. x. D	21. xi. F	20. xii. G	22. 19. i. B	17. ii. C	19. iii. E	17. iv. F	17. v. A	15. vi. B	15. vii. D	13. viii. E	12. ix. G
1135	1722	12. x. B	11. xi. D	10. xii. E	23. 9. i. G	7. ii. A	9. iii. C	7. iv. D	7. v. F	5. vi. G	5. vii. B	3. viii. C	2. ix. E
1136	1723	1. x. F	31. x. A	29. xi. B	29. xii. D	24. 27. i. E	26. ii. G	26. iii. A	25. iv. C	24. v. D	23. vi. F	22. vii. G	21. viii. B
1137	1724	20. ix. D	20. x. F	18. xi. G	18. xii. B	25. 16. i. C	15. ii. E	16. iii. F	15. iv. A	14. v. B	13. vi. D	12. vii. E	11. viii. G
1138	1725	9. ix. A	9. x. C	7. xi. D	7. xii. F	26. 5. i. G	4. ii. B	5. iii. C	4. iv. E	3. v. F	2. vi. A	1. vii. B	31. vii. D
1139	1726	29. viii. E	28. ix. G	27. x. A	26. xi. C	25. xii. D	27. 24. i. F	22. ii. G	24. iii. B	22. iv. C	22. v. E	20. vi. F	20. vii. A
1140	1727	19. viii. C	18. ix. E	17. x. F	16. xi. A	15. xii. B	28. 14. i. D	12. ii. E	13. iii. G	11. iv. A	11. v. C	9. vi. D	9. vii. F
1141	1728	7. viii. G	6. ix. B	5. x. C	4. xi. E	3. xii. F	29. 2. i. A	31. i. B	2. iii. D	31. iii. E	30. iv. G	29. v. A	28. vi. C
1142	1729	27. vii. D	26. viii. F	24. ix. G	24. x. B	22. xi. C	22. xii. E	30. 20. i. F	19. ii. A	20. iii. B	19. iv. D	18. v. E	17. vi. G
1143	1730	17. vii. B	16. viii. D	14. ix. E	14. x. G	12. xi. A	12. xii. C	31. 10. i. D	9. ii. F	10. iii. G	9. iv. B	8. v. C	7. vi. E
1144	1731	6. vii. F	5. viii. A	3. ix. B	3. x. D	1. xi. E	1. xii. G	30. xii. A	32. 29. i. C	27. ii. D	28. iii. F	26. iv. G	26. v. B
1145	1732	24. vi. C	24. vii. E	22. viii. F	21. ix. A	20. x. B	19. xi. D	18. xii. E	33. 17. i. G	15. ii. A	17. iii. C	15. iv. D	15. v. F
1146	1733	14. vi. A	14. vii. C	12. viii. D	11. ix. F	10. x. G	9. xi. B	8. xii. C	34. 7. i. E	5. ii. F	7. iii. A	5. iv. B	5. v. D
1147	1734	3. vi. E	3. vii. G	1. viii. A	31. viii. C	29. ix. D	29. x. F	27. xi. G	27. xii. B	35. 25. i. C	24. ii. E	25. iii. F	24. iv. A
1148	1735	24. v. C	23. vi. E	22. vii. F	21. viii. A	19. ix. B	19. x. D	17. xi. E	17. xii. G	36. 15. i. A	14. ii. C	14. iii. D	13. iv. F
1149	1736	12. v. G	11. vi. B	10. vii. C	9. viii. E	7. ix. F	7. x. A	5. xi. B	5. xii. D	37. 3. i. E	2. ii. G	3. iii. A	2. iv. C
1150	1737	1. v. D	31. v. F	29. vi. G	29. vii. B	27. viii. C	26. ix. E	25. x. F	24. xi. A	23. xii. B	38. 22. i. D	20. ii. E	22. iii. G

A.H.	A.D.	Muharram	Safar	Rabí' I	Rabí' II	Jumádá I	Jumádá II	Rajab	Sha'bán	Ramadán	Shawwál	Zú-l-Ka'dah	Zú-l-Hijjah
1151	1738	21. iv. B	21. v. D	19. vi. E	19. vii. G	17. viii. A	16. ix. C	15. x. D	14. xi. F	13. xii. G	39. 12. i. B	10. ii. C	12. iii. E
1152	1739	10. iv. F	10. v. A	8. vi. B	8. vii. D	6. viii. E	5. ix. G	4. x. A	3. xi. C	2. xii. D	40. 1. i. F	30. i. G	29. ii. B
1153	1740	29. iii. C	28. iv. E	27. v. F	26. vi. A	25. vii. B	24. viii. D	22. ix. E	22. x. G	20. xi. A	20. xii. C	41. 18. i. D	17. ii. F
1154	1741	19. iii. A	18. iv. C	17. v. D	16. vi. F	15. vii. G	14. viii. B	12. ix. C	12. x. E	10. xi. F	10. xii. A	42. 8. i. B	7. ii. D
1155	1742	8. iii. E	7. iv. G	6. v. A	5. vi. C	4. vii. D	3. viii. F	1. ix. G	1. x. B	30. x. C	29. xi. E	28. xii. F	43. 27. i. A
1156	1743	25. ii. B	27. iii. D	25. iv. E	25. v. G	23. vi. A	23. vii. C	21. viii. D	20. ix. F	19. x. G	18. xi. B	17. xii. C	44. 16. i. E
1157	1744	15. ii. G	16. iii. B	14. iv. C	14. v. E	12. vi. F	12. vii. A	10. viii. B	9. ix. D	8. x. E	7. xi. G	6. xii. A	45. 5. i. C
1158	1745	3. ii. D	5. iii. F	3. iv. G	3. v. B	1. vi. C	1. vii. E	30. vii. F	29. viii. A	27. ix. B	27. x. D	25. xi. E	25. xii. G
1159	1746	24. i. B	23. ii. D	24. iii. E	23. iv. G	22. v. A	21. vi. C	20. vii. D	19. viii. F	17. ix. G	17. x. B	15. xi. C	15. xii. E
1160	1747	13. i. F	12. ii. A	13. iii. B	12. iv. D	11. v. E	10. vi. G	9. vii. A	8. viii. C	6. ix. D	6. x. F	4. xi. G	4. xii. B
1161	1748	2. i. C	1. ii. E	1. iii. F	31. iii. A	29. iv. B	29. v. D	27. vi. E	27. vii. G	25. viii. A	24. ix. C	23. x. D	22. xi. F
1162	1748	22. xii. A	49. 21. i. C	19. ii. D	21. iii. F	19. iv. G	19. v. B	17. vi. C	17. vii. E	15. viii. F	14. ix. A	13. x. B	12. xi. D
1163	1749	11. xii. E	50. 10. i. G	8. ii. A	10. iii. C	8. iv. D	8. v. F	6. vi. G	6. vii. B	4. viii. C	3. ix. E	2. x. F	1. xi. A
1164	1750	30. xii. B	30. xii. D	51. 28. i. E	27. ii. G	28. iii. A	27. iv. C	26. v. D	25. vi. F	24. vii. G	23. viii. B	21. ix. C	21. x. E
1165	1751	20. xi. G	20. xii. B	52. 18. i. C	17. ii. E	17. iii. F	16. iv. A	15. v. B	14. vi. D	13. vii. E	12. viii. G	10. ix. A	10. x. C
1166	1752	8. xi. D	8. xii. F	53. 6. i. G	5. ii. B	6. iii. C	5. iv. E	4. v. F	3. vi. A	2. vii. B	1. viii. D	30. viii. E	29. ix. G
1167	1753	29. x. B	28. xi. D	27. xii. E	54. 26. i. G	24. ii. A	26. iii. C	24. iv. D	24. v. F	22. vi. G	22. vii. B	20. viii. C	19. ix. E
1168	1754	18. x. F	17. xi. A	16. xii. B	55. 15. i. D	13. ii. E	15. iii. G	13. iv. A	13. v. C	11. vi. D	11. vii. F	9. viii. G	8. ix. B
1169	1755	7. x. C	6. xi. E	5. xii. F	56. 4. i. A	2. ii. B	3. iii. D	1. iv. E	1. v. G	30. v. A	29. vi. C	28. vii. D	27. viii. F
1170	1756	26. ix. A	26. x. C	24. xi. D	24. xii. F	57. 22. i. G	21. ii. B	22. iii. C	21. iv. E	20. v. F	19. vi. A	18. vii. B	17. viii. D
1171	1757	15. ix. E	15. x. G	13. xi. A	13. xii. C	58. 11. i. D	10. ii. F	11. iii. G	10. iv. B	9. v. C	8. vi. E	7. vii. F	6. viii. A
1172	1758	4. ix. B	4. x. D	2 xi. E	2. xii. G	31 xii. A	59. 30. i. C	28. ii. D	30. iii. F	28. iv. G	28. v. B	27. vi. C	26. vii. E
1173	1759	25. viii. G	24. ix. B	23. x. C	22. xi. E	21. xii. F	60. 20. i. A	18. ii. B	19. iii. D	17. iv. E	17. v. G	15. vi. A	15. vii. C
1174	1760	13. viii. D	12. ix. F	11. x. G	10. xi. B	9. xii. C	61. 8. i. E	6. ii. F	8. iii. A	6. iv. B	6. v. D	4. vi. E	4. vii. G

1175	1761	2. viii. A	1. ix. C	30. ix. D	30. x. F	28. xi. G	28. xii. B	62. 26. i. C	25. ii. E	26. iii. F	25. iv. A	24. v. B	23. vi. D
1176	1762	23. vii. F	22. viii. A	20. ix. B	20. x. D	18. xi. E	18. xii. G	63. 16. i. A	15. ii. C	16. iii. D	15. iv. F	14. v. G	13. vi. B
1177	1763	12. vii. C	11. viii. E	9. ix. F	9. x. A	7. xi. B	7. xii. D	64. 5. i. E	4. ii. G	4. iii. A	3. iv. C	2. v. D	1. vi. F
1178	1764	1. vii. A	31. vii. C	29. viii. D	28. ix. F	27. x. G	26. xi. B	25. xii. C	65. 24. i. E	22. ii. F	24. iii. A	22. iv. B	22. v. D
1179	1765	20. vi. E	20. vii. G	18. viii. A	17. ix. C	16. x. D	15. xi. F	14. xii. G	66. 13. i. B	11. ii. C	13. iii. E	11. iv. F	11. v. A
1180	1766	9. vi. B	9. vii. D	7. viii. E	6. ix. G	5. x. A	4. xi. C	3. xii. D	67. 2. i. F	31. i. G	2. iii. B	31. iii. C	30. iv. E
1181	1767	30. v. G	29. vi. B	28. vii. C	27. viii. E	25. xi. F	25. x. A	23. xi. B	23. xii. D	68. 21. i. E	20. ii. G	2[illegible]. iii. A	19. iv. C
1182	1768	18. v. D	17. vi. F	16. vii. G	15. viii. B	13. xi. C	13. x. E	11. xi. F	11. xii. A	69. 9. i. B	8. ii. D	9. iii. E	8. iv. G
1183	1769	7. v. A	6. vi. C	5. vii. D	4. viii. F	2. xi. G	2. x. B	31. x. C	30. xi. E	29. xii. F	70. 28. i. A	26. ii. B	28. iii. D
1184	1770	27. iv. F	27. v. A	25. vi. B	25. vii. D	23. viii. E	22. xi. G	21. x. A	20. xi. C	19. xii. D	71. 18. i. F	16. ii. G	18. iii. B
1185	1771	16. iv. C	16. v. E	14. vi. F	14. vii. A	12. viii. B	11. xi. D	10. x. E	9. xi. G	8. xii. A	72. 7. i. C	5. ii. D	6. iii. F
1186	1772	4. iv. G	4. v. B	2. vi. C	2. vii. E	31. vii. F	30. viii. A	28. ix. B	28. x. D	26. xi. E	26. xii. G	73. 24. i. A	23. ii. C
1187	1773	25. iii. E	24. iv. G	23. v. A	22. vi. C	21. vii. D	20. viii. F	18. ix. G	18. x. B	16. xi. C	16. xii. E	74. 14. i. F	13. ii. A
1188	1774	14. iii. B	13. iv. D	12. v. E	11. vi. G	10. vii. A	9. viii. C	7. ix. D	7. x. F	5. xi. G	5. xii. B	75. 3. i. C	2. ii. E
1189	1775	4. iii. G	3. iv. B	2. v. C	1. vi. E	30. vi. F	30. vii. A	28. viii. B	27. ix. D	26. x. E	25. xi. G	24. xii. A	76. 23. i. C
1190	1776	21. ii. D	22. iii. F	20. iv. G	20. v. B	18. vi. C	18. vii. E	16. viii. F	15. ix. A	14. x. B	13. xi. D	12. xii. E	77. 11. i. G
1191	1777	9. ii. A	11. iii. C	9. iv. D	9. v. F	7. vi. G	7. vii. B	5. viii. C	4. ix. E	3. x. F	2. xi. A	1. xii. B	31. xii. D
1192	1778	30. i. F	1. iii. A	30. iii. B	29. iv. D	28. v. E	27. vi. G	26. vii. A	25. viii. C	23. ix. D	23. x. F	21. xi. G	21. xii. B
1193	1779	19. i. C	18. ii. E	19. iii. F	18. iv. A	17. v. B	16. vi. D	15. vii. E	14. viii. G	12. ix. A	12. x. C	10. xi. D	10. xii. F
1194	1780	8. i. G	7. ii. B	7. iii. C	6. iv. E	5. v. F	4. vi. A	3. vii. B	2. viii. D	31. viii. E	30. ix. G	29. x. A	28. xi. C
1195	1780	28. xii. E	81. 27. i. G	25. ii. A	27. iii. C	25. iv. D	25. v. F	23. vi. G	23. vii. B	21. viii. C	20. ix. E	19. x. F	18. xi. A
1196	1781	17. xii. B	82. 16. i. D	14. ii. E	16. iii. G	14. iv. A	14. v. C	12. vi. D	12. vii. F	10. viii. G	9. ix. B	8. x. C	7. xi. E
1197	1782	7. xii. G	83. 6. i. B	4. ii. C	6. iii. E	4. iv. F	4. v. A	2. vi. B	2. vii. D	31. vii. E	30. viii. G	28. ix. A	28. x. C
1198	1783	26. xi. D	26. xii. F	84. 24. i. G	23. ii. B	23. iii. C	22. iv. E	21. v. F	20. vi. A	19. vii. B	18. viii. D	17. ix. E	16. x. G
1199	1784	14. xi. A	14. xii. C	85. 12. i. D	11. ii. F	12. iii. G	11. iv. B	10. v. C	9. vi. E	8. vii. F	7. viii. A	6. ix. B	5. x. D
1200	1785	4. xi. F	4. xii. A	86. 2. i. B	1. ii. D	2. iii. E	1. iv. G	30. iv. A	30. v. C	28. vi. D	28. vii. F	23. viii. G	25. ix. B

A.H.	A.D.	Muharram	Safar	Rabí' I	Rabí' II	Jumádá I	Jumádá II	Rajab	Sha'bán	Ramadán	Shawwál	Zú-l-Ka'dah	Zú-l-Hijjah
1201	1786	24. x. C	23. xi. E	22. xii. F	87. 21. i. A	19. ii. B	21. iii. D	19. iv. E	19. v. G	17. vi. A	17. vii. C	15. viii. D	14. ix. F
1202	1787	13. x. G	12. xi. B	11. xii. C	88. 10. i. E	8. ii. F	9. iii. A	7. v. B	7. v. D	5. vi. E	5. vii. G	3. viii. A	2. ix. C
1203	1788	2. x. E	1. xi. G	30. xi. A	30. xii. C	89. 28. i. D	27. ii. F	28. iii. G	27. iv. B	26. v. C	25. vi. E	24. vii. F	23. viii. A
1204	1789	21. ix. B	21. x. D	19. xi. E	19. xii. G	90. 17. i. A	16. ii. C	17. iii. D	16. iv. F	15. v. G	14. vi. B	13. vii. C	12. viii. E
1205	1790	10. ix. F	10. x. A	8. xi. B	8. xii. D	91. 6. i. E	5. ii. G	6. iii. A	5. iv. C	4. v. D	3. vi. F	2. vii. G	1. viii. B
1206	1791	31. viii. D	30. ix. F	29. x. G	28. xi. B	27. xii. C	92. 26. i. E	24. ii. F	25. iii. A	23. iv. B	23. v. D	21. vi. E	21. vii. G
1207	1792	19. viii. A	18. ix. C	17. x. D	16. xi. F	15. xii. G	93. 14. i. B	12. ii. C	14. iii. E	12. iv. F	12. v. A	10. vi. B	10. vii. D
1208	1793	9. viii. F	8. ix. A	7. x. B	6. xi. D	5. xii. E	94. 4. i. G	2. ii. A	4. iii. C	2. iv. D	2. v. F	31. v. G	30. vi. B
1209	1794	29. vii. C	28. viii. E	26. ix. F	26. x. A	24. xi. B	24. xii. D	95. 22. i. E	21. ii. G	22. iii. A	21. iv. C	20. v. D	19. vi. F
1210	1795	18. vii. G	17. viii. B	15. ix. C	15. x. E	13. xi. F	13. xii. A	96. 11. i. B	10. ii. D	10. iii. E	9. iv. G	8. v. A	7. vi. C
1211	1796	7. vii. E	6. viii. G	4. ix. A	4. x. C	2. xi. D	2. xii. F	31. xii. G	97. 30. i. B	28. ii. C	30. iii. E	28. iv. F	28. v. A
1212	1797	26. vi. B	26. vii. D	24. viii. E	23. ix. G	22. x. A	21. xi. C	20. xii. D	98. 19. i. F	17. ii. G	19. iii. B	17. iv. C	17. v. E
1213	1798	15. vi. F	15. vii. A	13. viii. B	12. ix. D	11. x. E	10. xi. G	9. xii. A	99. 8. i. C	6. ii. D	8. iii. F	6. iv. G	6. v. B
1214	1799	5. vi. D	5. vii. F	3. viii. G	2. ix. B	1. x. C	31. x. E	29. xi. F	29. xii. A	1800. 27. i. B	26. ii. D	27. iii. E	26. iv. G
1215	1800	25. v. A	24. vi. C	23. vii. D	22. viii. F	20. ix. G	20. x. B	18. xi. C	18. xii. E	1801. 16. i. F	15. ii. A	16. iii. B	15. iv. D
1216	1801	14. v. E	13. vi. G	12. vii. A	11. viii. C	9. ix. D	9. x. F	7. xi. G	7. xii. B	1802. 5. i. C	4. ii. E	5. iii. F	4. iv. A
1217	1802	4. v. C	3. vi. E	2. vii. F	1. viii. A	30. viii. B	29. ix. D	28. x. E	27. xi. G	26. xii. A	3. 25. i. C	23. ii. D	25. iii. F
1218	1803	23. iv. G	23. v. B	21. vi. C	21. vii. E	19. viii. F	18. ix. A	17. x. B	16. xi. D	15. xii. E	4. 14. i. G	12. ii. A	13. iii. C
1219	1804	12. iv. E	12. v. G	10. vi. A	10. vii. C	8. viii. D	7. ix. F	6. x. G	5. xi. B	4. xii. C	5. 3. i. E	1. ii. F	3. iii. A
1220	1805	1. iv. B	1. v. D	30. v. E	29. vi. G	28. vii. A	27. viii. C	25. ix. D	25. x. F	23. xi. G	23. xii. B	6. 21. i. C	20. ii. E
1221	1806	21. iii. F	20. iv. A	19. v. B	18. vi. D	17. vii. E	16. viii. G	14. ix A	14. x. C	12. xi. D	12. xii. F	7. 10. i. G	9. ii. B

TABLE

FOR

CONVERTING ENGLISH INCHES INTO MILLIMETRES

AND THE

MEASURES OF MIONNET'S SCALE.

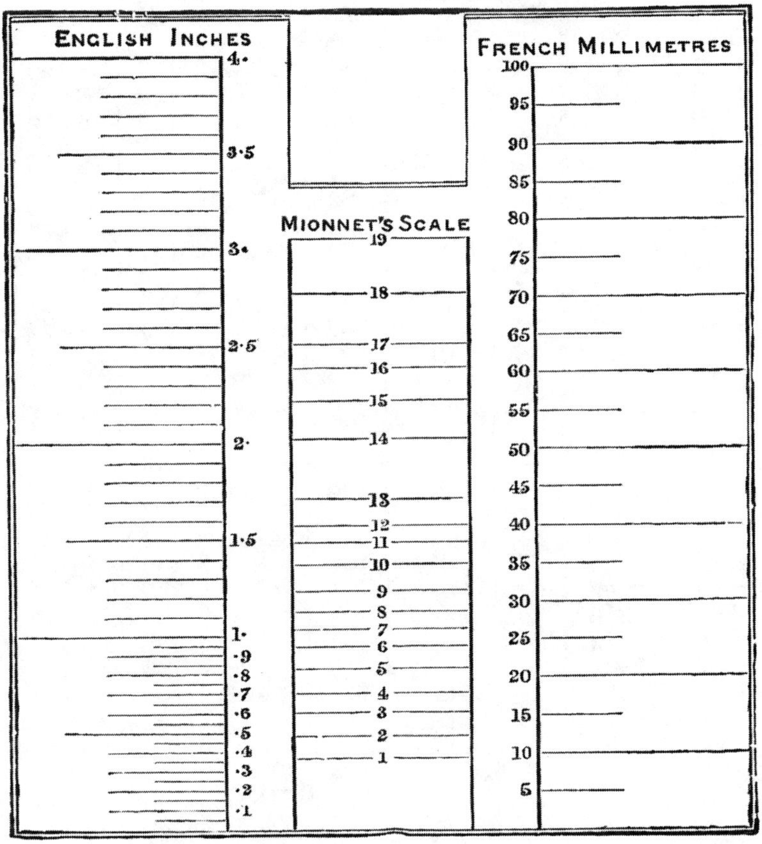

TABLE

OF THE

RELATIVE WEIGHTS OF

ENGLISH GRAINS and FRENCH GRAMMES.

Grains	Grammes.	Grains.	Grammes.	Grains.	Grammes.	Grains.	Grammes.
1	·064	41	2·656	81	5·248	121	7·840
2	·129	42	2·720	82	5·312	122	7·905
3	·194	43	2·785	83	5·378	123	7·970
4	·259	44	2·850	84	5·442	124	8·035
5	·324	45	2·915	85	5·508	125	8·100
6	·388	46	2·980	86	5·572	126	8·164
7	·453	47	3·045	87	5·637	127	8·229
8	·518	48	3·110	88	5·702	128	8·294
9	·583	49	3·175	89	5·767	129	8·359
10	·648	50	3·240	90	5·832	130	8·424
11	·712	51	3·304	91	5·896	131	8·488
12	·777	52	3·368	92	5·961	132	8·553
13	·842	53	3·434	93	6·026	133	8·618
14	·907	54	3·498	94	6·091	134	8·682
15	·972	55	3·564	95	6·156	135	8·747
16	1·036	56	3·628	96	6·220	136	8·812
17	1·101	57	3·693	97	6·285	137	8·877
18	1·166	58	3·758	98	6·350	138	8·942
19	1·231	59	3·823	99	6·415	139	9·007
20	1·296	60	3·888	100	6·480	140	9·072
21	1·360	61	3·952	101	6·544	141	9·136
22	1·425	62	4·017	102	6·609	142	9·200
23	1·490	63	4·082	103	6·674	143	9·265
24	1·555	64	4·146	104	6·739	144	9·330
25	1·620	65	4·211	105	6·804	145	9·395
26	1·684	66	4·276	106	6·868	146	9·460
27	1·749	67	4·341	107	6·933	147	9·525
28	1·814	68	4·406	108	6·998	148	9·590
29	1·879	69	4·471	109	7·063	149	9·655
30	1·944	70	4·536	110	7·128	150	9·720
31	2·008	71	4·600	111	7·192	151	9·784
32	2·073	72	4·665	112	7·257	152	9·848
33	2·138	73	4·729	113	7·322	153	9·914
34	2·202	74	4·794	114	7·387	154	9·978
35	2·267	75	4·859	115	7·452	155	10·044
36	2·332	76	4·924	116	7·516	156	10·108
37	2·397	77	4·989	117	7·581	157	10·173
38	2·462	78	5·054	118	7·646	158	10·238
39	2·527	79	5·119	119	7·711	159	10·303
40	2·592	80	5·184	120	7·776	160	10·368

TABLE

OF THE

RELATIVE WEIGHTS OF

ENGLISH GRAINS and FRENCH GRAMMES.

Grains.	Grammes.	Grains.	Grammes.	Grains.	Grammes.	Grains.	Grammes.
161	10·432	201	13·024	241	15·616	290	18·79
162	10·497	202	13·089	242	15·680	300	19·44
163	10·562	203	13·154	243	15·745	310	20·08
164	10·626	204	13·219	244	15·810	320	20·73
165	10·691	205	13·284	245	15·875	330	21·38
166	10·756	206	13·348	246	15·940	340	22·02
167	10·821	207	13·413	247	16·005	350	22·67
168	10·886	208	13·478	248	16·070	360	23·32
169	10·951	209	13·543	249	16·135	370	23·97
170	11·016	210	13·608	250	16·200	380	24·62
171	11·080	211	13·672	251	16·264	390	25·27
172	11·145	212	13·737	252	16·328	400	25·92
173	11·209	213	13·802	253	16·394	410	26·56
174	11·274	214	13·867	254	16·458	420	27·20
175	11·339	215	13·932	255	16·524	430	27·85
176	11·404	216	13·996	256	16·588	440	28·50
177	11·469	217	14·061	257	16·653	450	29·15
178	11·534	218	14·126	258	16·718	460	29·80
179	11·599	219	14·191	259	16·783	470	30·45
180	11·664	220	14·256	260	16·848	480	31·10
181	11·728	221	14·320	261	16·912	490	31·75
182	11·792	222	14·385	262	16·977	500	32·40
183	11·858	223	14·450	263	17·042	510	33·04
184	11·922	224	14·515	264	17·106	520	33·68
185	11·988	225	14·580	265	17·171	530	34·34
186	12·052	226	14·644	266	17·236	540	34·98
187	12·117	227	14·709	267	17·301	550	35·64
188	12·182	228	14·774	268	17·366	560	36·28
189	12·247	229	14·839	269	17·431	570	36·93
190	12·312	230	14·904	270	17·496	580	37·58
191	12·376	231	14·968	271	17·560	590	38·23
192	12·441	232	15·033	272	17·625	600	38·88
193	12·506	233	15·098	273	17·689	700	45·36
194	12·571	234	15·162	274	17·754	800	51·84
195	12·636	235	15·227	275	17·819	900	58·32
196	12·700	236	15·292	276	17·884	1000	64·80
197	12·765	237	15·357	277	17·949	2000	129·60
198	12·830	238	15·422	278	18·014	3000	194·40
199	12·895	239	15·487	279	18·079	4000	259·20
200	12·960	240	15·552	280	18·144	5000	324·00

PL. I.

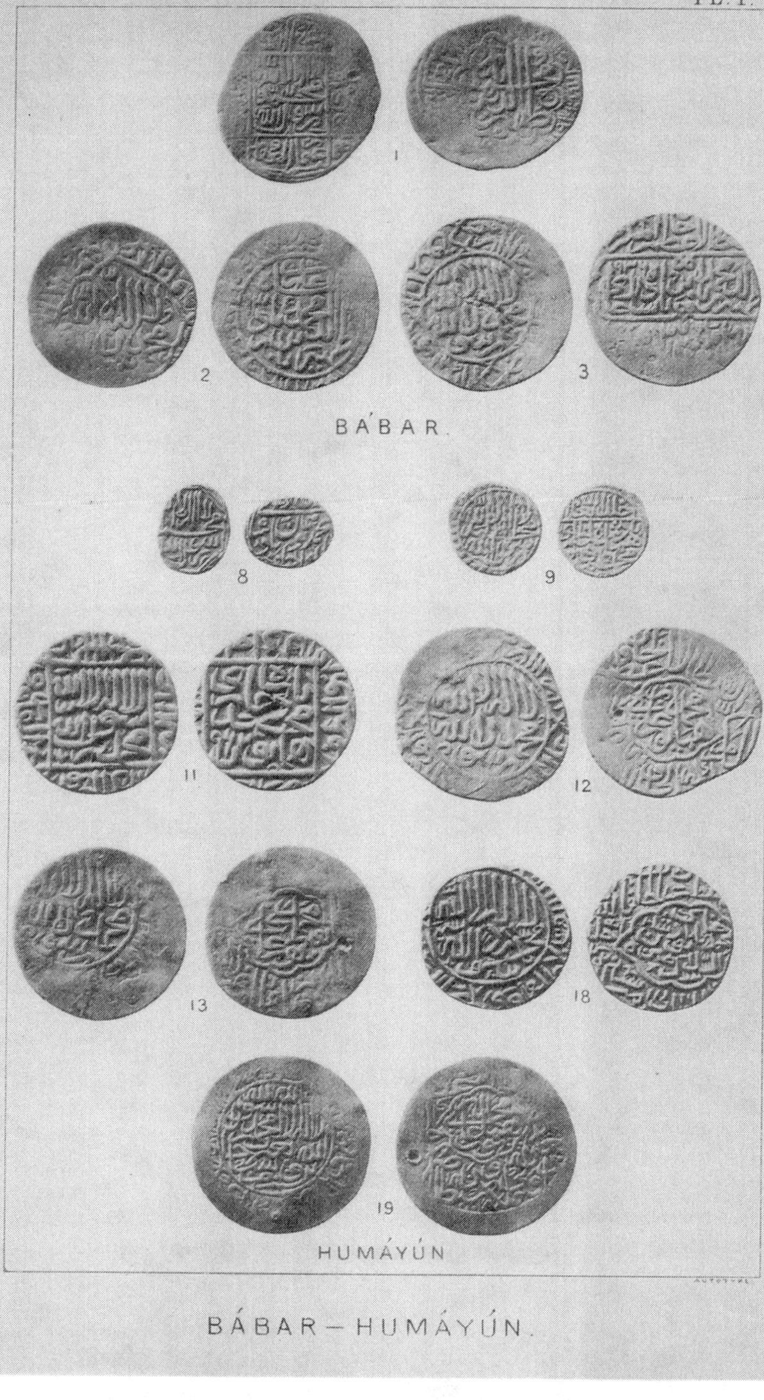

BÁBAR—HUMÁYÚN.

PL. II.

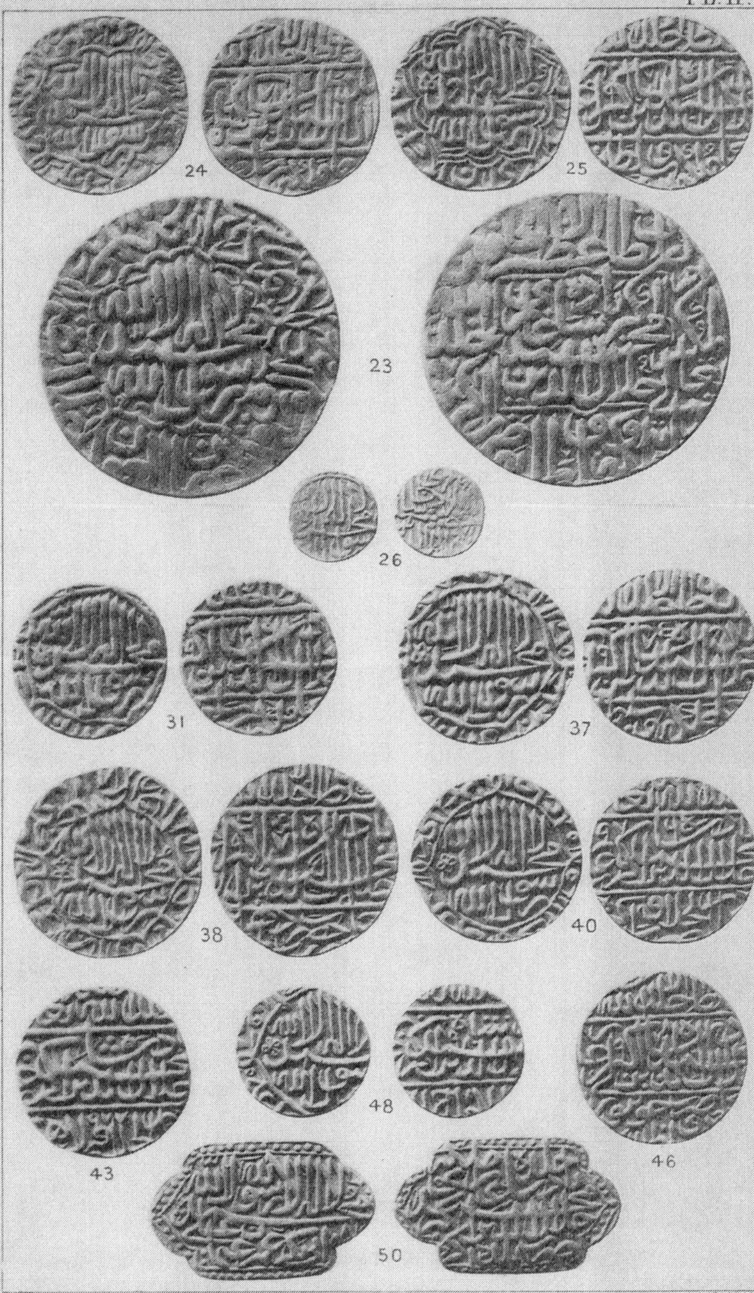

AKBAR: GOLD.

PL. III

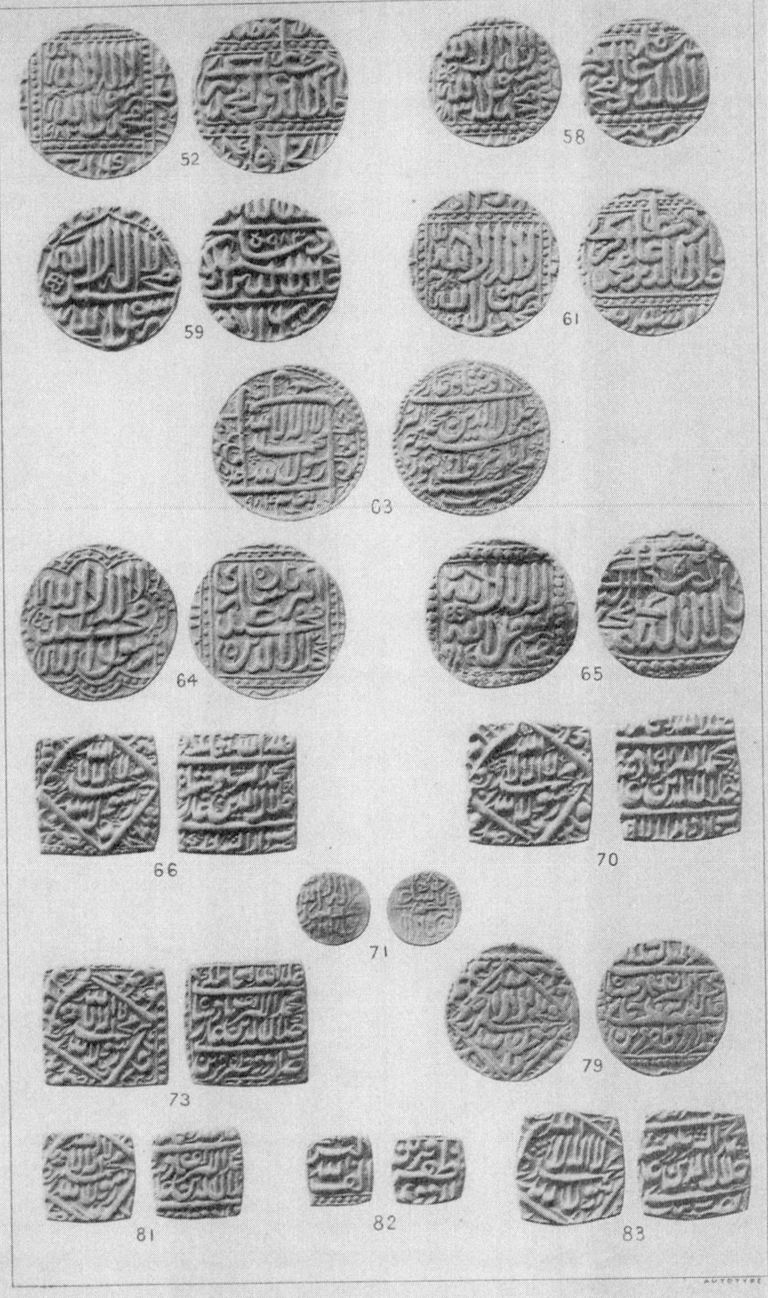

AKBAR: GOLD.

AKBAR: SILVER.

PL. V.

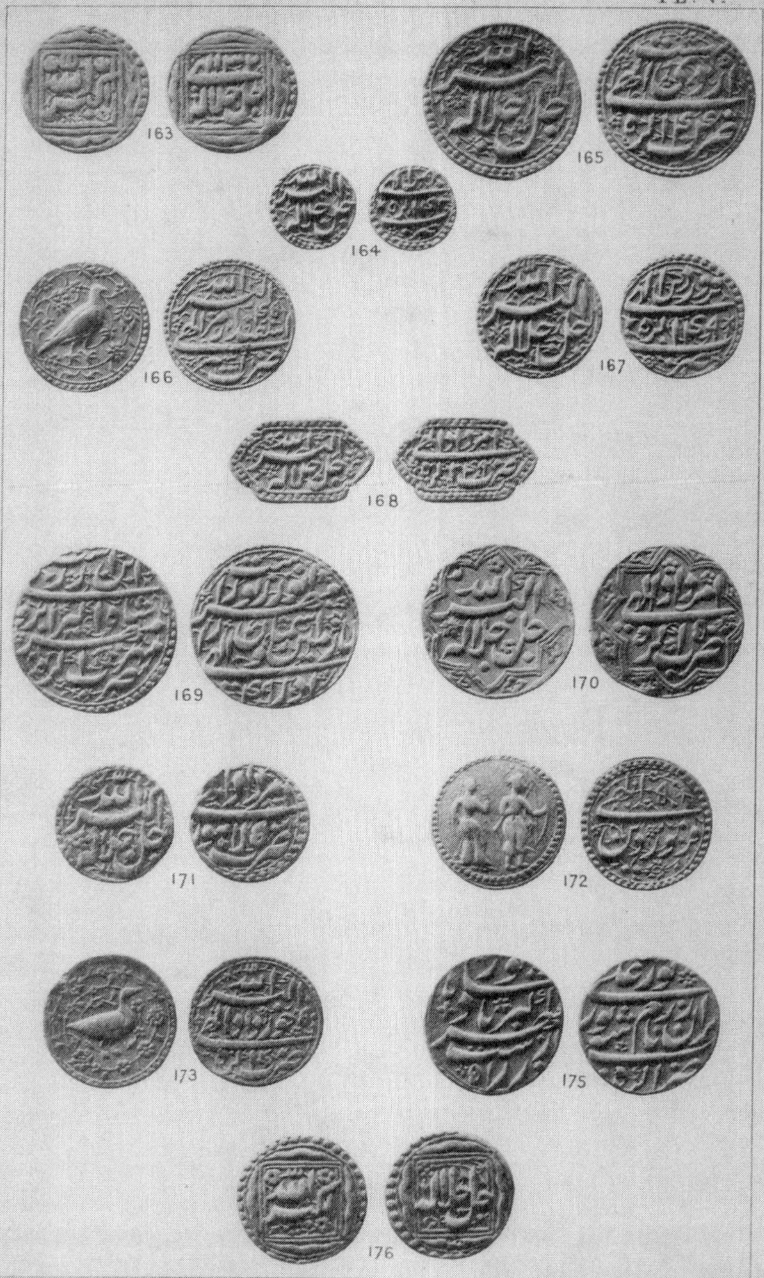

AKBAR: ILAHÍ GOLD.

PL. VI.

AKBAR: ILÁHÍ SILVER.

PL. VII.

AKBAR. SILVER. COPPER.

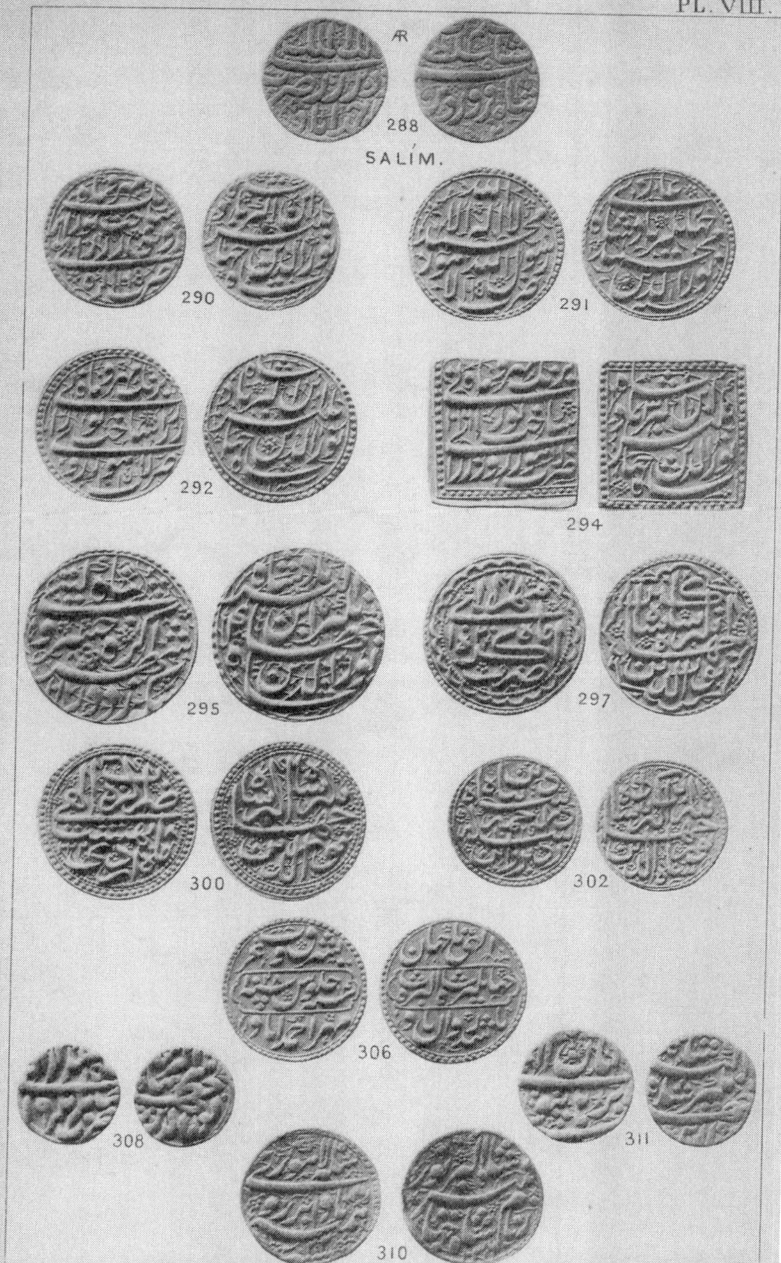

JAHÁNGÍR. GOLD.

305

312

313

314

315

317

318

319

AUTOTYPE.

JAHÁNGÍR. GOLD.

PL. X.

JAHÁNGÍR. ZODIACAL MOHRS.

PL. XI.

JAHÁNGÍR. ZODIACAL RUPEES & IMITATIONS.

PL. XII.

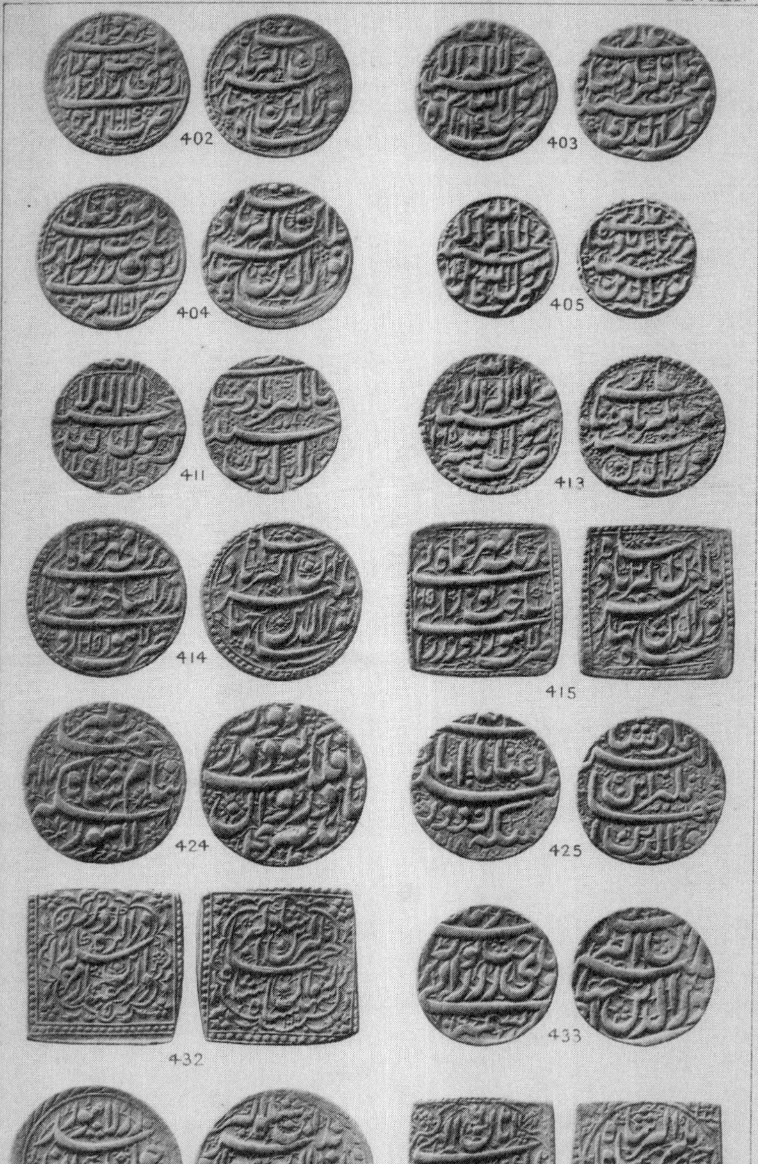

JAHÁNGÍR . SILVER .

PL. XIII.

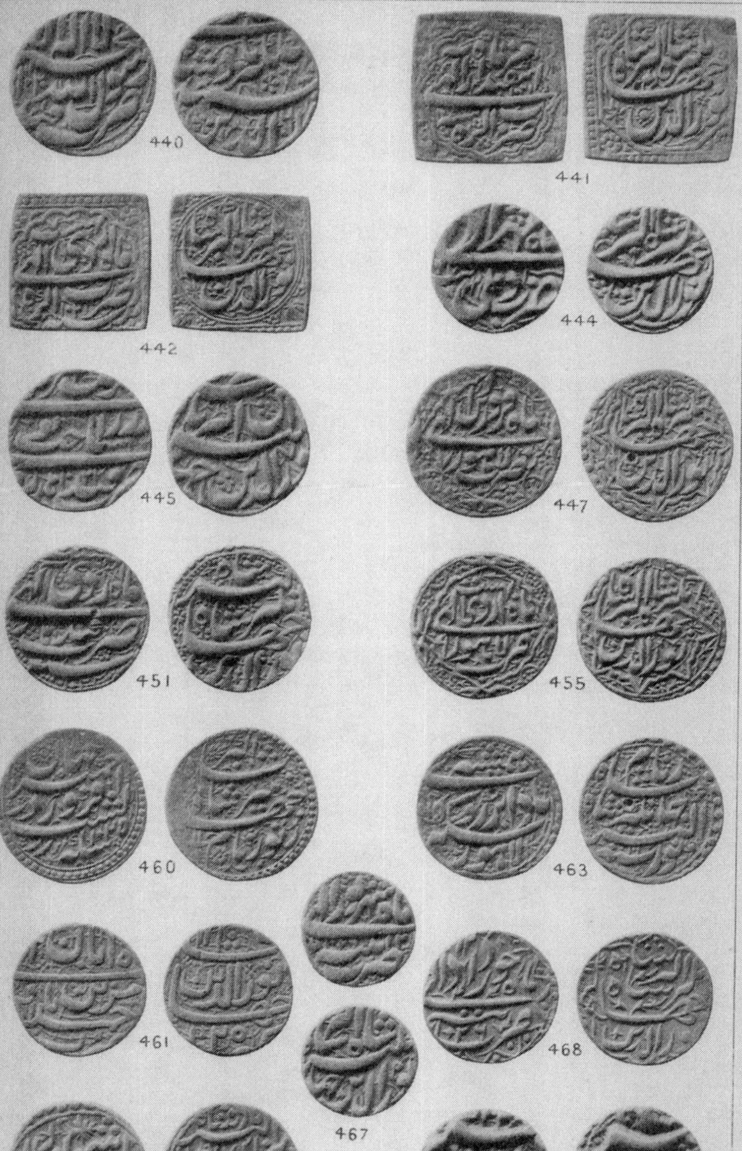

JAHÁNGÍR. SILVER.

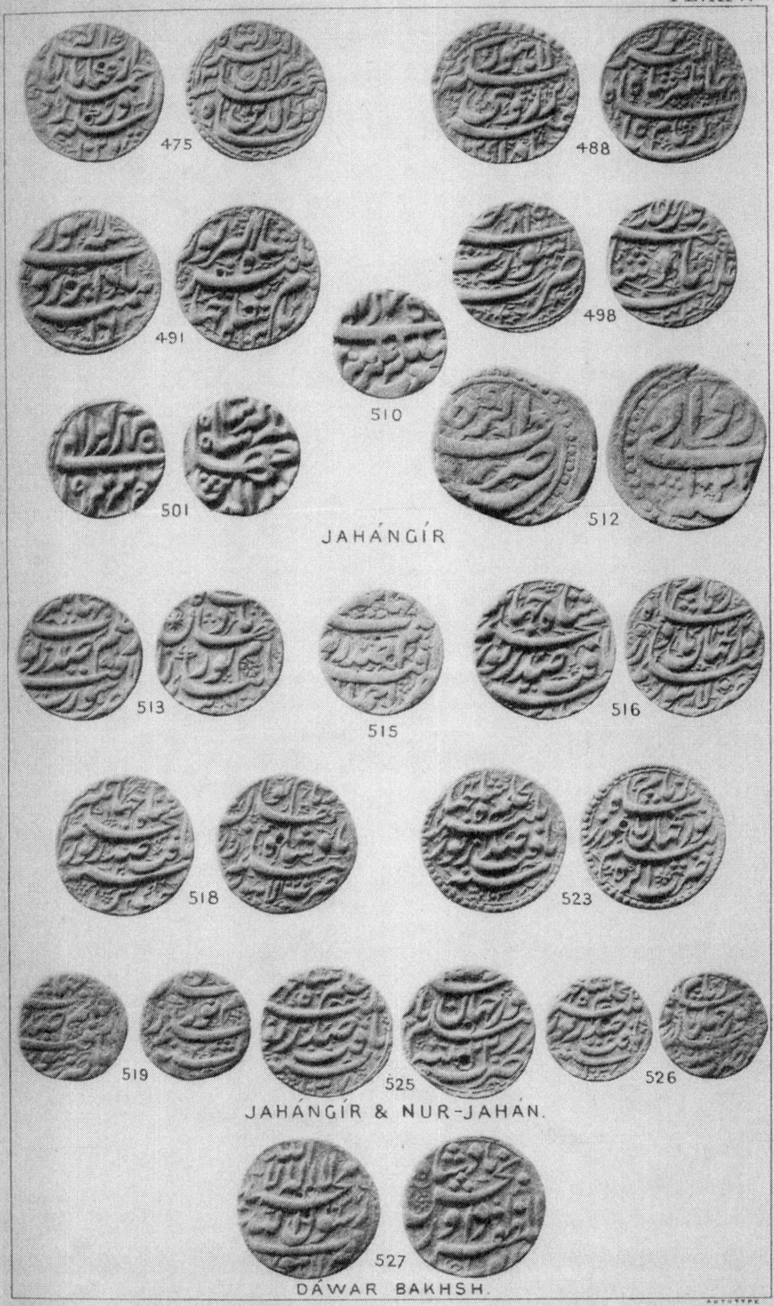

JAHÁNGÍR. NÚR-JAHÁN. DÁWAR BAKHSH.

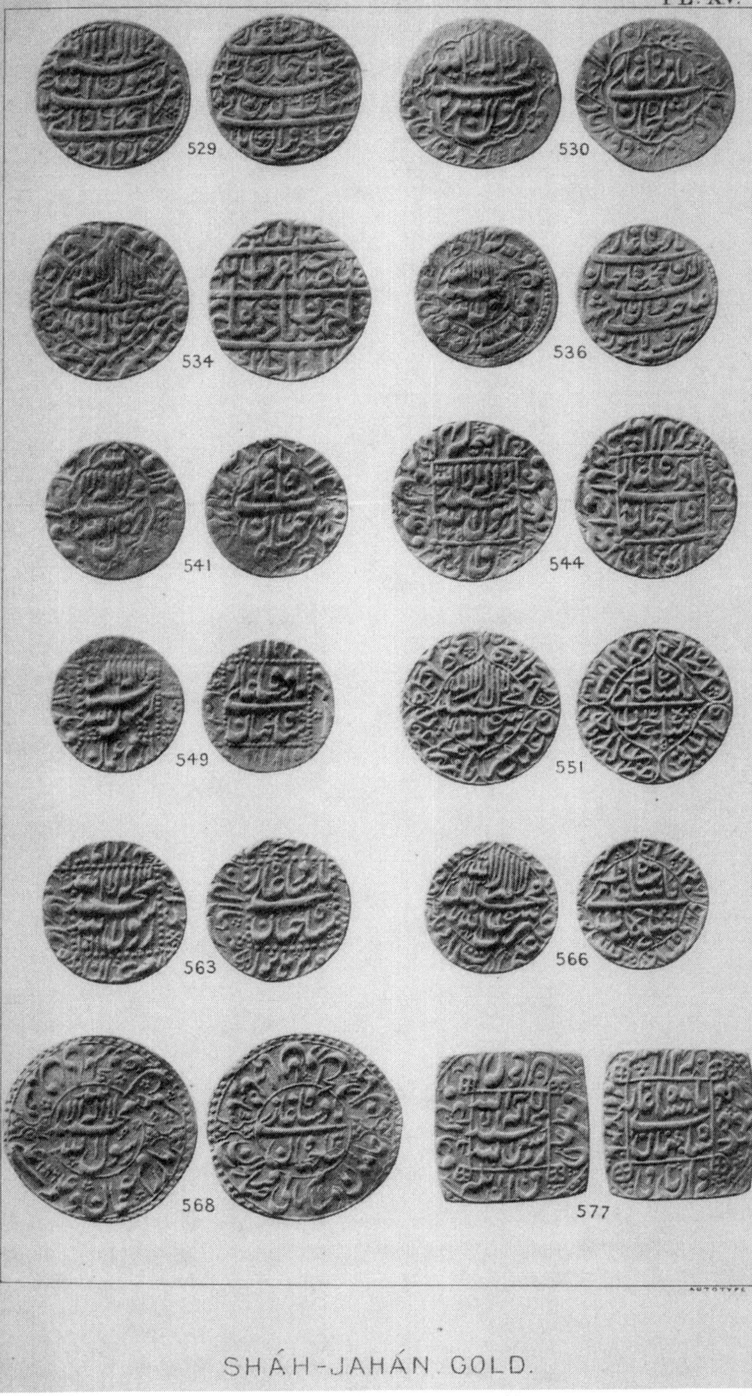

SHÁH-JAHÁN. GOLD.

PL. XVI.

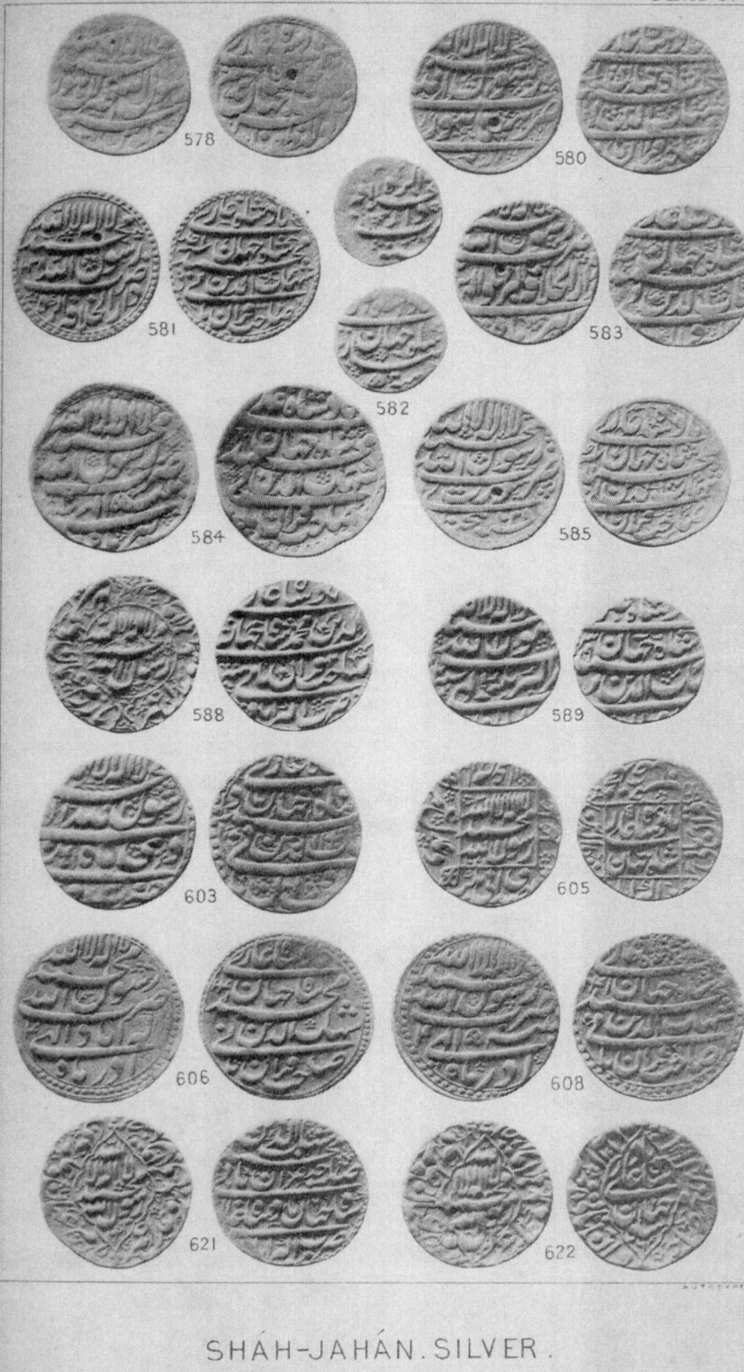

SHÁH-JAHÁN. SILVER.

PL. XVII.

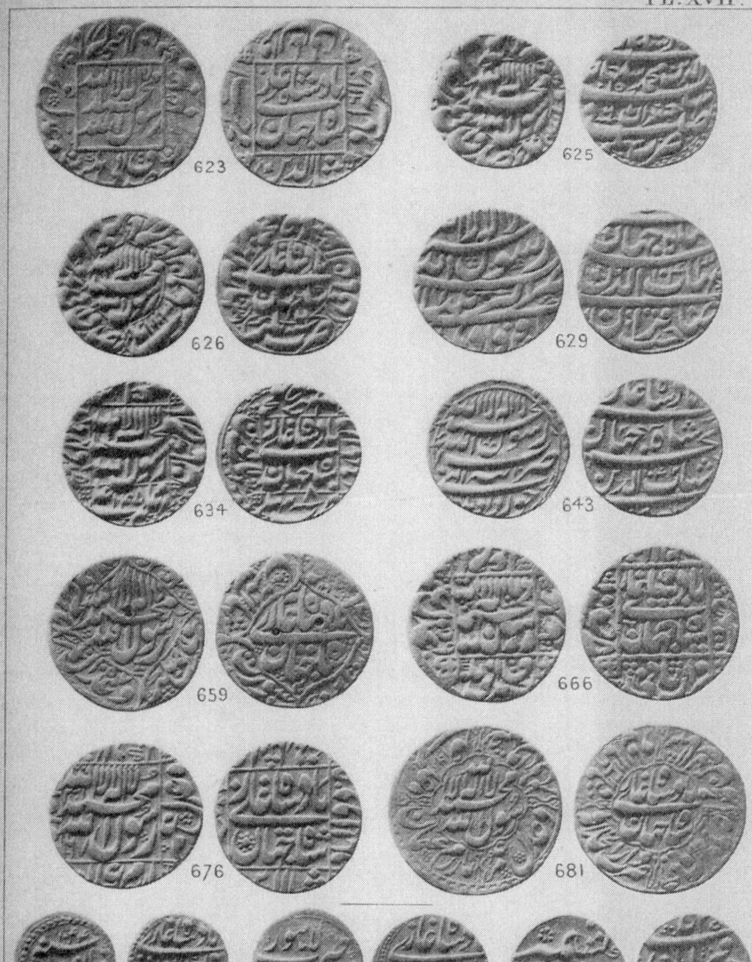

SHÁH-JAHÁN. SILVER & NISÁRS.

PL. XVIII.

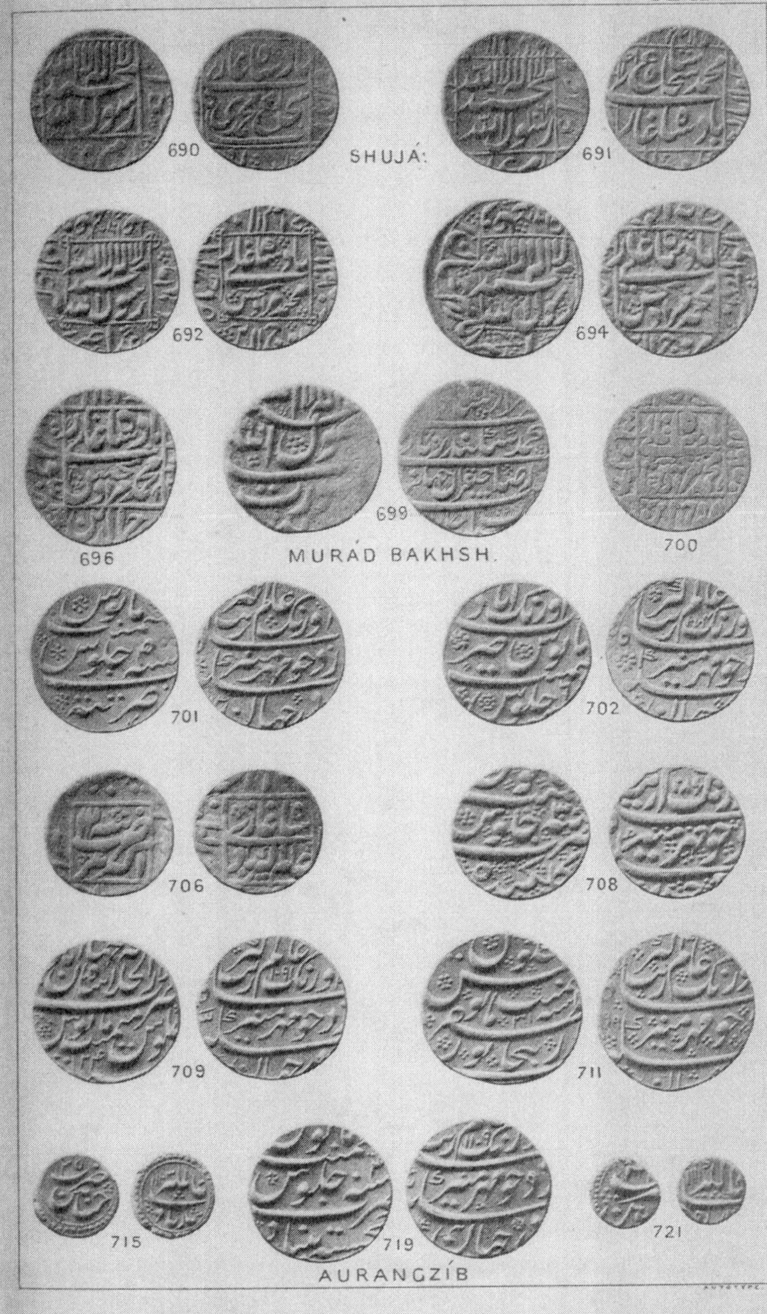

SHUJÁ, MURÁD BAKHSH, AURANGZÍB (GOLD)

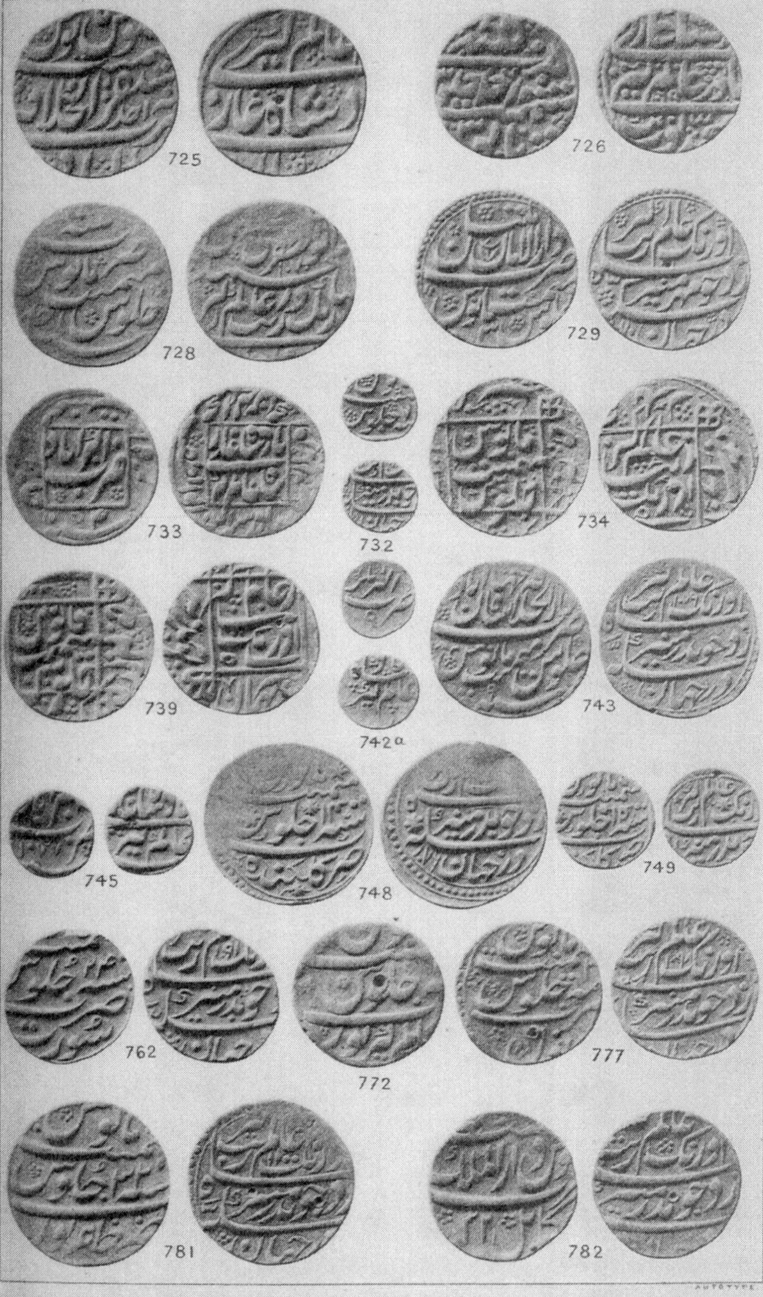

AURANGZIB. SILVER.

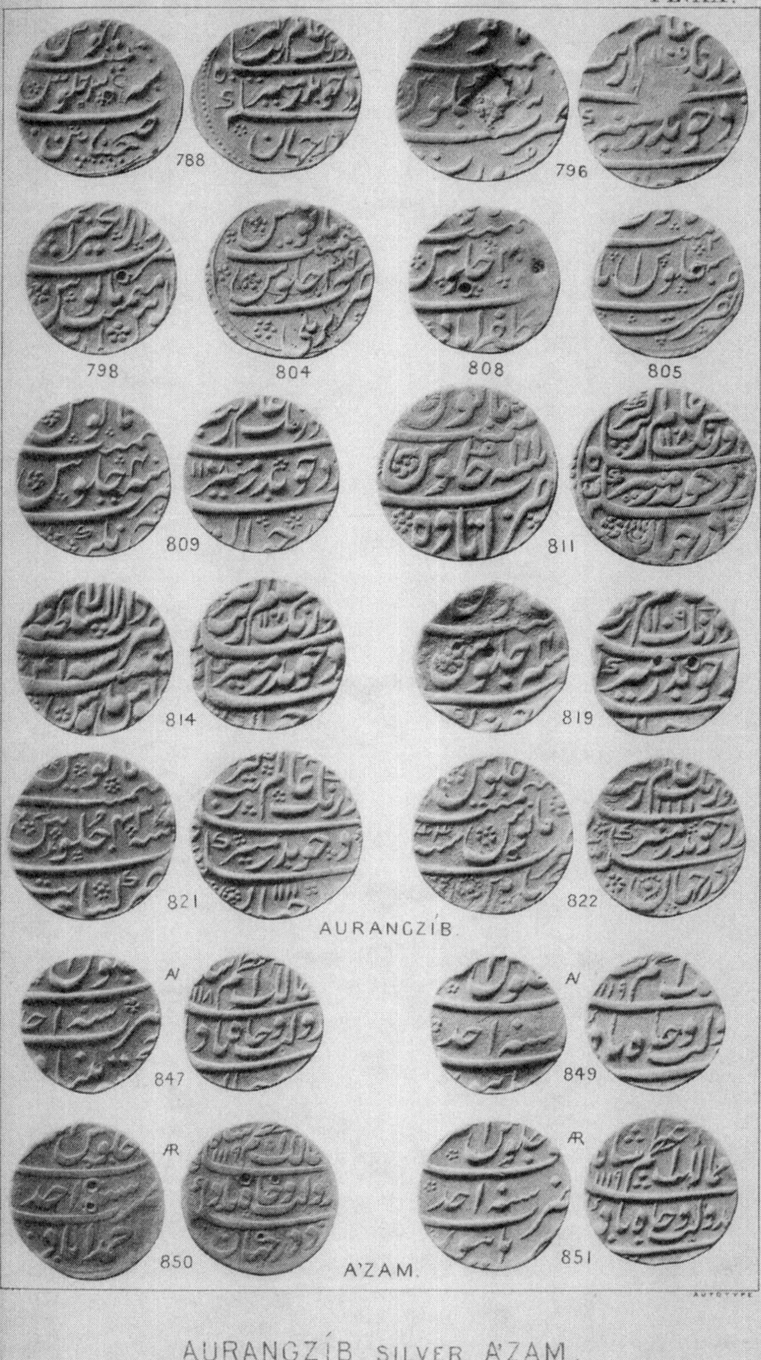

AURANGZÍB, SILVER. A'ZAM.

PL. XXI.

KÁM BAKHSH. BAHÁDUR.

PL. XXII.

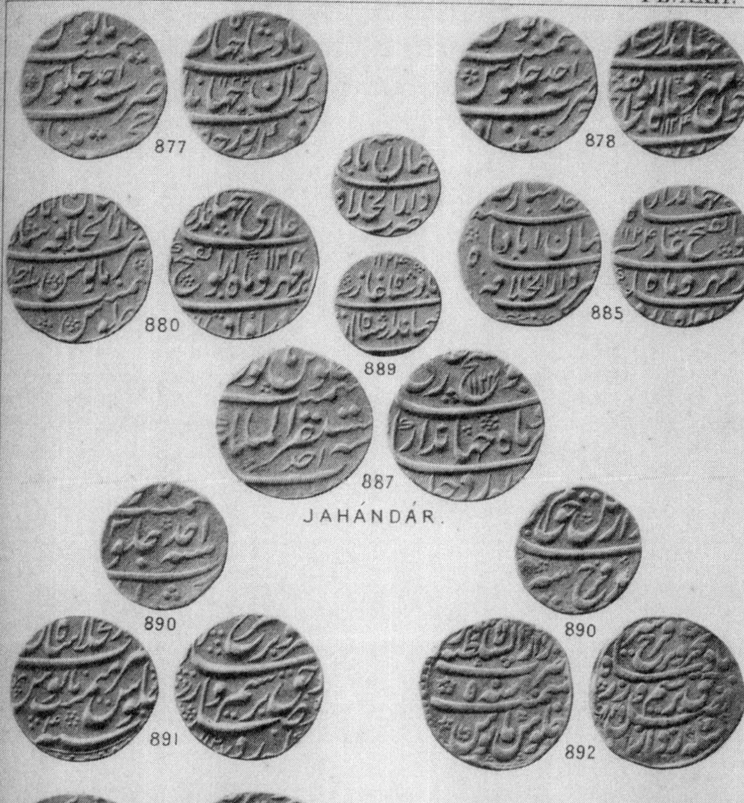

JAHÁNDÁR. FARRUKH-SIYAR, GOLD.

PL. XXIII.

FARRUKH-SIYAR, SILVER. RAFÍ-AD-DARAJÁT.

PL. XXIV.

AUTOTYPE.

RAFÍ'-AD-DAULAH. NÍKÚ-SIYAR. IBRÁHÍM.

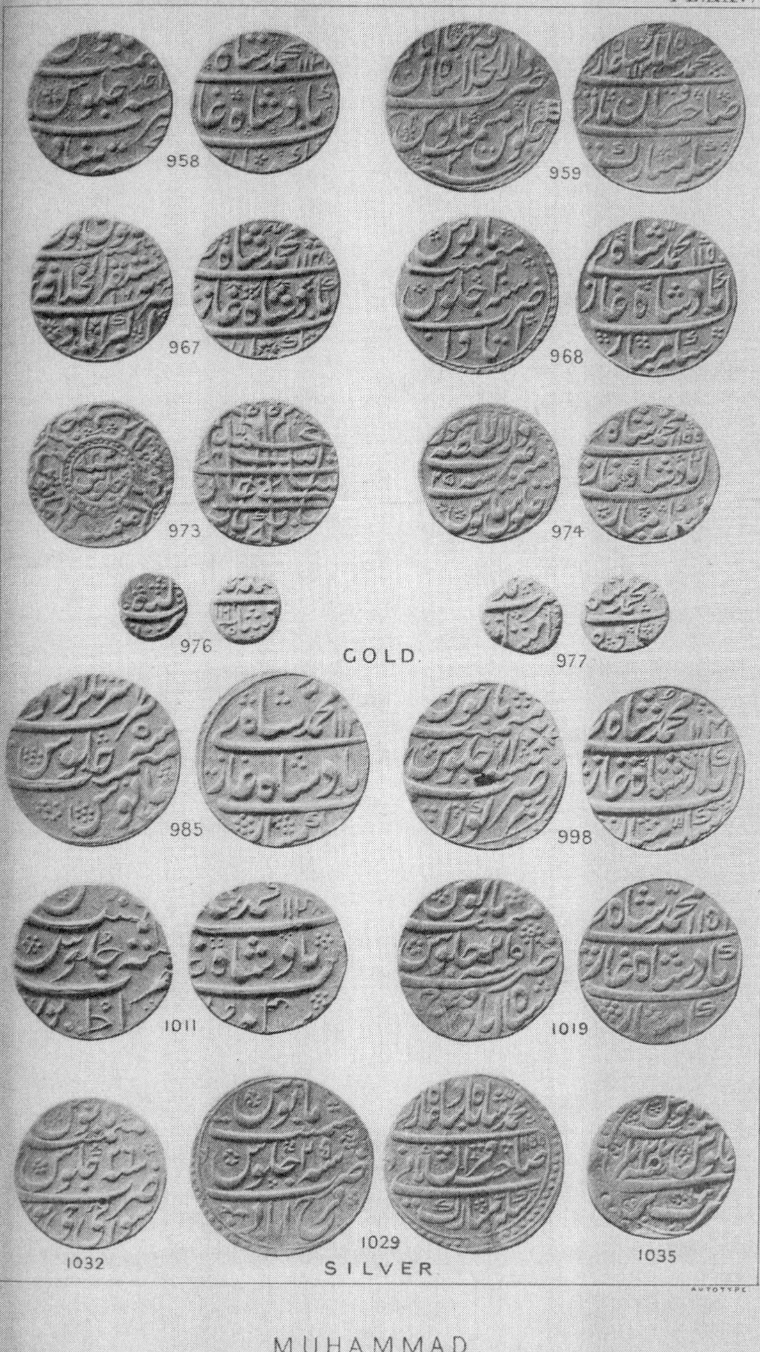
958
959
967
968
973
974
976
GOLD.
977
985
998
1011
1019
1032
1029
SILVER.
1035
AUTOTYPE

MUHAMMAD.

PL. XXVI.

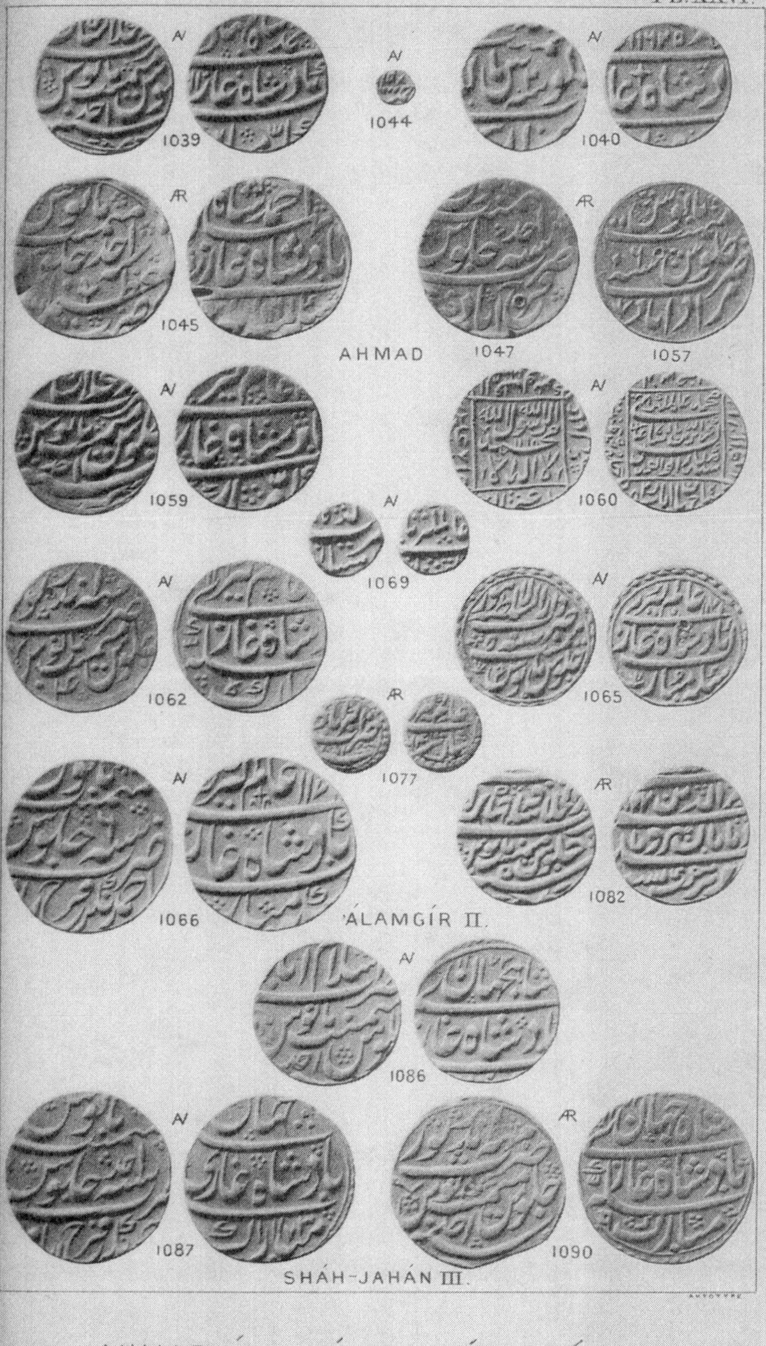

AHMAD. ʾÁLAMGÍR. II. SHÁH-JAHÁN III.

PL. XXVII.

SHÁH-ÁLAM.

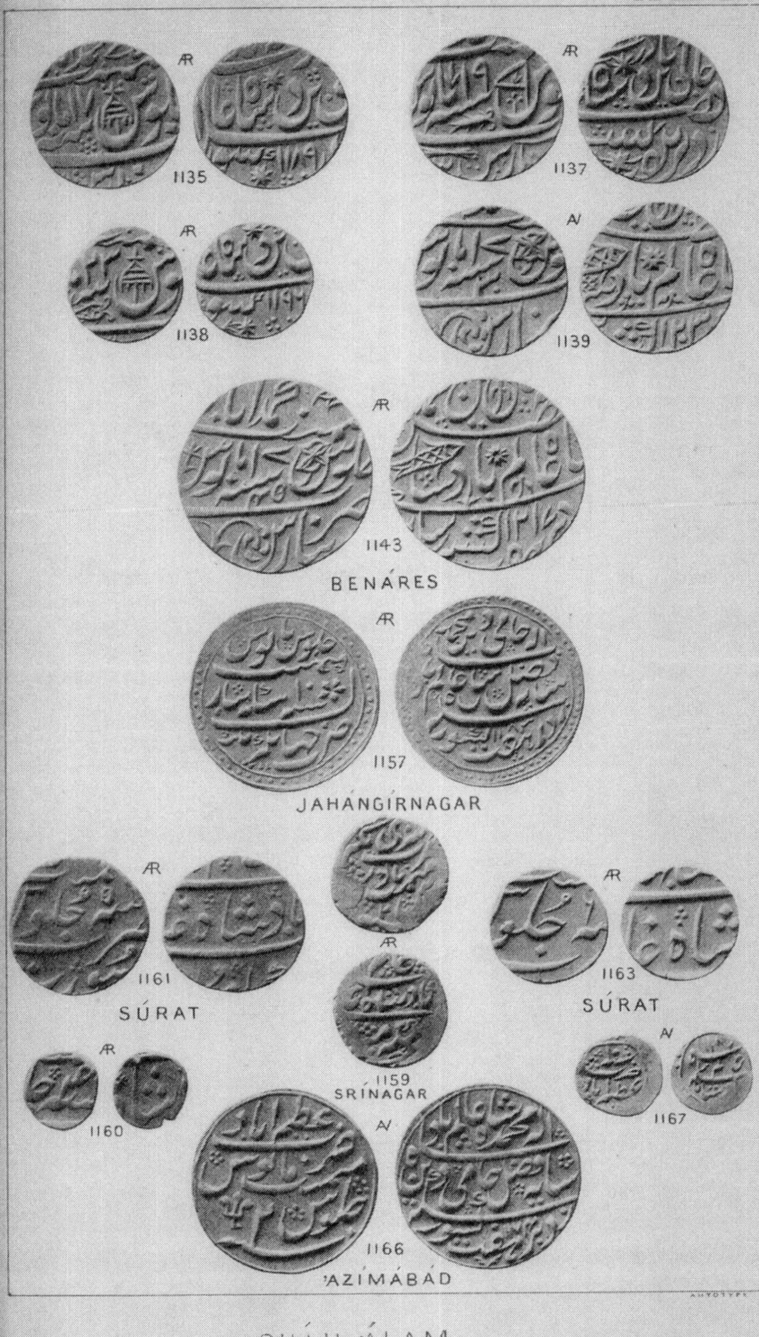
AR
1135
AR
1137
AR
1138
AV
1139
AR
1143
BENÁRES
AR
1157
JAHÁNGÍRNAGAR
AR
1161
SÚRAT
AR
AR
1163
SÚRAT
AR
1160
1159
SRÍNAGAR
AV
1167
AV
1166
'AZÍMÁBÁD

SHÁH-ÁLAM.

PL. XXIX.

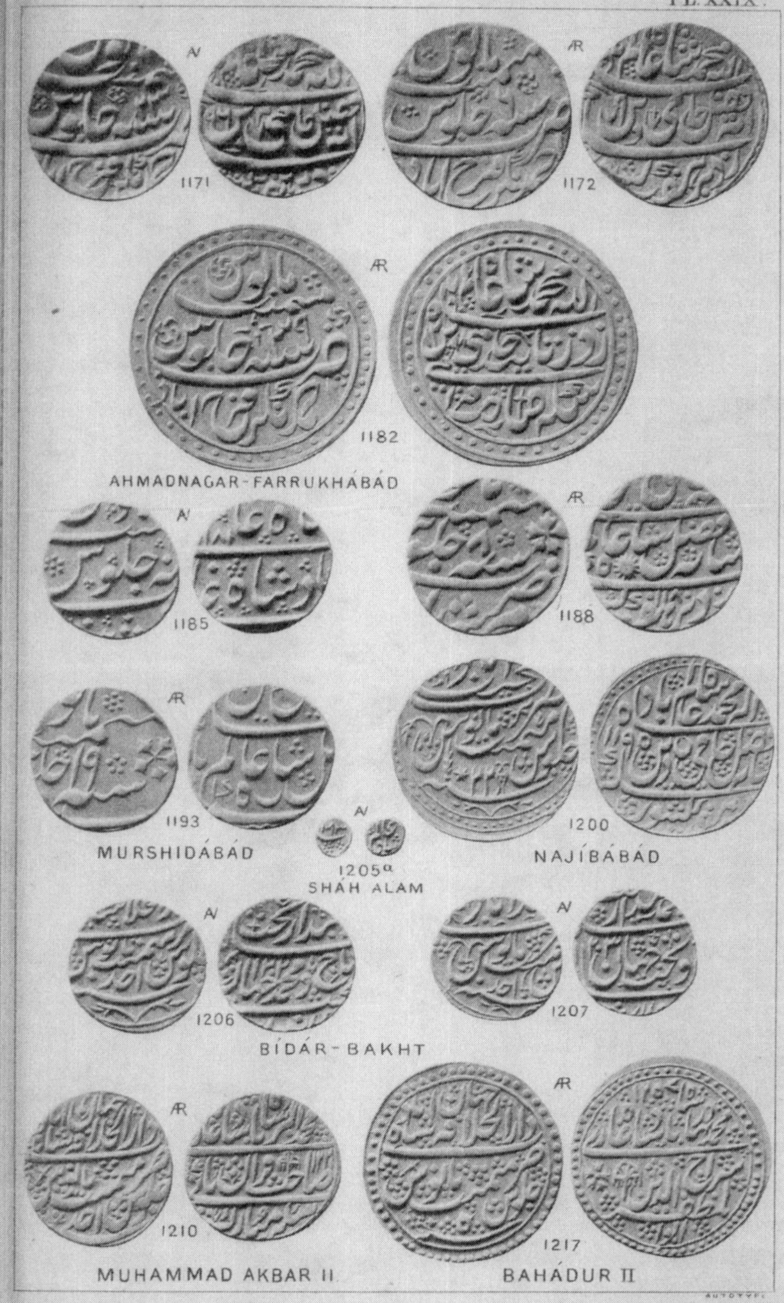

SHÁH-ʿALAM — BAHÁDUR II.

PL. XXX.

EAST INDIA COMPANY.- MURSHIDÁBÁD.

PL. XXXI.

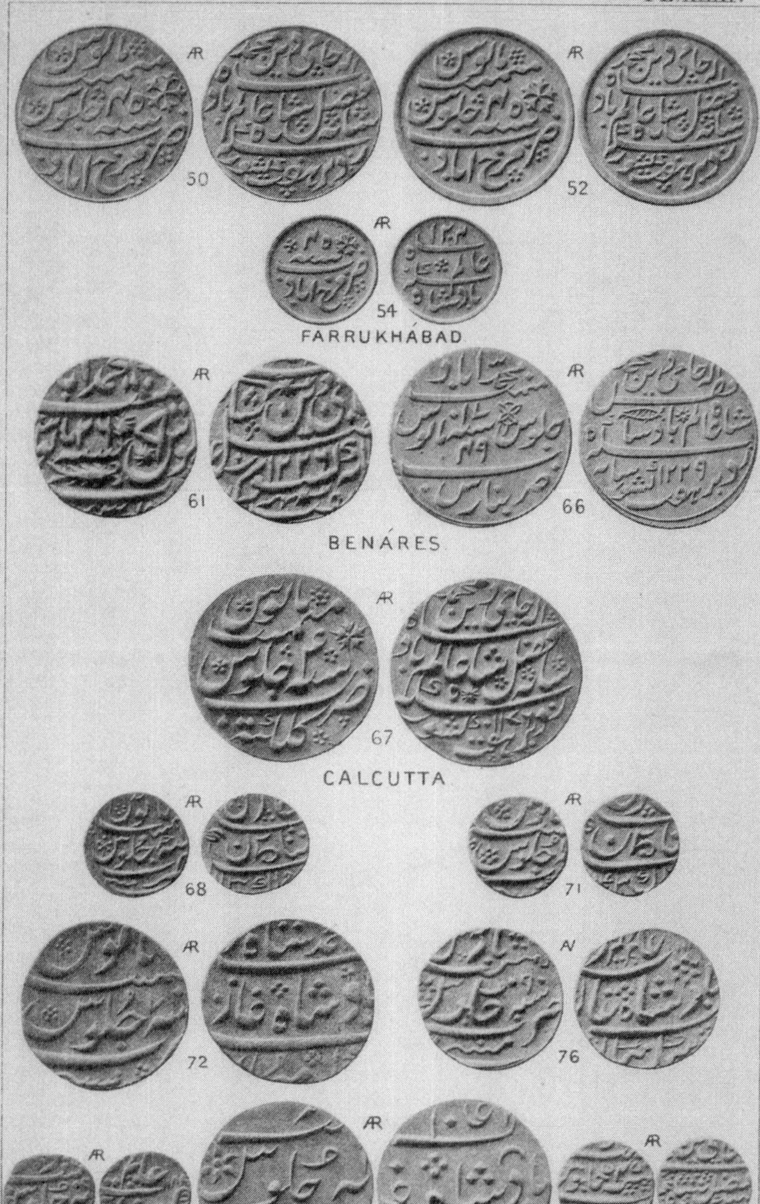

EAST INDIA COMPANY.

PL. XXXII.

EAST INDIA COMPANY. FRENCH COMPANY.

200-MOHR PIECE OF SHÁH-JAHÁN.